AF291494

American Rap Scenes

American Rap Scenes

An Analysis of 25 Locations

Lavar Pope

BLOOMSBURY ACADEMIC

NEW YORK • LONDON • OXFORD • NEW DELHI • SYDNEY

BLOOMSBURY ACADEMIC
Bloomsbury Publishing Inc, 1385 Broadway, New York, NY 10018, USA
Bloomsbury Publishing Plc, 50 Bedford Square, London, WC1B 3DP, UK
Bloomsbury Publishing Ireland, 29 Earlsfort Terrace, Dublin 2, D02 AY28, Ireland

BLOOMSBURY, BLOOMSBURY ACADEMIC and the Diana logo are
trademarks of Bloomsbury Publishing Plc

First published in the United States of America 2025

Copyright © Lavar Pope, 2025

Cover design by Louise Dugdale
Cover image: Oxygen/Getty Images

For legal purposes the Acknowledgments on pp. x–xi constitute an extension
of this copyright page.

All rights reserved. No part of this publication may be: i) reproduced or transmitted in any form,
electronic or mechanical, including photocopying, recording or by means of any information
storage or retrieval system without prior permission in writing from the publishers; or ii) used
or reproduced in any way for the training, development or operation of artificial intelligence (AI)
technologies, including generative AI technologies. The rights holders expressly reserve this
publication from the text and data mining exception as per Article 4(3) of the Digital Single Market
Directive (EU) 2019/790.

Bloomsbury Publishing Inc does not have any control over, or responsibility for, any
third-party websites referred to or in this book. All internet addresses given in this book were
correct at the time of going to press. The author and publisher regret any inconvenience caused if
addresses have changed or sites have ceased to exist,
but can accept no responsibility for any such changes.

Library of Congress Cataloging-in-Publication Data
Names: Pope, Lavar, author.
Title: American rap scenes : an analysis of 25 locations / Lavar Pope.
Description: [1.] | New York : Bloomsbury Academic, 2025. |
Includes bibliographical references and index.
Identifiers: LCCN 2024036207 (print) | LCCN 2024036208 (ebook) |
ISBN 9798765118962 (paperback) | ISBN 9798765118931 (hardback) |
ISBN 9798765118948 (ebook) | ISBN 9798765118924 (pdf)
Subjects: LCSH: Rap (Music)–History and criticism. | Hip-hop–History. |
Music and geography–US. | Rap musicians–Social conditions.
| Rap (Music)–Political aspects–US–History–20th century.
| Rap (Music)–Political aspects–US–History–21st century.
| African American neighborhoods–History. | Great Migration, ca.
1914-ca. 1970 | Human geography–US–History–20th century. |
Human geography–US–History–21st century. |
Rap (Music)–Production and direction–History.
Classification: LCC ML3531 .P65 2025 (print) | LCC ML3531 (ebook) |
DDC 782.421649–dc23/eng/20240812
LC record available at https://lccn.loc.gov/2024036207
LC ebook record available at https://lccn.loc.gov/2024036208

ISBN: HB: 979-8-7651-1893-1
PB: 979-8-7651-1896-2
ePDF: 979-8-7651-1892-4
eBook: 979-8-7651-1894-8

Typeset by Newgen KnowledgeWorks Pvt. Ltd., Chennai, India
Printed and bound in the United States of America

For product safety related questions contact
productsafety@bloomsbury.com.

To find out more about our authors and books visit www.bloomsbury.com
and sign up for our newsletters.

To Isaiah

Contents

Acknowledgments

First, I would like to thank God for giving me and my family the strength to survive the last few years of life developments and world events. This book is dedicated to my son and family with continued hope for a better generational future for our family in America. I would like to thank my wife, two daughters, son, mom, dad, stepdad, stepmom, and extended family (grandparents, aunts, uncles, and cousins) for their love and support. I am also grateful for my mother-in-law and my extended family of in-laws. I would like to thank two other family members, one who introduced me to rap music and the other who taught me that it was possible to make rap music from scratch. Jason Rodgers, my cousin, helped introduce me to some very important and raw rap albums released during the end of rap's Golden Age. Jay Bates, my uncle, also played a significant role in my continued interest in the rap album and mixtape formats and processes. He was the first person to show me that it was possible to make rap songs, albums, and mixtapes. Thank you. In early 2020, my family mourned the loss of my father-in-law. I want to thank him for everything that he did for me and our family. I miss him dearly and wish that he had the chance to meet his grandson and second granddaughter.

Second, thank you to teachers, colleagues, students, and anyone who has helped teach me. Thank you to my professors at University of California Santa Cruz, especially my dissertation chair Michael Brown. Previously, while I was at Lehigh University, I was fortunate to meet a group of professors, mentors, and colleagues who have helped me tremendously. These include Rick Matthews, Ted Morgan, Cleveland McCray, and Maggie Hagerman, among many others. I am also grateful to the professional organizations to which I belong: the National Conference of Black Political Scientists (NCOBPS), the Western Political Science Association (WPSA), the Midwest Political Science Association (MPSA), and the American Political Science Association (APSA). I express thanks to Todd Shaw, who introduced me to Adolphus Belk, who introduced me to Cedric Johnson. I want to particularly thank Cedric Johnson for his friendship and support. I also especially want to thank Lakeyta Bonnette-Bailey for her support, conversations, and care over the years. My introduction to these scholars was facilitated by NCOBPS, so many thanks to the organization and its leadership. Also, thank you Akil Houston for your sound advice and perspective.

Third, thank you to the people and institutions that made this research possible. This includes Loyola University Chicago and its faculty, staff, and students, especially the students at Arrupe College. I extend a special thank you to DC Cochrane, Aisha Raees, Giancarlo Tarantino, David Keys, and Brandon Sparkman—a few of my many great Loyola and Arrupe colleagues—for your support and listening to my ideas about this and other projects. Many thanks to Loyola and Arrupe for research support and funding. In particular, I would like to thank Associate Dean Jennie Boyle and Dean Fr.

Thomas Neitzke, SJ, for their support and helping foster an environment in which this research is a possibility. In addition, I would like to thank Loyola's Office of Research Services for their overall assistance and creation of funding opportunities for faculty. This book directly benefited from the office's Manuscript Publication Assistance (MPA) and Book Subvention grants. I also want to thank Come to Believe Network founder, president, and CEO Fr. Steve Katsouros, SJ, for his support as well. I absolutely want to thank Loyola's libraries, especially anyone in web intake, library loan, and book delivery roles. Admittedly, there were times when hundreds of books were ordered in a short time, and these books were delivered to my faculty mailbox. I was able to return the books via intercampus mail. When I say the research in this book was only made possible with this type of help, I sincerely mean it. Many thanks as well to Annette Alvarado for research strategies around scoping and systematic reviews. Thanks also to the Loyola libraries for recognizing my prior scholarship. Thank you to Kevin Leer at International Mapping for creating such detailed maps of the local sites. Additionally, I want to thank Rachel Moore (the book's acquisition editor), the book's anonymous peer reviewers, and the Bloomsbury Academic Music & Sound Studies team for helping shape, improve, and ready this book for publication.

Fourth, thank you to authors who published academic scholarship on this book's topics, and thank you to scholars who provided expert feedback on my previous research on the topic. For existing research, I want to thank Mickey Hess, Lakeyta Bonnette-Bailey, James Scott, Robin D. G. Kelley, Michael Hanchard, James Taylor, Mark Katz, Mark Mattern, and Dawn-Elissa Fischer. There are some specific areas of this book that were only made possible by the research of other scholars in significant ways. This includes Mickey Hess's work on local rap, as well as the regional and local analyses of other scholars. For census and population data, the work of Campbell Gibson and Kay Jung was vital to this book. For overall US city population and changes in migration, Richardson Dilworth's work helped form a significant part of this book's scope. For social movements, the University of Washington's "Mapping American Social Movements Project" was very important in summarizing chapter histories of groups and key organizational events. Also, thank you to a circle of colleagues whose longitudinal work on rap has been essential to the development of local rap scene analysis and this book: Matt Miller, Maco Faniel, Lance Scott Walker, Daudi Abe, Joe Coscarelli, and Langston Collin Wilkins. For extremely valuable feedback on my previous research, I want to thank Christopher Malone, Rickey Vincent, Najja Baptist, and Lakeyta Bonnette-Bailey. Their comments, feedback, and reviews related to *Rap and Politics* were extremely valuable in shaping this book.

Fifth, thank you to some of my closest friends and colleagues—many of whom are rap music practitioners. This includes the people who were essential to my first book— Young B, Relly Rell, Lights Out, Mac tha Kat, and many others. I also express thanks to two great friends who died too soon, Shotime and Mario a.k.a. "Skillz."

Finally, I want to thank you (the reader) for taking an interest in *American Rap Scenes*.

Figures

Tables

Introduction

American Rap Scenes focuses on the development of twenty-five local US rap music scenes by exploring the factors of settings, migrations, movements, music, and technology. Through this combined geographical and topical approach, *American Rap Scenes* presents evidence of local rap music as a product of physical location, migration, prior social movements, local musical traditions, and technological development. *American Rap Scenes* makes the case that rap is a distinct Black American musical creation with Latinx, Caribbean, and other global influences and that each local scene constitutes its own independent micro unit while simultaneously engaging with other scenes in regional, domestic, and global ways. The twenty-five scenes and five factors offer a strong coverage of rap's overall development in the US. By better understanding how each of these local scenes began, persisted, and evolved, we can better understand how each scene interacts, collaborates, and engages with other scenes regionally, domestically, and globally.

KRS-One's "Underground" challenges listeners to consider the rap scene from an "upside down perspective" (Figure 1) when he raps:

You could be platinum or gold, hot or cold / But it's the respect you hold that's underground / When the critics don't get, that for the streets you spit it / When your lyric they fear, that's underground.[1]

In the song's opening chorus, KRS-One makes it clear that anyone listening to him is underground. The first verse then opens with an announcement (or "thunder sound") and asks the listener to search in their "own town for the underground." He questions some rappers' motives (such as a desire to be on TV or to sell albums) and insists that if they are not an "MC," they are not underground. KRS-One is also abundantly clear that respect is at the center of the underground. In other verses, KRS-One mentions a series of artists and groups, including himself and his groups, who are considered underground. KRS-One was familiar with the South Bronx rap scene around the time of its construction, as Abrams explains that the rapper had "soaked in the atmosphere of the block parties" near Kool Herc's 1520 Sedgwick location.[2] Since its construction, underground rap has often been distinguished by use of topics highly reflective and relevant to local communities, calls to local struggles, and references to the histories of struggle in that geographic space. As Orejuela describes,

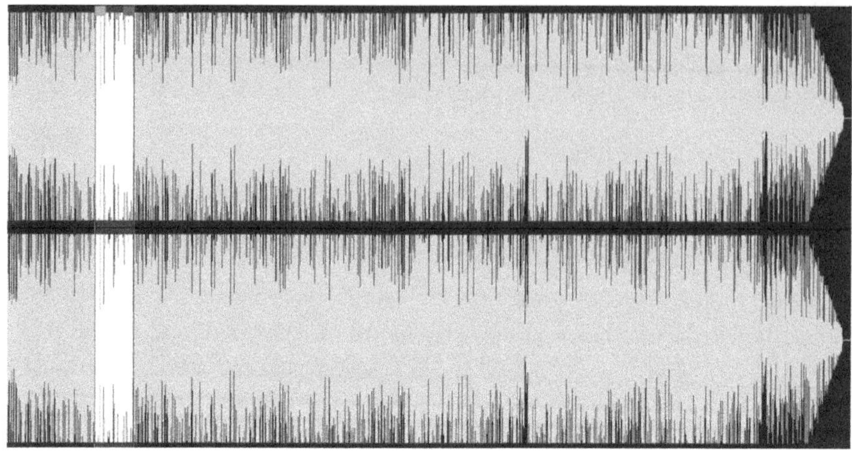

Figure 1 KRS-One's "Underground" Akai WAV snapshot with quoted material highlighted.

> Underground hip hop is an umbrella term that refers to independently produced, alternative styles that intentionally shift away from the dominant tastes and directions of commercial rap. It is the product of subterranean music scenes that are under the radar of the mainstream rap music fan base in part because they are formulated and supported by local performers and audiences.[3]

American Rap Scenes is about rap from these locations, recognizing an underground rap layer existing under the mainstream rap market and documenting both the underground layer and its relationship to the mainstream. To introduce book chapters, *American Rap Scenes* uses eight rap quotes in similar ways to KRS-One's quote. Other quotes are from Grandmaster Caz (South Bronx), CeeLo with Goodie Mob (Atlanta), Masta Ace with Masta Ace Incorporated (Brooklyn), Wise Intelligent (Trenton), Sir Quick Draw (Oakland), Bahamadia (Philadelphia), Busta Rhymes (Brooklyn/Long Island), and MF Grimm (Harlem).

This Introduction presents the book's main purpose and context, core terminology and themes, framework, methods, and main content and arguments.

Book Purpose and Context

Book Title and Main Contributions

The title, *American Rap Scenes*, references new developments in the field of local rap scenes study, presenting the argument that these twenty-five scenes represent a mass of rap's overall US development and that the factors visible on these scenes are likely visible on other scenes in the US (and perhaps elsewhere). *American Rap Scenes* also recognizes that these scenes are created on sites that are physically part of the US but that may be distinct in their political, economic, and social separation from other parts of the US (and sometimes even parts of their own local environment). Within these scenes, rap is sometimes used as a primary vehicle for expression, recognition of identities, raising awareness about issues, and enacting significant change. Participants on American rap scenes may have more in common with other participants on local scenes in the US (or elsewhere) than some neighboring areas in close proximity.

This title is rooted in findings of Hess's *Hip Hop in America*, which moved rap from a regional to a local level of analysis. The overall locational sequencing in *American Rap Scenes* is similar to *Hip Hop in America*, following rap's local development from East Coast, West Coast, Midwest, and South scenes. Since Hess's *Hip Hop in America*, there have been about seven new books on local rap scenes—each with some longitudinal-type of examination. These books have covered New Orleans, Houston, Seattle, Oakland, and Atlanta. These studies of local scenes indicate the likelihood that there will be more studies of these scenes and other local scenes in the US and elsewhere. One of the most recent studies is Coscarelli's *Rap Capital: An Atlanta Story*; although Coscarelli does not express it to be a comprehensive study of Atlanta, the book's coverage of nearly a decade of local rap offers tools for building longitudinal studies of this and other scenes. Atlanta is understood as a rap capital in the US, along with the New York City (NYC) and Los Angeles (LA) rap axis. These three sites tend to have a phenomenally higher output of mainstream rap activity (and perhaps underground) than most other sites. A main focus in *American Rap Scenes* is on documenting non-NYC, LA, and Atlanta scenes—especially smaller main cities and mid-sized locations.

Overall, *American Rap Scenes* adds a music scene analysis by exploring developmental factors on scenes. Geography, migration, movements, music, and technology are taken as factors in the production of US rap. The overall narrative here is of a *geography* in which people *migrate*, of youth *movements* in response to unresponsive electoral systems, of *music* rooted in the types of movements, and of the use of *technology* to manipulate and transform sound in the process of music making. *American Rap Scenes* sees rap's initial emergence as a projection of voices from marginalized groups of Black, Caribbean, and Latinx peoples in US cities. This research helps explain the specific experiences, identities, migrations, and social movements involving minoritized youth communities living through American and Global crises. Such crises might include the Middle Passage, Slavery, American Reconstruction, the Great Depression, the Great and Migration and Second Great Migrations, the Civil Rights Movement, the Racial Justice Movement, the War on Poverty, and the War on Drugs. Globally, this study helps in understanding more about colonization, slavery, and poverty.

The Book's Impetus

There are five main reasons *American Rap Scenes* was written. These impetus points include the following: (1) previous local and regional research on rap highlighted these scenes in increasing detail, specificity, and accuracy; (2) US city and population growth pointed to these cities as locations of major migrations of Black, Latinx, and Caribbean populations; (3) social movements such as the Black Panther Party for Self Defense (BPPSD), the Black Arts Movements, and other radical Latinx, Women's, and other identity groups harkened on issues such as colonization, slavery, migration, and contested land as related to these sites; (4) personal and team feedback from coursework, presentations, workshops, studies, grants, and proposals about these cities from students,, experts, and the general public helped in improving the author's thinking behind both sites and factors; and (5) tremendous technological advancements in rap production has occurred, creating new regional styles and a growing use and capability of DJ/production technology such as digital vinyl systems and music production consoles to create studio quality rap recordings in a home studio. These impetus points will be further discussed in the "More Scenes" chapter of this book, as the initial beginnings were crucial to the book's selection of scenes and might be useful in identifying additional scenes.

Frequently Asked Questions

What?

What is this book about? It is about factors (geographical, migrational, political, musical, and technological) on the development of local US rap scenes. The book is comparative, exploring the commonalities and differences on these scenes in terms of geography and place, migrations and identity formation, movements and representation, music creation and meaning making, and music production though manipulation and transformation of source material. This book sees rap scenes as part of an evolution of a site's ongoing changes around these factors. Particular themes within these factors reoccur throughout the book, such as the evolution of the local environment and geography; the proximity and timeline of Black, Latinx, and Caribbean migrations; the impact of the Civil Rights, Racial Justice, and Women's Movements; and the development of rap music and rap technologies on the site and elsewhere.

Where?

The *where* question is the easiest question to answer. *American Rap Scenes* explores the development of the following twenty-five local rap scenes in the US: South Bronx, NY; Manhattan, NY; Queens, NY; Brooklyn, NY; Staten Island, NY; Hempstead, NY; Philadelphia, PA; Newark, NJ and Jersey City, NJ; Boston, MA; Los Angeles, CA and Compton, CA; Oakland, CA and the San Francisco Bay Area; Seattle, WA and Portland, OR; Chicago, IL and Gary, IN; St. Louis, MO; Minneapolis, MN; Detroit, MI; Houston, TX; New Orleans, LA; Memphis, TN; Atlanta, GA; Miami, FL; Hampton, VA; Washington, DC and Baltimore, MD; Honolulu, HI; and San Juan, PR and Saint Thomas, VI.

Most scenes are located within the contiguous US—the exceptions are Honolulu, San Juan, and Saint Thomas. The twenty-five scenes represent about thirty-five different actual cities, counties, or sites. When available, the relationship of the city to the metro region is also considered. The sites include the following US states, territories, and commonwealths: California (four sites), District of Columbia, Florida, Georgia, Hawai'i, Illinois, Indiana, Louisiana, Maryland, Massachusetts, Michigan, Minnesota (two sites), Missouri, New Jersey (two sites), New York (seven sites), Oregon, Pennsylvania, Tennessee, Texas, Virginia, Washington, Puerto Rico, and the US Virgin Islands (USVI).

When?

The book's *when* questions focus on the last fifty years (since about 1973 to today), asking: When did rap music emerge on the scene, and what was its relationship to the local geography, migrational patterns, social movements, music history, and technological development? When did this musical scene solidify itself as sustainable? When was this contribution recognized by others outside of the scene? For most scenes, there is an interest in the following time periods: geography and place-making before 1870; migrations from 1870 to 1990; movements from 1950 to 1980; music from 1980 to the present day; and technology from 1980 to the present day. While *American Rap Scenes* focuses on the twentieth and twenty-first centuries, it also deals heavily in many historical periods related to the US and Black Americans.

How?

How does *American Rap Scenes* construct local rap scenes? For geography, the focus is on placemaking—incorporation, land and sea areas, and metro to city ratios. For migration, the focus is on the migrations of Black and Latinx populations during the 1870s and beyond. For social movements, the focus is on four organizations and a coordinated activity by student activists: the Black Panther Party for Self Defense (BPPSD), the Brown Berets, the Student Nonviolent Coordinating Committee (SNCC), the May 1970 anti-war student protests (the coordinated activity), and the Third World Women's Alliance (TWWA). For music, the focus is on development, specifically looking at established artists and groups on the scene and building historical and up-to-date artist lists based on current musical material, journalistic accounts, and academic studies of the scene. For technology, the focus on producers of rap, specifically looking at who produced the rap artists and groups on the local scene when possible.

Why?

So, why rap? Rap offers a historical record of a multigenerational Black music that is also regional and locale specific. It offers windows into the Black experience in the US and in the Americas. Rap is deeply rooted in West African drum traditions, musical patterns, songs of enslaved persons, protest songs, and the rich eclectic history of the music of the Black diaspora. Latinx and Caribbean peoples, some of whom were also connected to the Black diaspora or its culture, also became contributors to Hip Hop as early as its roots, founding, or construction—depending on who you ask. Much of rap is locally rooted, underground produced, raw, and unsanitized. Some rap still speaks to the identities, positions, and struggles of marginalized identities. Such rap can deal in power, protest, and the art of resistance, as "oppressed groups will develop and deploy the weapons of the weak to combat the oppression of the exploitative system."[4] When viewed as part of the Hip Hop movement, rap music contributes to a greater understanding of social movements involving minoritized communities in the historical aftermath of the Civil Rights Movement, Racial Justice Movement, and Black Arts Movement.

Why those specific twenty-five rap scenes? The scenes are mostly based on prior research on regional and local rap. Many scenes have histories of Black and Latinx migration and local political movements associated with this migration. Most are major or mid-sized cities, featuring major waterways, railways, and highways. Many of these sites have comparable data around population changes, political leadership, and economic industry, and the cities have production of musical content and uses of inventive technology on the scene. The scenes have plenty of music to create a database for analysis, and the scenes have a great amount of scholarly and journalistic literature for contextualization. Additional scenes beyond the twenty-five featured in the book and the reasoning around scene selection is a main topic of the "More Scenes" chapter.

Why *local* rap music? A focus on local rap achieves clarity and precision when speaking about the geographical, political, economic, and social conditions faced by minoritized populations since the 1970s. Rap is an essential form of communication initially created by groups of marginalized youth in US cities. Many local artists have offered deep critiques of their local conditions, and some local artists have offered systematic explanations for their conditions. Often, this local layer can effectively contextualize their local conditions with respect to other local, domestic, or global struggles both current and historical. Additionally, as Bennett writes, defining the scene also has value "as a conceptual framework for examining musical taste and collectivity."[5] Holt adds that cities are important sites for nightlife: "Where small towns and suburbs have little public life after midnight, night in the city is a time of activity among neo-bohemians, artists, and subcultures."[6] *American Rap Scenes* dwells in this space of local music scenes, with a specific focus on rap music scenes.

Core Terminology and Themes

Some core terminology is useful for understanding this book's analysis of US rap scenes and factors. These terms and sets of terms include the following:

rap music / Hip Hop culture
local / global
underground / mainstream

regional rap scenes / local rap scenes
comparative scenes approach

The rap music/Hip Hop culture distinction is necessary for better understanding the book's scope, possibilities, and limitations. The local/global distinction is discussed in combination with the underground/mainstream distinction. This two-part scale, a "dual axis continuum," has an axis for local-to-global and an axis for underground-to-mainstream. Much of the book deals in local or regional styles, so the regional/local scene distinction is important. The book uses a "comparative scenes approach," which builds from rap music scene and music scene studies.

Rap Music/Hip Hop Culture

Use of the term "rap" denotes a technical distinction, as a form of spoken word over an instrumental (or beat) and that spoken word over a beat being made into a consumable product through live performance or through physical or digital formats. Technology plays an integral role in this process, as DJing and its evolution into production have been essential for establishing rap as a commercial product. *American Rap Scenes* takes rap music and associated DJ and producer technology as integral to the spreading of Hip Hop culture. Essentially, the book sees rap music and DJ/production technology as serious contributions to Hip Hop culture, in the same ways that graffiti, breaking, and style have been taken as serious contributions to Hip Hop.

Rap music is one of five elements of Hip Hop culture constructed in the 1970s in the South Bronx. Keyes studies Hip Hop as a "recent" term and uses Hager's definition in *Hip Hop* as a "Funky music suitable for rapping; a collective term used to describe rap/graffiti/breaking/scratchin'". The term was invented by Starski, who used to chant: "To the hiphop, hiphop, don't stop that body rock."[7] Another tale of the origin of the term "Hip Hop" is that it started with slang for "hip" (cool) and "hop" (unusual dance). Hager's term, with the inclusion of graffiti, DJing, breaking, and rapping, really comes to embody Hip Hop culture. As defined by Bennett, rap music is a narrative in the "form of vocal delivery which is spoken in a rhythmic patois over a continuous backbeat, the rhythms of the voice and the beat working together."[8] Since 1979, rap music has generally been the element of Hip Hop most visible to the public. As early as 1984, Keyes identified rap as a "popular musical genre which makes extensive use of rhyme, nonsense syllables and music" and South Bronx and Harlem as its locational birthplace.[9] By the mid-1980s, Smitherman had published a highly influential book on rap and language entitled *Talkin' and Testifyin'*, seeing rap "in street corner, barbershop, beauty shop and other casual rap scenes," and recognizing it in activities such as signifying, capping, testifying, and toasting.[10]

Of course, the roots of rap and of Hip Hop culture run much deeper than its South Bronx emergence. While the core beginnings of Hip Hop start as early as the Middle Passage or colonization of the Americas, KRS-One understands Hip Hop as a concept that "started in 3114 BCE, based on the Mayan calendar."[11] That is to say that Hip Hop culture, as a "collective consciousness," started when time began to be marked in modern ways.[12] Hip Hop's cultural elements are deeply rooted in the "soul, soil, and spirit of Africa."[13] In addition to West African influences, the culture has deep Latinx and Caribbean influences as well as other influences from nearly every continent.

Local/Global

The local/global continuum is about product reach, and the underground/mainstream continuum is about target audience. This dual axis continuum provides a way of measuring *where* the rap impacts and *who* is impacted by the raps. Extremely local rap does not go beyond a block, neighborhood, or city. More expansive music would reach city, regional, or national audiences. Extremely global would be output to audiences worldwide. The analysis in *American Rap Scenes* includes local, global, underground, and mainstream artists and groups.

Underground/Mainstream

The other continuum is about the intended or target audience. This continuum runs from deeply underground to deeply mainstream. This underground extreme can be characterized by (at least) three distinct elements: (1) a DIY "do-it-yourself" culture, process, and release; (2) independent, local label ownership instead of major label ownership; and (3) functional obligation to represent local culture, crews, styles, and allegiances. These DIY products, at times, can sound and appear raw, unmastered, and unfinished. These aspects of the DIY product and culture share similarities with DIY dub, punk, and new wave subcultures, to name a few. Another main distinction is between local music production and industry-led music production. With many DIY products, local and independent labels create and own the product.

The continuum's other extreme end is wholly mainstream, when the intended audience is a worldwide market of buyers. Mainstream products are taken as those started, completed, and released by major record labels. As a continuum, there are many intervals in between the underground and mainstream extremes. Rap can also be "glocal," or somewhere between local production and global recognition. Also, it is difficult to completely separate "corporate music industry with the scene-based DIY industry." As Bennett and Peterson attest, the systems are "highly interdependent"; the corporate music industry uses the scene DIY for a "steady flow of new talent that gives a veneer of authenticity to their 'product,'" while the "DIY industry relies on the technologies created by the corporate industry."[14] However, the local and underground classifications are important, because lyrics, sounds, and artwork can be connected to the local experience and provide a deeper understanding of particular communities and the individuals who live in them. Additionally, as Perry emphasizes, a "revolutionary current exists in the underground communities of unsigned artists who pushed forward creative development without corporate involvement."[15] "Local underground artists" are seen as organic, "cultural workers" who can present their own image and thus "provide a good source when we seek feminist and other politically progressive messages in hip hop."[16]

As shown in Figure 2, both local/global and underground/mainstream distinctions are combined to produce a horizontal continuum (local/global) and a vertical continuum (underground/mainstream). This allows for a fuller understanding of rap's many forms and for a framework that respects the audience reached and audience targeted in rap from local scenes. It also calls for comparison of labels, artists, and styles in relation to one another. This dual axis continuum could also be used to plot nearly every artist or producer mentioned in *American Rap Scenes* with better accuracy than a simple local/global or underground/mainstream understanding.

Regional Rap Scenes/Local Rap Scenes

American Rap Scenes is made possible due to prior journalistic and academic studies of rap, especially those at the regional and local levels of analysis. For about ten years after Hip Hop's birth, it was mostly journalists and a handful of academics publishing

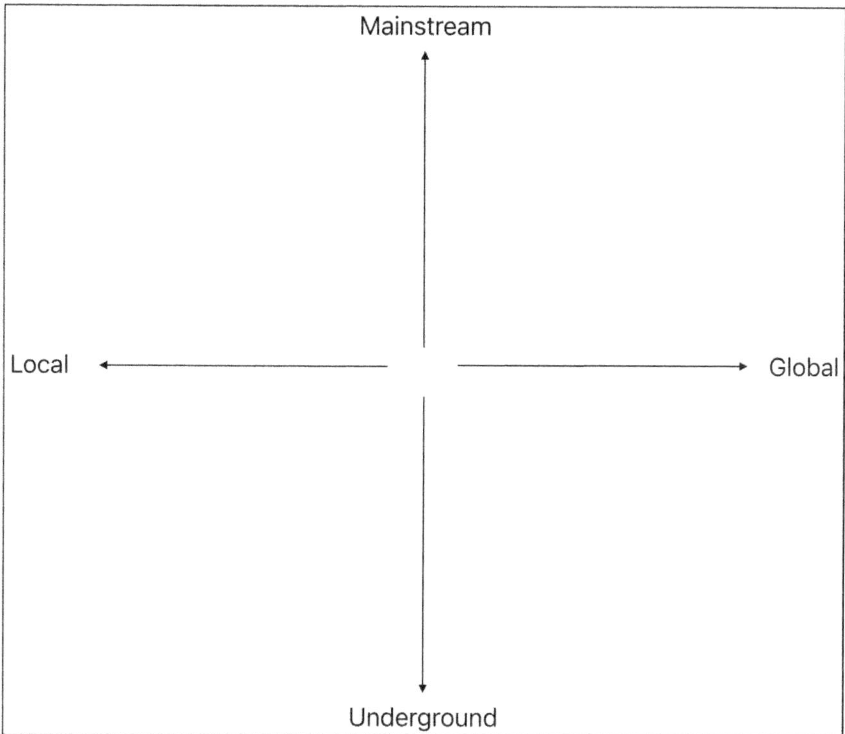

Figure 2 Local/global and underground/mainstream dual axis continuum.

about rap music and Hip Hop culture. In 1994, Rose's groundbreaking work on flow, layers, and the local emergence of rap contended that within ten years of rap music's emergence, Compton, Oakland, Detroit, Chicago, Houston, Atlanta, Miami, Newark and Trenton, Roxbury, and Philadelphia appropriated Hip Hop's "language, style, and attitude" to their adverse local conditions.[17] These various local Hip Hop scenes were linked to local instances of "alienation, unemployment, political harassment, social, and economic isolation."[18] However, to date and with few exceptions, the development of these local rap scenes has remained largely unexamined. There have been many topical examinations in the areas of location, proximity, and geography. Additionally, the studies of the earliest rap and Hip Hop scenes feature analyses of locations such as South Bronx, Harlem, or New Jersey. This is from 1979 to about 1982, which is the start of the recording industry's interest in rap. There, early locational and topical studies typically embraced the music and ethnographic detail or method. There were several regional studies of rap on the West Coast and in the South that also advanced locational studies of rap.[19]

In 2009, Hess's edited volume *Hip Hop in America* presented a detailed analysis of local scenes.[20] This volume presented a prototype for moving scholars beyond regional analysis into local analysis by providing an extremely detailed local mapping of rap. The scenes are grouped by regional emergence and by relative local emergence within the region. Each local scene is presented in a separate book chapter. Related to this local level analysis, there was also a great development of local rap scene ethnographic methods.[21] An additional text was highly influential to the design of *American Rap Scenes*. In 2010, Woldu covered the scope of Hip Hop writing to the date of publication. Covering multiple industries and fields, and quite remarkable in overall breadth, Woldu's article presents a "kaleidoscope" of Hip Hop writing and created three author groups: academic authors, journalists and cultural critics, and Hip Hop "devotees."[22] Examining "significant publications" from 1988 to 2008, through a "variety of lenses" to help "illuminate new directions" for Hip Hop's future, Woldu explains, "The earliest period of writing about hip-hop focused on the newly emergent 'party' music of the late 1970s through the early 1980s."[23] By the 1990s, writing on Hip Hop "in generalist and popular-culture magazines focused largely on 'gangsta rap'," and, in the 2000s, Hip Hop became "widely accepted as an academic discipline."[24] Woldu's text is essential to the shaping of this book's initial research, the scoping review design used, and the overall merging of locational and topical foci in *American Rap Scenes*. The book builds from this model and adds a scoping review, data analysis, and an expansion of some of the topics and themes mentioned by Woldu.

The local level of analysis offered by Hess and advances in Hip Hop scholarship led to studies that could offer a deeper analysis of US rap scenes and musical content. These studies, often longitudinal in approach, have involved scenes such as New Orleans, Houston, Oakland, Seattle, and Atlanta.[25] Focused on New Orleans and published in 2012, Miller's *Bounce* comprehensively covers decades of local rap history.[26] *Bounce* provided one of the first known longitudinal (long-range) analyses about local rap on a non-Bronx US scene. Miller's interest is on actual music collections and documenting the history of the New Orleans rap scene. *Bounce* set a standard for a thorough musical examination of rap scenes. Then in 2013, Faniel's *Hip-Hop in Houston* added to this field of local rap studies. It is historically, musically, and artistically focused.[27] It offers a deep description of the history of the Houston rap scene, focusing on the musical culture to trouble the "single origin narrative" of rap music.[28] Local rap was also examined in Walker's *Houston Rap Tapes* in 2018. Walker adds to local rap analysis by using extensive and candid interviews (with both mainstream and underground artists) to vividly describe the local scene by both industry and street accounts.[29] Walker's organization, thorough timeline, and other impressive resources make this an important contribution to the scene and to local studies of rap. Published in 2023, Wilkins's *Welcome 2 Houston* is the first study to operate largely on a local-to-neighborhood level and notes a "deep local pride" in these spaces of production and artistry.[30] Wilkins's analysis is about the "indigenization" of Hip Hop on the local Houston scene.[31] Wilkins looks at Houston within a "nation of streets concept," contending, "Economic practices, language, clothing styles, vehicle aesthetics and other cultural trends were now being shared between geographically distant streets."[32]

Focused on Seattle, Abe's *Emerald Street* provides a rich historical account with a thick description of all things related to the local scene. Published in 2020, it starts from the point of Hip Hop's arrival in Seattle, covering a timeline of Hip Hop from 1979 to 2015.[33] Abe's book is a master course in writing about a local scene's richness and formation, evolution, and impact. Focused on the Oakland and San Francisco Bay Area, my *Rap and Politics* builds a framework to examine the evolution of the music. It looks at the following: (1) the arrival of new racial and ethnic groups to the new urban setting; (2) the ascension of underground leaders and representation when subgroups find that the official political order is unwilling or unable to meet their interests; (3) the political, radical, and militant movements of the 1960s and 1970s; (4) comprehensive discourse banks created by the movements in the 1960s and 1970s, rappers in the 1980s and 1990s (generally, through the rap album), and rappers in the 2000s and beyond (generally, through the rap single); and (5) the local, regional, national, and international impact of the discourse bank.[34] These local studies of rap show the New Orleans, Houston, Seattle, and Oakland scenes building types of regional, local, or hyper-local sounds and production that are then connected to other US scenes and the international Hip Hop community.

Comparative Scenes Approach

This book's "comparative scenes approach" is a combination of local rap music scene analysis and music scene analysis—which have been somewhat separate literatures. Rap music scene analysis is more recent and is typically done by scholars of Hip Hop and rap with some elements of musicology or music scene analysis. This type of analysis has been rare throughout the study of Hip Hop and rap, but arguably, some of the most influential studies have seriously engaged rap music scenes. Meanwhile, music scene analysis has been more common in the work of cultural anthropologists or musicologists who consider an understanding of music scenes as an essential and uncompromisable starting point to understanding the music created from the scene.

For the most part and historically, most of these local analyses have been about musics other than rap (i.e., rock, alternative, blues, jazz, bluegrass) or about rap beyond the US. Yet, the music scene literature provides an important theoretical starting point in defining, understanding, and analyzing scenes. *American Rap Scenes* presents an approach that takes both rap music and music scene analysis very seriously. This inquiry of rap on the twenty-five scenes increases knowledge about the scenes and their "glocal" (local and global) connections.

Summary of Framework

American Rap Scenes asks, What is the role of geography, migration, social movements, musical tradition, and technology in shaping the development of local US rap scenes? Rap is largely locally produced—which requires an understanding of geography and placemaking. Geography is analyzed through physical area (land and water area), placemaking (or the establishment of city government), the overall urban history on the local scenes, and the physical relationship within the region and between scenes.

Rap involves Black identities and other identities associated with the West African diaspora. Rap is especially connected to Caribbean and Latinx identities (among many others). Such connections require an understanding of migrational patterns. Migration is analyzed through population changes and racial and ethnic demographic data. This shows patterns of Black migration to the North and return migration to the South and Latinx migration and immigration to cities. Caribbean migration and immigration to cities, while important, can be tremendously difficult to measure though US census data.

Rap follows the Civil Rights, Racial Justice, and Black Arts Movements and is part of the Movement of Hip Hop. These social movements involve(d) responses by descendants of migrants or immigrants who went beyond the limits of the political, economic, or societal order in cities (which was not accommodating them). Movements involve the establishment of government, the inaccessibility of this government to new arrivals of Black, Latinx, Caribbean peoples, and the quests for representation in both electoral and non-electoral political settings.

Rap's musical form varies greatly from locale to locale. This is largely an impact of migration of peoples and musical history on the scenes, as different cultures bring expertise in different musical instruments and genres. Musicology (or, more specifically, ethnomusicology) helps explain the different types of musics on the scene. The term "ethnomusicology" signifies "the division of musicology in which special emphasis is given to the study of music in its cultural context—the anthropology of music."[35] Forms of ethnomusicology use historical musicology and application of data and archives, especially those "who work in cultures lacking written records must rely on methods designed to investigate oral history."[36]

Rap's musical form is also highly dependent on technological invention; rap producers invent new sounds by manipulating and transforming popular music through DJ equipment and studio production equipment, respectively. Some consumer technologies (such as turntables) were initially used to manipulate sound, and then a rising number of production technologies (such as MIDI production consoles and digital audio workstations) were used to transform samples from popular music into new musical forms. There is also a key relationship between the local music scene, historical change, and the larger international "music culture." Straw discusses this interrelationship: "The manner in which musical practices within a scene tie themselves to processes of historical change occurring within a larger international music culture will also be a significant basis of the way in which such forms are positioned within that scene at the local level."[37] Technology plays a vital role in all of this.

Most of the core literature and data in *American Rap Scenes* were collected between December 2020 and August 11, 2023. This end date is associated with the 50th Anniversary of Hip Hop's construction at 1520 Sedgwick in the South Bronx. This book used these dates to form a scoping review of books, academic articles, and book chapters, finding more than eight hundred related to the factors and more than two thousand related to the scenes. These texts were then examined for relevancy for use in *American Rap Scenes*. The book also looked into theses and "grey" literature. Since this grey literature includes papers, presentations, and other non-published materials, these sources were not generally included in the study. This grey literature measurement, however, was taken to estimate popularity of the factors and locations as topics in Google Scholar and ProQuest. There were close to 1,000,000 search results (725,000 ProQuest dissertations and theses and close to 300,000 Google Scholar grey literature sources) related somehow to the core factors and locations. There is much more about this review process in Appendix A: Technical Appendix.

Summary of Methodology

The methodology is directly linked to the framework discussed above. In Chapter 1, Scenes, date of incorporation, 2020 population, 2020 Black percentage, 2020 Latinx percentage, city-to-metro area ratio, and land area (in square miles and square kilometers) are reported for most scenes. Sites with outlier rankings (as in top five or bottom five) are highlighted. Chapter 2, Geography, considers latitude-longitude, date of incorporation, geographical land and water areas, and population and population density. Chapter 3, Migration, considers the movement of Black populations from the 1870s and beyond and Latinx populations since 1970. This inquiry considers changes in total population, changes in Black population, and changes in Latinx population from the previous decennial census data. Chapter 4, Movement, considers local radical and militant chapter histories on the scenes as foundations of protest on the local scene, looking to the local chapter history or local event history of the following groups: the BPPSD, the Brown Berets, the SNCC, the May 1970 activity, and the TWWA. Chapter 5, Music, considers the history of music on location (local musicology) and brought to location (ethnomusicology), with a focus on rap artists and groups after the 1980s. A starter list of rap artists related to each local scene is provided in Chapter 1. Chapter 6, Technology, centers on producers involved with the production of rap and discusses producers derived from the rap artists above.

American Rap Scenes hopes to assist in a paradigm shift, where the development of local rap is taken seriously, carefully, and with a focus *on* and engagement *with* local, community-based sources. These community sources created in or by the local community's independent artists, labels, and organizations can take forms in music (singles, albums, mixtapes), print media (newsletters and pamphlets), and visual media (photographs and film). These local sources can be examined to achieve additional clarity and precision when speaking about the local geographical, political, economic, and social conditions faced by Black, Latinx, and other minoritized youth in US cities.

Book Content and Main Arguments

American Rap Scenes features seven chapters.

Chapter 1: "Scenes" focuses on twenty-five US rap music scenes. The chapter's main argument is that a scene analysis of US local rap would include factors such as geography, migrational history, social movements, musical history, and technology use in production. This chapter explores core evidence of these five factors on twenty-five US rap music scenes to set up the book's next five substantive chapters—on Geography, Migration, Movement, Music, and Technology. The information is organized by the following regions: East Coast, West Coast, Midwest, and South and Contested Islands.

Chapter 2: "Geography" underscores the importance of geography, placemaking, society, and governance as an essential background to rap scenes. The chapter analyzes data related to geographic size (total area, land area, and water area), township establishment date (oldest, most recent), population size (largest, smallest), Black population percentage (largest, smallest), Latinx population percentage (largest, smallest), and city to metro (high city percentage, high metro percentage). The chapter contextualizes this data with studies of regional and local rap geographies.

Chapter 3: "Migration" explores rap as a product of the migratory patterns of people of West African, Caribbean, and Latin American descent as well as the migratory patterns of people in general. The basis for this argument lies in the data related to demographic changes from the decennial census (changes in total population, changes in Black population, and changes in Latinx population) on the twenty-five scenes— which comprise about thirty-five city or administrative site locations. A comparative analysis of migration on the twenty-five scenes highlights the common themes of colonization, slavery, and Great and Second Great Migrations as related to rap scenes.

Chapter 4: "Movement" focuses on rap scenes as a product of social movements. The main argument is that social movement activity on the local scene helped act as precursors for the types of politics that eventually manifest in Hip Hop culture and rap music. Hip Hop culture is a social movement, with rap music being a main message carrier to outsiders of this movement activity. This argument is bolstered by data related to locational activity (organizations or events) from several movements with chapters and activity on the twenty-five scenes (or about thirty-five sites), including the BPPSD, the Brown Berets, the SNCC, the May 1970 anti-war protests held across the US, and the TWWA. The chapter contextualizes this local activity within US identity and movement politics, highlighting identity areas such as race, ethnicity, gender, class, and related intersections of these identities.

Chapter 5: "Music" explores rap music scenes through an ethnomusicology lens, specifically as a product of migratory musics and developing musics on a scene. West African, Black American, Jamaican, Puerto Rican, and other cultures helped create the music that exists and that evolves on a local scene. A comparative analysis of this musical development and an examination of the origins, foundation, emergence, connectivity, and legacy of rap is explored on the twenty-five scenes.

Chapter 6: "Technology" explores DJ and production technologies as vital catalysts in the growth of local rap scenes. DJs use turntables and other instruments to manipulate sound, and producers use music production consoles and other devices to transform samples. Rap production is built from these practices of manipulation and transformation by rap producers. The chapter also explores what happens after a song or album is finished, highlighting areas of its manufacture and distribution and Music 3.0 as related to local rap scenes. Understanding these production technologies and how final products are distributed will help in an understanding of how local rap expands to regional, domestic, and international locations.

Chapter 7: "More Scenes" focuses on the gains and limits of the locational approach, noting additional rap scenes in the US, worldwide, and in virtual spaces. The main argument is that there are many other scenes in need of further study, which is additional testimony to the localization (or glocalization) of rap and its impact. The chapter explores geography, migration, movements, music, and technology as factors on these additional scenes. The rationale for choosing the twenty-five scenes is explained through five main impetus points to the writing of the book. These points include the following: (1) prior research findings; (2) evidence of Black, Latinx, and Caribbean migration; (3) political, radical, and militant movement chapter histories; (4) changes in production and DJ technologies; and (5) evolving project feedback.

The Conclusion summarizes the major points and findings as related to geography, migration, movements, music, and technology, while highlighting applications to topical areas of place, identity, power, class, social change, media and technology, and methodology. Finally, the book concludes by looking at future directions, providing a survey template for local scenes and researchers. Ultimately, the argument is that researchers should continue a focus on rap's local development. It is key for the primary source material to be drawn from the local community to tell us about a local community. Ideally, these sources would be identified and selected with inputs from local communities or through community-centric survey and research methods. Overall, *American Rap Scenes* shows that the evidence of rap on the twenty-five scenes and elsewhere indicates that it is likely that these messages will continue to grow in other places, or, put differently, as long as there are racial, ethnic, class, gender, and other forms of oppression in the world, there will likely be rap resistance.

Conclusion

In sum, the book's main purpose is to explore the development of twenty-five US rap music scenes though five key factors—geography, migration, movement, music, and technology. The local scene is integral in building the capacity for comparative scene analysis. The goal is to push Hip Hop studies forward with a combined locational and thematic approach.

1

Scenes

Introduction

In "South Bronx Subway Rap (Original Version)," (Figure 3) Grandmaster Caz demonstrates how to transform the poor socio-economic conditions of the South Bronx scene into something greater:

South Bronx, New York that's where I dwell / To a lot of people it's a living hell
Full of frustration and poverty / But wait, that's not how it looks to me
It's a challenge and opportunity / To rise above the stink and debris
Ya gotta start with nothing and then you build / Follow your dream until it's fulfilled.[1]

As one of South Bronx's early creators of rap music, Grandmaster Caz provides a detailed, contextualized description of the local scene and how the local environment led to voiced resistance. He mentions the view from the "outsider" as context. With garbage overflowing, trains running constantly, ruined buildings, crime, and pollution, some outsiders see this as a "living hell." However, instead of the "frustration and poverty" noticed by outsiders, Grandmaster Caz suggests using self-determination to "rise above the stink and debris." He mentions dreams, from building to fulfillment, all in the first verse. The second verse doubles down on self-determination and praxis by proposing to use art as a weapon—even asking the listener to try to make their South Bronx "home" better. Perry outlines the type of tension related to such an urban scene: "Depending on one's perspective it is either a wasteland or a garden. Concrete as far as the eye can see, piercing the sky and covering the earth. And yet the smells, sounds, tastes, and the smaller frames of vision encase blacks and browns, piecing together their roots in this seemingly uprooted place."[2] In this type of environment, rappers began employing political messaging early. As Vernon underscores, the type of progressive self-determination expressed by Grandmaster Caz was the dominant messaging until rapping hit the mainstream.[3] Yet, while Grandmaster Caz and others were effective in providing snapshots of current conditions and resident responses on a single scene, much could be gained by taking a comparative and historical look at the factors, conditions, and range of responses on local rap music scenes.

This chapter is about music scenes, and more specifically rap music scenes. The term "music scene" was "originally used primarily in journalistic and everyday

                    American Rap Scenes

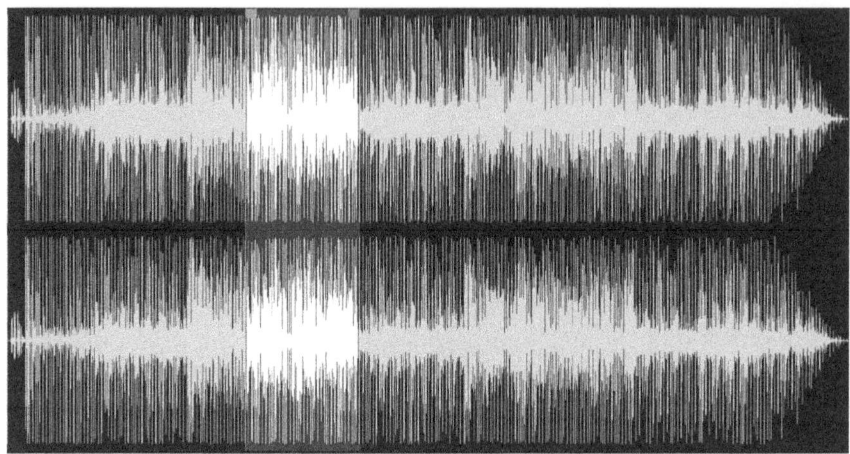

Figure 3 Grandmaster Caz "South Bronx Subway Rap (Original Version)" Akai WAV snapshot with quoted material highlighted.

contexts," and it "is increasingly used by academic researchers to designate the contexts in which clusters of producers, musicians, and fans collectively share their common music tastes and distinguish themselves from others."[4] It was first used in the 1940s by journalists attempting to "characterize the marginal and bohemian way of life of those associated with the demiworld of jazz."[5] Eventually, scene as concept grew to describe an entire culture of "music, dress, and deportment appropriate to a scene," and it grew into a "cultural resource for fans of particular musical genres, enabling them to forge collective expressions of 'underground' or 'alternative' identity and to identify their cultural distinctiveness from the 'mainstream.'"[6] Music scene perspectives have often centered on music venues, studios, performances, and other locations. Yet, a rap music scene perspective must also acknowledge the difficult environment on these locales and the ability of youth to transform these harsh conditions into something greater.

Music scene analysis has been helpful in better understanding the emergence of rap music scenes. To date, there has been very little focus on the conditions behind rap scenes. Music scene theorists have characterized an area of analysis beyond the music, as Straw writes:

Scenes, I suggest, might be seen as all of the following: as *collectivities* marked by some form of proximity; as *spaces of assembly* engaged in pulling together the varieties of cultural phenomena; as *workplaces* engaged (explicitly or implicitly) in the transformation of materials; as *ethical worlds* shaped by the working out and maintenance of behavioural protocols; as *spaces of traversal and preservation* through which cultural energies and practices pass at particular speeds and as *spaces of mediation* which regulate the visibility and invisibility of cultural life and the extent of its intelligibility to others. [7]

Straw outlines scenes as collectives, "spaces of assembly," workplaces, ethical worlds, "spaces of traversal and preservation," and "spaces of mediation." Applying this logic to local rap music scenes, rap locations should be marked by local residents as places to gather, work, create internal community standards, enact cultural change, preserve traditions, and create visibility and intelligibility of the scene to outsiders.

This chapter introduces twenty-five rap scenes, analyzed by five key factors throughout the book: geography and place, migrations of peoples, movements formed by people on the scene, musics of people who moved to the scene and musics already on the scene, and technologies on the scene. To date, rarely have the conditions behind scenes been considered as factors on music production on scenes. This is the function of the current chapter.

Scene Analysis in *American Rap Scenes*

Rooted in Cultural Studies, music scene analysis has been deeply centered on local city environments, with a growing focus on virtual scenes. Straw points out that the concept of scene has been used to "circumscribe highly local clusters of activity and to give unity to practices dispersed throughout the world," noting that scene "functions to designate face-to-face sociability and as a lazy synonym for globalized virtual communities of taste."[8] Straw also finds that scenes suggest "both the direction of a movement and its scale," and this might include "recurring congregation of people at a particular place," "movement of these people between this place and other spaces of congregation," "streets/strips along which this movement takes place," "all the places and activities which surround and nourish a particular cultural preference," "the broader and more geographically dispersed phenomena of which this movement or these preferences are local examples," or "the webs of microeconomic activity which foster sociability and link this to the city's ongoing self reproduction." The main question posed is important: "All of these phenomena have been designated as scenes. Is a scene the group of people, as they move from place to place? Is it the places through which they move?"[9] Meanwhile, Kruse emphasizes that "scene" encompasses "both the geographical sites of localized music practice and the social and economic networks that exist within these contexts."[10]

As a site of local production, Shank finds that the Austin, TX, alternative rock scene's "most significant sites" included "record stores, nightclubs, rehearsal rooms, city neighborhoods, streets and alleyways."[11] Shank's analysis also identifies geography within the scene as important, with a computer-drawn map showing highways and structures important to the locale. Music magazines and fanzines are also analyzed as part of the scene context. Scene analysis at the city level is important because, as Holt shows, "cities have been centers for live popular music since the late nineteenth century; their large populations providing audiences for both mass entertainment and for subcultures and niche genre scenes that only existed in large cities."[12] Klement and Strambach have asked how "new music genres emerge and lead to a diversification of music scenes," which relates to rap scenes.[13] Peterson and Bennett have also applied music scene analysis to rap music scenes.[14]

Overall, the work by Straw and others moves scholars beyond older notions of "musical community" into more complete notions of a "musical scene," which is "that cultural space in which a range of musical practices coexist, interacting with each other within a variety of processes of differentiation, and according to widely varying trajectories of change and cross-fertilization."[15] Ultimately, Straw finds, "The aesthetic values which dominate local alternative terrains are for the most part those of a musical cosmopolitanism wherein the points of musical reference are likely to remain stable from one community to another."[16] Bennett adds that scene qualities can be bound by musical taste (rather than by class or by community), constantly evolving, and transient in nature.[17] This is all helpful in defining the contexts for scene development and interaction between scenes. Similar to music scene analysis, rap scene analysis must consider the context of the creation of this material culture.

Local rap scenes in New Orleans, Houston, Seattle, and Oakland have been analyzed in more comprehensive and longitudinal forms. This specialized type of music scene analysis tends to highlight long-range changes on the scene through rap labels or their products, with some studies offering comprehensive listings of local, independent, and DIY labels. Some studies also highlight local club or live performance venues. Others look at conditions behind the music, such as local demographics, political leadership and organizations (electoral and non-electoral), print media (newspapers, music magazines, and fan magazines), broadcast media (including pirate radio), and shifts in the use of new technologies. Rap scenes would also likely include creative arts agencies, business and management, media, political institutions and structures, and social justice activist groups on a site. The material produced on rap scenes matters. Katz explains, "Most people around the world first experienced hip hop in electronically mediated form, whether through analog means in its early years or through digital streaming services, video-sharing platforms, or social media."[18] Someone's first contact with rap music might be though a product from a local scene—that scene could be nearby or in another part of the world.

Factors in *American Rap Scenes*

Focusing on five factors (geography, migration, movement, music, and technology) not only works within the music scene analysis tradition but also emphasizes the geographical and historical landscape of urban local rap scenes in the US.

First, the geography and placemaking are analyzed through site data related to the following: total area, land area, and water area; date of incorporation; 2020 population, racial and ethnic composition, city-to-metro area population distribution, and population density. Second, migration is analyzed by looking at changes in total population, Black population, and Latinx population from the prior US decennial census. Third, the social movements section considers the Black Panther Party for Self Defense (BPPSD), the Brown Berets, the Student Non-Violence Coordinating Committee (SNCC), the May 1970 anti-war protests, and the Third World Women's

Alliance (TWWA) activities or events on scenes. In the instance of three or more of these activities or events on a scene, all known activity on the scene is reported. This look into specific Black, Latinx, Women's, Student, and Intersectional groups highlights the presence of social movements with political, radical, and (at times) militant elements on the scene just before (and during) rap's emergence. This is designed to consider Hip Hop as a movement and rap as a growing form of protest. Fourth, for music as factor, the chapter builds a starter list of rap artists and groups related to each local scene. Fifth, for technology as factor, the chapter focuses on local producers on the scene who have created soundscapes for local rappers.

The rappers and producers listed are drawn from scene-specific journalistic and academic sources. Due to the volume of sources, they are not directly cited here. However, they are grouped by scene in Appendix B: List of Known Studies of Rap on Scenes from *American Rap Scenes*. More detailed information about this general data and sourcing is available in Appendix A: Technical Appendix. Further information and comparative analyses of these factors (geography, migration, movement, music, and technology) are offered in the book's next five chapters.

Table 1 shows the comparative geographical and social movement data for *American Rap Scenes*. There are three main codes used: T1, T5, and T10. These are indications of how each site compares to the others: T1 for the top site; T5 for one of the top five sites; and T10 for above most others in each given category. New York City (NYC) is considered at the separate site (borough) level and as a consolidated site. However, NYC data has an asterisk next to it—for example, T1*, T5*, or T10*. Each city's geographical rank is discussed below if the top site, one of the top five, or among the top sites in *American Rap Scenes*. Chapter 2 examines this data by looking at common characteristics of the sites with the highest and lowest trends in each category.

East Coast

South Bronx

The Bronx sits on 42 mi^2 (109 km^2) of land. It was established around 1898 and had a 2020 population of 1.47 million (43.8 percent Black and 56 percent Latinx), representing about 7.3 percent of the population of the New York metro area. At the time of Hip Hop's birth, the Bronx has had significant geographical, migrational, movement, musical, and technological factors present. There are geographical factors related to density, and there was a major population decline. Migration is also a factor, as the Black and Latinx percentages have been growing since the 1960s. The Latinx percentage in the Bronx is one the highest of the sites. The Bronx is also a movement scene (with the movement of Hip Hop as a primary factor), and it is also a music scene (with the first live raps) and a technology scene (with the first Hip Hop DJing).

Artists and groups associated with the South Bronx rap scene include Afrika Bambaataa, Antoinette, B-Lovee, Beatnuts, Big Punisher, Boogie Down Productions, Busy Bee, C-Rayz Walz, Camp Lo, Canibus, Cosmic Force, Coke La Rock, Cold

Table 1 Overview of Comparative Data on Scenes.

Scene Number	City or Site	Total Area (Highest)	Total Area (Lowest)	Land Area (Highest)	Land Area (Lowest)	Water Area (Highest)	Water Area (Lowest)	Oldest	Newest	Population (Highest)
1	Bronx		T10						T5	T10
2	Manhattan and Harlem		T5		T5			T5		T10
3	Queens	T10				T5		T10		T5
4	Brooklyn							T5		T5
5	Staten Island									
	New York City	T5*		T5*		T5*		T5*		T1*
6	Hempstead	T10						T5		
7	Philadelphia			T10				T10		T10
8	Newark		T5		T5	T5				T10
	Jersey City		T1		T1	T10				
9	Boston			T10	T10			T5		
10	Los Angeles	T5		T5		T10				T1
11	Oakland							T10		
	San Francisco	T10			T10	T1				T10
	San Jose	T10		T5			T5		T10	T10
12	Seattle					T5			T10	
	Portland	T10		T10					T10	
13	Chicago	T5		T5			T10			T5
	Gary		T5		T10		T1		T5	
14	St. Louis		T10				T10			
15	Minneapolis				T5				T5	
	St. Paul		T10		T10				T10	
16	Detroit			T10		T10				
17	Houston	T1		T1		T5				T5
18	New Orleans	T5		T10		T5				
19	Memphis	T5		T5						
20	Atlanta			T10				T5		
21	Miami		T10	T5					T5	
22	Hampton				T5					
23	Washington, DC									T10
	Baltimore									
24	Honolulu								T1	
25	San Juan			T10	T10			T1		
	Saint Thomas		T5		T5			T10		

Population (Lowest)	Density (Highest)	Density (Lowest)	Black % (Highest)	Black % (Lowest)	Latinx % (Highest)	Latinx % (Lowest)	City to Metro (High City)	City to Metro (High Metro)	3+ Social Movement Sites
	T5				T5			T10	
	T1						T10		
	T5				T10				
	T5								
									3
	T5*						T5*		3+*
								T5	
									3
	T10		T10		T10			T5	3
T5	T5				T10			T1	
	T10								
				T5	T5		T10		4
									4
	T10		T5						3
			T5		T10		T1		
			T5			T10			3
		T10	T10				T10		3
	T10				T10		T10		3
T5		T5	T1						
T5		T10	T10			T1			
T10				T10		T10		T10	
		T10	T5				T10		3
		T10			T5		T5		3
T10		T5	T5			T5	T5		3
		T5	T5			T10	T5		
		T10	T10			T5		T10	
		T10		T10	T5			T5	
T5		T5						T10	
			T5			T5	T10		3
T10				T1			T5		
T10				T10	T1				
T1		T1							

Crush Brothers, Corey Gunz, Cru, D-Nice, Diamond D & The Psychotic Neurotics, Disco King Mario, DJ John Brown, DMX, DreamDoll, ESG, Fat Joe, French Montana, Funkmaster Flex, Funky 4 + 1, Grandmaster Flash, Grandmaster Caz, Grandmaster Flash & The Furious Five, Grandmaster Melle Mel, Grand Wizzard Theodore, Ice Spice, Juggaknots, Just-Ice, Kay Flock, Keef Cowboy, Kool DJ AJ, Kool Herc, Kool Keith, Kool Kyle The Starchild, KRS-One, Lil TJay, Lisa Lee, Lord Finesse & DJ Mike Smooth, Lord Tariq & Peter Gunz, Love Bug Starski, Mr. Magic, Nairobe & Awesome Foursome, Nice & Smooth, Nine, Percee P, Pete Rock, Psycho Les, Remy Martin, Ron Suno, Showbiz and A.G., Slick Rick, South Bronx Movement, Sweet G, Swizz Beatz, T La Rock, T Ski Valley, Terror Squad, Tim Dog, Ultramagnetic MCs, Uneek (Bounce Squad), and the Universal Zulu Nation. Producers associated with the South Bronx rap scene include Afrika Islam, Afrika Bambaataa, Amadeus, Billy Nichols, Beatnuts, Buckshot, Buckwild, Ced-Gee, Diamond D, Kool DJ AJ, DJ Breakout, DJ Charlie Chase, DJ Jazzy Jay, DJ Kid Capri, Dj Louie Lou, Funkmaster Flex, Grand Wizzard Theodore, Grandmaster Flash, Jazzy Joyce, Juggaknots, Just-Ice, KRS-One, Lord Finesse, Minnesota, Mr. Magic, Nice & Smooth, Pete Rock, Showbiz, Ski Beats, South Bronx, Special K, Swizz Beatz, The 45 King, Tim Dog, Ultramagnetic MCs, and Yogi.

Manhattan and Harlem

Manhattan sits on 22.93 mi^2 (59.1 km^2) of land. It was established around 1624 and had a 2020 population of about 1.69 million (18.5 percent Black and 26.4 percent Latinx). Manhattan represented about 8.4 percent of the New York metro area population in 2020. Manhattan is a high-density scene, with more people living on less land area than most other sites. Harlem, a popular Black migration destination, is also part of Manhattan's census reporting. Manhattan, in addition, has a strong Latinx population. Manhattan is also a movement city, with Black freedom and arts movements in Harlem, with an important BPPSD chapter (that led NYC and organized East Coast Panthers), a legacy of student protests, at least twenty instances of SNCC organizational activity, and one of two US-based TWWA chapter offices. NYC, as a combination of boroughs, includes the Bronx, Brooklyn, Harlem, Queens, and Staten Island. NYC sits on 300.5 mi^2 (778 km^2) of land. Established in 1624, its 2020 population was around 8.8 million (20.2 percent Black and 28.3 percent Latinx), representing 43.7 percent of the New York metro area. NYC's Latinx percentage was 25.2 percent and 28.7 percent in 1970 and 1980, respectively. NYC is a high-population and high-density site, with one of the highest total, land, and water areas of the sites.

Artists and groups associated with the Manhattan and Harlem rap scene include A$AP Ferg, Afrika Bambaataa, Afrika Bambaataa & Soulsonic Force, Azealia Banks, Beastie Boys, Big Daddy Kane, Big L, Biz Markie, Boogie Boys, Brenda K. Starr, Bytches With Problems (BWP), Cam'ron, Cardi B, Cannibal Ox, CC Crew, Crash Crew, Cutmaster D.C., D&D All-Stars, Dave East, Def Squad, Delinquent Habits, Diplomats, Disco Four, Doug E. Fresh & The Get Fresh Crew, Dr. Jeckyll & Mr. Hyde, E.Bros, Eddie Cheeba, Fat Back Band, Fearless Four, Flipmode Squad, Frankie Cutlass, FunkMaster Flex, GM Grimm, Harlem World, Group Home, Harlem World Crew,

Ill Al Skratch, Immortal Technique, J-Live, Jean Grae, Jim Jones, Juelz Santana, Jungle Brothers, Kemo the Blaxican, Kool Moe Dee, Kurtis Blow, Lord Finesse, Mantronix, Mase, Missy D & The Melody Crew, Mr. Magic, Paulette and Tanya Winley, Pete DJ Jones, Pete Rock & C.L. Smooth, Posta Boy, Rebel Diaz, Rob Base & DJ E-Z Rock, Sean "Diddy" Combs, Smoke DZA, Spoonie Gee, Spyder D, Swizz Beats, The Last Poets, The Marvelous Three & Younger Generation, The Weathermen, Treacherous Three, Whodini, and Vast Aire. Producers associated with the Manhattan and Harlem rap scene include 88-Keys, Afrika Bambaataa & Soulsonic Force, Agallah, Arkatech Beatz, Arthur Baker, Big L, Bill Curtis, Biz Markie, Blockhead, Cannibal Ox, Chyskillz, D.I.T.C., Dame Grease, DJ Clark Kent, DJ Clue, DJ Hollywood, DJ Kurtis Mantronik, Doug E. Fresh & The Get Fresh Crew, El-P, EZ Elpee, Focus…, Frankie Cutlass, Grand Mixer DXT, Harry Fraud, Hurby Luv Bug, Jimi Kendrix, Juelz Santana, Just Blaze, Kanye West, Kid Capri, Knobody, Kurtis Blow, Mark Ronson, MC Tee, MF Grimm, Mr. Magic, Omen, Paul C, Pete Rock, Rick Rubin, Ron Browz, Scram Jones, Sean "Diddy" Combs, Sha Money XL, Swizz Beatz, Teddy Riley, The Heatmakerz, The Hitmen, The Ummah, True Master, and Vinylz.

Queens

Queens sits on 109 mi² (280 km²) of land. It was established around 1683 and had a 2020 population of about 2.4 million (20.7 percent Black and 28.1 percent Latinx), representing about 11.9 percent of the New York metro area. Queens is a geographical and migrational scene, with high total, land, and water areas and with one of the largest populations and highest densities of the sites. As a migratory scene, Queens had a population boom in the 1950s, and its Black and Latinx percentages subsequently grew in the 1980s and 1990s. Queens is a technology scene, given Marley Marl's role in transforming musical production.

Artists and groups associated with the Queens rap scene include 3rd Bass, 50 Cent, A Tribe Called Quest, Action Bronson, Akinyele, Awkwafina, Big Jus, Big Noyd, Brand Nubian, Capone, Cormega, CJ Fly, Craig G, DJ Red Alert, Havoc, Homeboy Sandman, Juice Crew, Jungle Brothers, K.M.D., Kool G Rap & DJ Polo, Large Professor, Lil Tecca, LL Cool J, Lost Boyz, MC Serch, MC Shan, Meyhem Lauren, Mobb Deep, Nas, Nikki Minaj, Noreaga, Onyx, Organized Konfusion, Pharoahe Monch, Prodigy of Mobb Deep, Q-Tip, Rich the Kid, Run-D.M.C., Roxane Shante, Salt-N-Pepa, Sweet Tee & DJ Jazzy Joyce, The Showboys, Tragedy Khadafi, and Vinia Mojica. Producers associated with the Queens rap scene include 50 Cent, Akinyele, Ali Shaheed Muhammad, Ayatollah, Biz Markie, DJ Hurricane, DJ Jam Master Jay, DJ Red Alert, Havoc, Irv Gotti, J-Zone, Juice Crew, K.M.D., Large Professor, Larry Smith, Marley Marl, Mathematics, MC Serch, Prince Po, Q-Tip, Rob Swift, Rockwilder, Salaam Remi, and Ty Fyffe.

Brooklyn

Brooklyn sits on 70.82 mi² (183.4 km²) of land. It was established around 1634 and had a 2020 population of about 2.7 million (26.7 percent Black and 18.9 percent Latinx), representing about 13.6% of the New York metro area. Brooklyn, one of the oldest sites, was an independent city from 1834 to 1898, and this impacts how data is reported. Brooklyn is a high-population and high-density site. It is also considered a migratory site, as there were major increases in Black and Latinx percentages from 1970 to 1990.

Artists and groups associated with the Brooklyn rap scene include 6ix9ine, All City, Angie Martinez, Audio Two, AZ, Big Daddy Kane, Bizzy Banks, Black Moon, Blackstar, Bobby Shmurda, Captain Steez (Capital Steez), Casanova, Chubb Rock, Count Coolout, Crooklyn Dodgers, Cut Master D.C., Dana Dane, Das Racist, Digable Planets, DJ Premier, Divine Sounds, EMC, Fabolous, Fivio Foreign, Foxy Brown, Gang Starr, Guru, GZA, Ill Bill, J.I., Jay Z, Jeru The Damaja, Joell Ortiz, Joey Bada$$, Junior M.A.F.I.A., La The Darkman, Lil Kim, Lil Mama, Lordz Of Brooklyn, M.O.P., Maino, Masta Ace, Masta Killa, MC Lyte, MC Peaches, Memphis Bleek, Mos Def, Ms. Melodie, Naomi Peterson, Necro, Notorious B.I.G., Ol' Dirty Bastard, Papoose, Paula Perry, Pop Smoke, Pumpkinhead, Queen Mother Rage, Queen Pen, Raekwon, Rampage, Sabac Red, Sauce Money, Sean Price, Sheff G, Shinobi Ninja, Sir Menelik, Shyheim, Sleepy Hallow, Smif-N-Wessun, Stetasonic, Talib Kweli, The Real Roxanne, Thirstin Howl III, T.J. Swan, Travis "Travitron" Lee, Unbeknownst (Masta Ace Incorporated), Uncle Murda, UTFO, X-Clan, Young M.A, and Your Old Droog. Producers associated with the Brooklyn rap scene include Afrika Baby Bam, Audio Two, Big Daddy Kane, Black Moon, Bluez Brothers, Da Beatminerz, Digable Planets, DJ Clark Kent (Brooklyn), DJ Premier, DJ Scratch, DJ Spinna, DR Period, Easy Mo Bee, GZA, Howie Tee, Jaz-O, Larry Smith, Max Perry, Mister Cee, M.O.P., Mr. Walt, Oddisee, Party Supplies, Pete Nice, Prince Paul, Reefa, Stetsasonic, Thirstin Howl III, Trackmasters, Wise, and X-Clan.

Staten Island

Staten Island sits on 58.5 mi^2 (152 km^2) of land. It was established in 1661 and had a 2020 population of about 495,000 (10.5 percent Black and 19.6 percent Latinx), representing 2.5 percent of the New York metro area. Staten Island is largely examined as a technology site, with RZA helping create the local rap scene through his innovative production and five-year plan for Wu-Tang Clan members.

Artists and groups associated with the Staten Island rap scene include All in Together Now Crew, Carlton Fisk, Cappadonna, Fes Taylor, Force M.D.'s, Ghostface Killah, GZA, Heart Foundation, Inspectah Deck, Lounge Lo, Method Man, NYOIL, Ol' Dirty Bastard, Raekwon, RZA, Streetlife, U-God, The U.M.C.'s, and Wu-Tang Clan. Producers associated with the Staten Island rap scene include 4th Disciple, Force M.D.'s, GZA, Inspectah Deck, RZA, and True Master.

Hempstead

Hempstead sits on 117.68 mi^2 (307.39 km^2) of land. It was established around 1624 and had a 2020 population of around 793,000 (17.3 percent Black and 21 percent Latinx), representing 3.9 percent of the New York metro area. Hempstead has more total area than most other sites. It is one of the areas of Long Island that experienced a large population boom in the 1940s and 1950s. Hempstead is a major rap technology site with the rise of Long Island producers in the 1980s and 1990s. Artists and groups associated with the Long Island rap scene include A+, Aesop Rock, Biz Markie, Busta Rhymes, Chuck D, Craig Mack, Curly J, De La Soul, DJ Red Alert, Doctor Dré & Ed Lover, EPMD, Eric B. & Rakim, Erick Sermon, Flavor Flav, Freddie Foxxx, Goretex, Grand Daddy I.U., JVC Force, Keith Murray, KMD, Leaders of the New School, Lil Peep, Lil Tecca, Method Man, MF Doom, Monsta Island Czars, Original Concept, PMD, Poetic, Prodigy of Mobb Deep, Public Enemy, Rakim, Roc Marciano, R.A. The Rugged Man, Son of Bazerk, Staxx B, TaBandzzz, Terminator X, Young Black Teenagers, Young Fazo, WillieFromTheDrive, and ZillaKami. Producers associated with the Long Island rap scene include Aesop Rock, Bomb Squad, Elvis Beatz, DJ Maseo, DJ Skribble, DJ SubRoc, Doctor Dré, EPMD, Eric "Vietnam" Sadler, Eric B. & Rakim, Hank Shocklee, Keith Shocklee, MF Doom, Prince Paul, Rick Rubin, Terminator X, and X-Ray da Mindbenda.

Philadelphia

Philadelphia sits on 134.36 mi² (347.98 km²) of land. It was established in 1682 and had a 2020 population of 1.6 million (43.6 percent Black and 15.5 percent Latinx), representing 25.7 percent of the Philadelphia metro area. Philadelphia has clear factors such as geography (with more land area than most sites) and migration (a higher population and higher Black percentage than most sites). Social movements are also seemingly a factor in Philadelphia, with a BPPSD chapter, SNCC organization activity, and at least four May 1970 student actions. Philadelphia has a rich musical tradition prior to Hip Hop and rap, and it features many innovations in DJ and production technology. Some of these early and highly influential pioneers were women.

Artists and groups associated with the Philadelphia rap scene include 2 Kannon, Army of the Pharaohs, Asher Roth, Bahamadia, Beanie Sigel, Black Landlord, Black Thought, Boyz II Men, C.E.B., Cash Money and Marvelous, Charlie Baltimore, Chief Kamachi, Cool C, Cosmic Kev, Dark Lo, Diplo, DJ Code Money, DJ Ease, DJ Jazzy Jeff & The Fresh Prince, DJ Lightenin' Rich, DJ Spinbad, DJ Too Tuff, DJ Ultraviolet, Doodlebug, EST (3 Times Dope), Ethel Cee, E-Vette Money, Eve, Freeway, Gillie da kid, Grandmaster Nell, Ice Cream Tee, Ital tha Ruffian, Jakk Frost, Jamal, Jedi Mind Tricks, Jewel T, Jill Scott, Jocko Henderson, JT, KUR, Kurupt, Lady B, Larry Larr, Last Emperor, Leaf Ward, Lil Uzi Vert, Major Figgas, Matt Ox, MC Breeze, MC Sport, Meek Mill, MFSB, Money B, Monie Love, Munk wit da Funk, Neef, Omillio Sparks, Ot7Quanny, OuterSpace, Philly's Most Wanted, PNB Meen, Questlove, Quilly Mills, Rahzel, Ram Squad, Reed Dollaz, Reef The Lost Cauze, Ruggedness MaddDrama, Schoolly D, Sha'Dasious, Shape of Broad Minds, Tech 9, The Goats, The Kartel, The Roots, Tierra Whack, Tommy Hill, Tone Trump, Too Brown, Traum Diggs, Tuff Crew, Will Smith, and Young Chris. Producers associated with the Philadelphia rap scene include Black Thought, Butcher Bros., CHOPS, Diplo, DJ Cash Money, DJ Code Money, DJ Jazzy Jeff, DJ Royal Rocker, Ice Cream Tee, Jahlil Beats, King Britt, Lady B,

MC Breeze, Neo da Matrix, OuterSpace, Philly's Most Wanted, Questlove, Rahzel, Reef The Lost Cauze, Schoolly D, Scott Storch, Scratch, Stoupe the Enemy of Mankind, The Beat Bully, and The Roots.

Newark and Jersey City

Newark sits on 24.14 mi^2 (62.53 km^2) of land. It was established in 1693 and had a 2020 population of about 311,000 (48.2 percent Black and 36.8 percent Latinx), representing 1.5 percent of the New York metro area. Newark has a smaller geographical area (in total, land, and water measurements), a lower population, and a higher density than most other sites. It has had a significant Black percentage of the population since the 1960s and a significant Latinx percentage since the 1990s. Newark is a social movement site, with a BPPSD chapter, SNCC organization activity, and a May 1970 student action. Additionally, Newark was a major site of the Black Arts Movement. The scene's participation in commercial recorded rap music occurs early with The Sugarhill Gang's 1979 song "Rapper's Delight," and women have been major participants on the scene both as artists and executives. Sylvia Robinson's hand in "Rapper's Delight," though anecdotal, is a sign of this integral role of women on the scene. Later, women rappers such as Queen Latifah, Lauryn Hill, and Rah Digga became prominent features of the scene. In addition, emphasis of underground sounds and roots also became a fixture on the scene. Jersey City sits on 14.75 mi^2 (38.2 km^2) of land. It was established around 1838 and had a 2020 population of around 292,000 (22.5 percent Black and 27.5 percent Latinx), representing about 1.5 percent of the New York metro area. Similar to Newark, Jersey City has a lower geographical area (total, land, and water areas), a lower population, and a higher population density than most other sites.

Artists and groups associated with the Newark or Jersey City rap scene include 3Breezy, Afrika Islam, Akon, Artifacts, Albee Al, Arsonal Da Rebel, Bandmanrill, Billy Roadz, Chill Rob G, Chino XL, Coi Leray, Dave Ghetto, Fetty Wap, G Smoke, George Clinton, Hasan Salaam, Heather B, Hoodrich Pablo Juan, Ignorant Intelligence, Joe Budden, Kanye West, Krown Rulers, Lakim Shabazz, Lauryn Hill, Lords of the Underground, Mariahlynn, Naughty By Nature, Neako, Outsidaz, Nikki D, Poor Righteous Teachers, Queen Latifah, R Rated, Rah Digga, Redman, Ronny J, Rufugee Camp All-stars, Sylvia Robinson, The Fugees (Tranzlator Crew), The Sugarhill Gang, Tsu Surf, Wise Intelligent, and Wyclef Jean. Producers associated with the Newark or Jersey City rap scene include !llmind, Afrika Islam, Akon, Artifacts, Cardiak, Double O, Eric IQ Gray, George Clinton, K-Def, Kanye West, Khalis Bayyan, Megahertz, Mr. Green, PMD, Pras, Queen Latifah, Redman, Sylvia Robinson, Tony D, Wyclef Jean, and Young Zee.

Boston

Boston sits on 48.34 mi^2 (125.2 km^2) of land. It was established in 1630 and had a 2020 population of around 675,000 people (23.5 percent Black and 19.8 percent Latinx), representing 13.7 percent of the Boston metro area. Geographically, Boston has a lower land area but higher water area than most other sites. Boston's Black percentage grew significantly in the 1980s and 1990s.

Artists and groups associated with the Boston rap scene include 7L, Akrobatik, Bell Biv DeVoe, Benzino, BIA, Big Shug, Big Smooth, Bobby Brown, Concrete Click, Cousin Stizz, E Dub, Ed O.G & Da Bulldogs, Edan, Edo G., Esoteric, Gang Starr, Guru, Insight, Jaysaun, Joyner Lucas, Kevin Fleetwood, Kevlar Omega, Killin Field, Kool Gee, Krumb Snatcha, La Coka Nostra, Made Men, Marky Mark and the Funky Bunch, Masspike Miles, Maurice Starr, MC Lyrical Infinity, MC Spice, Millyz, Mr. Lif, Natives in Black, New Edition, Poets of Wickedness, Polecat, Reks, Sage Francis, Scientifik, Slaine, Special Teamz, Street Poets, T.D.S. MOB, Termanology, The Almighty RSO, T-Max, The Devil'z Rejects, The Jonzun Crew, Token, Top Choice Clique, X-Caliber, and Y Society. Producers associated with the Boston rap scene include 7L & Esoteric, Akrobatik, Benzino, Chain Reaction, Che Pope, Danny Wood, DJ Fakts One, Edo G., Edan, FORCEFIELD, Hangman3, Karma, Kevin Fleetwood, Michael Jonzun, Mr. Lif, Papa D!, Sage Francis, Statik Selektah, Top Choice Clique, and Truth Elemental.

West Coast and Northwest

Los Angeles and Compton

Los Angeles (LA) sits on 469.5 mi^2 (1216 km^2) of land. It was established around 1850 and had a 2020 population of around 3.89 million (8.6 percent Black and 48.4 percent Latinx), representing about 29.5 percent of the LA metro area. When NYC sites are taken as separate boroughs, LA features the highest population among the sites. Geographically, LA is a large site, with high total, land, and water areas. LA's Latinx population grew in the 1980s and 1990s. LA is a social movement site, with a BPPSD chapter, the Brown Berets, SNCC organization events, and a May 1970 student protest. In the 1960s and 1970s, the BPPSD had well-documented conflicts with the US Organization over the future direction of the Black Power Movement. LA is analyzed as a scene in which prior musics and the use of production technology are considered primary factors.

Artists and groups associated with the LA rap scene include 1TakeJay, 2Mex, 2Pac, Ab Soul, Aceyalone, Aloe Blacc, Baby Keem, Bad Lucc, Beat Junkies, Black Eyed Peas, Blackalicous, Blxst, Buddy, Blueface, Bravo The Bagchaster, CJ Mac, Cypress Hill, D Smoke, D.B.A., Damani, Daz Dillinger, Defari, Delinquent Habits, Dilated Peoples, DJ Battlecat, DJ Mustard, Doja Cat, Dom Kennedy, Dr. Dre, Drakeo the Ruler, Earl Sweatshirt, Egyptian Lover, Everlast, Evidence, Fashawn, Fatlip, Frank Ocean, Funkdoobiest, G Perico, Gerardo, Ghetto Henchmen, Hittman, Hodgy Beats, Ice-T, Ice Cube, Jay Rock, Jurassic 5, K-Dee, Kalan.frfr, KAM, Kid Frost, Krondon, Kurupt, Lady of Rage, Likwit Junkies, Living Legends, Lootpack, Lord Zen, Luckyiam PSC, Mack 10, Madlib, Mestizo, MURS, N.W.A., Native Guns, Nate Dogg, New Breed Hustlas, Nipsey Hustle, O3 Greedo, OT Genasis, People Under the Stairs, Pharcyde, Phil da Agony, Project Blowed, Rage Against the Machine, Rakaa (Iriscience), Ras Kass, Rucci,

Schoolboy Q, Sick Jacken, Sinister, Snoop Dogg, South Central Cartel, Strate Crooked, Suga Free, Tash, Teena Marie, Tha Alkaholiks, Tha Dogg Pound, The D.O.C., The Watts Prophets, Thes One, Toddy Tee, T.H.U.G. L.I.F.E., Ty Dolla Sign, Ugly Duckling, Uncle Jamm's Army, Vince Staples, Warren G, WC And The Maad Circle, Westside Connection, Xzibit, U-N-I, and Zack de la Rocha. Producers associated with the LA rap scene include Aceyalone, Alchemist, Beat Junkies, Black Eyed Peas, Chilly Chill, Crazy Toones, Cut Chemist, D-Styles, D.O.C., Daz Dillinger, Digi+Phonics, Dilated Peoples, DJ Babu, DJ Battlecat, DJ Khalil, DJ Muggs, DJ Mustard, DJ Pooh, DJ Quik, DJ Rhettmatic, DJ Skizz, Double K, Dr. Dre, E-Swift, Egyptian Lover, Exile, Flying Lotus, FredWreck, Harv, Hit Boy, Hurt-M-Badd, Johnny "J," Kid Frost, Knxwledge, Kurupt, KutMasta Kurt, L.T. Hutton, Lootpack, Madlib, Mel-Man, Oh No, Ozomatli, Ras Kass, Sam Sneed, Sir Jinx, Soopafly, Suga Free, Tha Alkaholiks, The Baka Boyz, Tommy Brown, Tony G., Ty Dolla Sign, Tyla, Uncle Jamm's Army, Warren G, WC, Willie B, and will.i.am.

Artists and groups associated with the Compton rap scene include Arabian Prince, Bambi, B.G. Knocc Out, Baby Eazy-E (E3), Big Fase 100, Compton's Most Wanted, Coolio, CPO Boss Hogg, Curtis Young, DJ Quik, DJ Yella, Dr. Dre, Dresta, Eazy-E, Fo' Clips Elipse, Guerilla Black, Hi-C, Kendrick Lamar, King Tee, Lil Eazy-E, Mausberg, MC Eiht, MC Ren, Michel'le, Roddy Ricch, Spider Loc, Tha Chill, The Game, Tweedy Bird Loc, Tyga, Westside Boogie, YG, and Yo-Yo. Producers associated with the Compton rap scene include Arabian Prince, Curtis Young, DJ Lonzo Williams, DJ Quik, DJ Yella, Dr. Dre, MC Eiht, MC Ren, Sounwave, Suge Knight, Yolanda Whittaker, and Young D.

Oakland and San Francisco Bay Area

Oakland sits on 55.93 mi² (144.59 km²) of land. It was established in 1852 and had a 2020 population of around 440,000 (22 percent Black and 27.2 percent Latinx), representing 9.3 percent of the San Francisco Bay area. Oakland's Black population grew significantly from the 1960s through the 1980s. Oakland is a social movement site, with two BPPSD chapters (one as the founding site), the Brown Berets, an SNCC organization activity, and TWWA offices in the Oakland and San Francisco areas. Located in the headquarters of Silicon Valley, technology has also been a major influence on San Francisco Bay Area musical productions.

San Jose sits on 178.3 mi² (462 km²) of land. It was established around 1850 and had a 2020 population of around 1.01 million (3 percent Black and 31 percent Latinx), representing 50.7 percent of the San Jose metro area. Geographically, San Jose has a larger land area and lower water area than most sites. San Jose has a higher population than most sites and had a major population increase from the 1960s to the 1980s. San Jose has one of the lowest Black percentages of the sites and has a higher Latinx percentage than most other sites.

Artists and groups associated with the Oakland and East Bay rap scene include 3-Deep, 415, 2Pac, 3X Krazy, ACKTUP, All Ready Fresh, ALLBLACK, Ally Cocaine,

America's Most Wanted, Andre Nickatina (Dre Dog), Ant Banks, APG Crew, Audi and Mike Dee, B-Legit, Bailey, Beeda Weeda, Big Omeezy, Black Dynasty, Blackalicious, Capolow, Cassidine, Celly Cel, Champ Bailey, Charizma & Peanut Butter Wolf, Commanda C & DJ MF, Coolio Da Unda Dogg, D-Lo, D-Shot, Dangerous Dame, Del tha Funkee Homosapien, Dem HoodStarz, Digital Underground, DJ Shadow, Dru Down, E-40, E-A-Ski, East Side Oakland, Federation, Freddy B, Girlz N The Hood, Goapele, Haji Springer, Hieroglyphics, Hoodstarz, Iamsu!, Izz Thizz, J Stalin, J-Diggs, Jay Tee, Jel, Johnny Ca$h, JT The Bigga Figga, Kafani, Kamaiyah, Kaz Kyzah, Keak da Sneak, Key-Lo, Keyshia Cole, Latyrx, Lil Blood, Lil Bruce, Lil Rue, Lyrics Born, Mac Dre, Mac Mall, Mac Mill, Mac tha Kat, Master P, MC Jay & DJ Villian, MC Sirgeo, Messy Marv, Mhisani, Mistah F.A.B., Morocco Moe, Motorcycle Mike, Mr. Fresh & Master T.M.D., Mr. Kee, Mystik Journeymen, Nump, Nutt-So, Oaktown's 357, Peanut Butter Wolf, Philty Rich, Poohman, Professionals (aka Prafeshanals), Qing Qi, Rappin Ron & Ant Diddly Dog, Raw Fusion, Ray Luv, Scweez, Shotime, Sir Quick Draw (Em-Cee Quik), Sky Balla, Souls of Mischief, Spice 1, Symba, T-Kash, The A'z, The Ansārs, The Click, The Conscious Daughters, The Coup, The Delinquents, The Govenor, The Grouch, The Jacka, The Luniz, The Pack, The Team, Themselves, TKO, Too $hort, Traxamillion, TRU, Turf Talk, Underground Rebellion, Vitamin C, Yukmouth, and Zion I. Producers associated with the Oakland and East Bay rap scene include Amp Live, Andre Nickatina, Ant Banks, B. Branch, Big D the Impossible, Boots Riley, Celly Cel, Chief Xcel, CMT, Coolio Da Unda Dogg, Digital Underground, DJ Daryl, DJ Fuze, DJ K-OS, DJ Pam the Funkstress, DJ Shadow, Droop-E, Dru Down, E-40, E-A-Ski, K-Lou, Keak da Sneak, Live Squad, Lyrics Born, Master P, Mistah F.A.B, Numskull, Peanut Butter Wolf, Raphael Saadiq, Rappin Ron & Ant Diddly Dog, Raw Fusion, Rick Rock, Saweetie, Shock G, Studio Ton, The Conscious Daughters, The Coup, The Team, Thizz Entertainment, TRU, and Zion I.

San Francisco sits on 46.9 mi² (121.48 km²) of land. It was established around 1850 and had a 2020 population of around 808,000 (5.4 percent Black and 15.4 percent Latinx), representing 17 percent of the San Francisco metro area. San Francisco has the most water area of the sites, which contributes to its larger total area. However, it has a lower land area and higher population density than most sites. It has one of the lowest Black percentages of the sites. San Francisco is a social movement city, with a BPPSD chapter, the Brown Berets, and a May 1970 activity.

Artists and groups associated with the San Francisco or East Palo Alto rap scene include 11/5, Berner, Big Rich, C-Fresh, Cellski, Cold World Hustlers, Cougnut, D-Moe, Dan the Automator, Don Cisco, Dre Dog (Andre Nickatina), Ghetto Soldiers, Guce, Ill Mannered Posse, J. Espinosa, JT the Bigga Figga, Larry June, Lil Bean, Lil Kayla, Lil Pete, Mac Minister, MC Frontalot, Messy Marv, Mr. Sandman, Paris, Rappin' 4-Tay, RBL Posse, Sage the Gemini, San Quinn, Seff Tha Gaffla, Sway and King Tech, T-Bone, T-Lo, Totally Insane, Ya Boy, and Zay Bang. Producers associated with the San Francisco or East Palo Alto rap scene include Cellski, Dan the Automator, JT the Bigga Figga, Paris, Rappin' 4-Tay, Ray Luv, Rick Rock, Sage the Gemini, Sean T, Tone Capone, Traxamillion, and Zaytoven.

Seattle and Portland

Seattle sits on 83.9 mi² (217 km²) of land. It was established around 1865 and had a 2020 population of around 737,000 (6.8 percent Black and 7.2 percent Latinx), representing about 18.3 percent of the Seattle metro area. Geographically, Seattle has one of the highest water areas of the sites. Its location within the US is also a point of discussion as it is isolated from most other scenes (with the exception of Portland). Seattle has one of the lowest Black percentages of the sites, and it also has a lower Latinx percentage than most sites. Seattle had social movement activity in a BPPSD chapter and a May 1970 student activity. Seattle is identified as a technology scene, with PC technology developed in the region and a long-standing history of rap production on the scene. Portland sits on 133.4 mi² (346 km²) of land. It was established around 1851 and had a 2020 population of around 652,000 (9 percent Black and 10.3 percent Latinx), representing 26 percent of the Portland metro area. Portland has higher total and land areas and lower population densities than most other sites. Similar to Seattle, there is a lower Black percentage than most other sites. Portland is also a social movement site, with a BPPSD chapter, an SNCC activity, and a May 1970 student activity.

Artists and groups associated with the Seattle or Portland rap scene include "Nasty" Nes Rodriguez, 151, 3D, B-Mello, B-Self, Blaac, Blue Scholars, Boom Bap Project, Brothers of the Same Mind, Butterfly, Central District Posse, Check Team, Chelly Chell, Common Market, Crooked Path, Darkset, Dividenz, Double Odd, Duke and Double Rock, DURACELL Crew, Duragned Pitt, DVS Crew, Dyme Def, E-Dawg, Emerald City Players, Emerald Street Boys, Emerald Street Girls, Emperor P, Five Fingers of Funk, Funk Daddy, Gangsta Nutt, Gift of Gab, Grayskul, Grynch, Jace, Jam Delight, Khingz, Kid Sensation, KGodd, Lifesavas, Lil Kriz, Lil Mosey, Litefoot, Macklemore, Mad Rad, Marshall Law Band, MikeJack3200, Mr. Benjamin, Mr. Supreme, Nacho Picasso, No Good Therapy, Nocturnal Rage, Oldominion, Pete Miser, Porter Ray, Red Head Steve, Sarkastik, Shaabazz Palaces, Sharpshooters, Sir Mix-A-Lot, Twin G, Vitamin D, Wall Nut, West Coast Stone, Wordsayer, and Yeat. Producers associated with the Seattle or Portland rap scene include "Nasty" Nes Rodriguez, B-Mello, Boom Bap Project, Butterfly, DJ Sabzi, DJ Top Spin, Funk Daddy, Iame, Jake One, Jumbo, Kid Sensation, King Otto, Kylea, Mr. Hill, Mr. Supreme, Negus I, Nerdy B, Onry Ozzborn, Rev Shines, Ryan Lewis, Samson S., Shaabazz Palaces, Sir Mix-a-Lot, Sleep, Specs, Strath Shepard, Vitamin D, and Wordsayer.

Midwest and North

Chicago and Gary

Chicago sits on 227.7 mi² (590 km²) of land. It was established around 1833 and in 2020 had a population of around 2.74 million (29.2 percent Black and 28.7 percent Latinx), representing 28.6 percent of the Chicago metro area. Geographically, Chicago has one of the highest total and land areas of the sites. It also has one of the largest populations of the sites and a higher population density than most other sites. Chicago's Black and Latinx percentages are also higher than most sites. Chicago can be explained as a social movement site, with an important BPPSD chapter, SNCC organizational activity (at least thirteen events), and May 1970 protests (at least five events). Chicago is a main center of Black Arts Movement activity as well. Music is also a primary factor, with key Black musics (spiritual, blues, jazz) brought to Chicago via the Great Migration. Gary sits on 49.87 mi^2 (129.15 km^2) of land. It was established around 1906 and had a 2020 population of around 69,000 (78 percent Black and 8.7 percent Latinx). Gary has the lowest water area among the sites and one of the lower land areas. It has one of the lowest populations and lowest population densities among the sites.

Artists or groups associated with the Chicago or Gary rap scene include Ballout, BJ The Chicago Kid, CCA (Concord Affiliated), Bo Deal, Booka600, Boss Woo, Bump J, Casper, Chance the Rapper, Chief Keef, Chilldrin of Da Ghetto, Common (Common Sense), Crucial Conflict, cupcakKe, Da Brat, Daily Plannet, Do or Die, Dreezy, E.C. Illa, Family Tree, FBG Duck, Freddie Gibbs, Fredo Santana, G Herbo, Ghetto Mob, GLC, Go Getters, Iomas Marad, J. Davis Trio, Jeremih, JoJo Capone, Juice, Juice WRLD, Kanye West, Katie Got Bandz, KB Mike, Kid Sister, Kidz In the Hall, King Louie, King Von, L'A Capone, Lady XO, Landlords, L.E.P. Bogus Boys, Lil Durk, Lil Reese, Lil Zay Osama, Los Marijuanos, Louie P Newton, Lucki, Lupe Fiasco, M.C.G.'z, Maker, Matlock, Meaty Ogre, Mick Jenkins, Molemen, Mr Lee, Nacrobats, Nizm, No I.D., Noname, Panik, PGF Nuk, Polo G, Prime, Prince Dre, Psychodrama, Pugs Atomz, Qualo, Queen Kay, Qwel, R. Kelly, Really Doe, Rhymefest, Robust, Rusty Chains, Saba Pivot, SD, Shawnna, Sly Polaroid, Sno Boy, Sugar Ray Dinke, The Cool Kids, Twista, Typical Cats, Unorthodox Poets Society, Vakill, Verbal Kent, VIC MENSA, Visual (Ndvisual), Vyle, and Yungeen Ace. Producers associated with the Chicago or Gary rap scene include Daily Plannet, DJ Joey D, DJ Kid Scratch, DJ Moondawg, DJ Natural, DJ Sean Mac, DJ Twin, DJ V-DUB, Iomas Marad, Juice, Kanye West, Kaos, Kid Knis, Meaty Ogre, Molemen, No I.D., R. Kelly, Rhymefest, The Legendary Traxster, Tricky Stewart, Vakill, and Young Chop.

St. Louis

St. Louis sits on 61.72 mi^2 (159.85 km^2) of land. It was established around 1822 and in 2020 had a population of about 301,000 (44.8 percent Black and 4.2 percent Latinx), representing 10.7 percent of the St. Louis metro area. St. Louis has one of the lowest total and water areas of the sites. It also has one of the lowest population densities. Furthermore, St. Louis has one of the highest Black percentages and one of the lowest Latinx percentages of the sites.

Artists and groups associated with the St. Louis rap scene include .40 Cal, 3 Problems, 5ive, 10 Man & The Jihad Squad, 30 Deep Grimeyy, Abyss, Ali, AMR Dee Huncho, Big Boss Vette, BigBuckz Trey, BigBuckz Von, Bits & Pieces, Benji Brothers, Blaque Diamond, Chavis, Chingy, Colonel Lee, County Brown, Cujo the Malachi, D.O.A., Da Bangaz, Da Hol 9, Day1ss, Deadly Deuce, DJ Charlie Chan, DJ G.Wiz, DJ

Kut, Dr. Jockenstein, Ebony Eyez, Fadel Level, Flame, Flow, Freshanova, Gentleman Jim Gates, Golden Boys, Hard Knox, Huey, Illegal Assembly, J-Kwon, JCD, Jibs, Jiggy Keyz, Jizzle Buckz, JMC & Ronnin, Json, Jus Bleezy, King Odie, KoKo, LA4ss, Laudie On Da Track, Lil St. Louis, Out of Order, Mad Keys, Meela Li, Mo P., Murphy Lee, Nelly, Nuski2Squad, NWM Cee Murdaa, Penelope Jones, Pretty Willie, Rahli, Raw Reese, Raw Society, Raysta, Ruka Puff, San Da Don, Sav Karti, Scrips 'n Screws, Smino, Sexxy Red, Spaide Ripper, St. Lunatics, Sylk Smoov, Taylor Made, Tarboy, The Devastation Clic, Tonina, Vic Damone, Young Beano, and Zado. Producers associated with the St. Louis rap scene include Chingy, DJ Kut, Dr. Jockenstein, Gentleman Jim Gates, Jay E, Laudie On Da Track, Mall (TheWrath2BFelt), Metro Boomin, Steve Wills, The Trak Starz, and Zado.

Minneapolis and St. Paul

Minneapolis was established around 1867 and had a 2020 population of around 429,000 (18.4 percent Black and 9.8 percent Latinx), representing 11.6 percent of the Minneapolis St. Paul metro area. It has one of the lowest land areas of the sites explored. Artists and groups associated with the Minneapolis rap scene include Atmosphere, Benzilla, Beyond, Brother Ali, Carnage The Executioner, Castro, Contac, Desdamona, Dessa, Doomtree Collective, I.R.M. Crew, I Self Devine, Jimmy Jam and Terry Lewis, Headshots, Highlight Entertainment, K Banks, K Wood, Kaos, Kanser, Kode Blue, Lizzo, Los Nativos, Northside Hustlaz Clic, M.anifest, Micranots, Moochy C, Musab (Beyond), Paper Tiger, P.O.S, Raw Villa, Rhyme Sayers, Sandman, Semi. Official, Six Pak, Slug, Tanqueray Locc, The Dynospectrum, Toki Wright, Top Tone, Tori Fixx, Travis "Travitron" Lee, Truthmaze, and Villa Rosa. Producers associated with the Minneapolis rap scene include Ant, Brother Ali, Desdamona, DJ Kool Akiem, I Self Devine, Jimmy Jam and Terry Lewis, Lazerbeak, P.O.S, Paper Tiger, Toki Wright, Travis "Travitron" Lee, and Truthmaze.

Saint Paul was established around 1854 and had a 2020 population of around 311,000 (16 percent Black and 9.7 percent Latinx), representing 8.4 percent of the Minneapolis St. Paul metro area. Of the scenes examined, St. Paul has one of the smallest populations. It has lower total and land areas than most other sites, and, demographically, it has a lower population, lower Black percentage, and lower Latinx percentage than most other sites. Artists and groups associated with the St. Paul rap scene include 1 UP, Abstract Pack, Bay-G, Bobby Raps, Destiny Roberts, Delicious Venom, DMG, Down 4 Dirt, Endangered Species, Eyedea & Abilities, Frankie Bash, Heiruspecs, KayCyy, Lexii Alijai, Maria Isa, Orikal Uno, Quiet Loc, Shade Luv X, St. Paul Slim, XconviX, and Yung Gravy. Producers associated with the St. Paul rap scene include Cardo and DJ Abilities.

Detroit

Detroit sits on 138.7 mi^2 (359 km^2) of land. It was established around 1806 and had a 2020 population of around 639,000 (77.9 percent Black and 7.8 percent Latinx), representing 14.6 percent of the Detroit metro area. Detroit has a larger land area and lower population density than most sites. Since 1960, it has had ongoing population declines, major ones in 1980 and 2010, and others in 1990 and 2020. Detroit has one of the highest Black percentages of the sites, and it has a lower Latinx population than most other sites. Detroit is explored as a social movement site, with a BPPSD chapter, the Brown Berets, and a May 1970 student activity. Detroit is a centerpiece to the Black Arts Movement as well, and it is also a music city, with musics such as Black R&B, punk, and electro in production prior to rap.

Artists and groups associated with the Detroit rap scene include 42 Dugg, A.W.O.L., Aaliyah, Anybody Killa, Athletic Mic League, Awesome Dre & The Hardcore Committee, Baby Smoove, Babyface Ray, BabyTron, Big Herk, Big Meech, Big Sean, Binary Star, Bizarre, Blade Icewood, Black Milk, BMF, Boldy James, Bombsell, Bo$$, Bruiser Brigade, Champtown, Chedda Boyz, Cybotron, D12, Dabrye, Danny Brown, Detroit's Most Wanted, DJ Assault, DJ Virus, DeJ Loaf, DMT, Elzhi, Eminem, Esham, EZ-B and DJ Los, Fatt Father, Feloni, Gmac Cash, Guilty Simpson, Hush, Illa J, Icewear Vezzo, Insane Clown Posse (ICP), Invincible, J Dilla, Jamie Madrox, Jeff Mills, Juan Atkins, Kaos & Mystro, Kash Doll, Kid Rock, King Gordy, Kodac aka M80, M-City J.r., Mastamind, MC Breed, Molly Brazy, One Be Lo, Phat Kat, Prince Vince & The Hip Hop Force, Proof, Redbone, Royce Da 5'9," Sada Baby, Skilla Baby," Slum Village, Smiley, Spyder D, Street Lord Juan, Street Lordz, Swifty McVay, Tee Grizzley, Teejayx6, Tone Tone, Trick Trick, Underground Resistance, Veeze, and Will Youmans. Producers associated with the Detroit rap scene include Alius Pnukkl, Amp Fiddler, Antt Beatz, Apollo Brown, Athletic Mic League, Awesome Dré, Bass Brothers, Black Milk, Blitz, Bronze Nazareth, Carl "Butch" Small, Chic Masters, Cysion, D.J. Homicide, Dabrye, Davina, Decompoze, Denaun Porter, Denmark Vassey, DJ Clay, DJ HouseShoes, Duncan Hines, Eminem, J Dilla, Helluva, Jeff Bass, Jeff Mills, Juan Atkins, Karriem Riggins, Key Wane, Konphlict, Luis Resto, Mac Back on da Track, Magestik Legend, Nick Speed, One Be Lo, Prince Vince, Proof, Richard "3070" Davis, Rockwell, Royce Da 5'9," Slautah, Slum Village, Spyder D, Trackezoids, Vincent Eason, and Waajeed.

South and Contested Islands

Houston

Houston sits on 640.4 mi^2 (1659 km^2) of land. It was established around 1837 and had a 2020 population of around 2.3 million (22.6 percent Black and 44.5 percent Latinx), representing 32.4 percent of the Houston metro area. Geographically, Houston is one of the largest sites (total area, land area), and it has more water area than most others. Despite its large population, its large land size keeps its population density lower than most other sites. Houston had a large population boom from 1950 to 1980 and another in 2000 (with 1950 and 1960 being the largest booms). Houston's Black percentage has remained substantial, and its Latinx percentage increased greatly in 1980 and 1990. Houston is a social movement site, with a BPPSD chapter, the Brown Berets, and SNCC organization activity (at least two events). Houston is explored as a musical and technological site, with the long-standing Black traditions in music and with discoveries of new production methods by independent artists and labels on the scene.

Artists and groups associated with the with the Houston rap scene include 5th Ward Boyz, B L A C K I E, B-1, Big Gerb, Big Love, Big Mello, Big Mike, Big Moe, Big Pokey, Bloc Boyz Click, Botany Boyz, Boyz N Blue (Boss Hogg Outlawz), Brick WolfPack, Bun B, Bushwick Bill, Captain Jack, Chamillionaire, Choice, Cl' Che', Convicts, DeeBaby, Def Jam Blaster, Def IV, Devin the Dude, DJ Screw, Don Toliver, Dope-E, Drama Queen, E.S.G., Facemob, Fat Pat, Fat Tony, G-Dash, Ganxsta NIP, Geto Boys (Ghetto Boys), Gifted the Flame Throwa, Guerilla Maab, H.A.W.K., Icey Hott, J. Dawg, Jazzie Redd, Justice Allah, K-Otix, K-Rino, KenTheMan, Killa Kyleon, Klondike Kat, Lebra Jolie, Lez Moné, Lil Flip, Lil Jairmy, Lil Keke, Lil O, Lil Raskall, Lil Troy, Maxo Kream, MC Wickett Cricket, Megan Thee Stallion, Michael "5000" Watts, Mike Jones, Mike Moe, Monaleo, Mr. 3-2, Much Luvv, Nasty Nique Roots, Odd Squad, O.G. Style, OMB Bloodbath, OTB FastLane, Paul Wall, Paul Wall & Chamillionaire, Peso Peso, Pimp C, Point Blank, Prince Johnny C, Propain, PSK-13, Raheem, Rapid Ric, Real Chill, Ricky Royal, Rizzo Rizzo, Rob Quest, Romeo Poet, Pyrex, Royal Flush, Sauce Walka, Scarface, Shorty Mac, Sire Jukebox, Slicc, Slim Thug, Sosaman, Southside Playaz, Street Military, Propain, South Park Mexican, The Mighty D-Risha, The Terrorists, TisaKorean, Tobe Nwigwe, Top Dawg, Travis Scott, Trae Tha Truth, Tre-9, UGK, Willie D, Yungstar, and Z-Ro. Producers associated with the Houston rap scene include Crazy C, Curtis "DEF-C" Whycoff, DJ B-Do, DJ DMD, DJ Ready Red, DJ Screw, Dope E, Egypt "E", H.A.W.K., Icy Hott, J. Prince, J.B. Money, James Smith and Karl Stephenson, Jazzie Redd, Johnny "Tiger" Walker, K-Rino, Klondike Kat, Mike Dean, Mr. 3-2, Mr. Lee, Paul Wall, Pimp C, OG Ron C, Point Blank, Prince Johnny C, PSK-13, Raheem, Scarface, Suave House, Terrorists, Tony Draper, Von Won, and Z-Ro.

New Orleans

New Orleans sits on 169.5 mi^2 (439 km^2) of land. It was established around 1718 and had a 2020 population of around 383,000 (58.1 percent Black and 5.6 percent Latinx), representing 30.2 percent of the New Orleans metro area. Geographically, it is one of the sites with the highest total areas, highest water areas, and lowest densities. New Orleans also has a smaller population than most of the other sites and experiences large population decreases—especially in recent censuses. New Orleans has had a substantial and growing Black percentage, especially since 1960, and it has one of the lowest Latinx percentages of the sites. It could be described as a social movement city with a BPPSD chapter, an SNCC organization activity, and May 1970 protests (at least two events). New Orleans is also an examined as a musical city.

Artists and groups associated with the New Orleans rap scene include $uicideboy$, 39 Posse, 504 Boyz, 69 Boyz, AIA Litt, B.G., Baby T & Devious D, Bally-B, Big Mike, Bengie B, Big Freedia, Big Tymers, Birdman, Black Menace, BLÜ, BTY Young'n, Bust Down, By Any Means Necessary, C-Murder, Cash Money Millionaires, CeeFineAss, Cheeky Blackk, Chip, Choppa, Curren$y, Dee-1, D.J. Jimi, D.J. Jubilee, Da 187 Klick, Da

Mobsters, Derrick b, DJ Mouche, Dolemite, E.R.C., Fiend, Fila Phil, Final Approach, G5-j, Gangsta, Gank D., Ghetto Twins, Gregory D And D.J. Mannie Fresh, Hot Boys, Ice Mike, Jay Electronica, Jet Life, jo Vanity, Juvenile, Kane and Abel, Katey Red, Kidd Kidd, Kilo G, Kimmy P, KLC, Krazy, Lady Red, Lil D, Lil Slim, Lil' Wayne, Louis V Mob, M.C. Heavy, M.C. J' Ro', M.C. Possie, M.C. T-Tucker & DJ Irv, M.C. Thick, M.V.P., Mac, Magic, Manny Fresh, Master P, Mercedes, Mia X, Miss Chee, Mo B. Dick, Most Wanted Posse, Mystikal, Neon Calvin, New Jack Macks, Ninja Crew, Pallo Da Jiint, Partners-N-Crime, Pimp Daddy, Pimp Dogg, Play Beezy, Precious T, Ricky B., Rob49, Rocker's Revenge, Romeo, S. Tee, Short T, Silkk the Shocker, Silky Slim, Slick leo, Sonia C, Soulja Slim, Sporty T, Stone Cold Jizzzle, SupahBadd, T-Bo, T1O, TEC, Tec-9, The Knux, Tim Smooth, Tre-8, Treety, TRU, Turk, UNLV (Uptown N*gg*s Living Violently), Warren Mayes, WWE, Xcel N Choice, and Young Ro. Producers associated with the New Orleans rap scene include 69 Boyz, 504 Boyz, B.G., Beats by the Pound, Blaza, Bryan "Baby" Williams, Carlos Stephens, Cash Money Millionaires, Craig B, D.J. Fess, D.J. Jimi, D.J. Jubilee, DJ Daryl, Donald Robertson, Elray Holmes, Full Pack, Gregory D, Ivan Varnado, J. Diamond Washington, KLC, Krazy, M.C. T-Tucker, Manny Fresh, Mo B. Dick, N.O. Joe, Odell, Ronald "Slim" Williams, and Tha Real Roc.

Memphis

Memphis sits on 297 mi^2 (769 km^2) of land. It was established around 1826 and had a 2020 population of around 633,000 (66.4 percent Black and 7.7 percent Latinx), representing 47.3 percent of the Memphis metro area. Memphis has one of the highest areas (total and land) and lowest population densities of the sites. Memphis has a historical record of high Black percentages, and it has a lower Latinx percentage than most other sites. Memphis is discussed as both a musical and technological site, with the long-standing Black musics prior to rap on the scene and with the use of home studios in the production of their local underground sound.

Artists and groups associated with the Memphis rap scene include 8Ball & MJG, 10 WantedMen, 211, 901 Thugz, Action Pack, Al Kapone (M.C. Al), Ballistic, BARN YARD PIMPS, Blac Youngsta, BIG30, Big Bogie, Big Scarr, BINSU, Boss Bytch, C-Rock, Children of the Corn, Chopper Girl, Chrome, Crunchy Black, Dark Cappa, DHP, Dirty Boy Wolf Pak, DJ Paul, DJ Squeeky, DJ Spanish Fly, DJ Zirk, Double Trouble, Duke Deuce, Everlasting Gangsta, Finesse2Tymes, Frayser Boy, FreeSol, Fresco Trey, Gangsta Black, Gangsta Boo, Gangsta Pat, Gloss UP, Glo Rilla, H.O.H., Hypnotize Camp Posse, Icy-K, II Tone, Indo G, Inner-City Clique, Iron Mic Coalition, Jucee Froot, Juicy J, K Carbon, K-Rock, Kia Shine, Kingpin Skinny Pimp, Key Glock, Koopsta Knicca, La Chat, L.I., Lil Blunt, Lil Gin, Lil Wyte, Lord Infamous, Lord T. and Eloise, M.C. 12, Maniac, Marshall Law Productions, MC Rod, Men-E-Faces, MG, Mr.Sche, Mr. Quikk, Moneybagg Yo, Nasty Nardo, NLE Choppa, Playa Fly, Playa Panne, Playa G, Pooh Shiesty, Princess Loko, Project Pat, Project Playaz, Prophet Posse, Radical T, Red Bo$$, Rico, Scat Cat, Slim, Shawty Pimp, Slim Thug, Strange Nation, T-Tee, T-Rock, Taylor Boyz, Tela, Three 6 Mafia, Tom Skeemask, Tommy Wright III, Tunnel

Clones, Underground Sam, V-Dog, Yo Gotti, Young Dolph, and Z-DOGG. Producers associated with the Memphis rap scene include 8Ball, 8Ball & MJG, Chopper Girl, D.J. Diz, DJ Squeeky, DJ Paul, DJ Spanish Fly, Drumma Boy, E-Rokk, Iron Mic Coalition, Juicy J, Kia Shine, Lil Pat, Lord Infamous, M.D.B., Mac Shon, Maceo Da Man, MJG, Shawty Pimp, South O, Street Symphony, Tay Keith, Taylor Boyz, and Tommy Wright III.

Atlanta

Atlanta sits on 135.3 mi^2 (350 km^2) of land. It was established around 1847 and had a 2020 population of around 498,000 (48.2 percent Black and 5.6 percent Latinx), representing 8.2 percent of the Atlanta metro area. Geographically, Atlanta has a lower land area and a lower population density than most sites. It has a higher Black percentage than most sites and has had high Black percentages since the 1870s. Atlanta is a social movement site, especially around organizational activity; it had a short-lived BBPSD chapter and over fifty SNCC events. Atlanta and the region grew into a US and global capital of rap by the early 2000s.

Artists and groups associated with the Atlanta rap scene include $ofaygo, 2 Chainz, 12 Gauge, 21 Savage, Alley Boy, Andre 3000, Arrested Development, Baby D, Baby Tate, Bankroll Fresh, Big Gipp & Khujo, Big Boi, Big Rube, BKTHERULA, B.o.B., Bone Crusher, Cee-Lo, Childish Gambino, Cool Breeze, Crime Mob, D-Roc, Da Brat, D4L, DJ Kizzy Rock, DJ Smurf, Dae Dae, Dungeon Family, Fabo, Future, Goodie Mob, Gucci Mane, Gunna, Hard Boyz, Hitman Sammy Sam, iLoveMakonnen, JID, Jermaine Dupri, Kaliii, Kilo Ali, Killer Mike, Kris Kross, Latto, LightskinKeisha, Lil Baby, Lil Jon & The Eastside Boyz, Lil Keed, Lil Nas X, Lil Yatchy, Ludacris, M.C. Shy-D, Migos, Mojo, Money Man, Mr. Collipark (DJ Smurf), OJ Da Juiceman, Oomp Camp, OutKast, Pastor Troy, Playboi Carti, Prophetix, Raheem the Dream, Rich Homie Quan, Rich Kidz, Rocko, Run the Jewels, Shawty Lo, So So Def Bass Allstars, Soulja Boy, Success-N-Effect, T.I., T-Mo, TLC, Travis Porter, Tokyo Vanity, Trouble, Waka Flocka Flame, Witchdoctor, Ying Yang Twins, Young Dro, Young Jeezy, Young LA, Young Nudy, Young Ralph, Young Thug, and YoungBloodZ. Producers associated with the Atlanta rap scene include 21 Savage, 808 Mafia, B.o.B., Babyface, Big Gipp & Khujo, Cee-Lo, Childish Gambino, Colin Wolfe, Dallas Austin, Daryl Simmons, DJ Don Cannon, DJ GEE Supreme, DJ Len, DJ Spinz, DJ Toomp, El-P, Gucci Mane, Honorable C.N.O.T.E., Jazze Pha, Jermaine Dupri, Joe "The Butcher" Nicolo, Joel Peavy, L.A. Reid, Lex Luger, Lil Jon, London on da Track, Ludacris, Maestro, M.C. Shy-D, Mike Will, Mojo, Mr. Collipark, Mr. DJ, Nard & B, Nitti, Organized Noize, OutKast, Polow da Don, Ray Murray, Rico Wade, Shawty Redd, Sleepy Brown, Sonny Digital, Soulja Boy, Southside, Speech, The Hard Boys, and Young Nudy. It should be mentioned that many of the rappers and producers from this Atlanta list hail from College Park, GA, which is a city just south of Atlanta. While location is largely defined by the major or mid-major city limits in *American Rap Scenes*, it is understood that these cities and their nearby areas are porous. This issue of city limits is also a concern when defining other scenes and sites—such as Miami and the Hampton area.[19]

Miami

Miami sits on 36 mi² (93.23 km²) of land. It was established around 1898 and in 2020 had a population of around 442,000 (15.2 percent Black and 72.3 percent Latinx), representing 7.2 percent of the Miami metro area. Miami has a lower land area than most other sites. It is discussed as a migration scene, with one of the highest Latinx percentages of the sites and long-standing Black percentages higher than most sites. Miami is also regarded as a musical scene with a history in Black and Latinx musics prior to Hip Hop and early contributions to rap—some of the first in the South.

Artists and groups associated with the Miami rap scene include 2 Live Crew, 3RE Tha Hardaway, Ball Greezy, Beat Dominator, Beatmaster Clay D. & the Get Funky Crew, Big Z The Dollar Don, Bizzy Crook, Blac Haze, Brisco, C-Ride, City Girls, Denzel Curry, DJ Khaled, DJ Magic Mike, DJ Uncle Al, Dunk Ryders, Dynamix II, Flo Rida, Jacki-O, Jam Pony Express, Jason Derulo, JT Money, K. Foxx, Kat Dahlia, Kiddo Marv, Lil Pump, Luke, Madball & Uzi, Maggolulu Too, Maggotron Crushing Crew, MajorNine, Marty, MC A.D.E., M.C. Shy-D, Mike Smiff, Missy Mist, Palmerforce Two, Piccalo, Pitbull, Poison Clan, Poo Bear, Pretty Ricky, Redd Eyezz, Rick Ross, Ronny J, S-Diggie, Sean Kingston, Smokepurpp, Suki, T-Pain, Tafia, Tego Calderon, The Dogs, The Lost Tribe, The Sonarphonics, Third Degree, Trick Daddy, Trina, Vanilla Ice, and Yung Simmie, and Zoe Pound. Producers associated with the Miami rap scene include Ace Hood, Bigg D, Celph Titled, Cool & Dre, DJ Khaled, DJ Magic Mike, DJ Uncle Al, Gorilla Tek, Infamous, Jim Jonsin, Jimmy Dade, JT Money, Kane Beatz, Kevin "She'kspere" Briggs, Lil Jon, Luke Skyywalker, Mr. Collipark, Mr. Mixx, Righteous Funk Boogie, Ronny J, and T-Pain.

Hampton

Hampton sits on 136.27 mi² (353.95 km²) of land. Hampton was established around 1705 and had a 2020 population of 137,131 (48.6 percent Black and 6.13 percent Latinx), representing 7.62 percent of the Virginia Beach metro area. Hampton has one of the highest water areas of the sites. It also has one of the lowest populations and population densities of the sites. Hampton had massive population growth in 1960. The Black percentage has been significant since at least the 1890s. Hampton is discussed as a core technological scene, with many influential producers emerging from the site.

Artists and groups associated with the Hampton (and nearby) rap scene include 9th Level Productions, Alondo Jackson, Armed Forces, Bankroll Fresh, BEO Smook, Brigante, Cale Steph, Ced Hughes, Ceo Moc, Cocaine Mali, Danja Mowf, DRAM, Fam-lay, Gichi Dame, Grand Emir, Greer, Humanreck, Kenn Starr, Leikeli47, Lil Tracy, Low Down Boyz (LB'z), Magoo, Missy Elliot, N*E*R*D, No Malice, NVA, Pharrell, Poverty Stricken, Pretty Savage, Pusha T, Re-Up Gang, Sean Slaughter, Shane Dollar, Sista, Skavengaz, Surround by Idiots, The Archeville Cartel, The Clipse, The Legacy, The Neptunes, The Spokesman, The Verbal Assassins, Timbaland, Verbal Threat, Wu-Syndicate, X-Military, Young Crazy, and yvngxchris. Producers associated with the Hampton (and nearby) scene include Bink, Chad, Danjahandz, Devante Swing, Missy Elliot, Nottz, The Neptunes, Pharrell, Teddy Riley, and Timbaland.

Washington, DC and Baltimore

Washington, DC (DC) sits on 61.13 mi^2 (158.32 km^2) of land. It was established around 1798 and had a 2020 population of around 689,000 (44.7 percent Black and 11.3 percent Latinx), representing 10.8 percent of the Washington, DC, metro area. DC is the US capitol. It has a higher population than most other sites in this study. Since at least 1870, DC has had a significant Black percentage, and from 1950 to 1970, that percentage greatly increased. Musically, DC features a style of music known as go-go, which helps set the local soundscape for rappers.

Artists and groups associated with the DC rap scene include Baby Fifty, Backyard Band, Black Fortune, Chelly the MC, Chuck Brown, Ciscero, Cordae, DJ Kool, Experience Unlimited (E.U.), Fat Trel, Go-Go Mickey, Huck-a-Bucks, Jigga Flames, Junk Yard Band (JYB), LIL LO, Logic, MoneyMarr, No Savage, Nonchalant, Noochie, Oddisee, OP Tribe, Panacea, Phil Adé, Q da Fool, Rare Essence, Ras Nebyu, Rico Nasty, Shabaaz PBG, Shy Glizzy, SlimeGoon9, Tabi Bonney, TCB Band, Trouble Funk, Wale, What? Band, WillThaRapper, and XanMan. Producers associated with the DC rap scene include Carnage, Chris Barz, Chuck Brown, Cordae, Damu the Fudgemunk, DJ Kool, Grace Jones, Jigga!, Junk Yard Band (JYB), Kenny Beats, Kev Brown, Logic, Moe Shorter, Nonchalant, Oddisee, Reo Edwards, Rico Nasty, Roy Battle, XanMan, and Yung Manny.

Baltimore sits on 80.9 mi^2 (210 km^2) of land. It was established in 1796 and had a 2020 population of around 585,000 (61.6 percent Black and 5.6 percent Latinx), representing 20.6 percent of the Baltimore–Columbia metro area. Baltimore's Black percentage increased greatly between the 1960s and 1990s. Baltimore is a social movement city, with a BPPSD chapter, at least five SNCC organizational events, and at least five May 1970 student protests.

Artists and groups associated with the Baltimore rap scene include 3ohBlack, Baby Jamo, Big Flock, Blaqstarr, Bossman, D.King, DeScribe, DeStorm Power, Foggieraw, GlockBoyKari, Goonew, Height Keech, Ill Conscious, Jay Royale, JPEGMAFIA, K-Swift, K.A.A.N., King Los, Labtekwon, Lightshow, Lil Dude, Lil Gray, Lissen, Mumu Fresh, mererackz, Mike Hughes, NOE, Patron the DepthMC, Premo Rice, Rod Lee, Rome Cee, Rye Rye, Sintax the Terrific, Sweet Cherie, Tate Kobang, and Y-Love. Producers associated with the Baltimore music scene include Andre Johnson, Blaqstarr, Darren Frazier, Donnell Floyd, Ignatius Mason, JPEGMAFIA, K-Swift, Mike Neal, Moe Shorter, and Reo Edwards.

Honolulu

Honolulu sits on 60.5 mi^2 (156.7 km^2) of land. It was established around 1907 and had a 2020 population of around 350,000 (2.7 percent Black and 10.4 percent Latinx), representing 34.5 percent of the urban Honolulu metro area. Honolulu showed major general population increases in the 1950 and 2000 censuses, though there were population decreases in 1960 and 2010. Honolulu's population density is higher than most other sites in this study. It also has one of the lowest Black percentages of the sites.

Artists and groups associated with the rap scene in Hawai'i include Amphibeus Tungs, Audible Lab Rats (ALR), Bruno Mars, Bxmbz, Creed Chameleon, Dezman, Hoku Haiku, Ill Valley Productions, Juan P, Khia, MadeinTYO, Natural Vibrations, Sean Na'auao, Seawind, Shing02, Sudden Rush, Tassho Pearce, Tempo Valley, The Grouch, and Thomas Iannucci. Producers associated with the Hawaiian music scene include ATFC, CyrusFX, Ion Myke, Island Music, Jai Freedom Lewis, Joe Dub, Kohomua, Natural Vibrations, Old Joseph, Riseup, The Grouch, The Lab Rats, and Warren Clarke.

San Juan and Saint Thomas

San Juan sits on 47.9 mi² (199 km²) of land. San Juan was established around 1521 and in 2020 had a population of around 342,000 (12.4 percent Black and 98.1 percent Latinx), representing 16.4 percent of the San Juan metro area. San Juan has a higher land and water area than most sites. It has the highest Latinx percentage and a lower Black percentage than most other sites in this study. Artists and groups associated with the San Juan rap scene include Baby Rasta & Gringo, Bad Bunny, Calle 13, Chezina, Daddy Yankee, Dj Negro, DJ Playero, Don Chezina and Las Gaunabanas, Falo, Frankie Boy, Héctor el Father, Ivy Queen, Kendo Kaponi, Luny Tunes, Maicol & Manuel, MC Cassidy, MC Ceja, Mexicano 777, Ranking Stone, Residente, Rey Pirin, The Noise, Vico C, Wilfred y la Ganga, Wiso G, and Voltio. Producers associated with the San Juan rap scene include Baby Rasta & Gringo, DJ Blass, DJ Fat, Dj Joe, Dj Negro, DJ Nelson, DJ Playero, Echo, Eliel, Lito Y Polaco, Luny Tunes, Maicol & Manuel, Miguel Correa, Monserrate & DJ Urba, Naldo, Nely el Arma Secreta, Ñengo Flow, Nesty, Nico Canada, Noriega (producer with Luny Tunes), DJ Rafy Mercenario, Rey Pirin, Tainy, Tego Calderón, The Noise, Tony Touch, and Vico C.

Saint Thomas sits on about 32 mi² (83 km²) of land. It was established around 1657 and had a 2020 population of about 42,000. Saint Thomas has one of the lowest total areas and lowest land areas among the sites. Saint Thomas has the lowest population and lowest population density among the sites, although its population increased greatly in the 1970s and 1980s. Artists and groups associated with the US Virgin Islands scene include BB, Dem Rude Boyz, Dezarie, Midnite, R. City (Rock City, Planet VI), Rudeboy Jett, Too Much, Trendsettah, Verse Simmonds, and Young Fyah. Producers associated with the US Virgin Islands music scene include BB, Dem Rude Boyz, Dezarie, Funk Gumbs, Inner Visions, Jerry Meyers, Midnite, R. City, Rudeboy Jett, Trendsettah, Verse Simmonds, Wilfredo Micheals, and Young Fyah.

Conclusion

This chapter centered on rap music scenes, opening a study of twenty-five US rap scenes using the factors of geography, migration, movement, music, and technology.

2

Geography

Introduction

CeeLo Green's raps with his group Goodie Mob describe a geographical separation in an urban locale (Figure 4):

Me and my family moved in our apartment complex / A gate with the serial code was put up next / They claim that this community is so drug-free / But it don't look that way to me.[1]

This example, from the second verse of the song, carries a vivid description of a movement into new housing and an immediate response from security forces to put up coded gates, then false claims of safety from drug trafficking (with evidence of it all around), then a curfew for Black people, then the pressing of the "New World Order," and an ensuing "slaughter." Yet, it is the very end of the verse that shows the greatest connection to geography and the present chapter. CeeLo mentions his "mind will not allow him not to be curious" and then ultimately asks if the gate is for the protection of the people inside the gate or for the protection of the people outside of the gate.

Atlanta rapper CeeLo and the group Goodie Mob were at the foundation of the Atlanta rap scene, which is considered a third wave of US rap music (following scenes in the East and West). French explains that rap progressed geographically "from one major urban center to another in America in a leapfrog pattern," and the conclusion is vital:

In the 1980s, rap dispersed from New York City to distant urban centers of Los Angeles, Houston, and Oakland in a leapfrog manner. The last rap centers to develop were cities in the Midwest, which were closer to New York City than those on the West Coast. If rap music spread according to contagious diffusion, rap would reach Chicago and St. Louis before it would reach Los Angeles and Oakland.[2]

French finds that local rap developed in a leapfrog pattern and that it "followed the hierarchical diffusion pattern of leapfrogging from one large metro area to another."[3] This was based on "mapping 1124 rap artists" and finding three major Hip Hop centers in NYC, LA, and Atlanta, and then "secondary rap centers" in the "East

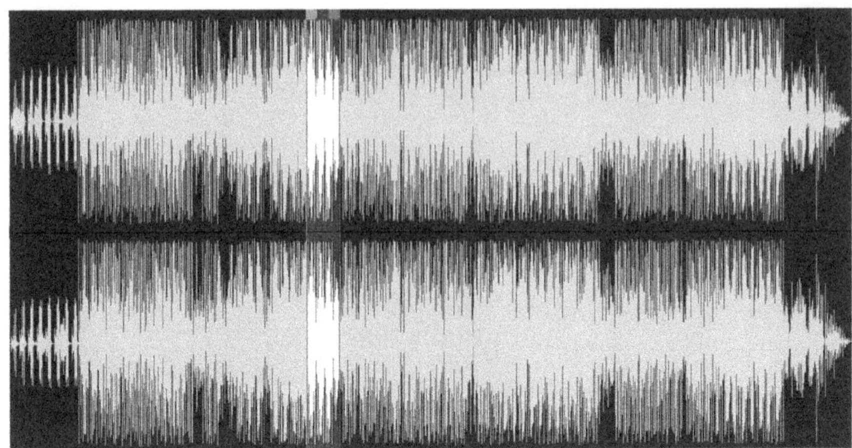

Figure 4 Goodie Mob "Cell Therapy" Akai WAV snapshot with quoted material highlighted.

Coast (Philadelphia), West Coast (The Bay Area), South (New Orleans, Houston, and Miami), and Midwest (Chicago and Detroit)." [4] French also found that rappers "from these centers developed local rap styles and used local slang to portray their locality." [5]

Comparative Analysis of Geography and Place

This chapter analyzes comparative geographical and place data from the twenty-five scenes. The scenes are analyzed as "sites," usually at the city or borough level. There are about thirty-five administrative sites examined. As of 2020, about 9.35 percent of the US population lived on one of these sites, and about 33.21 percent of the US population lived in the metro areas containing these sites. Table 2 shows the 2020 geographical characteristics. In 2020, the average total area was 146.04 mi^2 (378.24 km^2), the average land area was 115.35 mi^2 (301.06 km^2), and the average water area was 31.65 mi^2 (84.49 km^2). The average Black percentage on the sites was 30.46 percent, while the US average is about 13.6 percent. The average Latinx percentage on the sites was 23.31 percent, while the US average is about 18.9 percent. The average establishment or incorporation date for the US cities examined was about 1778.

Sites in the West, Midwest, and South—Houston, LA, New Orleans, Memphis, and Chicago—have the *most total area* of the sites in the study. This ranges from 671.7 mi^2 to 234 mi^2 (1,740 km^2 to 607 km^2), respectively. East Coast sites (Hempstead and Queens) and West Coast sites (San Francisco, San Jose, and Portland) are those with larger *total areas* than most other sites. The five locations with the *least total area* are in the East (Jersey City, Newark, and Manhattan), the Midwest (Gary), and the Caribbean (Saint Thomas). This ranges from 21.02 mi^2 to 50.6 mi^2 (54.48 km^2 to 131.05 km^2),

Table 2 Geographic Data.

Scene Number	City or Site	Coordinates	State or Territory	Total Area (mi²)	Total Area (km²)	Land Area (mi²)	Land Area (km²)	Water Area (mi²)	Water Area (km²)
1	Bronx	40°50′14″N 73°53′10″W	New York	57	150	42	109	15	40
2	Manhattan and Harlem	40°47′N 73°58′W	New York	33.58	87	22.83	59.1	10.76	27.9
3	Queens	40°45′N 73°52′W	New York	178	460	109	280	70	200
4	Brooklyn	40°41′34″N 73°59′25″W	New York	97	250	70.82	183.4	26	67
5	Staten Island	40°34′19″N 74°8′49″W	New York	102.5	265	58.5	152	44	110
	New York City	40.66°N 73.94°W	New York	472.4	1,224	300.5	778	172	445
6	Hempstead	40°42′17″N 73°37′02″W	New York	191.77	496.68	117.68	307.39	73.08	189.29
7	Philadelphia	40.01°N 75.13°W	Pennsylvania	142.7	369.59	134.36	347.98	8.34	21.61
8	Newark	40.72°N 74.17°W	New Jersey	25.88	67.04	24.14	62.53	1.74	4.51
	Jersey City	40.71°N 74.06°W	New Jersey	21.03	54.48	14.75	38.2	6.29	16.28
9	Boston	42.34°N 71.02°W	Massachusetts	89.61	232.1	48.34	125.2	41.27	106.9
10	Los Angeles	34.02°N 118.41°W	California	501.6	1,299	469.5	1,216	32.1	83

(Continued)

Table 2 (*Continued*)

Scene Number	City or Site	Coordinates	State or Territory	Total Area (mi²)	Total Area (km²)	Land Area (mi²)	Land Area (km²)	Water Area (mi²)	Water Area (km²)
11	Oakland	37.77°N 122.23°W	California	78.03	202.1	55.93	144.59	22.1	57.24
	San Francisco	37.73°N 123.03°W	California	231.89	600.89	46.9	121.48	184.99	479.11
	San Jose	37.30°N 121.81°W	California	181.4	470	178.3	462	3.1	8
12	Seattle	47.62°N 122.35°W	Washington	142.1	368	83.9	217	58.2	151
	Portland	45.54°N 122.65°W	Oregon	145	376	133.4	346	11.5	30
13	Chicago	41.84°N 87.68°W	Illinois	234.5	607	227.7	590	6.8	18
	Gary	41°35′44″N 87°20′43″W	Indiana	50.6	131.05	49.87	129.15	0.73	1.89
14	St. Louis	38.64°N 90.24°W	Missouri	66.17	171.39	61.72	159.85	4.45	11.53
15	Minneapolis	44.96°N 93.27°W	Minnesota	57.51	148.98	54	139.86	3.51	9.08
	St. Paul	44.95°N 93.10°W	Minnesota	56.1	145.31	51.97	134.61	4.13	10.7
16	Detroit	42.38°N 83.10°W	Michigan	142.9	370	138.7	359	4.2	11
17	Houston	29.79°N 95.39°W	Texas	671.7	1,740	640.4	1,659	31.2	81

18	New Orleans	30.05°N 89.93°W	Louisiana	349.8	906	169.5	439	180.4	467	
19	Memphis	35.11°N 89.97°W	Tennessee	304.6	789	297	769	7.6	20	
20	Atlanta	33.76°N 84.42°W	Georgia	136.3	353	135.3	350	1	2.6	
21	Miami	25.78°N 80.21°W	Florida	56.07	145.23	36	93.23	20.08	52	
22	Hampton	37.034946°N 76.360126°W	Virginia	136.27	352.95	51.46	133.28	84.81	219.67	
23	Washington, DC	38.90°N 77.02°W	District of Columbia	68.35	177	61.126	158.32	7.224	18.71	
	Baltimore	39.30°N 76.61°W	Maryland	92	238	80.9	210	11.1	29	
24	Honolulu	21.32°N 157.85°W	Hawai'i	68.4	177.2	60.5	156.7	7.9	20.5	
25	San Juan	8.40°N 66.06°W	Puerto Rico	77	199	47.9	199	29.1	75	
	Saint Thomas	18°20′N 64°55′W	USVI	32	83	32	83			
	Totals for All Cities or Sites*			4823.68	12,494	3,804	9,929	1,019	2,640	
	Site Averages			146.04	378.24	115.35	301.06	31.65	82.49	
	US Totals					3,533,038.28		269,995.13		
	Scene/US					0.11%		0.38%		
	US Averages									

respectively. Other Midwestern sites such as St. Paul, Minneapolis, and St. Louis also have smaller *total areas* than most other sites.

The five sites with the *most land area* are in the South (Houston and Memphis), West (LA and San Jose), and Midwest (Chicago). This ranges from 640.4 mi^2 to 178.3 mi^2 (1,659 km^2 to 462 km^2), respectively. Other sites in the South (New Orleans, Atlanta), Midwest (Detroit), and other locations (Philadelphia and Portland) also have more *land area* than most other sites. The five sites with the least *land area* are mostly in the East (Jersey City, Manhattan, Newark), with Saint Thomas and Miami as other locations. This ranges from 14.75 mi^2 to 36 mi^2 (38.2 km^2 to 92.23 km^2), respectively. Some East Coast (Bronx and Boston), West Coast (San Francisco), Midwest (Gary), and Caribbean (San Juan) sites also have less *land area* than most of the other sites.

The five cities *with the most water area* were in the West (San Francisco and Seattle), South (New Orleans, Hampton), and East (Queens). This ranged from 184.99 mi^2 to 58.2 mi^2 (479.11 km^2 to 151 km^2), respectively. East Coast (Staten Island and Boston), West Coast (LA), South (Houston), and Caribbean (San Juan) sites also have more *water area* than most of the other sites. The lowest five in *water area* were in the Midwest (Gary and Minneapolis), South (Atlanta), East (Newark), and West (San Jose). This ranged from 0.73 mi^2 to 3.51 mi^2 (1.89 km^2 to 9.08 km^2), respectively. Other Midwest sites such as St. Paul, Detroit, St. Louis, and Chicago also have less *water area* than most of the other sites.

The 2020 place and population data are shown in Table 3. The *oldest establishments*, townships, or incorporations are in the Caribbean (San Juan) and on the East Coast (Manhattan, Hempstead, Boston, and Brooklyn). These date from the years 1521 to 1624, respectively. Other sites in the Caribbean (Saint Thomas) and on the East Coast (Staten Island, Philadelphia, and Queens) were also established before most others.

The *most recent establishments*, townships, or incorporations are Honolulu in the Pacific, Gary and Minneapolis in the Midwest, the Bronx in the East, and Miami in the South. These date from the years 1907 to 1867, respectively. Sites in the West (Seattle, Oakland, Portland, and San Jose) and in the Midwest (St. Paul) were also established later than most others.

In 2020, the *largest site populations* were in the East with Brooklyn and Queens, the West with LA, the Midwest with Chicago, and the South with Houston (from about 3.9 million to about 2.3 million people, respectively). NYC is the largest city with 8.8 million people. Other sites with large populations include the East Coast sites Manhattan, Philadelphia, and the Bronx, and the West Coast sites San Jose and San Francisco. The *lowest city populations* are in Saint Thomas, Gary, Hampton, Jersey City, and St. Louis, (from 42,261 to 301,578 people, respectively). St. Paul, Newark, San Juan, Honolulu, and New Orleans are also cities with lower populations than most other sites. Gary and St. Louis have experienced waves of post-industrialization, as has Jersey City. Saint Thomas, San Juan, and Honolulu are also island sites.

Population density was measured by dividing the population by the land area on the site. All of the sites with the *highest population density* are in the East—Manhattan, Brooklyn, the Bronx, Queens, and Jersey City. This ranges from 74,211 to 19,827 people per square mile, respectively. Other East Coast sites (Boston and Newark),

Table 3 Place and Population: 2020 Data.

Scene Number	City or Site	Est./ INC.- Township*, county*, Town*	2020 Population	Population Density (Land Area, mi²)	Population Density (Land Area, km²)	2020 % Black	2020 % Latinx	2020 Metro Population	Metro Area	City/Metro Population
1	Bronx	1898	1,472,654	35,063.19	13,510.59	43.8	56.4	20,140,470	New York–Newark–Jersey City, NY–NJ–CT–PA metro area	7.31%
2	Manhattan and Harlem	1624	1,694,251	74,211.61	28,667.53	18.5	26.4	20,140,470	New York–Newark–Jersey City, NY–NJ–CT–PA metro area	8.41%
3	Queens	1683	2,405,464	22,068.48	8,590.94	20.7	28.1	20,140,470	New York–Newark–Jersey City, NY–NJ–CT–PA metro area	11.94%
4	Brooklyn	1634	2,736,074	38,634.20	14,918.62	26.7	18.9	20,140,470	New York–Newark–Jersey City, NY–NJ–CT–PA metro area	13.58%
5	Staten Island	1661	495,747	8,474.31	3,261.49	10.5	19.6	20,140,470	New York–Newark–Jersey City, NY–NJ–CT–PA metro area	2.46%
	New York City	1624	8,804,190	29,298.47	11,316.44	20.2	28.3	20,140,470	New York–Newark–Jersey City, NY–NJ–CT–PA metro area	43.71%
6	Hempstead	1624	793,409	6,742.09	2,581.12	17.3	21	20,140,470	New York–Newark–Jersey City, NY–NJ–CT–PA metro area	3.94%
7	Philadelphia	1682	1,603,797	11,936.57	4,608.88	43.6	15.5	6,245,051	Philadelphia–Camden–Wilmington, PA–NJ–DE–MD MSA	25.68%

(Continued)

Table 3 (*Continued*)

Scene Number	City or Site	Est./ INC.-Township*, county*, Town*	2020 Population	Population Density (Land Area, mi²)	Population Density (Land Area, km²)	2020 % Black	2020 % Latinx	2020 Metro Population	Metro Area	City/Metro Population
8	Newark	1693	311,549	12,905.92	4,982.39	48.2	36.8	20,140,470	New York–Newark–Jersey City, NY–NJ–CT–PA metro area	1.55%
	Jersey City	1838	292,449	19,827.05	7,655.73	22.5	27.5	20,140,470	New York–Newark–Jersey City, NY–NJ–CT–PA metro area	1.45%
9	Boston	1630	675,647	13,976.98	5,396.54	23.5	19.8	4,941,632	Boston–Cambridge–Newton, MA–NH MSA	13.67%
10	Los Angeles	1850	3,898,747	8,304.04	3,206.21	8.6	48.4	13,200,998	Los Angeles–Long Beach–Anaheim, CA MSA	29.53%
11	Oakland	1852	440,646	7,878.53	3,047.56	22	27.2	4,749,008	San Francisco–Oakland–Berkeley, CA MSA	9.28%
	San Francisco	1850	873,965	18,634.65	7,194.31	5.4	15.4	4,749,008	San Francisco–Oakland–Berkeley, CA MSA	18.40%
	San Jose	1850	1,013,240	5,682.78	2,193.16	3	31	2,000,468	San Jose–Sunnyvale–Santa Clara, CA MSA	50.65%
12	Seattle	1865	737,015	8,784.45	3,396.38	6.8	7.2	4,018,762	Seattle–Tacoma–Bellevue, WA MSA	18.34%
	Portland	1851	652,503	4,891.33	1,885.85	9	10.3	2,512,859	Portland–Vancouver–Hillsboro, OR–WA MSA	25.97%

13	Chicago	1833	2,746,388	12,061.43	4,654.89	29.2	28.7	9,618,502	Chicago–Naperville–Elgin, IL–IN–WI MSA	28.55%
	Gary	1906	69,093	1,385.46	534.98	78	8.7			
14	St. Louis	1822	301,578	4,886.23	1,886.63	44.8	4.2	2,820,253	St. Louis, MO–IL MSA	10.69%
15	Minneapolis	1867	429,954	7,962.11	3,074.17	18.4	9.8	3,693,729	Minneapolis–St. Paul–Bloomington, MN–WI MSA	11.64%
	St. Paul	1854	311,527	5,994.36	2,314.29	16	9.7	3,693,729	Minneapolis–St. Paul–Bloomington, MN–WI MSA	8.43%
16	Detroit	1806	639,111	4,607.87	1,780.25	77.9	7.8	4,392,041	Detroit–Warren–Dearborn, MI MSA	14.55%
17	Houston	1837	2,304,580	3,598.66	1,389.14	22.6	44.5	7,122,240	Houston–The Woodlands–Sugar Land, TX MSA	32.36%
18	New Orleans	1718	383,997	2,265.47	874.71	58.1	5.6	1,271,845	New Orleans–Metairie, LA MSA	30.19%
19	Memphis	1826	633,104	2,131.66	823.28	66.4	7.7	1,337,779	Memphis, TN–MS–AR MSA	47.33%
20	Atlanta	1847	498,715	3,685.99	1,424.90	48.2	5.8	6,089,815	Atlanta–Sandy Springs–Alpharetta, GA MSA	8.19%
21	Miami	1898	442,241	12,284.47	4,743.55	15.2	72.3	6,138,333	Miami–Fort Lauderdale–Pompano Beach, FL MSA	7.20%

(Continued)

Table 3 (*Continued*)

Scene Number	City or Site	Est./ INC.-Township*, county*, Town*	2020 Population	Population Density (Land Area, mi²)	Population Density (Land Area, km²)	2020 % Black	2020 % Latinx	2020 Metro Population	Metro Area	City/Metro Population
22	Hampton	1705	137,131	2,664.81	1,028.89	48.6	6.13	1,799,674	Virginia Beach–Norfolk–Newport News, VA–NC metro area	7.62%
23	Washington, DC	1790	689,545	11,280.72	4,355.39	44.7	11.3	6,385,162	Washington–Arlington–Alexandria, DC–VA–MD–WV MSA	10.80%
	Baltimore	1796	585,708	7,239.90	2,789.09	61.6	5.6	2,844,510	Baltimore–Columbia–Towson, MD MSA	20.59%
24	Honolulu	1907	349,800	5,781.82	2,232.29	2.7	10.4	1,016,508	Urban Honolulu, HI MSA	34.41%
25	San Juan	1521	342,259	7,145.28	1,719.89	12.4	98.1	2,081,265	San Juan–Bayamón–Caguas, PR MSA	16.44%
	Saint Thomas	1657	42,261	1,320.66	509.17					
	Totals for All Cities or Sites*		31,004,149					110,082,245		
	Site Averages	1778.03	939,519.67			30.46	23.31	5,200,950.18		17.13%
	US Totals		331,449,520					331,449,520		
	Scene/US		9.35%					33.21%		
	US Averages					13.6	18.9			

the West's San Francisco, the South's Miami, and the Midwest's Chicago also feature population densities much higher than other sites. The sites with the *lowest population density* are Saint Thomas, Gary, Memphis, New Orleans, and Hampton. This ranges from 1,320 to 2,664 people per square mile, respectively. Houston, Atlanta, Detroit, St. Louis, and Portland also feature population densities much lower than other sites. This measurement is far from perfect, as not all land on a site is inhabitable or available to local residents.

The sites with the *highest Black percentages* are in the Midwest (Gary and Detroit) and South (Memphis, Baltimore, and New Orleans). These range from 78 percent to 58.1 percent, respectively. Newark and the Bronx on the East Coast, Atlanta and DC in the South, and St. Louis in the Midwest are also sites where the Black percentage is higher than in most sites. The sites with the *lowest Black percentages* are in the Pacific and the West—Honolulu, San Jose, San Francisco, Seattle, and LA. These range from 2.7 percent to 8.6 percent, respectively. Portland, Staten Island, San Juan, Miami, and St. Paul are additional sites where the Black percentage is lower than other sites.

The sites with the *highest Latinx percentages* are San Juan, Miami, Bronx, LA, and Houston. These range from 98.1 percent to 44.5 percent, respectively. Newark, Queens, and Jersey City, on the East Coast, as well as San Jose and Chicago, in the West and Midwest, respectively, are also sites where the Latinx percentage is higher than most others. The sites with the *lowest Latinx percentages* include St. Louis and sites in the South—New Orleans, Baltimore, Atlanta, and Hampton. These range from 4.2 percent to 6.1 percent, respectively. The Midwest (Detroit, Gary, and St. Paul), West (Seattle), and South (Memphis) are additional sites where the Latinx percentage is lower than most other sites.

The relationship of the city to the metro area was also examined. A city-to-metro area ratio measures how many people in the metro area live within the city limits. This can be an indication of the site's regional influence or an indication of other sites in the metro area also having significant populations. It can also be an indication of how the metro area is defined. The sites with the *highest percentage of city-to-metro area ratio* are San Jose, Memphis, Honolulu, Houston, and New Orleans. This ranges from 50.6 percent to 32.4 percent, respectively. LA, Chicago, Portland, Philadelphia, and Baltimore are additional sites with high percentages of city-to-metro area ratios. The sites with the *lowest percentage of city-to-metro area ratio* are Jersey City, Newark, Staten Island, Hempstead, and Miami. This ranges from 1.5 percent to 7.2 percent, respectively. The Bronx, Hampton, Atlanta, Manhattan, and St. Paul are additional sites with lower ratios of city to metro area.

The sites in the book include about thirty-two metropolitan statistical areas (MSAs) or metro areas. The New York area appears nine times, the San Francisco area twice, and the Minneapolis area twice. There are twenty-two states, districts (DC), or territories (e.g., PR, VI) examined. Many of the sites are in New York (seven) or California (four). The five *most populous* metro areas or MSAs were the following:

New York–Newark–Jersey City, NY–NJ–CT–PA metro area
Los Angeles–Long Beach–Anaheim, CA MSA

Chicago–Naperville–Elgin, IL–IN–WI MSA
Houston–The Woodlands–Sugar Land, TX MSA
Washington–Arlington–Alexandria, DC–VA–MD–WV MSA

The populations of these top areas ranged from about 20.1 million to about 6.4 million.

The five *least populous* metro areas or metropolitan statistical areas examined were the following:

Urban Honolulu, HI MSA
New Orleans–Metairie, LA MSA
Memphis, TN–MS–AR MSA
Virginia Beach–Norfolk–Newport News, VA–NC metro area
San Jose–Sunnyvale–Santa Clara, CA MSA

The populations of these metro areas or MSAs ranged from about 1 million to 2 million people.

Rap Geographies: From Regional to Local

East Coast

There are four distinct regions of rap in the US. Sigler and Balaji establish a regional grouping of "Northeast ('East Coast'), South (i.e., 'Dirty South'), West (i.e., 'West Coast'), and the Midwest."[6] The East Coast sites (the Bronx, Queens, Newark, Jersey, and NYC) have a higher population density than many others. While the sites in NYC have larger areas and higher populations, the New Jersey sites have lower populations but less land areas, resulting in higher population densities. The East also features some of the earliest establishment dates in NYC, Brooklyn, Queens, Hempstead, Boston, and others.

The South Bronx construction of Hip Hop led to a regional claim to authenticity that NYC eventually benefited from. George explains that contempt of "New Yorkers for non-New York rap began with the disdain in Manhattan for New Jersey's Sugar Hill Gang." Then a series of battles for geographical authenticity ensued: the Bronx versus Queens, New York versus Philadelphia, New York and Philadelphia against the Northeast.[7] By this time, rap was beginning to grow well beyond the East Coast and Northeast. In the mid-1990s, Rose documented that Compton, Oakland, Detroit, Chicago, Houston, Atlanta, Miami, Newark and Trenton, Roxbury, and Philadelphia appropriated Hip Hop's "language, style, and attitude" to their adverse local conditions.[8] Later, Samuels connected local rap's growing popularity with its ease of production: "Rap quickly spread from New York to Philadelphia, Chicago, Boston, and other cities with substantial black populations. Its popularity was sustained by the ease with which it could be made."[9] By 2000, Forman noted that rap had "grown more regional and even local."[10] Forman noted a regionalization and localization still very pronounced in rap: "Within U.S. rap culture, artists and fans alike reflect an acute awareness that people in different parts of the country produce and enjoy regional variations on the genre; they experience rap differently, structuring it into their social patterns according to the norms that prevail in a given urban environment."[11]

West Coast and Northwest

The West Coast sites have higher land areas in LA and San Jose and higher total and water areas in LA and San Francisco than most other sites. The establishment dates are more recent than other sites, as in the cases of Oakland and San Jose. San Francisco is a high population density site, when compared to sites in the West and to sites in the South.

LA opened rap regions beyond the East Coast. Quinn's study of LA even necessitates a regional distinction of the types of raps found on the West Coast, such as the "evolving classifications and connotations of the terms gangsta rap, reality rap, hardcore rap, player rap, and so on."[12] Regionally, the West Coast also has a connection to the South. Quinn describes a deliberate, "slightly southern" flow linking first-generation and second-generation Black "Westerners" to the "toasts, stories, icons, and heroic figures of the South."[13] Viator looks at LA's unique contribution to the rap world and finds "the Bronx West" as a "poor model for examining the unique, homegrown, and socially insulated youth dance scenes that emerged far from the South Bronx, Brooklyn, and Queens but that developed concurrently."[14] Viator finds that the LA scene operated "quite differently" from the Manhattan club scene, as "LA nightclubs in the early 1980s were a virtual wasteland for contemporary urban music and for the record companies seeking to expose crowds to it."[15] Instead, "LA DJs crafted their own scene, a do-it-yourself alternative to industry gigs" by "organizing 'mobile' dance parties in rented spaces, including garages, school gyms, hotel ballrooms, and conference centers, all over Los Angeles County."[16] Sides offers an assessment of Compton that is also telling, noting, "But if the material circumstances of Compton were typical of Americas declining suburbs, its location was not; its geographic proximity to the heart of the nation's film and music industry further shaped Comptons transformation to metonym."[17] Keyes finds that the radio station KDAY (in LA) was an important transmitter of these styles to larger audiences and in spreading West Coast rap music.[18]

Oakland and Seattle have also been the subject of close scholarly inquiry. In the case of Oakland, my *Rap and Politics* maps out a fifty-year political narrative of three eras of local discourses starting in mid-1960s' West Oakland.[19] By looking at the local scene's music, comparing the local music to the Billboard Charts at the given time, I claim that the type of rap shown to exist in Oakland could actually exist in at least twenty-five other North American cities or sites.[20]

For Seattle rap, geographical isolation is a factor, as Abe writes in *Emerald Street*: "Aside from Portland, Oregon, the next biggest city south is San Francisco, eight hundred miles away. Minneapolis is the next major city due east, nearly 1,700 miles away."[21] Abe "chronicles decades of Seattle rap history" and makes the case that "Seattle's regional isolation" has created a "sheer geographic and cultural reach."[22] Abe's musical timeline runs from 1979 to 2015 and offers a map of key locations. According to Abe, The Sugarhill Gang's "Rapper's Delight" "sent cultural shockwaves through young people" in the Central District and the South End.[23] At the time, NYC was seen as the center of the rap world, and "serious doubts were cast on the legitimacy of nearly all material that came from elsewhere."[24] There are two main goals of Abe's text, and each goal has a relationship to Seattle's geographical position. First, Abe aims "to shine light on a rich but often overlooked and underappreciated aspect of Seattle's cultural history," and, second, Abe hopes "to position Seattle's contribution within the larger national and international narrative" of Hip Hop.[25] *Emerald Street* provides a rich historical account with a thorough description of how Hip Hop was formed on the local scene and how rap developed since the 1980s.[26]

Midwest

The Midwest sites have *land areas higher* than most sites in Chicago and Detroit, and *land areas lower* than most sites in Gary, St. Louis, and St. Paul. Many of these sites also have lower water areas, such as Chicago, Gary, St. Louis, Minneapolis, St. Paul, and Detroit. Most of these are located near large bodies of water in the Great Lakes or the Mississippi River. Similar to the sites in the West, many locations in the Midwest were more recently established (Gary, Minneapolis, St. Paul) than other sites examined.

While regional development in the West and South has been the subject of scholarship, little concentration has been given to the Midwest as a region, or in the way of individual scenes. There are a few exceptions to this, such as some coverage of Chicago, Minneapolis, and Detroit. Analysis of rap scenes in the Midwest are largely at the chapter or article level. In some cases, there are several theses and dissertations but few comprehensive or longitudinal peer-reviewed studies of these Midwest scenes. Some of this is explained by local musical development, as French argues: "The relatively lower total number of rappers from the Midwestern cities of Chicago, Detroit, and St. Louis was due to the fact that rap diffused into these cities at a later time."[27] Abrams explains that before "Eminem, Nelly, and Kanye West emerged," the music in the Midwest "took elements from both the East and West Coasts."[28] At the time of Common Sense and No ID emerging on the Chicago rap scene, Chicago rap was closer to house music, with artists such as Fast Eddie, Vitamin C, JMD, and Kool Rock Steady.[29]

South and Contested Islands

In the South, some sites have high total and land areas (Houston, Memphis), others have high total areas due to high water areas (New Orleans), and others have lower total areas. The sites with lower total areas include Miami and Hampton; however, these sites are located in metro areas that are much larger. Most of the sites in the South tend to have lower population densities than most other sites.

The South as a region also developed as an academic topic. Sarig claims that the rise of Southern Hip Hop was the "first large-scale break from New York's dominance."[30]

This claim was based on a reading of data that showed the West Coast (defined as "the Bay and L.A. combined") never contributing "more than 25 to 35 of acts on the rap charts, even at its peak."[31] This also might be an indication that LA and Bay Area rap was localized in many of its forms. Sarig's analysis offers four key reasons why Southern Hip Hop has been so successful: (1) the southern heritage; (2) the social aspects of the music (e.g., "call and response"); (3) inversion of the Great Migration and new "Northern transplants"; (4) and the Southern strategy, which included a "a strange alchemy."[32] Palmer's study of the South takes a mixtape approach, with a deep curation of sources, extensive web resources, and thorough bibliographical sources.[33] In a discography section, there are carefully curated rap lists, such as songs by women, the South and West collaborations, South and Midwest collaborations, a regional South singles collection, "unpredictable" collaborations, controversial songs, songs with drug references, and essential album recommendations listed by artists.[34] Palmer lists several compilations, while also providing a media center containing publications from magazines; local papers; films with descriptions; radio stations for Miami, Atlanta, New Orleans, Houston, and Memphis; and even a glossary from Bay Area native and rapper E-40.[35] One area called "Deep Representation Cuts" included the following: Arrested Development's "Tennessee," David Banner's "Mississippi," 8Ball and MJG's "Memphis City Blues," Jermaine Dupri's "Welcome to Atlanta" (featuring Ludacris), Juvenile's "Nolia Clap," Lil Scrappy's "FILA," Petey Pablo's "Raise Up (NC)," Pitbull's "Welcome to Miami" off of his *MIAMI* album, Scarface's "Southside Houston Texas," and Ying Yang's "Georgia Dome."[36] In regional analyses of the South, some of the cities examined by Sarig, Palmer, and others (e.g., Miami, Houston, Memphis, New Orleans, and Atlanta) became the focus of more localized examinations.[37]

In Faniel's *Hip-Hop in Houston*, the deep, historical, longitudinal examination of the local scene *is the method*, and this could be used to build local scenes elsewhere. The possible gains from looking at local sites are expressed by Faniel:

> But we cannot dialogue or even historicize hip-hop culture without including regional and local sites, as the persons and practices within these sites were and are participators and creators in what we call hip-hop culture. Regional and local hip-hop cultural developments were not just modulations of East Coast and West Coast hip-hop; the culture progressed from local and regional domains. Thus, the history must be understood as a fragmentary development in which sedimentary parts come together to represent the nature of hip-hop.[38]

Faniel makes it very clear that these "localities and regions that appropriated the culture increased its stock value."[39] Walker's analysis of Houston shows the rich media history as well. Although not a longitudinal study of local rap, Walker makes extensive use of photographs and very detailed interviews of "DJs, radio personalities, and the like." These individual historical accounts present the "passions, regrets, memories, and hopes" of the local musicians on the scene.[40] Then, similar to Faniel, Wilkins finds, "Local hip hop culture has made a major impact around the nation and around the world. Yet it has not received its proper respect within the city."[41] Wilkins's recent text is one of the first known books to reach a neighborhood level of rap analysis. Wilkins identifies three pockets or zones of Black life in Houston—North, South, and Southwest—all of them away from the downtown center.[42] Wilkins notes that the neighborhoods within these parts of Black Houston are the result of 150 years of segregated practices whose "genesis lay in racist political practice."[43] Black local residents have had restricted mobility in Houston, which also creates a social and physical attachment to the neighborhoods.[44] Wilkins explains how middle-class flight and a local recession (from an earlier boom cycle) changed life for Black Houstonians.[45]

Covering New Orleans, Miller's *Bounce* is one of the first known books to offer a comprehensive analysis of local rap on a city scene other than South Bronx.[46] In fact, it might be one of the first books to cover more than ten years of rap history on any local US scene in a comprehensive manner.[47] In the decade since *Bounce*, attention to the local scene has gotten more focused, especially in the areas of framework and method.[48] *Bounce* adds additional clarity, scope, and attention to the actual music collections and analysis.

The Hampton scene encompasses the 757 area code and includes Chesapeake, Portsmouth, and Norfolk as major borders, as well as other locations such as Newport News. Hampton is located midway between NYC and Florida, likely influencing a balanced sound that seems partially East Coast and partially South. Cannady claims that in the late 1980s, Teddy Riley "landed in the Hampton Roads area as if it was a musical territory to be conquered."[49] The boardwalk and beach have also been considered as major factors in scene growth. Another unique geographical factor is the relative mid-size of many cities in the area. The area is known as the "Seven Cities," which describes a collection of "small bergs."[50] It is also located fairly close to other Virginia scenes, such as Alexandria, DC, Richmond, and Petersburg. Hampton is one of many examples in which placemaking and society are complex. In the 1500s, it was called Kecoughtan, after the native inhabitants, and was a highly organized society at the time.[51] As Fairfax documents, Spanish and English invaders arrived first, and then enslaved Blacks were forced to work the land—the slave labor increasing especially between 1660 and 1680 during which Virginia slave laws and codes allowed for more "domestic terrorism of African people."[52]

The DMV scene involves multiple major cities; it is also known as the "DMV (DC, Maryland, Virginia) Music Movement."[53] The geography, music, and social movement are three integral parts to this name, and, as Thomas writes, "it is a description of how local artists have unified in the hopes of pushing the entire region to a greater level of success within the music industry."[54] According to Thomas, the rapper 20 Bellow "got tired of saying DC, MD, & VA" and started a website called "dmvundaground" to approach local artists and put them "on the site for free as a way to showcase them."[55]

The "Contested Islands" (Honolulu, San Juan, and Saint Thomas) also have some important characteristics. These sites are located on islands, and islands typically have lower populations than interior US sites. For Honolulu, its establishment date is later than most sites, and it has a population density lower than most other sites. For San Juan and Saint Thomas, the establishment dates are some of the earliest in this study.

These were the first European contact points with what colonizers perceived to be the New World.

Geography Themes

Explaining Regional and Local Rap Geographies

It is important to identify reasons for the growth of regional and local rap. French's "leapfrog" theory offers a compelling explanation. The study looks at diffusion of rap music by looking at hometowns of 1,124 rap artists and "the year of their debut album" as an indication of the "potential commercial success of a new rap artist."[56] The study found the top fifteen cities with the following number of rappers from 1979 to 2015:

1 New York City (314)
2 Los Angeles (162)
3 Atlanta (88)
4 New Orleans (48)
5 Houston (43)
6 Oakland (41)
7 Philadelphia (38)
8 Chicago (31)
9 Detroit (30)
10 Miami (25)
11 Memphis (17)
12 Boston (13)
13 San Francisco (12)
14 St. Louis (11)
15 Vallejo, CA (10)[57]

French notes a high concentration of products from NYC, LA, and Atlanta and that "the gap to the next tier of cities was sizable (New Orleans, Houston, Oakland, Philadelphia, Chicago, Detroit, and Miami), as no other city produced more than 50 rappers with albums."[58] There are some essential observations made by French, such as Philadelphia's Schoolly D becoming "the first non-New York City metro area rapper to release an album" in 1985.[59] This case validates the leapfrog pattern and occurs slightly before the LA rap floodgates open—skipping over areas much closer to NYC. If the Bay Area (which includes Oakland, San Francisco, and Vallejo data) were to be taken as "one entity, then there were 63 rappers from this conurbation," ranking it third behind Atlanta.[60] This Bay Area data is another case confirming the leapfrog pattern. During the 1990s rap era, French finds 77 "rappers with debut rap albums" and that the popularity of Hip Hop music "ignited diffusion to smaller urban centers in New Orleans (26 new rappers), Houston (24 new rappers), Oakland (20 new rappers), and Atlanta (18 new rappers)."[61] Finding "only a few rappers with albums from the Midwest in the 1990s" and a "post-millennium growth" of rap in cities such as Atlanta, French's study offers scholarship and evidence consistent with other sources. However, French also emphasizes, "Other cities like Philadelphia, Memphis, and Dallas continued to grow in rap talent over time. Midwestern rap nodes in St. Louis, Kansas City, Chicago, and Detroit continued to gain recognition in the 2000s."[62] This growth of the Midwest is a significant point and rises far beyond anecdotal evidence.[63]

Another explanation for the growth of regional and local rap styles involves the locale offering a sort of authenticity for artists and labels. Regional identity, according to Sigler and Balaji, "continues to factor prominently in how rappers articulate their identities, and more importantly, how corporations market them."[64] Sigler and Balaji find that rappers "continue to identify themselves with particular regions, cities, and specific neighborhoods in order to take advantage of their sign value."[65] The regional or local attachment for selling records is also presented in Balaji's study of Gorilla Zoe in Atlanta, writing the "local gatekeepers" "are vital to a corporation's efforts to build a rapper, not only from a perspective of hip-hop legitimacy, but also from an economic one in which the corporation seeks the maximum return on investment." In this analysis, the "localized and geographically specific" is used by corporations to sell a product but "still conform to the bottom line."[66]

Overall, this identity attachment to a local scene is seen as a selling point for the music and for labels looking to attach to a geography, as Sigler and Balaji write: "The construction of place at the regional scale is reinforced and articulated in part by the hip-hop industry and the political economy thereof. As the music industry has consolidated over time and mediums of distribution have changed, hip-hop has experienced a market-driven cultural shift toward an increasingly regionalized notion of place."[67] Sigler and Balaji examine four categories for place: "geographic setting, mise-en-scène, apparel, and place "representation."[68] For setting, Sigler and Balaji look at urban/rural/suburban, ghetto, road/street, and house/home.[69] For mise-en-scène, Sigler and Balaji examine skylines, luxury vehicles, "friends and neighbors," and "misogynistic representation of women."[70] For apparel, Sigler and Balaji examine luxury goods, conspicuous jewelry, "any sports apparel," and "local sports apparel."[71] For place representation, Sigler and Balaji look at place specific, regional, and "negativity toward other regions."[72] Sigler and Balaji find very few "disses" of other regions, and they instead see regional claims as a "stamp of authenticity"—finding the regional mentioning occurring in 40 percent of the videos examined.[73]

There is concern if the local attachments are inauthentic and used only for selling records. Seeking an attachment to a local scene brings along a need to represent that scene's culture (which might include a scene's street culture). As Rose explains, such street culture attachment can create a dangerous web of violent, Black male street cultures for the purposes of entertainment. The story Rose illustrates is that policies destroy Black communities, then Black men are seen as more violent (and treated with more violence), then rap's street stories are associated with this violence (but as "authentic black expression"), then this "activates a familiar kind of racial voyeurism and expands the market for their particular stories of crime and violence."[74] Rose sees this process as an infinite loop: "This creates economic opportunity for performing and celebrating violent storytelling. Round and round we go."[75] There are also issues with using "luxury goods" to gauge rapper attachment to local scenes, and this is part of the framework employed by Sigler and Balaji. As Perry notes, luxury goods and jewelry are excess elements "celebrated elsewhere in American life" and "deemed disgraceful when associated with poor black people."[76] Overall, if the regional analysis offered by Sigler and Balaji is accurate, it should be further analyzed within the literature around rap messaging critical analysis of race, gender, and other identities.

Or, perhaps these regional and local rap claims are more than just a "stamp of authenticity." Much of the current study looks at the background of the scene. This local micro-level of rap music helps us gain accuracy and precision in regard to the core messages being communicated by local youth and can help connect trends, patterns, and relationships between local scenes. Many local rap artists are able to offer deep critiques of their local conditions, and some artists begin to offer historical or systematic explanations for their current conditions. These explanations can be compared with other struggles locally, regionally, nationwide, and worldwide.

Local Rap Geographies Matter

Local rap geographies should be considered (or explicitly dismissed) in studies of rap drawn from US cities. Discussion of geography is important because rap music is part of a culture in which its "practitioners turn *space*, an abstract construction, into *place*—that is, a local reality defined by proximity, meaningfulness and experiential attachment."[77] A large, measurable, sign of place is the establishment of society or governance, populations of peoples, and markets. These spaces are also defined by human interaction, as Baur and others find: "People do not just imagine space. (Physical) space is created, shaped and changed by human practice—sometimes intentionally guided by human imagination, sometimes as an unintentional by-product of other human (inter)actions."[78] Fossett explains that city spaces are part of systems that are "hierarchically structured":

> Cities are embedded in regional, national, and global systems that are hierarchically structured. In systems, the relative positions of cities change over time. Some cities grow in relative size and influence, while others decline. These matters constitute the core concerns of economic and ecological theories explaining macrospatial population distribution.[79]

One factor in city growth (or "relative size and influence") is population, which is impacted by migration. Changes in population can change the fortune of a local environment. The locales examined in this book are part of the nearly ninety thousand local governments in the US, which by Anzia's calculations, spend "roughly a quarter of the nation's public money."[80] Moreover, local governments allocate essential services, as "they are responsible for public education, infrastructure, housing, public safety, public health, and other important services. The policies they make touch the day-to-day lives of virtually everyone living in the US, and they play a significant role in shaping broader social outcomes including the size of government and economic, political, and racial (in)equality."[81] Ultimately, as Anzia argues, "the decision makers and politics are primarily local."[82]

Local conditions (and the experiences of these conditions) have been intrinsic to rap's geographical spread in the US. In the case of some NYC scenes, Baker stresses that "the Bronx, Brooklyn, Queens—called by the Reagan/Bush era black 'holes' or urban blight—became concentrated masses of a new style, a hybrid sonics hip-hoppingly full of that piss, sass, and technological vinegar."[83] Given the histories of Black arts, musical innovation, and language development on NYC locales, it is not surprising that rap emerges on the scene. Spady, Meghelli, and Alim write that Hip Hop Nation Language Varieties (HHNLV) refers "both to the sociolinguistic variation found within the diverse regions in the U.S." and "to the syncretization of Black American Hip Hop nation language with local, street language varieties across the globe where Hip Hop is taken up by youth as a site of identity formation."[84] Kaltmeier and Raussert add, "Rappers use words to portray their local scene, their local reality. They rap about what is happening in their neighborhood, on their street, and in their families."[85] Klaess documents that fans and listeners calling in to request their favorite rap songs operated at a neighborhood or street level of geographical attachment. In the shout out,

> place names, nicknames, and bonds of friendship and kinship reach through the affective geographies of hip-hop in a stylized vernacular. It was this ability to interpellate listeners into a new hip-hop public, to envelop existing communities, while simultaneously generating new affiliations, real and imagined, that made radio such a compelling machine for community building.[86]

This neighborhood attachment is also related to representation and a desire to be seen (or heard) within this environment.

Many Parts of the State

This book uses elements of an American Political Development (APD) approach when looking at sites. This historically grounded approach combines "two important ideas and techniques within a single coherent approach,"—first, the concept of "intercurrence," and, second, "an empirical program that is focused on concrete shifts in governing authority."[87] There are three main claims to APD investigations that also apply to this book. First, intercurrence involves "the claim that political institutions are never simply created anew but are instead forged within the context of already existing institutions."[88] Second, political cultures are not "created anew but are instead forged within the context of already existing" cultures. Third, in reference to the US state, APD scholars argue that "there are in fact many *parts* of the state, each with its own internal purposes, culture, and rules."[89]

These three points are very fitting for the sites from which rap emerges. The new institutions are built on top of historical institutions on site, the political cultures are forged on top of existing site cultures, and new trends on the sites represent new "parts" of the state—sometimes with new "purposes, cultures, and rules." Race and class have been main shapers of APD, as Fortner writes that racism "has profoundly shaped" APD and that class "remains a significant variable in the study of city politics and urban public policy."[90] This leads Fortner to "a theoretical approach that attends to both the historical development of White supremacy in American cities and their evolving political economy."[91] Given the development of race and class over APD, it is not surprising that other identities (e.g., those around gender, sexual orientation, and related intersections) have also experienced struggle over the course of APD. In addition to helping better explain race and class in America, Lucas asserts that the APD approach helps explain "American politics, including its urban politics and development of the American state," which "cannot be understood without attending to the cities in which that development often originated and occurred."[92] Lucas's recommendation for future research is helpful here:

> Urban governance institutions always have a history—one that usually stretches back further than we imagine. To describe a city's institutions is to describe a series of layers, with new forms of governance, often embodying new conceptions of political authority, layered atop and alongside already existing institutions. To understand the development of urban governance over time, and the operation of urban governance institutions today, requires that we develop the theoretical and methodological resources with which to examine these layered institutions, to sort them into coherent patterns, and to understand how they have developed across cities, across policy tasks, and across time.[93]

Combined, the notion that there are several parts to the state and that new layers or forms of governance are "layered atop and alongside already existing institutions" provides a way of thinking about what happens when Black migrants arrive on the sites.

Others have found the "many parts of the state" to be more of a geographical distinction. Woodard insists that US regions are more symbolic of "nations," identifying eleven nations in the US with definitive characteristics and control of part of the continent at a given time. Woodard marks the origins and "spheres of dominance" of eleven regional areas discussed as "nations": El Norte, New France, Tidewater, Yankeedom, New Netherland, Deep South, Midlands, Greater Appalachia, The Left Coast, The Far West, and First Nation.[94] Woodard claims,

> These 11 nations have been hiding in plain sight throughout our history. You see them outlined on linguists' dialect maps, cultural anthropologists' maps of material culture regions, cultural geographers' maps of religious regions, campaign strategists' maps of political geography, and historians' maps of the pattern of settlement across the continent.[95]

Others have combined geographical and identity elements into their analysis. For Black Americans, common occurrences across geographical distance have been taken as a sign of a common community. Hunter and Robinson posit that there are actually six regions to Black America: Up South, Down South, Deep South, West South, Out South, and Mid South.[96] This definition is in place of the traditional regional terminology of "the Midwest, Northeast, Southeast, Pacific, Northwest, and Southwest," and Hunter and Robinson find "many and multiple Souths" as part of this new geography at "the intersections of race, place, and enduring patterns of inequality."[97] Drawn within these regions, they outline "Chocolate Cities," which they define as follows:

> Chocolate cities are a perpetual, political, and geographic tool and shorthand to analyze, understand, and convey insights born from predominantly Black neighborhoods, communities, zones, towns, cities, districts, and wards; they captured the sites and the sounds Black people make when they occupy place and form communities. Chocolate cities are also a metaphor for relationships among history, politics, culture, inequality, knowledge, and Blackness.[98]

They also emphasize, "Chocolate cities are geographic concentrations of Black life—neighborhoods, small towns, and entire cities—where Black people make and revise place through tight knit community networks of place makers, cultural production, and the consolidation of political and economic power."[99] Hunter and Robinson ultimately declare that "Black people in Philadelphia, Clarksdale, Newark, San Jose, Memphis, Detroit, Harlem, Kansas City, Tulsa, Oakland, Seattle, Los Angeles, Dallas, New Orleans, Boston, and Atlanta see a Chocolate city."[100]

While *American Rap Scenes* uses the more traditional East, West, Midwest, and South distinctions, Woodard's point about the regions being spheres of dominance (with definitive characteristics) is important. Hunter and Robinson's recognition of Black city life is also important in understanding the diversity of identities within the US and how they might be connected at regional and cross-regional levels.

Geography and Placemaking

Scene thinking, as Woo, Rennie, and Poyntz point out, involves "shared practices of meaning-, place- and community-making."[101] Place must be defined. As Enos asks, "What geographical area defines place?" "Is place a city? A town? A neighborhood?" If a city, then is it a "single city defined by municipal boundaries" or a metropolitan area?[102] Enos decides that "in the American context, I think the metropolitan area—geographically connected clusters of cities—is often a good choice of unit to represent the local environment."[103] This presents a key issue with "scenes" and "sites." While "scenes" offers a coverage of a larger metropolitan area (and has porous borders), "sites" is limited to more rigid definitions based on city or borough boundaries.

American Rap Scenes uses latitude–longitude, area and landmass, and population and demography to better understand the sites and rap scenes. To better compare scenes, additional data related to urban density, regional population changes, city administrative boundaries, local government, and road and sea transportation would seem especially relevant. Highways, waterways, railways, locations of ports and centers of commerce, gathering, and play remain essential in understanding these urban sites. Centers of music making, such as studios, night clubs, and festival grounds are also important for defining the scene within the site.

Society and Governance

The establishment of society and of governance is also important to the background of the scene. Governance dates are accessible and can be referenced with specific dates, although Indigenous Americans can certainly claim societies well before European documentation of site governance. In North America, the ancestors of Indigenous Americans arrived as early as forty thousand years ago, Vikings made contact in some areas as early as a thousand years ago, and Europeans arrived about five hundred years ago.[104] This type of site background adds perspective and a grounded analysis.

Over APD, Dilworth shows that patterns in major American cities have involved state and city divisions at the outset. Then as new immigrants arrived in the cities, they began to outnumber the elites in the cities. The immigrants often faced poor conditions and ethnic conflict, especially until new urban leadership from the immigrant class or new leadership from the site became more responsive to the immigrant class. All of this happened through a mobilization of the party politics machinery.[105]

These changes in a site's governance are interrelated with labor and migration. Dilworth outlines the following major themes: "Government and Politics"; "Industry, Commerce, and Labor"; and "Race, Ethnicity, and Immigration."[106] Judd and Swanstrom see three main types of politics (growth, governance, and metropolitan fragmentation) running throughout US urban history. Growth involves great expansion, building, and construction, while governance involves managing or pacifying competing groups and interests, and metropolitan fragmentation involves a new "patchwork" political rule and urban sprawl.[107] These types of issues in governance in a geographical place are essential in defining the background of a musical scene, as this is (or was) the environment to which migrants entered.

Conclusion

Geography is important to understanding rap scenes in the US. A scene's basic geography, place, society, and governance are established by others before the mass migrations of new peoples, discussed in the next chapter.

3

Migration

Introduction

Masta Ace Incorporated's "Born to Roll" captures an encounter (Figure 5) between a Black man and a police officer during a vehicle pull over, something that many Black men in America have experienced. The officer commands,

*Black boy, Black boy, turn that sh*t down / You know that America don't wanna hear the sound / Of the bass drum, jungle music, go back to Africa/ N*gg* I'll arrest ya if you're holding up traffic.*

The Black driver responds,

I'll be damned if I listen, so cops save your breath /And write another ticket if you have any left / I'm breaking eardrums while I'm breaking the law / I'm disturbing all the peace 'cause Sister Souljah said "War."[1]

In this incident, the police officer commands the Black driver to turn his music down and associates it with African drum music, to which the Black driver responds by essentially saying that he is not listening to the officer, directing the officer to "write another ticket" if he has any leftover (implying he writes too many tickets). The Black driver counters that his music is not disturbing the peace, because "we are at war" (according to rapper Sister Souljah). As soon as he drives away from the traffic stop, the Black driver warns, he will turn the music's volume right back to where it was before. Through this entire struggle, the bass is what provides this stirring power in the streets. The song's mention of African "jungle music" is a key connection to the present chapter—especially given rap music's origins in West African drum traditions, reggae and dub music, and even European music that has been "Africanized" into patterns and traditions that fit West African drum structures and patterns. Another key connection to the present chapter is the officer's suggestion to "go back to Africa."

As this chapter shows, at times Black Americans have been met with hostility when arriving to cities that had experienced decades of White American and European immigrant population growth prior to the Great Migration of Blacks. The officer's suggestion is an example of this hostility lasting multiple generations. Yet, the driver being told to "go back to Africa" is especially offensive given the

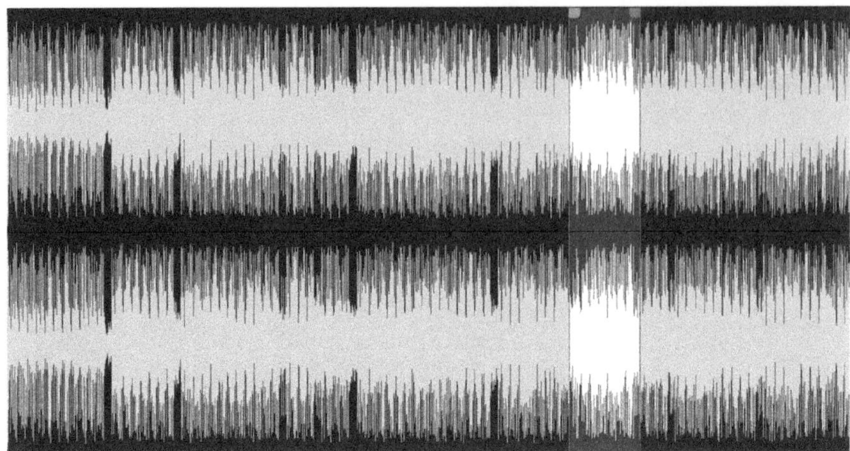

Figure 5 Masta Ace Incorporated "Born to Roll" Akai WAV snapshot with quoted material highlighted.

likelihood that the officer's ancestors did not help build America with free labor. It is also offensive given that the Black American driver's ancestors have likely been in America longer than the White officer's ancestors. In fact, even during the nineteenth- and early-twentieth-century Back-to-Africa movement, Smitherman explains many Black Americans expressly felt that "America was their country of birth, one which they had helped to build through more than two hundred years of free labor."[2]

Rap speaks about the Black experience in the Americas, and the foundation of rap is in Black oral tradition. Smitherman explains,

> Through song, story, folk sayings, and rich verbal interplay among everyday people, lessons and precepts about life and survival are handed down from generation to generation. Until contemporary times, Black America relied on the word-of-mouth for its rituals of cultural preservation.[3]

This analysis, from rap's very early history, is essential in understanding the value of such music to Blacks in the US. Smitherman recounts rap's ability to *keep* Black traditions over time, through various forms, through multiple generations—understanding the historical depth of this method of communication from slavery until the birth of rap. Rap is about "life and survival" and transitions "from generation to generation." As Smitherman shows throughout *Talkin' and Testifyin'*, these communication needs are outgrowths of slavery, colonization, and the struggles during and after the Great and Second Great Migrations. Although Black communication traditions have been kept by other means, as Weheliye finds, the sonic is "the principal modality in which Afro-diasporic cultures have been articulated."[4]

This chapter explores rap as a product of Black America and of the migratory patterns people of West African descent, with key contributions from Caribbean, Latinx, and other peoples. The first part of the chapter analyzes data around demographic change, specifically, changes in total population, changes in Black population, and changes in Latinx population—using US decennial census data. This statistical data includes about thirty-five individual sites. The focus is on evidence of migrational patterns and its impact on rap. This chapter also explores the concept of "internal colonization" and the themes of (forced) Black migration, US slavery and resultant Black American struggle, and the Great and Second Great Migrations to Northern and Western US cities.

Comparative Analysis of Migration

For migration, the following statistical data was analyzed for each site: total population change, US population percentage, Black population percentage 1860–1990, and Latinx population percentage 1970–1990. US census data, or secondary research using official US census data, were the main sources for this chapter. The census was ordered in Article I, Section 2 of the US Constitution, and the decennial census has been conducted in years ending in "0" since 1790. For most sites, data is available for much of US history, but one major limitation is in data from US territories. For the most part, US territory data is not comparable to mainland US census data until the 1950s or 1960s—with Hawai'i as somewhat of an exception. Population data from San Juan and Saint Thomas can also be less comprehensive than census data from the interior US.

The summary of population data is shown in Table 4. This includes population of the scenes, US total population, North American total population, and global population. Ratios were taken to estimate what percentage of the US, North American, and global population lives on these sites. The percentage of the US population living on these sites ranges from 18.59 percent in 1950 to 9.35 percent in 2020. The North American percentages are similar: 17.36 percent in 1950 and 8.29 percent in 2020. For the percentage of the global population these sites represent, it was 1.13 percent in 1950, less than 1 percent since then (and at about 0.40 percent in 2020).

While the core focus is on migrational data from 1950 and beyond, it is necessary to look at what occurred before the 1950s. By the time that many Blacks moved to US cities, there were urban power structures already set up by other newcomers—largely non-US-born European Whites. From 1850 to 1900, there was tremendous population growth on these sites. There is further discussion and evidence around this point in Appendix A: Technical Appendix. From 1900 to 1920 and from 1940 to 1970, there was continued growth at a time when some Black migrants were arriving in US cities. However, after the 1970s, there was either very slow growth or a decline in total population until 2020. The 2020 census was the first to show signs of growth in many of these sites.

This chapter focuses on the population data from 1950 to 2020 as shown in Table 5. By this time, large, sweeping changes in population were less likely than in prior census

Table 4 Population of Scenes Information.

Year	1950	1960	1970	1980	1990	2000	2010	2020
Population of Scenes	28,135,235	28,950,268	29,454,887	27,462,120	28,776,677	29,235,582	29,209,107	31,004,149
US Population	151,325,798	179,323,175	203,211,926	226,545,805	248,709,873	281,421,906	308,745,538	331,449,281
North American Population	162,089,353	194,177,008	221,865,907	247,761,304	275,860,329	313,205,695	345,272,107	373,956,671
Global Population	2,499,322,157	3,019,233,434	3,695,390,336	4,444,007,706	5,316,175,862	6,148,898,975	6,985,603,105	7,840,952,880
Scenes/US	18.59%	16.14%	14.49%	12.12%	11.57%	10.39%	9.46%	9.35%
Scenes/North America	17.36%	14.91%	13.28%	11.08%	10.43%	9.33%	8.46%	8.29%
Scenes/Global	1.13%	0.96%	0.80%	0.62%	0.54%	0.48%	0.42%	0.40%

Table 5 Changes in Population of Scenes (Percentage) 1950–2020.

Scene Number	City or Site	1950	1960	1970	1980	1990	2000	2010	2020
1	South Bronx	4.06%	−1.82%	3.29%	−20.57%	2.98%	10.70%	3.94%	6.32%
2	Manhattan and Harlem	3.71%	−13.36%	−9.37%	−7.21%	4.15%	3.34%	3.17%	6.83%
3	Queens	44.94%	−3.79%	9.78%	−4.79%	3.19%	14.23%	0.06%	7.83%
4	Brooklyn	1.48%	−4.05%	−0.96%	−14.26%	3.13%	7.16%	1.60%	9.24%
5	Staten Island	9.81%	15.89%	33.09%	19.18%	7.63%	17.09%	5.63%	5.76%
	New York City	5.86%	−1.39%	1.45%	−10.43%	3.55%	9.36%	2.08%	7.69%
6	Hempstead	66.79%	71.27%	8.22%	−7.87%	−1.74%	4.17%	0.51%	4.43%
7	Philadelphia	7.26%	−3.34%	−2.69%	−13.36%	−6.08%	−4.29%	0.56%	5.10%
8	Newark	2.10%	−7.65%	−5.63%	−13.90%	−16.41%	−0.61%	1.31%	12.42%
	Jersey City	−0.72%	−7.66%	−5.63%	−14.21%	2.24%	5.04%	3.14%	18.11%
9	Boston	3.97%	−13.01%	−8.05%	−12.18%	2.01%	2.59%	4.83%	9.40%
10	Los Angeles	30.98%	25.82%	13.60%	5.35%	17.48%	6.00%	2.65%	2.80%
11	Oakland	27.27%	−4.43%	−1.63%	−6.15%	9.70%	7.32%	−2.19%	12.78%
	San Francisco	22.19%	−4.52%	−3.33%	−5.13%	6.63%	7.29%	3.67%	8.54%
	San Jose	39.18%	114.31%	118.31%	41.20%	24.28%	14.40%	5.70%	7.11%
12	Seattle	35.10%	11.96%	−4.71%	−6.97%	4.54%	9.13%	8.04%	21.09%
	Portland	22.42%	−0.25%	2.67%	−4.24%	19.36%	20.99%	10.33%	11.77%
13	Chicago	6.60%	−1.95%	−5.17%	−10.75%	−7.37%	4.03%	−6.92%	1.88%
	Gary	19.86%	33.16%	−1.63%	−13.38%	−23.24%	−11.92%	−21.85%	−13.95%
14	St. Louis	4.99%	−12.46%	−17.04%	−27.18%	−12.45%	−12.23%	−8.30%	−5.55%
15	Minneapolis	5.96%	−7.45%	−10.04%	−14.61%	−0.69%	−0.40%	4.27%	12.38%
	St. Paul	8.21%	0.66%	−1.09%	−12.82%	0.74%	1.83%	2.84%	9.28%
16	Detroit	13.93%	−9.70%	−9.50%	−20.39%	−14.57%	−7.46%	−24.97%	−10.46%
17	Houston	55.04%	57.38%	31.40%	29.39%	2.22%	19.81%	7.46%	9.77%
18	New Orleans	15.35%	10.01%	−5.43%	−6.06%	−10.87%	−2.47%	−29.06%	11.68%
19	Memphis	35.18%	25.64%	25.33%	3.66%	−5.57%	6.51%	−0.49%	−2.13%
20	Atlanta	9.60%	47.13%	1.95%	−14.48%	−7.29%	5.70%	0.85%	18.74%
21	Miami	44.78%	17.01%	14.80%	3.59%	3.37%	1.09%	10.20%	10.71%
22	Hampton	1.15%	1396.11%	35.31%	1.52%	9.11%	9.48%	−6.19%	−0.21%
23	Washington, DC	20.98%	−4.76%	−0.97%	−15.62%	−4.92%	−5.74%	5.19%	14.60%
	Baltimore	10.55%	−1.12%	−3.54%	−13.14%	−6.45%	−11.53%	−4.64%	−5.68%
24	Honolulu	36.69%	−16.66%	10.43%	12.37%	3.26%	−1.58%	−9.09%	3.72%
25	San Juan	32.80%	100.94%	2.56%	−6.13%	0.67%	1.07%	−10.65%	−13.42%
	Saint Thomas	22.62%	17.29%	78.75%	53.22%	8.55%	6.26%	0.89%	−18.15%
	Population of Scenes		2.90%	1.74%	−6.77%	1.15%	5.25%	−0.09%	6.15%
	US Population		18.50%	13.32%	11.48%	9.78%	13.15%	9.71%	7.35%
	North American Population		19.80%	14.26%	11.67%	11.34%	13.54%	10.24%	8.31%
	Global Population		20.80%	22.39%	20.26%	19.63%	15.66%	13.61%	12.24%

eras. From 1950 to 2020, a key reportable threshold seems to be sites with population changes of more than 15 percent. Cases of 15 percent or more of the total population changing on the sites (with any negative values indicated with amount) are listed below:

1950: Brooklyn, Hempstead, LA, Oakland, San Francisco, San Jose, Seattle, Portland, Gary, Houston, New Orleans, Memphis, Miami, DC, Honolulu, San Juan, Saint Thomas

1960: Staten Island, Hempstead, LA, San Jose, Gary, Houston, Memphis, Atlanta, Miami, Hampton, Honolulu (−16.66 percent), San Juan, Saint Thomas

1970: Staten Island, San Jose, St. Louis (−17.04 percent), Houston, Memphis, Hampton, Saint Thomas

1980: South Bronx (−20.57 percent), Staten Island, San Jose, St Louis (−27.18 percent), Detroit (−20.39 percent), Houston, DC (−15.62 percent), Saint Thomas

1990: Newark (−16.41 percent), LA, San Jose, Portland, Gary (−23.24 percent)

2000: Staten Island, Portland, Houston

2010: Gary (−21.85 percent), Detroit (−24.97 percent), New Orleans (−29.06 percent)

2020: Jersey City, Seattle, Atlanta, Saint Thomas (−18.15 percent)

The sites experiencing deep population losses tend to be in areas most impacted by deindustrialization, urban renewal, or environmental factors. South Bronx, New Orleans, DC, Newark, Honolulu, and Saint Thomas lost more than 15 percent of their total population at least once between 1950 and 2020. St. Louis, Detroit, and Gary lost more than 15 percent of their total population twice during the same period.

There are also sites experiencing a substantial increase in population, especially after 1980. Population increases of at least 15 percent occurred in the following locations after 1980: Staten Island (1980, 2000), Jersey City (2020), LA (1990), San Jose (1980, 1990), Portland (2000), Seattle (2020), Houston (1980, 1990, 2000), and Atlanta (2020). None of the sites examined in *American Rap Scenes* had a population growth of over 15 percent in 2010.

Table 6 shows the percentage of the US Black population between emancipation and 1990. Within this study, in 1990, Newark (58.5 percent), Oakland (43.8 percent), Detroit (75.7 percent), and Atlanta (67.1 percent) represented the highest Black percentages in the East, West, Midwest, and South. When compared to other regions, the South has some striking data in terms of Black percentage. From 1870 to 1990, the Black population percentage was usually above 25 percent in Houston, New Orleans, Memphis, Atlanta, DC, and Hampton. Miami's Black population percentage was 25 percent in 1910, 1920, 1980, and 1990. Baltimore's Black population percentage has been above 25 percent since 1960.

The data also shows the Northern movement of Blacks to sites in the East, North, and West after the Great Migration and during part of the Second Great Migration. In addition to the scenes in the South with a Black population of over 25 percent (see above), the following sites also had Black populations over 25 percent:

Table 6 Black Percentage on Scenes 1860–1990.

Scene Number	City or Site	1860	1870	1880	1890	1900	1910	1920	1930	1940	1950	1960	1970	1980	1990
1	South Bronx					1.2	1	0.7	1	1.7	6.7	11.5	24.3	31.8	37.3
2	Manhattan and Harlem					2	2.6	4.8	12	15.8	19.6	23.4	24.7	21.7	22
3	Queens					1.7	1.1	1.1	1.7	2	3.3	8.1	13	18.7	21.7
4	Brooklyn					1.6	1.4	1.6	2.7	4	7.6	14.1	25.2	32.4	37.9
5	Staten Island					1.6	1.3	1.3	1.6	1.9	2.8	4.4	5.3	7.3	8.1
	New York City		1.4	1.6	1.6	1.8	1.9	2.7	4.7	6.1	9.5	14	21.1	25.2	28.7
6	Hempstead											3.4	5.8	9.3	12.1
7	Philadelphia	3.9	3.3	3.7	3.8	4.8	5.5	7.4	11.3	13	18.2	26.4	33.6	37.8	39.9
8	Newark	1.8	1.7	2.4	2.3	2.7	2.7	4.1	8.8	10.6	17.1	34.1	54.2	58.2	58.5
	Jersey City	1.1	0.9	1.1	1.3	1.8	2.2	2.7	4	4.5	6.9	13.3	21	27.7	29.7
9	Boston	1.3	1.4	1.6	1.8	2.1	2	2.2	2.6	3.1	5	9.1	16.3	22.4	25.6
10	Los Angeles	1.5	1.6	0.9	2.5	2.1	2.4	2.7	3.1	4.2	8.7	13.5	17.9	17	14
11	Oakland	1.2		1.7	1.3	4.5	2	2	2.6	2.8	12.4	22.8	34.5	46.9	43.9
	San Francisco	2.1	0.9	0.7	0.6	0.5	0.4	0.5	0.6	0.8	5.6	10	13.4	12.7	10.9
	San Jose		1.2	0.7	1	1	0.6	0.5	0.4	0.4	0.6	1	2.5	4.6	4.7
12	Seattle		1.2		0.7	0.5	1	0.9	0.9	1	3.4	4.8	7.1	9.5	10.1
	Portland	0.6	1.8	1.1	1	0.9	0.5	0.6	0.5	0.6	2.6	4.2	5.6	7.6	7.7
13	Chicago	0.9	1.2	1.3	1.3	1.8	2	4.1	6.9	8.2	13.6	22.9	32.7	39.8	45.4
	Gary						2.3	9.6	17.8	18.3	29.3	38.8	52.8	70.8	80.6
14	St. Louis	2.1	7.1	6.3	5.9	6.2	6.4	9	11.4	13.3	17.9	28.6	40.9	45.6	47.5
15	Minneapolis	0.3	0.8	0.8	0.8	0.8	0.9	1	0.9	0.9	1.3	2.4	4.4	7.7	13

(Continued)

Table 6 (*Continued*)

Scene Number	City or Site	1860	1870	1880	1890	1900	1910	1920	1930	1940	1950	1960	1970	1980	1990
	St. Paul	0.7	0.9	1.1	1.1	1.4	1.5	1.4	1.5	1.4	1.8	2.6	3.5	4.9	7.4
16	Detroit	3.1	2.8	2.4	1.7	1.4	1.2	4.1	7.7	9.2	16.2	28.9	43.7	63.1	75.7
17	Houston	22.2	39.3	39.2	37.6	32.7	30.4	24.6	21.7	22.4	20.9	22.9	25.7	27.3	28.1
18	New Orleans	14.3	26.4	26.7	26.6	27.1	26.3	26.1	28.3	30.1	31.9	37.2	45	55.3	61.9
19	Memphis	17.2	38.5	44.3	44.5	48.8	40	37.7	38.1	41.5	37.2	37	38.9	47.6	54.8
20	Atlanta	20.3	45.6	43.7	42.9	39.8	33.5	31.3	33.3	34.6	36.6	38.3	51.3	66.6	67.1
21	Miami						41.3	31.3	22.7	21.4	16.2	22.4	22.7	25.1	27.4
22	Hampton				47.1	54.5	60.2	64.6	56	70.3	62.8	78.6	74	63.9	58.4
23	Washington, DC	18	32.5	32.8	32.8	31.1	28.5	25.1	27.1	28.2	35	53.9	71.1	70.3	65.8
	Baltimore	13.1	14.8	16.2	15.4	15.6	15.2	14.8	17.7	19.3	23.7	34.7	46.4	54.8	59.2
24	Honolulu Island and County												0.7	1.2	1.3
25	San Juan														
	USVI												72.5		76.6

1960: Bronx, Manhattan, Philadelphia, Newark, NYC
1970: Brooklyn, Newark, Oakland, Gary, St. Louis, Detroit, USVI
1980: Bronx, Newark, Jersey City, Oakland, Gary, St. Louis, Detroit, NYC
1990: Bronx, Brooklyn, Newark, Oakland, Chicago, Gary, St. Louis, Detroit

By 1990, the Black population percentage was above 50 percent in Newark, Memphis, New Orleans, Atlanta, DC, Baltimore, Hampton, and the USVI. The Black population percentage in Detroit and Gary was above 75 percent. Honolulu, San Juan, and USVI have limited comparative data for Black percentages; however, what is available and comparable is reported.

This book also explores the growth of Latinx populations on the sites (Table 7). The data is extremely limited due to survey methods used by the US census and changes in how Latinx identity has been expressed on the US census. The most comparable data are between 1970 and 1990. Sites with a Latinx population percentage above 25 percent between 1970 and 1990 included the following:

1970: South Bronx, Miami
1980: South Bronx, LA, Miami
1990: South Bronx, Manhattan, Newark, LA, San Jose, Houston, and Miami

It should be further noted that by 1990, the Bronx (42.3 percent), LA (39.9 percent), and Miami (62.5 percent) had Latinx population percentages much larger than the 25 percent threshold. It would be interesting to explore whether rap from these scenes reflects a higher number of Latinx rappers and producers, given the higher Latinx group percentages than other sites. Puerto Rico and USVI census information was not comparable to the ethnicity data from the other sites in the years reported; it is therefore not reported here.

Migration and Rap Music Scenes

East Coast

In the years before Hip Hop emerged, roughly sixty thousand homes were demolished in the South Bronx.[5] Chang writes, "By the end of the [1960s], half the whites were gone from the South Bronx."[6] When leaving, they were "fighting back tears" and "stepping on the gas."[7] Jonnes adds, "The middle-class Italian, German, Irish, and Jewish neighborhoods disappeared overnight. Impoverished black and Hispanic families, who dominated the southern end of borough, drifted north. Businesses and factories relocated."[8] The devastation (or desolation) was so bad that it warranted visits from President Jimmy Carter, Pope John Paul II, Mother Theresa, and Ronald Reagan (who was running for president against Carter in 1980).

Robert Moses's Cross Bronx Expressway "negatively impacted the environment with noise and air pollution, particularly affecting people of color."[9] The rubble in

Table 7 Latinx Percentage on Scenes 1970–90.

Scene Number	City or Site	1970	1980	1990
1	South Bronx	27.7	33.9	42.3
2	Manhattan and Harlem	20.3	23.5	26.0
3	Queens	7.7	13.9	19.5
4	Brooklyn	20.1	17.6	15.1
5	Staten Island	4.2	5.4	8.0
	New York City	16.2	19.9	24.4
6	Hempstead	3.4	8.9	18.5
7	Philadelphia	2.4	3.8	5.6
8	Newark	12.2	18.6	26.1
	Jersey City	9.1	18.6	24.2
9	Boston	2.8	6.4	10.8
10	Los Angeles	17.1	27.5	39.9
11	Oakland	7.6	9.6	13.9
	San Francisco	11.6	12.3	13.9
	San Jose	19.1	22.3	26.6
12	Seattle	2	2.6	3.5
	Portland	0.3	0.6	0.8
13	Chicago	7.4	14	19.6
	Gary	8.1	7.1	5.7
14	St. Louis	1	1.2	1.3
15	Minneapolis	0.9	1.3	2.1
	St. Paul	2.1	2.9	4.2
16	Detroit	1.8	2.4	2.8
17	Houston	11.3	17.6	27.6
18	New Orleans	4.4	3.4	3.5
19	Memphis	0.4	0.8	0.7
20	Atlanta	1	1.4	1.9
21	Miami	45.3	56	62.5
22	Hampton	1.3	1.4	2.0
23	Washington, DC	2.1	2.8	5.4
	Baltimore	0.9	1	0.9
24	Honolulu Island and County	2.5	5.2	4.6
25	San Juan USVI			

the South Bronx was apparent in the photographs of President Carter's 1977 visit. Essentially, everything south of Fordham Road, around twenty square miles, was considered the South Bronx.[10] In addition to the different Black populations, there were also significant Latinx populations in the South Bronx, and Flores writes,

"It is Puerto Ricans who most directly shared with Young African Americans the demographic base and creative stage of hip hop in its origins."[11] Additionally, Flores explains, "The experience of being 'in between,' so deeply familiar to Puerto Ricans in the US, thus harbors the possibility of an intricate politics of freedom and resistance."[12]

The Bronx's general population declined by 25.57 percent in 1980, which was also around the time of rap's first commercial releases. If it were a city in its own regard, the Bronx's general population would be comparable to Philadelphia at the time.[13] The Black population percentage was 31.8 percent in 1980 and 37.3 percent in 1990. The Latinx population percentage was 27.7 percent in 1970, 33.9 percent in 1980, and 42.3 percent in 1990. Other NYC sites also show important migrational trends. Manhattan's Latinx population percentage reached 26 percent in 1990. NYC's Black population percentage was 25.2 percent in 1980 and 28.7 percent in 1990.

Harlem in the 1940s, according to Wilkerson, was a "mature and well-established capital" of Black cultural life with thousands of Blacks still arriving from Florida, North Carolina, South Carolina, Georgia, Virginia, Jamaica, and the Caribbean.[14] Similar to most other NYC scenes, Harlem's scene is interconnected with the Caribbean and Latin America. A film called *Feel the Noise* uses this connection to tell a fictional story that starts with a Harlem rapper's run-in with local criminals before fleeing to Puerto Rico, where he "finds his salvation in Reggaeton" through a "spicy blend" of Hip Hop, reggae, and Latin music. While the story sees Puerto Rico as the "spiritual home of Reggaeton," it ends with "an explosive performance at NYC's Puerto Rican Day Parade."[15]

Queens had a population boom in 1950 with a 31.01 percent total population increase. Queens has the largest public housing area in North America in the Queensbridge Houses. Brooklyn's Black population percentage was 25.2 percent in 1970, 32.4 percent in 1980, and 37.9 percent in 1990. Brooklyn has been described by words such as "enclaves" and (later) "gentrification." Beatboxing and toasting, two traditions typically associated with Caribbean music, are also often tied to Brooklyn. The film *Do the Right Thing* is based in Brooklyn's Bedford-Stuyvesant neighborhood and involves ethnic conflict. The drama unfolds "on the hottest day of the year" around an Italian pizzeria in a neighborhood with a "web of race relations" involving Blacks, Latinx, Italian Americans, West Indians, and Korean Americans.[16] This fictional tale, based on real incidents in NYC at the time, features Long Island rap group Public Enemy on the soundtrack.

Hempstead has had population increases of 66.79 percent and 71.27 percent in the censuses of 1950 and 1960, respectively. Long Island has represented upward mobility for some Black people, something that is reflected (and challenged) by some second-generation rappers who emerge from Long Island. Philadelphia's Black population percentage was 26.4 percent in 1960, 33.6 percent in 1970, 37.8 percent in 1980, and 39.9 percent in 1990. Philadelphia is the site of one of the first studies of Black migration—with Du Bois's work on the city.[17] Newark's Black population percentage was 34.1 percent in 1960, 54.2 percent in 1970, 58.2 percent in 1980, and 58.5 percent in 1990. Newark's Latinx population percentage was 26.1 percent in 1990. Boston's Black population percentage reached 25.6 percent in 1990.

West Coast and Northwest

LA's Latinx population percentage was 27.5 percent in 1980 and 39.9 percent in 1990. Most Black migration to LA happened during the military employment boom around World War II.[18] Yet, even from the nineteenth century, LA has been "an important site" for Black migration, and it included two great periods of "peacetime migration"— between 1910 and 1920 and from the late 1950s to the early 1960s.[19] Aspirations such as owning property, better employment, and the chance of escaping the South's racism were cited as reasons for Westward movement.[20] Cross finds that most Black people in LA "have some family connection to the southern states of Louisiana, Texas, Arkansas, Oklahoma, and Kansas," and that LA Black culture is deeply rooted in these states.[21] Studies of LA have also connected its blues history, early geography, and housing crises.[22]

LA was a major center for civil unrest in the 1960s and 1990s, when citizens responded to state brutality. Concerns over police brutality have been a central topic in movements and music from LA. There is concern that LA officials have been applying "carceral power," especially toward its most vulnerable residents. Johnson explains,

> During the Reagan-Bush years, Los Angeles became a crucial national stage for an emerging, popular cultural criticism of carceral power. Part of the city's unique role in this regard, was derived from its status as the global capital of music, television, and film production. At a deeper level, Los Angeles had served for sometime as an active laboratory for modern police and strategies, unlike other American cities, it faced an unfathomable wave of crime and gang violence that precipitated even more intense police militarization.[23]

In Oakland, the Black population percentage has been significant, reaching 34.5 percent in 1970, 46.9 percent in 1980, and 43.9 percent in 1990. San Jose had total population increases of 114.31 percent in 1980 and of 118.31 percent in 1990. San Jose and San Francisco continue to have some of the lowest Black percentages of the sites examined. Seattle and Portland are similar in this regard. Seattle and Portland, however, also have lower Latinx percentages than most other sites—which is different from LA and Oakland.

Abe writes about the first Black person arriving to Seattle in 1858, before migration of Black Americans to Rainer Valley and (later) immigration from Southeast Asia, Latin America, and the African continent.[24] This ethnic diversity runs counter to the national attention given to "software, coffee, and grunge." Abe writes about a unique Black experience in Seattle. Black men voted in the 1800s, some issues in the 1960s were more effectively addressed in Seattle than in other cities, and there was Black business and artisan success on the scene. Its location within the US is also important, as it is isolated from most other major US cities (with the exception of Portland).

Midwest and North

Chicago provides extraordinary insight into Black Midwest migration. Of the scenes examined, Chicago has the one of the largest populations and one of the largest Black percentages—reaching 32.7 percent in 1970, 39.8 percent in 1980, and 45.4 percent in 1990. This has influenced Chicago over time, as Garb understands the city's politics "determined by changing social geography, a fragmented, urban government, and a dynamic, rapidly swelling, urban populace, as well as national events and global flows of capital and labor migrations."[25] The early newcomers to Chicago "made powerful demands on local government," and until 1910, the Black population percentage in Chicago was under 2 percent.[26] When Blacks began migrating to the city, according to Wilkerson, they were "hemmed in and isolated into two overcrowded sections of the city—the South Side and the West Side" with restricted access to jobs, mortgages, and schooling.[27] These signs in Chicago were of an early *de facto* segregation and could produce results equal to those in the segregated South, with parents in Chicago working long hours for bad housing, leaving children open to local gangs, crime, and drugs, and "few ways out of the situation."[28] Of Chicago's geographical boundaries, Enos finds race as integral, stating, "In Chicago the boundary between north and south is the boundary between white and Black … everyone in Chicago knows the boundary is there and must accept that the other side is a place you shouldn't go."[29] Poverty in Chicago's suburbs has also been an ongoing issue. Agnew explains, "In Chicago itself, recent research suggests that poverty is also on the move, away from the South Side, increasingly abandoned or undergoing spotty gentrification, towards the inner ring of suburbs. Across the US, and in absolute terms, poverty in the suburbs now exceeds that in cities."[30]

Gary had the highest Black population percentage of the sites. Gary had a population decline of 23.24 percent in 1990 and of 21.85 percent in 2010. Gary's Black population percentage reached the following totals: 29.3 percent in 1950, 38.8 percent in 1960, 52.8 percent in 1970, 70.8 percent in 1980, and 80.6 percent in 1990. St. Louis also has a history of Black migration, with its population percentage reaching 28.6 percent in 1960, 40.9 percent in 1970, 45.6 percent in 1980, and 47.5 percent in 1990. Of the sites explored, St. Louis has the lowest Latinx population percentage. Two northern sites in the Midwest, Minneapolis and St. Paul, tended to have lower Black and Latinx percentages than other sites. Schell also mentions migration to Minneapolis and St. Paul from "places like Laos, Ghana, Puerto Rico, Vietnam, Iran, Mexico, and Liberia."[31] Detroit showed a general population decline of 20.39 percent in 1980 and of 24.97 percent in 2010. Detroit's Black population percentage was 28.9 percent in 1960, 43.7 percent in 1970, 63.1 percent in 1980, and 75.7 percent in 1990. Detroit is a model for urban flight from the city during the 1960s, after reactions to rioting. Then, the wars on poverty, crime, and drugs were heavily felt in Detroit.

South and Contested Islands

Houston's population increased by 55.04 percent in 1950 and by 57.38 percent in 1960. Houston's Black percentage was over 30 percent during every census from 1870 to 1910. From 1970 to 1990, the Black percentage was above 25 percent, except in 1920 (when it dipped to 24.6 percent). Houston's Latinx percentage reached 27.6 percent in 1990. New Orleans's total population decreased by 29.06 percent in 2010. New Orleans's Black percentage was never under 25 percent between 1870 and 1990, ranging from 26.1 percent to 61.8 percent. In Memphis, the total population increased by 25.64 percent in 1950 and by 25.33 percent in 1960. Memphis's Black percentage was never under 35 percent between 1870 and 1990, ranging from 37 percent to 54.5 percent.

Atlanta's general population increased by 47.13 percent in 1960. Atlanta's Black percentage was never below 30 percent between 1870 and 1990, ranging from 31.3 percent to 67.1 percent. Relocation and trauma seem to be issues faced by some Atlanta rappers. Gucci Mane, from Alabama originally, recounts an early childhood move and a stop at a Knights Inn in Atlanta that forever changed his life, as his mom and siblings saw their new reality.[32] Concern about a horrific string of Black child murders in the city was also a lasting influence on Atlanta rappers.[33] In 1980, a three-year old Kanye West and his mother left Atlanta for Chicago. Miami's Black percentage shows the following record: 1860 (41.3 percent), 1870 (31.3 percent), 1980 (25.1 percent), and 1990 (27.4 percent). Miami's Latinx percentage was at 45.3 percent, 56 percent, and 62.5 percent during the 1970, 1980, and 1990 censuses. Hunter and Robinson show Miami to be one of "many chocolate cities … born from the network of enclaves built by varying populations of the African diaspora."[34] The diversity of Miami (even within its Black and Latinx communities) is uniquely reflected in the music. Hampton is located near Cape Henry, where in 1607, the "first permanent English settlers touched ground in North America." Hampton is also near Jamestown, where in 1619, the first African peoples to be used as chattel slaves (called African "servants" at the time) were brought into the country.[35] Hampton had population increases of 1396.11 percent and 35.31 percent in 1960 and 1970, respectively. The Black percentage was never under 45 percent from 1890 to 1990, ranging from 47.1 percent to 78.6 percent.

DC's Black percentage was never under 25 percent from 1870 to 1930, ranging from 25.1 percent to 32.8 percent. Baltimore's Black population was 34.7 percent in 1960, 46 percent in 1970, 54.8 percent in 1980, and 59.2 percent in 1990. DC and Baltimore have shown deep, direct, and clear roots to West African music—especially with go-go music. Lornell and Stephenson claim that it is difficult, or even impossible, "to separate go-go music from its cultural background."[36] The rhythm, call-and-response, and forms of expression show overt connections to West African traditions, and these musical roots feature "interlocking percussion ensembles of the savanna."[37] Lornell and Stephenson explain that when "the pitched percussion instruments work together in syncopation; instead of producing a single meter, the drummers work a feeling of two (duple meter) against three (triple meter) to create a polymeter."[38] In addition, migration and immigration are factors in DC, and there are rich examinations of race in the urban development of DC.[39] Lornell and Stephenson connect DC migration with music, as they note that about 75 percent of DC is non-White, and DC's majority population is Black American "with strong familial roots in the tobacco-growing counties that constitute rural eastern Virginia and North Carolina."[40] DC's Black life "informs and helps to shape its rhythmic impulse, the lyrics of its songs, its audience, and the ways in which the music is presented and consumed."[41] There are also calls for DC's statehood.[42]

Honolulu's general population *increased* by 36.69 percent in 1950 and then *decreased* by 16.66 percent in 1960. In Hawai'i, non-Hispanic Whites are a minority, and Pidgin is a commonly spoken language in both society and song. Relatedly, for participants and supporters of the Hawaiian Sovereignty Movement, Hawai'i is seen as a sovereign kingdom illegally annexed and occupied by the US and then confirmed as legal by the occupier's court system—the US Supreme Court.

San Juan has the highest Latinx percentage of the sites examined. Since 1493, Puerto Rico has been occupied by another nation. Puerto Rican migrational patterns have been associated with construction of identity, racial subordination, caste-like systems, and a sort of dual (yet colonized) citizenship through the Jones–Shafroth Act.[43] Puerto Rican artists were early participants in Hip Hop and rap in the US, and, later, the San Juan scene became the main producer of *reggaeton*—which then influenced US rap. The USVI is the least populous scene explored in this book. The USVI was the center of slave transport and sugar plantations in the very early Americas. Owned by Denmark at the time, the USVI was used as a starting point of many Black American routes to the new world during the Middle Passage.

Migration Themes

Internal Colonies and Hyperghettos

The concept of "internal colonization" is important in understanding migration and rap. The concept is that within areas of a country, there are racial or ethnic enclaves (such as cities, neighborhoods, and territories) that are effectively separate from the rest of the nation, region, or locale. Within these areas or sections, internal colonization explains that there is "a state within a state," and that the people living in these areas have been colonized. However, the colonization is being led internally instead of externally by a separate nation. This concept effectively describes the political, economic, social, and technological differences between internal colonies and other domestic locations. Blauner, Gutiérrez, and Wacquant are leading authors in this area, although the basic concept stretches back to colonization of the Americas.

Gutiérrez shows that the Black and Latinx use of "internal colonization" was adapted by Latin American scholars, who adopted it from Indigenous Americans. Then Black and Chicano activists applied it to describe the ghetto or barrio from the 1950s to the early 1990s.[44] The core belief is that "there were 'domestic' or 'internal' forms of colonialism operant within nation states," and this theory has been used to explain Black and Latinx: "territorial concentration, spatial segregation, external administration, the disparity between their legal citizenship and de facto second-class standing, their brutalization by the police, and the toxic effects of racism in their lives."[45] The internal colonization process is characterized by forced entry, a cultural impact, external administration, and then applied racism.[46] Culturally, the impact is troubling, as Blauner describes it as a "policy which constrains, transforms, or destroys indigenous values, orientations, and ways of life."[47]

Wacquant's study of Chicago's South Side Woodlawn neighborhood between the 1950 and the 1990s is particularly important because of the stages of Black struggle outlined in the analysis. In Chicago, Wacquant found that "physical disrepair and institutional dilapidation of the neighborhood" communicated a second-class or third-class citizenship to its residents and could even have a potential social impact.[48] The epochs (or historical periods) include structural obstacles and forms of second- or third-class citizenship. The "hyperghetto," according to Wacquant, is the fourth application of the "ghetto" in the US.[49] The first was slavery, the second was Jim Crow, and the third was the early ghetto. Under the hyperghetto, there is an interplay between ghettos and prisons, severe underclassness, and state technology applied to uphold this.[50] Elsewhere, Wacquant similarly describes "four peculiar institutions" impacting Black Americans: Slavery from 1619 to 1865; Jim Crow from 1865 to 1965 in the South; the Ghetto from 1915 to 1968 in the North; and the Hyperghetto since 1968, with the prison as a primary growth location.[51]

Black Migration to Northern Cities

Over time, US cities became "points of destination for new arrivals" and had waves of Irish, German, Italian, Hungarian, and other Eastern European peoples in addition to Black migrants from the South, and then (later) increases of immigrants from Latin American countries.[52] Immigrants have often faced hostility and violence partly due to "fears that the new arrivals would threaten the economic positions of established residents."

Black "migration was highly concentrated in the top five destinations—New York City, Chicago, Detroit, Philadelphia, and Los Angeles," according to Boustan and the National Bureau of Economic Research.[53] William Collins characterizes cities as "hubs for innovative ideas and political organization," directly impacted from "the movement of Black Americans to many of the nation's largest cities," with many also becoming "centers of Black political power, particularly Chicago and New York."[54] Then, "as the racial composition of these boundary neighborhoods began to change," some White "neighborhoods intensified their efforts to 'defend' their communities, forming neighborhood associations to limit black entry through overt violence and intimidation or more subtle legal and social pressures."[55] These cities are also impacted by resources allocated to suburban communities, as "movement to the suburbs was facilitated by new housing construction on the suburban ring and by state and federal road-building programs that enabled residents of these bedroom communities to quickly and easily commute by car to jobs in the central city."[56]

Jones discusses Black experiences in US ghettos in three parts or "cities." The "first city ... comes about over a period of about 70 years."[57] Later, the "second city" was built from the remains of the old, with new, substantial economic issues. Jones outlines, "This is the jobless ghetto produced by a convergence of globalism, the suburbanization of investment, technological change, common urban renewal, and other transformations. The result is that the 21st century ghetto is a postindustrial wasteland."[58] Of this second city, "the real ghetto arises as a result of migration, economic, and global forces that concentrated poor blacks in urban enclaves."[59] Finally, in the "third city," wars on poverty, crime, and drugs led to further destruction in urban communities.

(Forced) Black Migration

It is vital to establish timelines for the Black American journey, as Hip Hop and rap were formed from the migrations of these and other peoples. This initial migration was driven by US slavery, US colonization, and the aftermath of these long-standing traditions. Wilkerson calculates that for US slavery, we must remember that from 1619 to emancipation is 246 years, which is *only* 12 generations.[60] Then in the twentieth century, after being in the country for four centuries, Blacks still had to "step aside and fall further down the economic ladder with each new wave of immigrants from all over the world, after generations as burden bearers."[61] For US colonization, 1492 is the date most commonly associated with European contact with North America. The complex colonization journey involves West African, Caribbean, Spanish, Ingenious people of the Americas, and many other peoples.

The US application of slavery and colonization is explained by a concept known as "ascriptivism," which used "ascribed" elements of one's personhood to limit them from accessing the political order. Ascriptivism involves inclusion and exclusion, and to be included at the time of the early US republic, one needed to be a property-owning White male with Anglo-Saxon roots. Smith understands this early US republic as guided by Anglo-Saxon principles from 1066 and explains,

> Such consciousness of themselves as bearers of a superior cultural or racial heritage remained vivid as Congress and the states dealt with various groups they saw as below the circle of full members of the civic body—British loyalists, blacks, Native Americans, and women.

Smith adds that these "ascriptive myths" were valuable "in preserving the supremacy of the white, propertied, European-descended but largely native-born male gentry who were the chief architects of the new governments."[62]

Colonization and the related slave trade helped set up a "core racial triangle" in the US involving "White settlers, indigenous peoples, and enslaved Africans" and this, according to Patricia Collins, "became the foundation to the new American nation-state."[63] This core racial triangle "provided an important continuity to American national identity," and this relationship between the three racial groups became integral to national identity in America and its encoding in the new nation-state, and it "has been repeatedly reworked" in the historical eras that followed.[64] Still, "the extent of the violence against Native Americans, Puerto Ricans, Chicanos, African Americans, native Hawaiians, and other groups who were incorporated into the US though conquest and slavery remains routinely ignored or distorted."[65] Smith's analysis also explains capture of the "Contested Islands." "Ascriptive myths" were used to acquire various islands after the Spanish-American War in 1898—including Puerto Rico and the final annexation of Hawaii. Smith describes how the purchase, occupation, and administration of these lands are of conflicting American civic ideals—between imperialism and anti-imperialism. As a form of imperialism, the island acquisitions used "liberalism, republicanism, and racism to contend that America's lucky new subjects should be tutored in enlightened civilization and self-governance." In contrast, under anti-imperialism, it is understood that "a liberal constitutional republic should have no subjects."[66]

Rap and Black American Historical Stages

Historical eras are important to the analysis, as some of the most vivid and insightful rap tales will refer to some of these eras. In fact, sometimes rappers with the ability to reference these eras are the ones most effective in expressing social and political issues. For Black Americans, key historical migration stages could be outlined in a series of about six distinct stages (as adopted from *Uneven Roads* and *The African Americans* documentary):

- **Stage 1 (1500–1800): Colonialism and Slave Trade**
    - Era of slave triangle and colonialism
    - Jamestown beginnings in 1604
    - First chattel slavery in 1619
    - Whiteness is only defined in comparison to Blackness
    - Blacks were essentially enslaved persons or subject to slavery at any time

- **Stage 2 (1800–60): Slavery Deepens and Revamps**
    - Cotton gin is invented
    - South expands
    - Slavery becomes more brutal and unstable
    - Slave revolts, such as Nat Turner's Revolt, occur
    - Early abolitionist movement begins

- **Stage 3 (1861–96): Civil War Amendments**
    - 13th, 14th, and 15th Amendments pass
    - Reconstruction begins, with Blacks largely joining the Republican Party
    - Bureau of Investigation (the Federal Bureau of Investigation's predecessor) is created to secretly investigate cases of voter intimidation in the South
    - Separate but equal is law (*de jure*) and in practice (*de facto*)
    - Biological racism is a leading theory in the US academy

- **Stage 4 (1897–1940): Jim Crow and Legal Resistance**
    - Legal and direct action challenges to separate but equal occur
    - Women's issues come more to the forefront

- Class issues come more to the forefront
- W. E. B. Du Bois and Booker T. Washington have key debates over strategy

- **Stage 5 (1940–68): *De jure* to *De facto***
  - Civil Rights campaign galvanizes
  - Racial Justice campaign erupts in cities
  - COINTELPRO targets and destroys Black radical and other groups
  - The "War on Poverty" and "War on Crime" emerge

- **Stage 6 (1968–present): Still Seeking Equality**
  - Employment, voting, housing discrimination, and affirmative action remain concerns
  - The impact of the "War on Drugs," unequal sentencing, policing, and other issues remain
  - Black Lives Matter movement (mainly) created in response to the killings of Black boys and men by police officers or citizens using unauthorized lethal force[67]

Throughout this history, US slavery and the Great Migration are two key areas of migration for Black Americans—to the US (via the Caribbean) while enslaved and then northward to US cities upon emancipation.

US Slavery and Black American Struggle

Toward the end of the 1400s, Portugal became the first European country to enter the African slave trade.[68] Moore stresses that there was such great demand created for enslaved persons by "the new Europeans colonies" that the practice of slavery increased exponentially, "destabilizing large areas of West Africa" as regions began to war with each other just to provide new slave captives.[69] Between 1530 and 1890, about twelve million people from Africa were captured into bondage and transported as enslaved persons to South America, Brazil, the Caribbean, and the North American South.[70] Most of the twelve million who were enslaved came from the Savannah region, Bantu-Kongo tribes, and other rainforest and "coastal littoral regions."[71] Jones is even more descriptive: "Before being sold into captivity, most of these Africans lived in the kingdoms of the Ashanti, the Ibo, Niger, and Benin. Today these regions are known as Senegal, Gambia, Liberia, the Ivory Coast, Ghana, Guinea, and Nigeria. Others came from present-day Angola, which is in South Africa, or central Africa."[72]

Smith writes that the Dutch and English began bringing Blacks from Africa in the 1620s "perhaps initially as indentured servants."[73] By the 1660s, legal codes began to be used throughout the colonies to define "the formal status of chattel slavery."[74] By 1750, there were about 235,000 Blacks and a million Whites in the colonies; most Blacks lived in "Southern Atlantic colonies, where virtually all were slaves."[75] Blacks, according to Smith, "were too essential as slaves for many colonists to countenance criticism of their presence or to consider accepting them as equals."[76] This example of ascriptive exclusion shows a Saxon mythology being used to imply "a connection between a people's unique cultural traits and their shared ancestry, and it was often used to distinguish British Americans biologically as well as culturally from Native-Americans and African-Americans whom they disdained as savages."[77] This was imported from Europe, adopted, and codified in the US constitution. This civic identity is deeply rooted in exclusion. It was not until 1807 that the US stopped importing enslaved Blacks.

During US slavery, Moore explains that most Blacks imported as enslaved persons were between nine and ten years old when entering the New World, and these children "did not necessarily represent the most knowledgeable culture bearers of their respective ethnic groups."[78] Myers specifies locationally that "many of these slaves first worked on the British, French, Dutch, or Spanish sugar-growing islands of the Caribbean before being brought to the USA."[79] Thus, as Whiteley, Bennett, and Hawkins show, "African slaves and their descendants faced a double-step, geographical dispersal, first from Africa, to the slave states of the Americas during the Atlantic slave trade, and secondly, through their ulterior migrations to diverse countries."[80] Smitherman shows that, combined, the age of the imported enslaved persons and the diversity of their place of origin in Africa led to a Black community in which there would always be enslaved persons "who could speak no English at all."[81] An additional factor was that the "majority of slaves lived on large farms or plantations located some distance from the master's house," and this atmosphere "allowed the slaves to maintain traditional cultural values and preserve a sense of self and identity that would provide the foundation for the development" of Black culture.[82] On the African continent, griots had carried news of "wars, births, deaths, and other events."[83] Griots also combined "the functions of living history book and newspaper with vocal and instrument virtuosity," which was part functional history book and part professional singer.[84] Sarig details this impact on tradition:

> Oral tradition was central to slaves because it was the only way memories of the African heritage and new American experience could be processed into cultural expression. For the most part, slaves were not allowed to gain literacy, and the tools to create visual art were often beyond reach. But the mind and spirit of African-Americans cannot be killed as long as slave masters valued their physical labor. So the voice became the primary instrument of expressing—talking, rhyming, singing. And because even certain types of oral communication between slaves raised the suspicion of masters, blacks developed a tradition of codes, metaphors, and euphemisms that was both a matter of creative expression and survival.[85]

Sarig explains, "All of the spoken forms that are recognized as precursors to rapping— playing the dozens, signifying, testifying, toasting, shuckin' and jivin'—have roots in slavery."[86] Thus, in Black America, "the oral tradition has served as a fundamental tool vehicle for getting over."[87]

Great Migrations and Arrival to US Cities

Data from the Great and Second Great Migrations help explain the social movements and musical resistance that eventually arises in US cities.[88] Wilkerson shows that in six decades, six million Black southerners "left the land of their forefathers and fanned out across the country for an uncertain existence in nearly every other corner of America."[89] This movement of people would "transform urban America and recast the social and political order of every city it touched."[90] In fact, Wilkerson shows that "a good portion of all black Americans alive" left Virginia, North Carolina, South Carolina, and Texas as well as the "backwoods of" Alabama, Arkansas, Florida, Georgia, Kentucky, Louisiana, North Carolina, Tennessee, and Oklahoma for the North, Northeast, West, and Northwest.[91] This movement of people "grew out of the unmet promises made after the Civil War" and "helped push the civil rights revolutions of the 1960s."[92]

As to why Blacks left the South, there are at least two main reasons, one related to opportunity (in the North) and the other related to terror (in the South). The opportunity explanation forms an understanding most compatible with Civil Rights requests for integration. William Collins connects the Great Migration and the Civil Rights Movement though opportunities, as "both sprang from a context of economic and political deprivation, and both encompassed purposeful efforts by millions of people to make more of their lives' potential than was possible in the Jim Crow South."[93] These connected geographical and political movements are certainly helpful in explaining why people moved, their expectations, and the aftermath.

Fear of Southern terror is another helpful explanation for Black migration. Cobb emphasizes a brutal, vivid reality of Black Americans (at least in part) fleeing the South to escape its "blood rituals," emphasizing a study between 1879 and 1920, during which "roughly 3,500 victims (mostly Black men)" were lynched, dismembered, and had the remains of their dead bodies distributed "to the gleeful white masses"—with "the penis reserved as the prize token."[94] There were also major changes to laws around how to patrol and catch enslaved persons who had escaped. As Hunter notes, courts at local, state, and federal levels were "inundated with lawsuits involving slave owners" who wanted the Fugitive Slave Act of 1793 to be enforced with more rigor.[95] They found a friend in US President Zachary Taylor, who—with the "quick stroke of his pen"—authorized the Fugitive Slave Act of 1850.[96] This new act "was a significant policy shift, wherein local, municipal, and even individual slave owners would be the enforcers of America's fugitive slave laws."[97]

Regardless of whether opportunity in the North or terror in the South provides the better explanation, many Blacks left the South for a better future, and this was a continuous, steady flow, as "it was a statistically measurable demographic phenomenon marked by unabated outflows of black émigrés that lasted roughly from 1915 to 1975."[98] It peaked during war years and generally headed North and West along "three main tributaries." One stream from Florida, Georgia, North Carolina, South Carolina, and Virginia went "up the eastern seaboard" and populated the cities of "Washington [DC], Philadelphia, New York, [and] Boston."[99] A second stream "traced the central spine of the continent" from Mississippi, Alabama, Tennessee, and Arkansas to "the industrial cities of Cleveland, Detroit, Chicago, Milwaukee, [and] Pittsburgh."[100] A third stream occurred later and was from Louisiana and Texas to "the entire West Coast."[101] This migration was partially driven by recruiters from the North getting paid "a dollar per head" to deliver Black labor to foundries and slaughterhouses.[102] With Black populations already in some of these cities, there were some divides between "old-timers" and "new arrivals." Old-timers sometimes saw the new arrivals as reminders of "the Jim Crow world they all sought to escape."[103]

Some of the difficult aspects of "The South" followed Black migrants after the Great Migration, such as "issues of discrimination, police brutality, and white domination." Hunter writes, "Race-based oppression awaited Black migrants and residents wherever they made their homes and persists across many key measures, such as the achievement and mortality gaps."[104] Even after emancipation, the Black experience was impacted by Reconstruction and the New Deal. Of the New Deal, Katznelson highlights that most Blacks "were farmworkers or domestics, and people in these categories did not qualify" for much under the policy, and this "feature of the new landmark law contradicted the strongly stated recommendation" by President Franklin D. Roosevelt's Committee on Economic Security—the report used for congressional action.[105] Additionally, in the 1930s, the Federal Housing Administration "refused to guaranteed mortgages in Black communities."[106]

The impact of the Great and Second Great Migrations can be understood by looking at population growth on US cities. William Collins calculates, "In 1910, less than two percent of the non-southern population was Black. A few cities had sizable Black populations, but for the most part, only a small share of the urban northern population was Black."[107] This migration, previously understudied, "bore the marks of immigrant behavior" and "plotted a course to places in the North and West that had some connection to their homes of origin."[108] The impact of this "persistent influx" of Black migrants to the North was felt in the labor and housing markets, which created competition for existing Black residents "in an economic setting already constrained by weakening labor demand and northern racism." This new migration, according to Boustan and the National Bureau of Economic Research, expanded the supply of Black workers already "competing for a limited set of jobs open" to Black applicants, "keeping Black wages low in the North."[109] Immense class and educational differences between Black migrants were also present. Overall, the migrational routes of musical practices and instruments seem especially important in helping produce the different regional and local styles of Black music. A main question is whether the different tributaries of Black migration produced different sounds in different regions.

Rap grows out of this migrational dynamic and emerges prominently in the South Bronx as a form of Black musical resistance. As observed in Toop's *Rap Attack*, "despite a vicious circle of poor education, poor neighborhoods, unemployment, underemployment and drugs, Black and Hispanic youth have made and are continuing to make a cultural statement that is being absorbed by youth of all races, sexes, classes and nations."[110] Rap music was able to emerge and grow in the Bronx and Harlem, despite being "two of the most depressed urban ghettos in the US," where functional illiteracy was "44% for Black youth and 56% for Hispanic youth" and where "unemployment [was] at 50–60% for these two groups."[111] Given this background, Connell demonstrates how the "neighborhood and the ghetto became the focus of funk and then hip-hop cultures, both in a discursive sense (through the subjects and sounds of songs themselves) and physically (as the site of 'authentic' performances and cultural roots, and through hip hop sub-cultural experiences)."[112]

The musical emergence of rap is not a trivial matter. As Whiteley, Bennett, and Hawkins show, more popular music researchers are beginning to acknowledge that "the search for social and cultural meanings in popular music texts inevitably involves an examination of the urban and rural spaces, in which music is experienced on a day-to-day basis."[113] The continued impact of these trends is also important as Toop hypothesizes that the "whole point of hip hop resides not in 'moves' or 'dress' but in the moods and meanings these take in a specific milieu." Toop continues, "Removed from its heritage and emotional context, there is only form without content. The content will remain in the ghetto, to create another form another time down the road."[114]

Conclusion

Rap music is a product of US Black migrations and other factors. Analysis of census information for total population and Black and Latinx population percentages shows the demographic changes occurring on the local sites. Meanwhile, the concept of internal colonization and its roots in slavery and Northern migration to sites is effective in explaining the future shape that many of these sites would take for Black and Brown residents.

Movement

Introduction

Wise Intelligent's "Mr. Rocket Launcher" (Figure 6) provides an insightful political analysis in the last lines of the first verse:

Now this the problem with the song that I sang / 'Cause I don't place the blame on the gangs that bang / I push the blame on the tie and jacket / 'Cause you reap a lot of profit from the bombs and the rockets.[1]

Hailing from Trenton, NJ, and a member of the Poor Righteous Teachers, Wise Intelligent presents his scene as a location of dire straits and gives the core reasons behind these conditions. When certain themes impact citizens on the scene (such as segregation, the drug war, gun violence, and the expansion of this strife), the rapper blames the mayor, the governor, and, ultimately, the profitability of weaponry and war. The chorus of the song intends to awaken listeners during their day-to-day activities. Wise Intelligent explains it through a series of activities including driving nice cars, smoking weed, and managing a handgun, and he presents it as something his listeners might be doing while listening. The song's rupture seems to come when he raps "listen ya teacher" and run downs a list of local, state, and national entities with "no love" for the listener and then lists nicknames these entities have for Black youth in inner cities. These nicknames include "Ganja Smuggler, Coka Dealer, Uzi Hustler, Original Gangster, and Rocket Launcher."

This is a powerful use of rap as political rhetoric. This rhetoric can be contrasted with direct political action, which has been the traditional way social movement protest has been analyzed. An example of this occurs when Bynoe challenges the Hip Hop generation to think about the type of impact they want to create:

I submit that it is time for the Hip Hop generation, particularly young Black Americans, to construct a more sophisticated dialogue about what constitutes leadership, politics, and political action. This understanding should be premised on the principle that political power comes from influence and influence comes from the ability to deliver (or deny) money, votes, or both to a political candidate, legislator, or political party.[2]

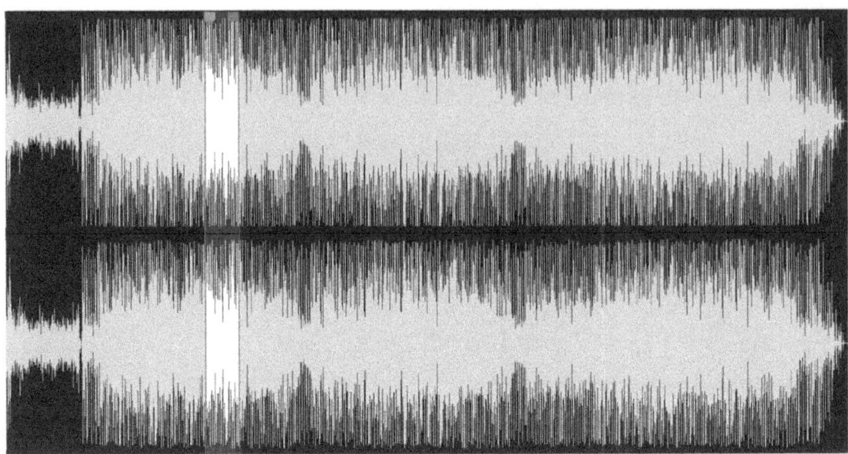

Figure 6　Wise Intelligent "Mr. Rocket Launcher" Akai WAV snapshot with quoted material highlighted.

Shabazz and others also argue that political power is achieved mainly through economics and "a loyal, growing constituency."[3]

The Wise Intelligent and Bynoe quotes above contrast one another and provide an essential frame for the present chapter. While Wise Intelligent alerts listeners to a system of oppression, Bynoe challenges readers to think about converting Hip Hop activity into real electoral power. Combined, the two quotes underscore the need to look at both rhetoric and political action when exploring rap's relationship to identity-based social movements. Additionally, while both quotes seem to be in regard to Black Americans, the quotes are actually quite intersectional. Wise Intelligent also raps about class, and Bynoe also writes about age and (implicitly) about class.

Race, class, and age are important identity politics areas related to rap. Such identity movements can be seen as political movements, as McFarland shows: "Identity is political. Identity as self/collective-concept determines behavior and is essential for the establishment and maintenance of any level of grouping."[4] Hip Hop and rap are rooted in social movement aims, as Asante explains: "When we consider hip hop's origins and purpose, we understand it is a revolutionary cultural force that was intended to challenge the status quo and the greater American culture."[5]

As Eyerman and Jamison add, social movements are not just "political activities"; rather, "they provide spaces for cultural growth and experimentation, for the mixing of musical and other artistic genres, and for the infusion of new kinds of meaning into music."[6] Rap then emerged "as an electrified folk poetry of the streets, as a way for young blacks to speak their minds, and as its influence has spread and many of its artists have become commercially successful, the older tensions between highbrow and lowbrow reappear."[7] Overall, Redmond analyzes about music generally as follows: "Music is a method. Beyond its many pleasures, music allows us to do and imagine things that may otherwise be unimaginable or seem impossible."[8] With specific regard to Blacks, Redmond explains, "Within the African diaspora, music functions as a method of rebellion, revolution, and future visions that disrupt and challenge the manufactured differences used to dismiss, detain, and destroy communities."[9]

This chapter analyzes local site activity of the Black Panther Party for Self Defense (BPPSD), the Brown Berets, the Student Nonviolent Coordinating Committee (SNCC), May 1970 anti-war protests held across the US, and the Third World Women's Alliance (TWWA). Members of these organizations and others associated with related activities were often COINTELPRO targets. In fact, many identity-based movements (e.g., Black, Latinx, Anti-War, Women, and Class movements) were targeted by the FBI's COINTELPRO. These types of social movements acted as precursors for the countercultural aspect of Hip Hop culture and rap music on US sites. This chapter also considers rap's relationship to politics (electoral and radical, Black alternatives); the Black Arts Movement; and racial, ethnic, gender, class, and intersectional identities.

Rap and the Movement of Hip Hop

Comparative Analysis of Movements on Scene

This data in this chapter are based on the site locations of four organizations in the US and a coordinated set of actions, between 1960 and 1982. Table 8 shows five types of social movement activity in these cities around the end of the 1960s until the early-1980s: the BPPSD, Brown Berets, SNCC, May 1970 action, and TWWA. The BPPSD data is from 1969 to 1982.[10] Brown Beret activity is measured from 1967 to 1977.[11] SNCC is measured from 1960 to 1970.[12] The May 1970 action is taken at the university level.[13] The TWWA organizations were in NYC and the Bay Area from 1971 to 1975. These movements have local, regional, and national (and sometimes international) chapters or activities. The analysis below highlights locales with three or more of the five organizational chapters or activities on site. This method is not meant to diminish other sites or chapter history but rather to identify scenes most associated with a range of these types of youth movements. A BPPSD, Brown Beret, SNCC, May 1970, and TWWA organization on a single scene is a sign of tremendously radical youth politics in the US before Hip Hop and rap.

The groups also represent intersectional approaches, local chapter histories, and, above all and eventually, targets of the FBI's COINTELPRO. Each group (or coordinated activity) could also be characterized as radical, and some groups were even self-characterized as militant at one point. There is some diversity in the groups selected, as one group emerged centered on race, one on ethnicity, one as a student organizing group, one as a collection of student protests, and one as a Black radical women's group. The idea of looking at local chapter history came from initial research on BPPSD chapters and the organization's relationship to race, class, gender, and its

Table 8 Social Movements on Scenes.

Scene Number	City or Site	BPPSD	Brown Berets	SNCC	May 1970	TWWA	3+ on Site
1	Bronx	•					
2	Manhattan and Harlem	•			• (6)		
3	Queens	•			•		
4	Brooklyn	•			•		
5	New York City Staten Island	•		• (~20)		•	3
6	Hempstead				•		
7	Philadelphia	•		•	• (4)		3
8	Newark	•		•	•		3
	Jersey City	•					
9	Boston	•			• (4)		
10	Los Angeles	•	•	• (4)	•		4
11	Oakland	• (2)	•	•		•	4
	San Francisco	•	•		•		3
	San Jose						
12	Seattle	•	•		•		3
	Portland	•		•	•		3
13	Chicago	•		• (13)	• (5)		3
	Gary				•		
14	St. Louis				•		
15	Minneapolis	•			•		
	St. Paul		•		•		
16	Detroit	•	•		•		3
17	Houston	•	•	• (2)			3
18	New Orleans	•		•	• (3)		3
19	Memphis	•			•		
20	Atlanta			• (~50)			
21	Miami				•		
22	Hampton				•		
23	Washington, DC	•			• (5)		
	Baltimore	•		• (5)	• (4)		3
24	Honolulu						
25	San Juan Saint Thomas			•			

intersections. Chapter 1 in this book highlights sites with more than three of these actions or groups (BPPSD, Brown Berets, SNNC, May 1970, and TWWA) and sites with over five SNCC or university-level events in May 1970. LA and Oakland have four types of this social movement activity. NYC, Philadelphia, Newark, San Francisco, Seattle, Portland, Chicago, Detroit, Houston, New Orleans, and Baltimore have three types of this social movement activity. Some sites have fewer recorded events than others, and these include Staten Island, San Jose, Honolulu, and Saint Thomas. Yet, land contestation and other issues such as colonization remain in locations such as Honolulu, San Juan, and Saint Thomas. These issues, when raised by local groups, can sound somewhat similar to the colonization and internal colonization concerns raised on the mainland sites.

BPPSD chapters were on many sites, and most local chapters were eventually destroyed by the COINTELPRO program or its influence. Witt recounts, "Panther Offices in Los Angeles, Oakland, Sacramento, Chicago, and Des Moines were either riddled with bullets or bombed by the police during this era of Panther persecution."[14] Additionally, "Breakfast for Children program food and donations were stolen in Chicago, Los Angeles, and New York."[15] However, with the Milwaukee chapter, there was less of an "emphasis on guns" and more of an emphasis on community programs.[16] This may have led to fewer killings of Milwaukee BPPSD chapter members as Witt finds a "relatively unique feature" of the chapter to be that "no Milwaukee Panther was ever killed by the police, which is not something that all of the branches and chapters could claim."[17] Local and BPPSD chapters also conflicted over the changing political direction of the Panthers. Jeffries found that "each branch or chapter had its own unique set of circumstances" and "applied the party's ten-point program and platform accordingly."[18] Members of branches and chapters also differed in terms of "socioeconomic makeup, experience with the criminal justice system, political acumen, and level of political consciousness."[19] There were significant regional clashes between the West Coast (Oakland-based) and East Coast (NYC-based) Panthers, especially toward the middle and end of the BPPSD story and especially on key strategies of the movement—including choosing whether to use militant, radical, or electoral politics as a guiding strategy.

Derived from Civil Rights and Black Power traditions such as the BPPSD, Perry points out a "radical commitment to otherness" in Hip Hop.[20] Even movements in this chapter *not* founded by Black Americans remain important to US sound culture and the development of rap music. Keyes reasons, "With the radical shift in U.S. politics in the 1960s—Civil Rights and Student Movements, Vietnam War, Black Nationalism, Feminist Movement—non-black youth gravitated toward African American blues sound culture as statements and gestures countering the 'establishment' or hegemony."[21] Rabaka articulates the diversity of interests that later develop in "The Hip Hop Movement," a movement she finds to be "simultaneously a multicultural, multi-racial, mutli-national, multi-lingual, multi-religious, and extremely multi-issue musical and socio-political macro-movement composed of several often seemingly uncoordinated micro-movements."[22]

Rap's Local Movement in the US

East Coast

East Coast sites Manhattan, Philadelphia, and Newark had high levels of social movement activity. Each of the sites had a BPPSD chapter and May 1970 student action, and Philadelphia and Newark also had SNCC organizational activity. In NYC, there was a BPPSD chapter, at least twenty instances of SNCC organizational activity, and a TWWA chapter office.

If Hip Hop is a social movement, DJ Kool Herc's party at 1520 Sedgwick Avenue in South Bronx would be its high-water mark—as the main elements were present. One of the elements, rap, became the voice of the movement. Later, there were high-profile media events that crossed over to audiences outside of the birthplace of rap, such as the initial release and airplay of "Rapper's Delight," Deborah Harry's appearance on Saturday Night Live (SNL) with the Funky Four Plus One More, *Washington Post*'s August 1980 article that made use of the term "rap" for the first time, and ABC 20/20's special report on rap.[23] This process happened alongside an identity change in rap, including the new use of "rapper" instead of "emcee" (the term used by early creators). This change was shaped by news reporters, journalists, and executives such as Sylvia Robinson rather than participants on the early Hip Hop scene.[24]

The conditions of the South Bronx from the 1960s to the birth of rap are very well documented, and Hip Hop and rap activity were direct response to the movements in state, market, and society. Economic shifts had caused shifts in social conditions, as Chang introduces: "Here was the unconstructed South Bronx, a spectacular set of ruins, a mythical wasteland, an infectious disease … [most] of New York City north of 110th Street was reimagined as a new kind of 'South' a global south just a subway ride away."[25] Horsfall mentions similar conditions in decay, rap as the response "in one of the poorest" US congressional districts, and its residents feeling "abandoned and fearful they would become victims of crime."[26] In this environment, "rap was an indigenous response." It expresses Black life, communicates inner-city struggles, and provides a "cathartic hope for the future."[27] Jonnes adds, "Along with the poor came their perennial problems: crime, drug addition, unemployment. They also brought a smoldering sense of injustice."[28] A BPPSD Information Center opened on Boston Road in response to these early problems. However, according to Chang, the "long hot summer" of 1968 was a "bad season" for the BPPSD to begin their New York recruitment, and the Panthers found themselves in a battle with J. Edgar Hoover's COINTELPRO initiatives. Ogbar adds, "In the early 1970s, the Puerto Rican Young Lords emerged as the most visible expression of Puerto Rican nationalism of their time. They explicitly modeled themselves after the Black Panther Party and worked as close allies with the Panthers in New York and elsewhere."[29]

As the BPPSD was being destroyed, Chang notes that local conditions were ripe for street gangs in South Bronx—as gangs added a delegitimized structure and were able to monetize off the "weak, elderly, drug addicts, store-owners, unaffiliated youths, [and] each other." In short time, these gangs became the "real law on the streets" in the eyes of some residents.[30] This was a rapid process, as within three years, the gangs had "colonized the borough." Police and media estimated eleven thousand members, "70 percent were Puerto Rican, the rest [were] Black."[31] Reeves describes an environment "eviscerated by arson scams" and resembling a "war-torn planet."[32] This left two main options for empowerment—street power through neighborhood gangs *or* a newly emerging Hip Hop culture. Turning to gang warfare was one option, as there was a "resurgence and growing power of street gangs."[33] In fact, it is only after a ceasefire that Hip Hop was able to fully take shape. Lamotte writes about early block parties:

> While clashes between neighbourhood gangs intensified in the 1970s and 1980s, the ceasefire of 1971 reconciled black and Latino gangs in the South Bronx. This peace treaty had a profound impact on the South Bronx, particularly because of the personal involvement of Afrika Bambaataa, a young warlord of the Black Spades (one of the larger gangs in the South Bronx, presided over by Bam Bam).[34]

An alternative option to street power (instead of gang membership) was a newly emerging style and music. Kajikawa insists that Flash's key technique in "manipulating breakbeats with greater accuracy and speed allowed him to create a more reliable, rhythmic framework for dancers, and for his MCs to launch increasingly elaborate rap routines."[35] In fact, Kajikawa writes that Grandmaster Flash's "quick mix theory" "Africanizes" any slice of sound, aligning it with other Afro-diasporic forms.[36] This became a cultural revolution with the release of the first mainstream rap products on radio airwaves, circumventing the disparagement of major labels or "their Negro executives in charge of 'black music' departments (many of whom saw no future in 'ghetto music')."[37] Brewster writes about early Hip Hop DJ culture and maintains that from 1974 to 1979, Hip Hop was not "heard beyond the Bronx" and that Hip Hop's "first five years were centered on nothing more complicated than throwing the best party."[38] This changed significantly after rap's growth in recognition and popularity. As Darzin writes in a review of the first Hip Hop film *Wild Style*, Hip Hop had finally "hit the big time."[39]

Hess shows some significant historical events in NYC prior to Hip Hop's emergence: Malcolm X was assassinated in Upper Manhattan in 1965; the Last Poets formed in 1969; Taki 183 began drawing "his nickname and street number ... in subway stations during his train rides to high school in Midtown Manhattan"; and the New York Times profiled Taki 183 and Philadelphia for graffiti activity in 1970.[40] In Staten Island, the Nation of Islam and Five Percent Nation have been influences on Black movements. RZA's 5-year plan is also symbolic of a political movement, especially when considering its overall background and philosophy. Patrin details RZA had a life changing event in Steubenville, OH, involving a gunfight and then began "struggling between an Islam-rooted spirituality and his own desperate-measures situation."[41] After this life changing event, RZA put his energy into music and created the 5-year plan for Wu-Tang Clan members.

Philadelphia starts the graffiti movement in the US. Cornbread and Cool Earl graffiti appears as early as 1967, and even during Hip Hop's emergence, the New York Times highlighted Philadelphia as the "Graffiti Capital of the World." MOVE was also a presence in Philadelphia. MOVE was a revolutionary organization that combined the ideology from the BPPSD with animal rights and communal living. They had two major encounters with law enforcement: a 1978 shootout and a 1985 bombing of their headquarters. In Newark, there have been struggles related to government-funding initiatives, fraud within public leadership, and other related issues that have limited Newark's development.[42] The role of women MCs in Newark and Trenton, such as Lauryn Hill, Queen Latifah, and Rah Digga (to name a few) is also noteworthy. Rah Digga, Mullins claims, is "paving the way and leading a new species of female MCs to just feel confident enough to come with raw rhymes and not have to worry about exploiting themselves sexually to succeed."[43] Lauryn Hill also paved her own way, as Iandoli shows she "became a pop music darling without having to compromise her mission to create an honest work that reflected all sides of her musical persona."[44]

West Coast and Northwest

On the West Coast, LA, Oakland, San Francisco, Seattle, and Portland each have significant social movement activity. Each site had a BPPSD chapter, and LA, Oakland, and San Francisco also had Brown Beret chapters. Most of the West Coast sites had SNCC or May 1970 student activity, and LA and Portland had both.

Regarding LA rap, Viator writes of it as "a West Coast phenomenon that was, in the tradition of the blues, a form of blunt self-expression, and thus a potent, if not immediately obvious, response to systems designed to silence and control black people."[45] Black youth in LA were being doubly terrorized by the local police and local gangs.[46] This condition is apparent in the music of N.W.A. and others on the scene. Shortly after the LA riots, Bohlman claims that musicology needed to "begin to 'face the music'" and accept LA rap as "music" worthy of analysis.[47] His work directly addressed a "moral panic" formed over types of LA rap. The carceral state is also a factor in the day-to-day lives of Blacks in LA. The anecdotal case of Dr. Dre going to jail over unpaid parking tickets exemplifies this.[48] It was in the crucial moments after release that he began to push his music, and the whole situation seems similar to 2Pac's rap beginnings with Digital Underground on "Same Song" after being slammed to the ground and arrested for jaywalking in Oakland. 2Pac later sued the Oakland Police Department. These experiences show the carceral state's direct impact on helping to produce the types of resistance that later emerge on the LA and Oakland scenes.[49]

In early-1980s Oakland, as the BPPSD was experiencing the last signs of collapse, local youth began using underground rap as a primary mode of political expression and drew heavily on the radical and militant elements of Panther discourse throughout the 1980s, 1990s, and 2000s. This was apparent in both artwork and lyrics and over a range of local rap styles (including a deep investment in the production of gangster rap). Rap offered hope amid increasingly worsening social conditions, which were partly led by factors such as government disinvestment in neighborhoods and continued investment in new forms of military surveillance. As in other places, this local situation intensified with the wars on crime and drugs, economic changes with middle-class White and Black tax bases leaving Oakland post-1960s and again in the 1970s, and the destruction of many of the grassroots political and social organizations of the late 1960s and 1970s.

Studying Seattle women rappers and Hip Hop artists, Gupta-Carlson finds participants "called attention to that invisibility through the creation of women-centered networks" through a variety of techniques such as "a monthly Ladies First Concert aimed at raising money for anti-rape and domestic violence programs" and "an organization known as B-Girl Bench that hosts deejay and break-dancing practice sessions for women." Gupta-Carlson describes the events:

> Many of these events such as Ladies First limit performers on the main stage to female artists. This limit calls attention to gender-based inequalities within the culture of hip-hop as well as society at large. At the same time, the events remain participatory in that men are not excluded from the audience and often attend the events to support women artists as well as the anti-rape and domestic violence efforts that Ladies First raises money for.[50]

The internet "also helped artists in cities as Seattle network with each other and helped make their art accessible beyond their immediate locality." Gupta-Carlson analyzes a transformation of the scene, mentioning 1980s and 1990s Seattle Hip Hop artists "break-dancing after school at Westlake Center, writing graffiti in empty spaces, and rapping at the Pike Place Market."[51] Then as "they entered their twenties and thirties, they began to work as independent artists, creating record labels, clothing lines, and workshops and classes to earn income and to promote their work."[52]

Midwest and North

The Midwest had several social movement cities. Chicago had a BPPSD chapter, SNCC organizational activity (at least thirteen events), and May 1970 protests (at least five events). Minneapolis had a BPPSD chapter and May 1970 action. St. Paul had a Brown Beret chapter and May 1970 activity. Detroit had a BPPSD chapter, Brown Berets, and May 1970 student activity. The National Afro American League held its first convention in Chicago and laid out its six point program.[53] When discussing Chicago and the Great Migration, Martin Luther King Jr.'s August 5, 1966, Chicago march can be seen as turning point for King, who saw and felt the "unresolved tensions in the North in the wake of the Great Migration."[54] When King arrived, a "fist-shaking crowd of some four thousand residents had gathered in advance," and "they cursed King with epithets from a knoll overlooking the march."[55] So, Chicago was a prominent site for the Civil Rights Movement, Nation of Islam, BPPSD, Chicago Freedom Movement, and Black Arts Movement. Hip Hop also arrived fairly early in the form of graffiti. In 1978, Angel moved to "Chicago from New York and tags in the northwest Chicago neighborhood of Logan Square. He and local tagger Berto (or B-Boy-B) form the Angel Berto Crew

(ABC).["56] Chicago has a long-standing history of using Hip Hop for political action. By 2004, Hip Hop was being used to register over seventeen thousand young voters through the Chicago Hip-Hop Political Action Committee.[57] Minneapolis and Detroit have produced rappers focused on the advancement of women. In Minneapolis since the 1990s, there seems to be an increased role or recognition of the role of women on the scene. Th B-Girl Be Summit is likely a leading source of this.[58] Women's role in Detroit rap music has also been explored by both journalists and academics.[59] Farrugia and Hay discuss the influence of women and role of gender identity on the scene.[60] They note that in Detroit, it is impossible to talk about one Hip Hop community, because of the diversity of music and interests on the scene.[61]

South and Contested Islands

In the South, Houston, New Orleans, Atlanta, and Baltimore each had BPPSD chapters and SNCC organizational activity (with as many as fifty events in Atlanta alone). Additionally, Houston had Brown Berets, and New Orleans and Baltimore had May 1970 protests. For Houston, Long finds that for Blacks in particular, the "role of systemic and systematic racism in urban planning" stretching back to the 1920s "directly relates to the rise of Hip Hop entrepreneurialism in the city."[62] Before rap emerged in Houston, Hip Hop had a presence as a visual culture and in the form of breaking. Then Grandmaster Flash's "Superrappin'" hit the early scene, and some of the first Houston rap songs were made from artists in MacGregor Park. The sideshow (parking-lot pimping) culture was created during this time. Eventually, as Walker observes, the "music got darker."[63] The Ghetto Boys turned into the Geto Boys and went full horrorcore, and there was a struggle between Northside and Southside acts and labels until the 2000s (when the mainstream rap industry became interested in the scene's sound).[64] Walker explains about the Northside/Southside "beef":

> What did happen in the new millennium was that the Northside/Southside beef was finally put out of its misery, and a movement that had been brewing in north Houston for years swept into the mainstream and put the Bayou City back on the map in a way the city had never experienced. And it benefited every side of town. In the past, records by artists from Houston had made a splash here and there, but this was the first time mainstream hip-hop was interested in the whole *city*.[65]

Overall, in Houston rap, there is a prominently voiced opposition to the disparity in the educational system, politics of the Bush Presidents, prison–industrial complex, and military–industrial complex. Rappers remarked about the changes in drugs (and policy) and how they destroyed the community, commenting on changes from heroin and pills to crack sourced from Miami.[66] Houston, like other scenes, has also built generational legacies in rap. Megan Thee Stallion is the "first child of a female rapper to become a female rapper," as she "carefully watched her mother write rhymes and deliver them during recording sessions, because her mother opted not to put her in day care."[67]

In New Orleans, Cohn writes about the city's eighteen wards as "gerrymandered political districts" with roots in the nineteenth century, and that the three main project housing locations associated with New Orleans rap have been Magnolia, Calliope, and Melpomene.[68] Rap has been discussed in reference to other urban changes as well. In the context of New Orleans, Cohn adds, "In the ghetto, it's taken for granted that crack was planned, a payback for Civil Rights ... Among other legacies, Ronald Reagan deserves to be remembered as the godfather of gangsta rap."[69] Rap has been used in response to urban strife on the scene. Crawford and Russell document "life in New Orleans as the city's major public housing projects are torn down" and finds a general use of music—DJing, rapping, and production—as a vital part of this story (for both coping and for representation).[70] Local rapper and author 10th Ward Buck writes, "When that music comes on you kind of forget about the struggle—the bills or the house note, or you broke up with your boyfriend or girlfriend or your kid is tripping. You kind of forget about it for the moment. Even in death."[71] 10th Ward Buck stressed that every "bounce artist that sung a song did it for the audience," their ward, or their partner.[72] When discussing Atlanta and DC BPPSD chapters, Jeffries notes operational issues because "many blacks could envision that one day they too would enjoy the middle-class accoutrements of nice homes, good schools, and well-paying jobs in Atlanta." Then in DC, the Black middle-class acted as a "strong magnet for those who found themselves at the margins of society yet so close to the seat of power" in DC.[73] In other words, the BPPSD may have been too radical for middle-class aspirants in Atlanta and those centered on impact via direct electoral power in DC.

"Contested Islands" also contain a type of social movement resistance. The Hawaiian Sovereignty Movement understands Hawai'i as illegally annexed by the US (with the annex upheld by the US Supreme Court). Bee and Bee find a direct link between migration and protest in Hawai'i, and they write about local resistance in the form of a protest song:

> They were protesting the forced signing of an oath of allegiance to the new Provisional Government of Hawai'i (which comprised mainly Hawaiian subjects of American descent and US citizens and foreign residents, whose intentions were to seek more power and control for themselves, through voting rights and the privileging of white American plantation owners' interest, and ultimately for the future annexation of Hawai'i to the US).[74]

Bee and Bee specify: "Awareness of the illegal overthrow of the Hawaiian monarchy in 1893 was widely publicized, as was the past history of the silencing of Hawaiian people through their language and culture."[75] In addition, Pidgin—the unofficial language of Hawai'i—is also sometimes used in raps and other music. Over time, Honolulu became known for having a multiethnic population. There has a been a close relationship with styles from the mainland, and musical migration through media, military bases, and concert series. In Hawai'i, citizens have fought against increased real estate prices and steep economic ladders. Local residents often work multiple jobs for survival. There are also issues with drugs mentioned in local rap, particularly methamphetamines and opiates.

Puerto Rico has some similar land contestations as Hawai'i. Flores writes,

> Indeed, if there is consensus on any issue, it is that Puerto Rico is a "colony." Whether the preferred option is annexation, increased autonomy, or national sovereignty, and whether the theoretical perspective is primarily guided by ideas of democracy, socialism, feminism, anti-imperialism, or anti racism, all programs are propounded with the purported aim of decolonization—that is, the recognition of an ongoing condition of subordination and external tutelage and the need to put an end to it.[76]

Giovannetti finds that Puerto Rico's rap scene "emerged from the marginalized youngsters of the depressed urban areas and housing projects and thereby became a statement of presence and an expression of social discontent."[77] Thus, North American rap and underground rap from Puerto Rico shared "similar urban and social origins" as both were "started among and mostly listened to by the socially oppressed peoples in their societies."[78] Jonnes describes ongoing struggles for independence, as the

> Puerto Rican diaspora hails from a nation that has languished in a dependent and tightly controlled political status for its entire history, a condition that has persisted throughout the 20th century. To this day, more than 100 years since U.S. troops landed on the island in 1898 and the growing world power set up a government of military occupation, Puerto Rico remains strapped with an unresolved and vigilantly manipulated place in the world of modern nations.[79]

Puerto Rico is geographically among the milieu of islands that make up the Caribbean. Many of the islands have been impacted by European colonization and the slave trade. Hutchinson emphasizes that "a number of Caribbean islands still fit the definition of colonies, as they are controlled by overseas powers" and "the USA maintains control of the US Virgin Islands, Puerto Rico, and the military base at Guantanamo in Cuba."[80]

The USVI, according to the US Census Bureau, is an "organized, unincorporated territory."[81] It was Columbus's first known contact with the Americas, as the US Census Bureau also details that:

> The European discovery of the islands occurred when Columbus first sighted Santa Cruz, now known as St. Croix. Exploring further, he found the islands of St. Thomas, St. John, Tortola (part of what is now the British Virgin Islands), and others, and named them collectively Las Virgenes (a name that means the Virgins, supposedly for the 11,000 virgins of St. Ursula).[82]

It was controlled by Denmark, and Harrigan and Varlack reveal that under Denmark, there was a rich history of slave revolts, and these revolts brought about fears of the "potential power" of enslaved persons. In addition to natural disasters, such as frequent hurricanes and droughts, the Danish slaveholders also used extra work and starvation techniques to reduce the number of enslaved persons.[83] After applying these means, there were so many deaths that enslaved persons on St. John responded by rising up and taking "control of the entire island, massacring any whites before outside force could retake it," and then "several isolated incidents on St. Croix were put down by extremely harsh measures."[84] The USVI was controlled by Denmark until the 1917 US purchase of the land. In 1927, USVI residents were granted US citizenship.

Movement Themes

Rap and Politics

Rap is part of the social movement of Hip Hop. Rap is based in Black Dialect, or as Smitherman writes, "an Africanized form of English," which "developed over time in Black America during conditions such as slavery and oppression."[85] The language includes "Euro-American speech with Black 'meaning, nuance, tone, and gesture.'"[86] Rapping has been part of Black America "since English became a language of the slaves," and colloquial language expressed in rhyming couplets is a "powerful tool of resistance, a way of delineating community and of communicating history."[87] Rap is important because it has been the only apparent opening for some Black youth, and as Lipsitz emphasizes, "people can take action only in the venues that are open to them; oppressed people rarely escape the surveillance and control of domination. Consequently they frequently have to 'turn the guns around,' to seize the instruments of domination used to oppressed them and try to put them to other uses."[88] Eyerman and Jamison also describe how cultural traditions can be turned into social movement power: "Cultural traditions are mobilized and reformulated in social movements, and this mobilization and reconstruction of tradition is central, we contend, to what social movements are, and to what they signify for social and cultural change."[89]

Music, as part of this cultural tradition, can be used to bring about social change. Mattern shows that "music is a tool or resource that increases political capacity, especially for people who have historically been blocked from participation in more traditional and institutionalized means. It thus increases political capacity by increasing opportunities for participation in communal and public life."[90] Mattern sees "alternative political arenas" in the form of people "acting in concert," and as a "different people identify with a particular kind of music, they internalize some of its meaning, and it becomes part of their identity."[91] There are also disagreements and conflicts throughout the process, which is reflective of a community.[92] There are also "confrontational" forms of "acting in concert," in which one community uses "musical practices to resist or oppose another community" (such as protest music).[93]

Rap grows from using oral tradition as a form of transformation. Sarig shows that oral tradition was "central to slaves" and the "only way the memories of their African heritage and the new American experience could be processed into cultural expression."[94] Literature and visual arts were prohibited or inaccessible, and "the voice became the primary instrument of expression—talking, rhyming, singing."[95] Yet, as these types of "oral communication between slaves raised the suspicion of masters," Blacks created and layered a "tradition of codes, metaphors, and euphemisms that was both a matter of creative expression and survival."[96] Rap's historical development is an "everyday form of resistance," similar to the types of resistance discussed by Scott. With slave resistance, Scott notes that high-profile struggles by leaders such as Nat Turner or John Brown were "rare, heroic, and foredoomed," and argues that the "grinding conflict over work, food, autonomy, [and] ritual" were types of day-to-day forms of slave resistance.[97] Rap music consists of some "historical reflection" or Black "everyman," as Perry shows, by discussing racial and national history and their personal experience within that history.[98]

Electoral and Radical Black Politics

Rap's use of politics is also related to both Black electoral and alternative Black organizations in the US. Politically, the first Black mayors in major cities in the North and West were "participants or sons of the Great Migration"—including Carl Stokes (Cleveland), Tom Bradley (LA), Coleman Young (Detroit), Harold Washington (Chicago), Wilson Goode (Philadelphia), David Dinkins (NYC), and Willie Brown (San Francisco).[99] While this migration has brought exceptional "gains for a sizable segment" of the Black population (such as Black mayors), it has continuously failed large numbers of poor and working-class Black Americans "who continue to deal with higher unemployment rates than Whites, poorer housing, bad schools, and disparate health outcomes."[100] When migrating to these cities, parents increased possibilities for children "to grow up free of Jim Crow and to be their fuller selves," but a "generational divide arose between the migrants and the children."[101] This was in addition to continued issues faced by middle-class Blacks, many issues still unresolved since the Great and Second Great Migrations.[102] Some US cities have undergone "urban renewal," which has sometimes involved "systematically uprooting" Black people (and others) from "valuable" parts of the city into "projects."[103]

Rap is also related to the radical, Black organizations in the 1960s that arose as alternatives to Black electoral systems and bourgeois capitalism. Kelley identifies several movements at the heart of radical Black resistance in the US: Universal Negro Improvement Association (UNIA), Nation of Islam (NOI), African Blood Brotherhood (ABB), Revolutionary Action Movement (RAM), Black Workers Congress (BWC), Republic of New Africa (RNA), and National Black Feminist Organization (NBFO).[104] Kelley describes the ABB as "a secret underground organization founded by the Caribbean-born editor Cyril Briggs."[105] RAM was "influenced by uprisings and revolutions in Africa, Asia, and Latin America."[106] The BWC held a "radical anticapitalist vision."[107] The RNA was based in Detroit. The BPPSD founders, Seale and Newton, saw Black liberation as only possible by "upending the deeply racist American infrastructure, starting with the police." The Panthers were a "media organization" in addition to a "political party, and anticolonist government, a node in an international network of revolutionaries, a community organization that organizes children's breakfast programs, and a paramilitary operations sworn to 'police the police.'[108] One surviving aspect of this radical Black tradition is the NOI, which holds "the most apparent influence in explicitly religio-political lyrics, particularly from groups like Brand Nubian or the Poor Righteous Teachers."[109] After the destruction of groups such as the BPPSD, the Black Arts Movement became one of the centerpieces of Black culture in US cities.

The Black Arts Movement in US Cities

The Black Arts Movement was built from Black creative activity that proceeded it and had been acting as a counterpart to the Black Power Movement for some time.[110] Eyerman and Jamison note that after World War I, "there was a great upsurge of creative activity" among Black Americans" and "within the neighborhoods which were created or transformed, small clubs and meeting halls, restaurants, movie houses, theaters, and dance halls sprang up in the black sections of Chicago, Detroit, Cleveland, Philadelphia, and especially New York."[111] Migration was a factor, as the "newly arrived refitted their traditional cultures to fit the urban environment and lifestyle."[112] Over time, generational differences emerged in the use of poetry, as Nielson and Dennis write that Black Arts poets differed from their "literary and musical predecessors" by using "coded language and euphemism" and that "they were explicit and provocative, often using violent rhetoric to signal their break from earlier black art forms that they believed were a failure, artistically and politically, because they were too beholden to, and therefore uncritical of, white America."[113] Perkins adds that the Last Poets and Gil Scott-Heron "invoked the most accessible form" of Black cultural nationalism in "message and word play—to reeducate and awaken the masses."[114] Sonia Sanchez, Nikki Giovanni, and Muhammad Ali were also part of this tradition.[115] The evolution of Afro Diasporic forms into popular music also continued during the soul and Black Arts Movement, with popular culture venues such as *Soul Train* fueling music, dancing, and ethnic pride. Hip Hop's dance predecessor was a "street dance movement" composed of "popping," "locking," and "boogaloo" styles.[116]

Locationally, RudeWalker shows that the "Black Arts Movement developed from local and regional grassroots activism across the country, with particularly vibrant activity in the San Francisco Bay Area, Chicago, Detroit, New York, Newark, and New Orleans."[117] Collins looks at some similar sites and adds Harlem, Brooklyn, Philadelphia, Watts, Cleveland, Tampa, Cincinnati, Baltimore, Kansas City, Pittsburgh, and DC as locations with Black Arts Movement activity between 1964 and 1968.[118] Smethurst argues that Black colleges, especially in the South, were important in the Black Arts Movement as well.[119] Some city hubs were especially well known for Black arts. RudeWalker sees Detroit, Newark, and Chicago as the "three vital hubs" of "Black Arts Movement activity." Detroit had Broadside Press run by Dudley Randal. Newark had Black electoral and activist politics as well as Amiri Baraka. Chicago *has* Third World Press run by Haki Madhubuti, had Chicago's Black Arts Magazines run by Hoyt W. Fuller, and also had the Organization of Black American Culture (OBAC).[120]

In the 1970s, there were also advancements in Black arts, music, and overall culture. Essentially, RudeWalker shows that Black Arts poets advanced "the toast form": "Black Arts poets incorporated into their work not only traditional toast stories, but a modernized version of the toast form in which speakers toast in the first person, casting *themselves* as the larger-than-life heroes."[121] Bynoe also notes rap's roots in both the "Beat poets of 1950s and 1960s" and the "Black Arts movement poets of the 1960 and 1970s."[122] Bynoe specifies that rap's "tales of sexual prowess, illegal empires," and other narratives are "following in the tradition of the toasters who rapped about Stagolee and Shine and who played the dozens with their cronies on street corners."[123] Rap picks up on aspects of the spoken word movement, which includes "poems, stories, [and] monologues," and this type of spoken word is "often viewed as an intelligent alternative to rap music."[124] Later, as Perkins shows, a second wave of rappers included some that documented "the pain, anguish, and social and moral crises of their generation."[125]

The Black Arts Movement, according to Dickerson, provided key "intellectual dynamism" using a praxis (around poetry and activism) that "emboldened and emblazoned artists to stand in the communal gap as a trusted activist, thereby generating more expansive space for those who could be deemed community movers and shakers beyond the preacher and the teacher."[126] Ultimately, as Salaam shows, these Black Arts Movements followed a "local/national/local model" and were made of "far-flung and uncoordinated activities across the country (grassroots/local)."[127] This decentralization of the Black Arts Movement helped produce a core focus on performance and publication.[128] The local-to-national model and focus on performance and production is directly relevant to the later development of US rap scenes. Overall, both the Black Arts Movement and rap grew out of Black oppression, as Kelley demonstrates: "Social movements generate new knowledge, new theories, new questions. The most radical ideas often grow out of a concrete intellectual engagement with the problems of aggrieved populations confronting systems of oppression."[129] This confrontation and "intellectual engagement" by Blacks in the 1960s and the 1970s also included a radical Black politics that (sometimes) began to understand race, ethnicity, and gender (and the intersections between these and other identities) as highly related to the Black condition in the US.

Identities

Race

Rap has been associated with Black social movements, from its beginnings in an oral tradition, which included communication during slavery and throughout differing stages of freedom. There have also been several groundbreaking studies in the areas of Black political ideology and rap music.[130] Roberts highlights the Black American tradition created during slavery, including the "folk heroic creation," and notes that there was a "a profound and enduring relationship" between African and Black American "cultures and oral traditions" post-emancipation.[131] Roberts understands this "as historically continuous Afrocentric" activity.[132] Smitherman observed,

In Black America, the oral tradition has served as a fundamental vehicle for gittin ovuh. That tradition preserves the Afro-American heritage and reflects the collective spirit of the race. Through song, story, folk sayings, and rich verbal interplay among everyday people, lessons and precepts about life and survival are handed down from generation to generation. Until contemporary times, Black America relied on the word-of-mouth for its rituals of cultural preservation.[133]

Studies on the music of the Civil Rights Movement in the US and in the African diaspora confirm this tradition.[134] Jones observes that the Civil Rights Movement "represented a kind of second reconstruction" by "securing citizenship for blacks in the South who still sweltered under a caste system enforced both by law and private violence."[135] Jones also insists that "the civil rights movement was directed by the black middle class leading from the pulpit," but the "new militancy was driven by the black underclass and led from the street."[136] This movement from the Black underclass would include the BPPSD and other Black radical groups. By the 1990s, sensing the ways in which Black communities were being destroyed, some rappers began to respond using tools of resistance learned from the BPPSD and other radical groups. For example, Gaines argues that 2Pac's "T. H. U. G. L. I. F. E. ideology was comparable to the Black Panther Party's 10 Point Platform," using "African American language tenants," and "speaking to a nation of peoples."[137] Gaines echoes that "being trapped" is a sentiment expressed by many Black youth.[138] Rappers, including Oakland-based 2Pac, began using what has now become known as Hip Hop Nation Language in their lyrics.

The Hip Hop Nation is global, beyond US, racial, and ethnic boundaries, but still largely Black American–centered.[139] Ultimately, Perry establishes that Hip Hop is seen as Black American music for four main reasons: (1) its use of "African American Vernacular English"; (2) its "political location in society distinctly ascribed to black people, music, and cultural forms"; (3) its development from Black oral cultural; and (4) its development from Black musical culture.[140] Barone even suggests that Hip Hop "provided the cultural framework for the anti-racist Black Lives Matter movement"— which would be a global movement creating another global movement.[141]

Ethnicity

Ethnicity is vital to understanding the politics of rap. Puerto Rico is important given its original colonization in 1493, racial and ethnic diversity, and location as a central meeting ground of Latin American, Caribbean, and African musics. Puerto Rican contributions to NYC rap at the construction of Hip Hop are also very important. Rivera documents the "joint practices of Puerto Ricans, African Americans, and West Indians" within NYC Puerto Rican music.[142] She expresses concern over the dismissal of Puerto Rican and Caribbean contributions to origin scenes.[143] There is certainly an interconnection between African, Latin American, and Caribbean cultures with a "history of shared cultural expression between African Americans and Caribbean people in New York" dating back to the "early days of slavery in the Americas."[144]

Through migration in the Caribbean and from the Caribbean to the US, this shared history continued strong throughout the nineteenth century.[145] Rivera ultimately argues that the "colonial relationship between Puerto Rico in the US ... is a prominent factor that sets Puerto Ricans apart from other Latinos," making their condition in the US more similar to Blacks in the US than perhaps other Latinos.[146] In her analysis, early Puerto Rican contributions to the early South Bronx and East Harlem rap scenes went more unquestioned than Puerto Rican contributions to early Brooklyn rap. Rivera explains rifts in Brooklyn, which seemed "to be greater," with "transethnic interaction less pronounced in other neighborhoods, particularly those with greater ethnic residential segregation."[147] In addition to outlining many rap contributions made by NYC Puerto Ricans, Rivera shows a dialogue between the island of Puerto Rico, the Caribbean, and other Latin American countries.[148] There is contemporary relevance in this area of migration and language. Flores contrasts the "crippling of bilingual programs and services and ... 'English Only' crusade" with Latino rap carrying "an ensemble of alternative perspectives and an often divergent cultural ethos into the mainstream of U.S. social life."[149]

Gender

Of the many studies of the gender expressions in rap, Gaunt's analysis of everyday games that Black girls play and its impact on rap is one of the most thorough explanations. Gaunt writes that women are rarely "taken seriously as creative and influential artists who contribute to the art form itself."[150] Positing Black girls' play as central to "understanding African American expressive culture and black popular musical aesthetics," Gaunt notes a generational passing of these games and musical behaviors.[151] Geographically, Gaunt shows, "Studies of handclapping games, cheers, and double-dutch have documented African American play in major urban cities in the Northeast (Philadelphia, D.C., and New York City), in the South (Texas and Alabama), and in the West (Los Angeles)."[152] The games in the 1960s were translocal and transcended "divisions of geography, and thereby class, age, national origin, and migration."[153] Gaunt insists that the role of Black girls in culture keeping is vast: "The result is a national sense of black communal memory and experience (or identity) defined by musical practices that involve key strategies of black linguistic play and musical movement. These are black girls' first public interactions in rural and public communities."[154] Then, Gaunt poses an important question about how Black men use these games in their raps: "But what do we make of hip-hop, an art form predominantly associated with males and masculinity, sampling from the familiar chants and beats of female musical expression?"[155]

There is a rich scholarship about gender expression in rap and its impact on society. One side of this analysis emphasizes concerns from women and allied groups over rap content, and another side focuses on the amplification of women voices and roles. Concerns over rap's content (and its impact) from women and allied groups became a leading form of critique—and rightfully so. However, it also triggered a "moral panic" around rap in which artists were blamed for all the ills they rapped about. Perry calls the "moral panic" a "dispersed panic of citizens confronted by hip hop's texts and arguments."[156] Guerra and Alberto add that the mainstream media and groups were "essentially focusing on the diverse masculine elements of gangsta rap," which triggered a moral panic, failing to "recognize the genre's political dimensions."[157]

Another side of gender analysis in rap has looked at women rappers and their influence. A leading (and persuasive) historical connection has been made between Black women MCs and Black women jazz and blues musicians of the past. Pough explains that, historically, Black women have been at the forefront of musical movements in the US, as "the first to put the blues on wax," and that they were the "the majority of the early blues singers, thus laying the foundation for the blues culture."[158] Woldu adds that these Black blues women traveled through Georgia, Alabama, and Mississippi and "moaned and groaned their way through the period, singing of no-good men, the joys of drinking, and proclaiming an unabashed delight in their own sexuality."[159] For specific artists, Keyes mentions "Ma Rainey, Bessie Smith, Ida Cox, Victoria Spivey, Alberta Hunter, Edith Wilson, Clara Smith, and Trixie Smith," and explains,

> While African American women found a home in the urban blues commercial market of the 1920s, black men commercially dominated the more rural or downhome styled Southern blues recordings defined by an acoustic guitar sound embellished with slides produced by a bottleneck or jack knife, raspy to smooth vocals, and harmonica and/or upright piano accompaniment (a fixture at barrelhouses or honky-Tonks.[160]

As a gender analysis, Perry adds that artists such as "Ma Rainey, Billie Holliday, Tina Turner, Gladys Knight, and Chaka Khan" had actually "entered artistic spaces gendered as male."[161]

Similar to Pough, Keyes finds women rappers to be "more closely allied to the women blues singers, known as classic blues singers, of the 1920s."[162] Keyes adds that "Berry Gordy's Motown captivated national audiences" several decades after these blues singers.[163] The love raps of Isaac Hayes, Barry White, and Millie Jackson were also important to early raps as they were "essentially monologues, recorded over a simple melody, that spoke to matters of the heart," and Millie Jackson is considered the "mother of women rappers" through these sounds.[164] Women were also the "majority of the workers" in the Civil Rights Movement.[165] In addition to Black women playing a foundational role in keeping Black folklore and games alive, they played formative roles in the industry, with various women such as Cindy Campbell, Sylvia Robinson, and Roxane Shanté as critical to the development of early rap.[166] In *Rap Attack*, Toop mentions early participation by women rappers (especially in groups and in production), including Funky Four Plus One More, Lady D, CC Crew, Naomi Peterson, Cosmic Force, Paulette and Tanya Winley, Lady B, and Sequence.[167]

Yet, rap remains dominated by male listeners, and as Harrison and Arthur explain, the more underground the music, the more male the listenership. Recent analysis on rap's listenership shows it to be a "minority music genre whose main audience is single men under 24, who are mainly students taking upper secondary or graduate studies."[168]

However, increasingly, "it publicizes unfailingly hierarchical identity politics—in some cases subverting and in others upholding existing relations of power—while being deeply concerned with the politics of identity; it speaks truth to power as it perpetually undermines and/or destabilizes our understandings of what is real."[169] Timothy Brown notes that while "evaluating blackness," Hip Hop "masculinity also perpetuates the patriarchal practice of providing limited identities" for Black men.[170] These identities can be "counterproductive" and can sometimes take the "values of boasting and stylistic expression to the extreme."[171] At a local level, Gupta-Carlson conveys that women Hip Hop artists rely upon local "personalized networks" for both promotion and for social justice mission.[172] This artist work "highlights the personal nature" of Hip Hop and "resembles daily democracy" with change coming about "as a result of tireless citizen activity," including "the collection of signatures, the gathering and presenting of evidence, the holding of meetings, [and] the rallying of people behind a particular cause."[173]

Class

Harrison and Arthur find that since Hip Hop's emergence, its "practitioners and affiliates have served and continue to serve as leading youth-culture taste-makers through their abilities to appropriate, innovate off of, and productively consume the cultural materials and symbols that capitalist society throws at them."[174] Klaess writes about the initial radio rejection of rap in relationship to Blackness and class. Rap was considered untried, it could be hard to understand vocally by some listeners, it had production perceived to be worse than mainstream R&B releases, and the image of "the young, dark-sinned rapper from the rubble of the Bronx" was in stark contrast to the projection of "Black middle-class respectability" stations had been trying to cultivate for years prior.[175] Lusane connects the emergence of Hip Hop with the labor market:

> It was, then, perfectly logical that Hip Hop culture should initially emerge most strongly in those cities hardest hit by Reaganomics with large minority youth populations—New York, Los Angeles, Houston and Oakland. For many of these youth, rap became not only an outlet for social and political discourse, but also an economic opportunity that required little investment other than boldness and a competitive edge. In a period when black labour was in low demand, if one could not shoot a basketball like Michael Jordan, then the entertainment industry was one of the few legal avenues available for the get-rich consciousness that dominated the social ethos of the 1980s.[176]

To be more specific, in the 1970s and the 1980s, many US urban centers experienced a loss of employers. Asante reports, "American Airlines, Boeing, Compaq, Dell, Eddie Bauer, Chevron, Hewlett-Packard, Honeywell, IBM, JCPenney, TWA, McDonald's, Microsoft, Motorola, Nordstrom, Pierre Cardin, Revlon, Sony, Texas Instruments, Victoria's Secret, and Toys "R" Us, to name a few."[177] The changes around employment opportunities happened alongside "disinvestment" in cities after the 1980s, as Wacquant explains that "city policy shifted away from supporting lower-class residents and districts towards attracting corporations and beefing up middle-class amenities … leaving [the urban poor] mired in rampant joblessness, crushing poverty, and escalating crime, as the predatory commerce of the street grew to fill the vacuum left by the ebbing of the formal economy."[178]

Intersectionality

Rap is largely an intersectional music, and topical rap analysis "has often been on gender, identity, politics, and religion."[179] Calderon and Hall show both "personal identity" and "social identity" categories as important to forming an intersectional approach. Music, *one* aspect of the personal identity categories, is related *many* of the social identity categories. Personal identity categories can include elements such as political affiliation, favorite food(s), favorite music, favorite film(s), hobbies, talents/skills/abilities, birth order, other (attribute that is relevant to who you are), favorite book(s), geographic identification, and personality traits.[180] Social identity categories have a contrasting and interlocking relationship with personal identity categories and can include race; ethnicity; sexual orientation; religion or spiritual affiliation; socioeconomic class; age; gender; sex; national origin; physical, psychological, mental and learning ability; and others.[181]

Rap has been associated with intersectional identities since its origins, even with just race and ethnicity being two intersectional examples. However, the intersection of class and gender is another area that needs to be considered throughout rap's development. Rap can respond to types of long-standing forms of "ascriptivism," which is defined as the use of race, ethnicity, gender, sexual orientation, or any other attribute of personhood to limit someone's standing in the political, economic, and social order.[182] Early analysis of US rap linked race and class, with Smitherman noting that the speech of Blacks, poor groups, and other groups had been "used as weapon to deny them full access to full participation in the society."[183] There are many intersections beyond race and class. Collins emphasizes many additional intersections: "Under racism, sexism, class exploitation, heterosexism, and similar systems of oppression, elite groups use their power to uphold privilege through the economic, political, or ideology domination of Blacks, women, poor people, and LGBT people."[184]

Smith reports that conflicting ideals of citizenship and identity have been a hallmark of US politics since its outset, and Hannah-Jones offers an intersectional approach while looking at the impact of the slave trade on the 1619 US "founding."[185] Smith confirms that for the "nation's ascriptively defined political subordinates," such as women, Native Americans, and Blacks, "the constitution was again largely silent or ambiguous, so that it disrupted the status quo as little as possible." Smith discusses "silence and ambiguity" about slavery as important in reaching a compromise on the issue.[186] This ascriptivism was likely rooted in a colonialism around "divide-and-conquer" strategies to dominate several minoritized identity groups. According to McFarland,

> colonialism, capitalism, and other forms of domination require a divide-and-conquer strategy; a separation of the colonized, working class, or other dominated

group into rival sectors. Colonialism and capitalism used xenophobic nationalism, racism, and sexism as tools of division. Patriarchal systems pit men against women and different groups of women against each other.[187]

Regarding divisions around gender, the US constitution uses "Masculine pronouns" thirty times, which is indicative of the gender politics during the US colonial era.[188] Smith writes about women and the colonial era, stating, "The fact that they are not mentioned at all reflects the agreement between colonial leaders and home officials that ordinarily women had no proper place in the public realm and only a subordinate one in the home."[189] Rap deals in these intersectional spaces and in multiple identity areas. For example, the "Black Hip Hop generation" has coped with life chances being greatly impacted by "joblessness, illiteracy, unplanned pregnancy, criminal activity, drugs, and alarmingly high rates of HIV."[190] Often, these crises have been met with Republican bootstrap and Black conservative ideologies. South Bronx, at the time of Hip Hop's emergence, was NYC's "most dispossessed borough" and the most poverty-stricken congressional district in the US.[191] So, race, ethnicity, and class are just starting points for understanding rap's intersectionality. It would be tremendously difficult to separate these factors, as Collins argues: "Race intersects with class to such a degree in the US that race often stands as a proxy for class. Yet social class also produces fundamental group-based differences that are often masked by the inordinate attention paid to racism."[192] Pough uses the term "representative publicity," which includes public spaces and publicity around issues that need "to be looked at in terms of race, class, gender, and sexuality."[193]

Race, Gender, and Class

Women rappers started in groups with one female MC, as "only one woman per male crew could exist."[194] MC Sha-Rock (of the group Funky Four Plus One) is widely regarded the first female MC.[195] The first all-female groups were South Carolina's The Sequence and the Bronx's The Mercedes Ladies. The Sequence was highly influenced by R&B and disco, and The Mercedes Ladies were MCs and DJs formed between 1976 and 1977 with a true rap sound (influenced by Grandmaster Flash).[196] In the new MC Debbie D era, women began as solo MCs.[197] The solo rapper trend grew during and after the Roxanne Shanté battles and with the emergence of Salt-N-Pepa. Both of these acts "paved the way for other women rappers by recording very successful songs that were responses to the hit records of men who were their contemporaries."[198] Over time, the influence of The Mercedes Ladies and others could be seen in groups and DJs such as BWP, JJ Fad, and Jazzy Joyce, as well as solo artists such as Dimples Dee, Sparky D, The Real Roxanne, Pebblee Poo, Yo Yo, and many others.[199] MC Lyte, Queen Latifah, Missy Elliott, Foxy Brown, Monie Love, and Trina also emerged as rap stars.[200] There are also Hip Hop–oriented women singers such as Amel Larrieux, Angie Stone, Alicia Keys, Erykah Badu, Harmony, Jill Scott, Ledisi, and Me'Shell Ndegéocello (to name a few). Additionally, Harvey mentions that women groups such as BWP originated a type of messaging in women's rap.[201] Lauryn Hill's solo album messages have also been analyzed as a unique space for politics; as Pough adds, "invoking her own name personalizes the political message."[202] This also opens up the opportunity for discussion of mental health and other similar struggles.[203] By the time Nicki Minaj hits center stage, Iandoli writes, she was being viewed as *the star* female rap artist, arriving "from what the mainstream perceived as a massive drought."[204]

Collins finds that Hip Hop feminism in "rap, autobiography, film, and magazines" acts to "challenge the misogynistic ideas and behaviors of their Black male counterparts and Black community norms."[205] The choice of a public venue is understandable, because "young Black women are so maligned within Black popular culture, it stands to reason that young Black women and girls will defend themselves in this public area."[206] Yet, like other forms of historical oppression, Black women have been limited from fully accessing rap in some ways. As Tyree and Williams show, "Black women's oppression in U.S. society is rooted in them being both a woman and Black, and this, too, worked to stifle their presence in rap music, which is dominated by Black men rappers and predominantly male executives (both Black and white)."[207] Historically, Collins observes Black feminism to be one of four shapers of Black politics and finds it "experienced a renaissance in the 1970s and 1980s."[208] Collins also recognizes several radical Black women groups in this space, among them, "Third World Women's Alliance, Black Women's Liberation Group of Mount Vernon/New Rochelle, The National Black Feminist Organization, the National Alliance of Black Feminists, Black Women Organized for Action, and the Combahee River Collective."[209] Additionally, Collins finds pronounced differences between the Black Women's Club Movement and the White Women's Club Movement. Yet, authors also stress the importance of intersectionality in the women's movement, with Pough noting,

> Black woman thinkers and activists in the 1970s helped to shape the renewed women's liberation movement … It was the voices of Black women, lesbians, and Black lesbians, who spoke out against the rampant racism and homophobia in the women's movement. These same voices soon after were joined by poor and working-class women who began to speak out against the decidedly middle-class orientation of the public face of the women's liberation movement. Without these dissident and disrupting voices feminism today would look a whole lot different.[210]

Pough also shows that discussion of Black women's sexuality "began to address issues of gender," finding that "the women's liberation movement was too focused" on White, middle-class women's issues to actually engage Black women's "specific needs and issues."[211] A detailed, long-range view of feminism as related to rap is also covered in the aptly titled "Oppositional Consciousness within an Oppositional Realm: The Case of Feminism and Womanism in Rap and Hip Hop, 1976–2004."[212]

Race, Gender, and Sexuality

Sexuality is another critical intersectional space related to rap. Kolarič mentions that it took nearly twenty years for "a noticeable change to occur in the way rap music dealt with homophobia."[213] Kolarič's rap analysis is formed after an examination of homophobia over American Political Development—starting in the seventeenth century.[214] This allows Kolarič to thoroughly examine the issue of homophobia in rap:

> I will focus on how the time at which the music was recorded influenced homophobia in the lyrics; How homophobic language has been used as double entendre or other figures of speech to comment on social issues; Religious influences on homophobia and rap; And whether any past movements, such as Black Arts, had an influence on this issue. [215]

Additional studies on sexuality (and intersectionality) exist in Oware's "Brotherly Love," Miller-Young's "Hip-hop Honeys and Da Hustlaz," Johnson's "Dirty South Feminism," Eave's "Interanimating Black Sexualities and the Geography Classroom," Skegg's "Two Minute Brother," and Lane's "Black Women Queering the Mic."[216] Gilman and Weinbaum's *Next to the Color Line* presents additional perspective on this issue.[217]

Overall, an intersectional approach is important to the study of rap, because it is not really possible to separate Blackness from "its intersections with location, class, gender and other markers of social position."[218] Youth politics also help shape rap politics. Dimou and Ilan outline different types of politics within "youth leisure practices," including the "politics of identity and becoming," "politics of defiance," "politics of affective solidarity," and "politics of different experience."[219] Relatedly, of the Hip Hop generation, Barone shows that "these young people came of age in an environment that severely disadvantaged them due to enormous unemployment rates, leisure poverty and violence."[220] The generation responded by creating "local political cultures and creative economies."[221] While the "generation benefited from federal civil rights laws," it also dealt with "racial discrimination; AIDS/HIV; the prison industrial complex; discrimination based on sexual orientation; gender equity; and economic advancement."[222] Given this legacy, there are tremendous gains in understanding the politics of rap. In the 1980s, Smitherman noted how "this kind of understanding can help bridge the linguistic and cultural gap" between racial groups and "facilitate communication."[223] George notes that it is important to remember that most "MCs are not social activists by training or inclination" but are rather "entertainers whose visibility and effectiveness as messengers are subject to the whims of the marketplace."[224] However, MCs have filled the role of community advocate since the foundation of rap.

Conclusion

This chapter focused on social movements as precursors for rap on twenty-five US sites. The chapter centered on rap as related to Black Movements, Latinx Movements, Women's Movements, Class Movements, and Intersectional Movements.

5

Music

Introduction

Oakland rapper Sir Quick Draw describes being trapped in a chain of rhymes in his song "Rapaholic." In his fifth and final verse (Figure 7), he raps,

On and on in a continuous chain / There's a million raps in the back of my brain
I rap and rap until I'm out of breath / And my raps don't give me any rest.[1]

In the song's verses, Sir Quick Draw passes on alcohol and hard drugs but is instead trapped by his raps. There are inward questions in "Why must I do this? / Why must I cap?" The rapper also mentions the consequences, including needing to rap all day and night. Sir Quick Draw's rhymes transform a discourse about addiction and poverty into one about making music. At the time of Sir Quick Draw's 1987 raps, Oakland was part of the diffusion of rap to the West Coast and was already developing rap styles unique from its West Coast counterparts in LA, Seattle, and elsewhere. This diffusion is important to the present chapter. Sir Quick Draw's raps provide an example of the continued adaptation of rap to specific local scenes and rap as a growing form of postindustrial street power on these locales. Meanwhile, his seriousness about rapping provides a direct response to challenges about the authenticity of rap from these new locales.

Sir Quick Draw's raps are clever, especially when he states them as such within his own rhymes. This is an example of true MCing according to the definition offered by Harris and colleagues:

Emceeing represents the talented vocalist who has mastered the art of the rhyme. MC is short for "emcee" or "Master of Ceremonies." Rather than subject the audience to a vulgar and base display of unimaginative lyrics, the clever and intellectually agile artist can regale the crowd with clever wordplay, creative constructs, marvelous metaphors—all in the name of celebrating their life via Hip Hop. This element has allowed us collectively to recognize local and culturally relevant performers and support the organic growth of talent already within our midst.[2]

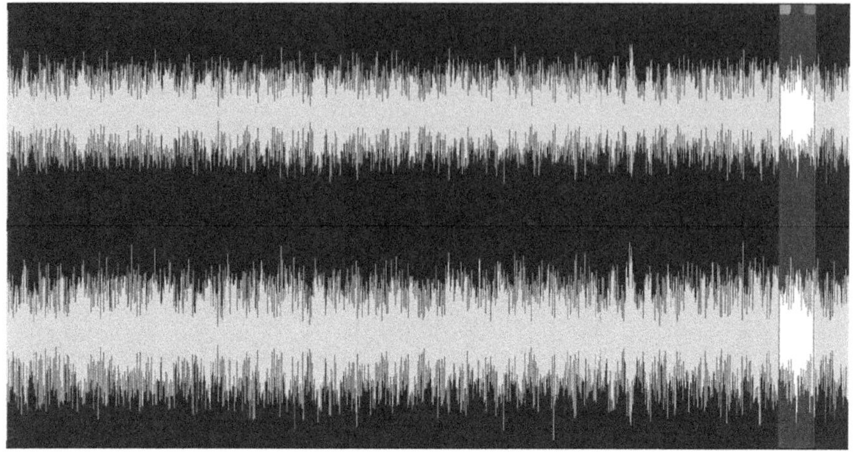

Figure 7 Sir Quick Draw "Rapaholic" Akai WAV snapshot with quoted material highlighted.

Rappers have also defined what it takes to be an MC, as in the case of New York rapper Kool Moe Dee's 1987 album *How Ya Like Me Now* with liner notes "grading" twenty-five rappers in ten areas on a scale of 0 to 10 (10 as the highest).[3] The ten areas exhibit what Kool Moe Dee values in an MC: vocabulary, articulation, creativity, originality, versatility, voice, records, stage presence, sticking to themes, and innovating rhythms. The list was reintroduced to evaluate more than thirty rappers in the 1999 rap era.

This chapter explores rap as a form of music with foundational roots in West African and Black American cultures, with clear influences of Jamaican, Puerto Rican, and other cultures. The chapter emphasizes that local rap is influenced by both musics on the scene and musics brought to the scene by migrants. The focus is on local rap from the 1980s to the 2020s, and topically, there is special attention given to the origins, foundation, emergence (narrative and musical), development, and connectivity of rap on scenes.

Comparative Analysis of Local Rap Development

East Coast

In the South Bronx, Ewoodzie explains a process of change within rap's first local scene: "DJs were the dominant figures, but somewhere along the way, MCs began to chip away at the power of DJs."[4] Then, "by 1978, all crews had MCs—not just one or two, but three or four. With the development of routines, MCs became the main source of entertainment while DJs were relegated to the background."[5] From 1975 to 1979, "rap styles were an assortment of party rhymes, nursery rhymes, boasts, and comic book inspired joke rhymes."[6] Coke La Rock was the first rapper, and it was only after T La Rock invented a more complex style that other NYC-area MCs (e.g., LL Cool J, KRS-One, Rakim, Slick Rick, Kool G Rap, and Big Daddy Kane) began further modernizing the rap style. Ewoodzie highlights MC battles as central moments in the local struggle. A battle on May 1, 1979, was a turning point in MCs, routines, and even group composition (with a solo MC taking control of the microphone during the "group" battle).[7] Ultimately, these first MCs became known as "rappers," and the music they produced (known as "rap music") began to overshadow the DJ.[8]

Hip Hop origins are deeply tied to Harlem, especially with regard to rap. Some would even claim that the foundational elements of Hip Hop were also present in Harlem at the time of Hip Hop's emergence in the South Bronx. Others have made similar claims about Brooklyn or Manhattan DJs as predecessors to Kool Herc. Harlem's foundational contributions to Hip Hop would include the long-standing history of Black music, poetry, and radicalism. Harlem boasted one of the first rap records with Kurtis Blow's "Christmas Rappin'" and one of the first reality records in Kurtis Blow's "The Breaks." The scene is immensely influential, and Mael's study of Harlem rap provides an "untold history of how Harlem helped ignite the revolution that changed music and American culture."[9] Queens rappers and producers were very important in moving rap styles and technology forward. While Marley Marl and others will be discussed in Chapter 6, it is important to highlight the range of innovations from rappers and groups with Queens associations—such as Roxane Shanté, LL Cool J, Prodigy of Mobb Deep, A Tribe Called Quest, Jungle Brothers, MC Serch, MC Shan, and Run-D.M.C.

Studying Brooklyn, Cooper documents "key periods in the evolutionary process of the sound system with a centralized focus on Brooklyn, while pinpointing the various style elements of this cultural development in the boroughs of New York."[10] Cooper strikes a key balance between highlighting Brooklyn contributions on Hip Hop and highlighting other NYC boroughs' influence on Brooklyn. Cooper describes the environment in which the Brooklyn "bum rush" became popular and rap's emergence in neighborhoods such as Bed-Stuy, Fort Greene, Brownsville, Bushwick, and East New York.[11] In addition, Mike Tyson, an iconic figure for rappers, is also from a section of Brooklyn. People from Brooklyn's scene had great influence on other scenes, as the cases of GZA (Staten Island) and Travis "Travitron" Lee" (Minneapolis) demonstrate. GZA is a rapper on both Brooklyn and Staten Island scenes. Travis "Travitron" Lee "moves from Brooklyn to Minneapolis" and begins a Hip Hop imprint in 1981.[12] Other artists have come to Brooklyn and solidified their group or sound on the scene—as in the cases of Digable Planets (Seattle, Philadelphia, and DC) and Gang Starr (Boston and Houston). The Brooklyn scene is very active, and by 1984, Uncle Ralph McDaniels's *Video Music Box* "appears on WNYC-TV in New York."[13] Between 1985 and 1990, UTFO, Just-Ice, Audio 2, Das EFX, MC Lyte, Gang Starr, and Big Daddy Kane had major album or single releases. As Black Moon released its debut album, Masta Ace was developing a new sound for the Delicious Vinyl label in LA.[14] Geographically, French notes that Brooklyn MCs were part of the struggle for a "territorial rap battle in New York," after the killing of Notorious BIG.[15] Meanwhile, many Long Island MCs and groups were important in pushing rhyme styles. These included rappers and groups such as such as Rakim, MF Doom, Eric Sermon, Biz Markie, Aesop Rock, De La Soul, and Craig Mack.

Philadelphia was "another early East Coast center for rap music" according to French.[16] Philadelphia has a reputation of changing what is possible in rap and Hip Hop. Boasting tagging before NYC, Philadelphia also released some of the first rap records with Jocko Henderson's "Rhythm Talk" and Lady B's "To the Beat." Many of the first women DJs and rappers were from Philadelphia. In the 1980s and 1990s, the Philadelphia scene pushed both ends of rap messaging—from the mid-1980s extreme gangster raps (Schoolly D) to family-friendly raps (DJ Jazzy Jeff & Fresh Prince). Schoolly D's "Park Side Killers (PSK What Does it Mean?)" is hailed as the foundational gangster rap song. Through a mixture of rapping, heavy scratching, and deep bass, the rapper communicated new rules in obtaining street power. The song started with a sound selector pan, break beats, and deep record scratching of two phrases ("The Official Adventures" and the word "fresh")—both made popular by early South Bronx and NYC DJs such as Grandmaster Flash.[17] Schoolly D's music influenced rappers in places such as LA and Oakland.[18]

In the early 1990s, Philadelphia's scene also advanced live instrumentalization, jazz, and neo-soul styles with groups and artists such as The Roots and Jill Scott. DJ Jazzy Jeff's 1998 Grammy award is also testament to the scene's fairly early legacy. Philadelphia produced early groups such as the Tuff Crew and Krown Rulers, a member of Digable Planets (Doodlebug), a TV show called Urban X-pressions, and future artists such as Meek Mill, Gillie Da Kid, Lil Uzi Vert, and Lil Dicky. Diplo and DJ Drama, also from the scene, became major influences in the DJ and production worlds and on other scenes. Boston was also one of the first sites outside of NYC to gain attention. Boston has had an important influence on rap journalism. The electro production style of the Jonzun Crew, Kevin Fleetwood's "Sweat it Off," and early influence of other East Coast scenes seem to be important starting points for Boston rap.

West Coast and Northwest

Two of the first LA rap records were released in 1981 and 1982, with Disco Daddy & Captain Rapp's "The Gigolo Rap" and Ronnie Hudson and the Street People's "West Coast Poplock." Compared to other US scenes (especially scenes not in NYC or on the East Coast), this was quite early to have an indigenous form of local rap. These early LA records were also sonically distinct from NYC raps of the time, which was not the case for early rap on most other scenes. By the 1980s, LA was mostly known for gangster rap, and French describes "Compton, South Central, and Long Beach City" as the main areas of this music.[19] The persona of the gangster rapper was important to the scene's reputation as well. Harvey reports Detroit native Boss becoming "obsessed with rappers like Ice-T and N.W.A., enough to move to Los Angeles, adopt a gangsta persona, and earn a lucrative record deal."[20] Slightly before the heyday of N.W.A., local policing and politics were already main subjects of criticism. Harvey points to the example of the original version of the song "Batteram" offering a deep critique of LA mayor Tom Bradley, LA police chief Daryl Gates, and

US president Ronald Reagan. The critique was so deep that much of it was edited out of the released version.[21]

N.W.A. defined both gangster and mainstream styles of rap for about twenty years. Their debut album *Straight Outta Compton* was released in 1988 and featured the album-titled song, "Gangsta Gangsta," and "F*ck tha Police." Some songs were banned from radio play, and the video for "Straight Outta Compton" was unambiguously banned by MTV. Yet, the group's proto-political song "Express Yourself" was eventually okayed by MTV and helped N.W.A. emerge as one of the most popular groups on the network. MTV was even forced by fan demand to retroactively play the video for "Straight Outta Compton." The social conditions and environment of Compton are so infamous that it is featured in two *Grand Theft Auto* (GTA) games. The first to feature a Compton-like scene is *GTA: San Andreas*. Butler explains this game as featuring "'ghetto life' in a number of urban environments that are strikingly reminiscent of some of the best known, almost iconic places of African American subculture, among them an area called 'Ganton' (obviously a rendition of L.A's Compton)."[22] GTA plays on the "'sonic map' of Compton" by calling on existing knowledge of rap "both on the lyrical level as well as through the regular sampling of police and crime scene noises in this genre."[23] Butler shows that "our hearing has been sonically prefigured through … previous media images of this specific urban space and its subjects: in conjunction with our genre expectations, then, which contribute to setting the stage for the soundscape we are about to encounter."[24] These sonic cues are powerful, as Butler argues that "we are thus prepared and enabled to imagine a neighborhood without any visual impression at hand, with the given sonic cues rendering the environment perhaps more instantly and comprehensively than the sequencing of visual impressions would allow."[25]

Quinn's study of LA rap considers "how lyrical battles are waged" and the "language, cultural and social, and movement building" around the scene.[26] Orejuela and others have noted the underground rap scene in LA. Orejuela highlights LA's Leimart Park arts scene, Fifth Street Dick's Coffee Company, and The Good Life Café as alternative rap spaces during the late 1980s and early 1990s.[27] By December 1989, The Good Life Café began reserving Thursday nights for local youth to perform, setting codes of conduct, and creating a participatory, crowd-driven envioroment.[28] This environment produced Freestyle Fellowship and members of Jurassic 5. Other types of scenes also exist in LA. For example, Zanfagna's study of LA Christian and gospel rap draws comparisons to Atlanta, Houston, Harlem, and Chicago scenes.[29] According to Perry, gospel rap "maintains the morality and messages" of Black Protestant "church communities."[30] Given its large size and many types of rap styles, it might be necessary to look at LA as multiple scenes or at the neighborhood level of analysis.

Oakland's rap differed from LA in the use of reality over allegory and in the reliance on underground sounds over Billboard sounds. In LA, the gangster rap transformation was rapid and was quickly adapted to mainstream audiences. In Oakland, the gangster rap transformation was defined by a longer trend and was only partially adapted to outside audiences. Then Oakland's rap transformed into "mobb" styles before transforming into "hyphy" styles.

Midwest and North

Chicago is a city with a history of musical styles brought by migrants and immigrants. Before rap was a major Chicago export, musics such as polka, ragtime, waltzes, jazz, big band, blues, R&B, soul, house, and Latin music were major exports from the scene. It took some time for indigenous Chicago rap to take shape, and when it did, its first form was still largely house-oriented until the next wave of Chicago rap (Common, Da Brat, Twista) took shape. Harkness writes about "three tiers" to the Chicago rap scene:

> The corporate tier consists of internationally established artists, such as Kanye West, Common, Twista, and Lupe Fiasco, who are tied to the major music corporations. The independent tier includes locally and regionally successful rappers who operate without aid from the major labels. These artists, whose number is very few, earn a modest living from music sales, live performances, and merchandise. The underground tier consists of rappers who are trying to launch careers in the music industry, hoping to be the next big name out of Chicago.[31]

Harkness focuses on the underground tier, further explaining,

> The musicians constituting this scene have no affiliation to the large music corporations, but occasionally have contracts with small, independent record labels. They hold concerts in local nightclubs and makeshift, unlicensed settings such as warehouses and house parties. Chicago's underground gangsta rappers perform at the handful of clubs willing to hire gangsta-rap acts, venues often situated on Chicago's West and South Sides, as well as some inner-ring suburbs.[32]

Musical elements of the nearby St. Louis scene stand out, from the presence of crews and groups or "cliques," to the diversity of jazz, rap, and country music. Additionally, the myth of Stagger Lee, which is a major influence on rap, is deeply rooted in St. Louis folklore. The folk song is originally set in St. Louis on Christmas Day in 1895. The importance of radio on St. Louis rap is also telling. Prior to rap's emergence on the scene, several prominent DJs had already risen to prominence on the national scene. Additionally, one infamous event occurred on a local East St. Louis radio station, when Gentlemen Jim Gates became the first DJ to "break" Sugarhill Gang's "Rapper's Delight" in 1979.

In Detroit, there have been many impactful Black musicians and artists. Berry Gordy and Motown were influential, as were some punk rock forms from the counterculture group MC5 and proto-punk innovators Death. The influence of techno and electro production in 1980s Detroit seems influential to the strong DIY scene in the 1990s and 2000s. Cybotron and Underground Resistance created a local format that future rappers and groups employed.

Regionally, rappers from the Midwest and South are connected by a form of rap flow. Rappers from Memphis, Cleveland, Chicago, and other places helped popularize triplet flow, which Duinker defines as an accompaniment to trap beats.[33] In particular,

Cleveland group Bone Thugs-n-Harmony and Memphis group Three 6 Mafia helped influence this flow—especially prior to 2000.[34] By 2015, Brooklyn rapper Desiigner employed total triplet flow on the song "Panda," showing the commercial appeal of this rap form. However, this form of rapping is largely regionally produced from artists in the South and Midwest.[35]

South and Contested Islands

The South has sonic and lyrical differences from other regions, as Westhoff finds: "Southern rap lyrics are full of hyper-regional slang. Formal structures and metaphor-heavy rhymes are often forsaken in favor of chants, grunts, and shouts, like when Lil Jon yells out, 'OK!' Many MCs have distinctive, atonal voices."[36] Westhoff shows sonically that "the music features tinny percussion, danceable rhythms, and big bass, often courtesy of the Roland TS-808 drum machine, which you can recognize as that low, round, subwoofer sound."[37] Houston's DIY and independent business models are legendary and can be seen as a form of self-determination. There are three thorough accounts of Houston's rap scene. Faniel's account is historical, musical, and cultural, offering a longitudinal, deep examination.[38] Walker's account is interview-based and resource-rich. He uses the mixtape approach in book design and layout, referring to many different voices on the scene.[39] Wilkin's account is comprehensive and current, presenting Houston's scene analysis at the neighborhood level.[40] He finds three different types of musical artists on the scene—street-based artist such as DJ Screw, underground artists seeking to connect to other scenes, and Christian Hip Hop artists.[41] This inclusion of Christian Hip Hop on the scene speaks to the analysis of LA's scene in Zanfagna's work.[42] Wilkins also sees Houston's Hip Hop scene in "places of production, performance, and engagement," which includes "bars, nightclubs, recording studios, radio stations, and recording labels scattered throughout the city."[43]

DJ Screw was at the center of Houston's unique sound, entrepreneurship, and developmental history. Walker accounts for DJ Screw's work by stating, "You heard it first in the streets, and it was heavy. It was enchanting. It was mystical. It made Houston feel different from anywhere else on the planet."[44] In addition to "Screw-associated acts" such as Fat Pat, Lil' Flip, and Big Moe, Screw's sound was immensely unique and identifiable to the scene. In terms of the music, it is argued that once someone hears a song's screwed version, they "can never hear it the same again, there is no such word as 'unscrewed.' "[45] Walker also highlights the musical transformation led by DJ Screw's music: "Screw took everybody's favorite songs and ripped them wide open, tearing into the fabric of the original sound, decompressing, adding earth, adding sky, and adding *voice*."[46] Houston sent its youth to college and military sites "in the state, in the country, and around the world, and they took their Screw tapes with them."[47] Indeed, if you ask someone, how or when they first heard "screwed" or "chopped and screwed" rap, chances are a Houston or Texas native was involved in that introduction. Music in Houston is well accounted for in scholarly publications and archival collections, and this is partially a testament to the respect for the legacy of Houston's Black and Latinx musical traditions.

Much of New Orleans rap has centered on two local record labels—Cash Money Records and No Limit Records. Both were created by local natives, with one created in New Orleans (Cash Money) and the other a relocated label from the Richmond, CA, area to New Orleans (No Limit). The sheer amount of music produced by No Limit after Master P's move back to New Orleans and the massive impact of Cash Money Records were great influences on the local scene. New Orleans jazz has been an influence as well, in addition to other local musics. Queens rap group Showboys' song "Drag Rap" was sampled by local artists, becoming known as the "Triggerman" beat.[48] The Queens song was released in 1986, with lyrics about a story set during the US prohibition era. "Drag Rap" also influenced the Memphis scene. In Miller's quintessential study of New Orleans rap, the music is essential to the analysis. Through this thorough and longitudinal analysis of the music, Miller is able to present a greater understanding of the local community struggle.[49]

Miller introduces the musical background to New Orleans rap and examines sound before lyrics. Much of the local sound revolves around funk and soul producers who had an "ultra-local focus in lyrics, musical style, and artistic personae."[50] Miller documents local rap through four stages: (1) from an initial "rap-lite" labeling to more developed local forms; (2) competition between bounce and other local rap forms; (3) bounce music as a form of political expression; and (4) local rap as a form of micro politics.[51] Later, on the New Orleans scene, there is a growth in popularity of music from openly gay rappers using call and response techniques. The style produces some of the first openly gay, bisexual, and transgender rappers in the US.[52] Kehrer writes that "over the past decade, queer and trans rappers have been the dominant force in New Orleans bounce, a dance-centric hip hop genre specific to that city."[53] Kehrer explains that these rappers "self-identify as gay and reclaim a once pejorative term to openly express their sexual and gender identities through their performances," and that locally there is "a largely visible group of openly queer and trans artists who are not only accepted, but in many cases are leading figures."[54]

Memphis rap has fused musical genre and cultures and created underground empires from music produced and recorded in basements, attics, and shotgun houses. Local music has been directly tied to the city's roots in soul, blues, jazz, gospel, funk, and rock and roll. This long-standing tradition of Memphis as a Black music recording powerhouse is important, because it is one of only few cities in the US to have this type of deep tradition in so many types of music. Similar to New Orleans, the "Triggerman" beat from the Showboys' "Drag Rap" was also essential to the scene. In the 1990s, Memphis rap artists used the legacy of the Civil Rights Movement and soul music to describe the struggles and lifestyles of the local Black community. DJ Spanish Fly was one of the local artists to speak on the topics of drugs and poverty in the community. Memphis has also prominently featured women rappers. Local Memphis youth also adopted DIY production technology, as made famous by groups such as Three 6 Mafia and films such as *Hustle and Flow*. Memphis has a long, storied history in horrorcore, especially in raps presenting disturbingly descriptive tales of violence and destruction (sometimes described to be the root of satanic forces). These tales (similar to some styles from other locations such as Detroit, Houston, and

Cleveland) were partly a reflection of the destruction created by urban disinvestment, drugs, and poverty.

Atlanta rap was made popular, according to French, through albums from artists and groups such as Arrested Development, Kris Kross, OutKast, and Lil Jon.[55] Coscarelli shows that Atlanta was later to arrive at the types of "innovations in Black music" seen in other cities, which is surprising given Atlanta's "stature as an early Southern center and driver of civil rights."[56] Comparatively, in the South, there was Nashville country, Memphis blues, New Orleans jazz, and Miami R&B/soul. Because there was not an indigenous rap form, there was a local notion that Atlanta rap had to catch up to other rap scenes. Coscarelli notes the "Big Bang" for Atlanta Hip Hop happening at Freaknik, showing that although LaFace and So So Def were already on the scene, Miami bass was the still the popular music being used at "parties in public parks, skating rinks and school dances" before Atlanta rap's "local independent boom."[57] Early Atlanta record labels such as Savory Records and Shurfine formed the basis of the rap scene; then R&B and rap-crossover acts took over much of the next stage of local rap development. Early rap artists such as MC Shy D also provided a scene basis, while OutKast, Organized Noise, Goodie Mob, and other groups were great ambassadors of the scene for national and global audiences. Childish Gambino is also a part of the scene, as a rap artist and also as a producer of the TV show *Atlanta*, which is a fictional show based on three individuals (two of whom are cousins) trying to "break" music on the Atlanta scene. When Atlanta grows its local form of industry music, it begins to dominate national and international charts. The music of this era "included up-tempo beats, Snap Rap, Trap, and Crunk," and did not "focus on the social ills within Southern inner cities."[58] Later, a new trap style of rap grows out of Atlanta, which does focus on many of the "social ills within Southern inner cities."

Miami is one of the first scenes in the South to feature a local form of rap. Emerging around the same time (or earlier) than Houston rap, Miami's sound was featured in the South for full decades before the development of some of the other scenes. Much of Miami's industry rap has been quite popular, but there are also independent labels. There is also legendary use of pirate radio in Miami. Other unique factors include 808 bass (brought by Queens producer Marley Marl), the rise of "booty music" (brought by Riverside, CA, transports), and the central role in defending artistic freedom (based on reactions to "booty music").

Hampton's rap scene has been greatly influenced by talent shows, high school marching bands, and drum majors and majorettes. This local music tradition has featured big bass, dance, and sound. Cannady shows that local high school and college marching bands created a "unique expression of self" that involved rhythm and choreography—which were used in both field and studio translations of the music.[59] Hampton's scene has made essential contributions through the "extraordinary efforts of a few rappers and producers."[60] There also seems to be a lot of relocation and travel among some of its newer artists to places such as Texas and New York. One of the area's artists, Lil Tracy, was born in New Jersey to parents from the groups Digable Planets (Ishmael Butler) and SWV (Coko) before emerging on the Seattle and Virginia Beach scenes.

Honolulu has a diversity of styles on the scene. Osumare reports that the Big Island Hip Hop "scene is ironically caught between rural hip-hop wannabes and one of the most Hawai'i-relevant rap groups that the islands have produced, Sudden Rush."[61] In terms of musical styles, Osumare declares that Jamaican reggae and Jawaiican music are "sure to please any local Hawai'i audience."[62] Yet, "in most cases, rap music has been the main promoter of hip hop culture in Hawaii after the initial break dance craze," and examples of this promotion of Hip Hop include the I-94 and Xtreme Radio Hawaii stations programming complete shows with mainland rap artists.[63] Additionally, mainland acts performed live shows in Hawai'i, also spreading rap there. The list of artists between 1987 and 1999 included Run-DMC, Beastie Boys, LL Cool J, Whodini, N2 Deep, Lighter Shade of Brown, Cypress Hill, House of Pain, Ice Cube, Snoop Dogg, Dr. Dre, Fugees, Big Markie, Coolio, OutKast, De La Soul, Black Eyed Peas, Yellow Man, and Lauryn Hill.[64]

For Puerto Rico, Aparicio, Jáquez, and Cepeda discuss the "impact of Jamaican music (reggae and dancehall) and rap music in Puerto Rico, and the development of two distinct, yet sometimes interconnected, identities in lifestyles that are related to these musical influences."[65] According to Flores, Vico C, Rubén DJ, Lisa M, "and many of the lesser known rappers of the day" were said to be working beyond "just a slavish import or imitation of North American expressive modes" as "rap on the island had taken on a life of its own, adapting themes—in Spanish—the realities of everyday life in Puerto Rican society, and influenced musically more by Caribbean styles like merengue and reggae than by any recent innovations in the US."[66] Even the NYC scene has tremendous connectivity to Puerto Rico, as Charlie Chase was active on the early scene and used his name to play on "Chasin' the Flash" in his rivalry with DJ Grandmaster Flash.[67] The nearby USVI scene has remained a remarkably rich musical site, despite its relatively small population when compared to the other scenes.

Themes and Local Rap

Origins

Origins, foundations, and emergence are important concepts for fully understanding US rap. The traditional origin story is really an "emergence" story, when the first DJs in the South Bronx (Kool Herc, Afrika Bambaataa, and Grandmaster Flash) began mixing "loops" (or repeated sounds) from soul artists such as James Brown and Sly Stone into the first Hip Hop breaks. There are also Hip Hop "origins" (generational musical traditions being passed down) and Hip Hop "foundations" (the practice of Hip Hop techniques and styles predating Kool Herc's party).

Rap's musical origins are in West African drum traditions that were continued in the US. Keyes shows that Black American music has about three lines or paths—Sacred Traditions, Secular Traditions (non-Jazz), and Secular Traditions (Jazz).

The first line, Sacred Traditions, begins in the 1700s and includes:

1700s: folk spiritual
1890s: folk gospel
1900s: gospel hymn
1930s: traditional gospel
1950s: gospel choirs
1970s: contemporary gospel

The second line, Secular Traditions (non-Jazz) begins in the 1600s and includes:

1600s: field work songs
1880s: rural blues
1940s: urban blues, rhythm and blues
1960s: Civil Rights songs
1970s: funk, disco, rap
1980s: techno funk, house music, and go-go

The third line, Secular Traditions (Jazz), also begins in the 1600s and includes:

1600s: syncopated dance music
1800s: ragtime
1920s: swing bands
1940s: jazz bebop
1950: hard bop, cool styles[68]

Rural blues and folk gospel were the major styles of Black music moving to cities after emancipation. Connell shows that blues "artists such as Robert Johnson, Son House and Skip James" used music to articulate "intimate attachments and reactions to physical places," and that these "migratory and transient experiences were littered throughout blues songs dedicated to themes of escape, songs of wandering and leaving home."[69]

Lornell's analysis of "down-home blues" and travel defines blues as follows: "The product of multigenesis in the Deep South (east Texas, Mississippi, Louisiana, and Alabama), blues was a synthesis of the traditions that preceded it: dance tunes, minstrel songs, secular ditties, and spirituals."[70] There are three main lines of musical migration identified by Lornell: (1) from Southeast or "Piedmont" to the East Coast areas including DC, New York, Boston, and Albany (with Pittsburgh slightly to the West of this migration); (2) from the Mid-South or "Delta" to the Midwest and North areas including St. Louis, Chicago, Detroit, Milwaukee, and Minneapolis; and (3) from the Southwest or "Texas" to locations further West such as San Francisco and LA.[71] Myers notes that blues lost popularity in the 1960s and 1970s "representing to African-Americans the resignation and complacency of a past era."[72]

Wilkerson shows Black migration changed American culture and music, bringing the blues, and birthing "whole genres of music" such as "jazz, rock, rhythm and blues" and eventually Hip Hop.[73] Wilkerson determines that Black migration essentially provided "the soundtrack to the twentieth century" and would "transform American music as we know it."[74] Three of the most influential figures in jazz—Miles Davis, Thelonious Monk, and John Coltrane—were products of the Great Migration.[75] Musically, "people all over the world were enriched by the music the migrants carried north with them," including artists such as Louis Armstrong and 2Pac, and the musical style of groups like the Rolling Stones.[76]

The rap tradition also includes signifying, playing the dozens, and other forms of Black American street culture, and uses musics such as disco and funk, other Black musics, television themes, advertising jingles, and video game soundtracks "through sampling, cutting, mixing, and scratching."[77] Dub may have also influenced the South Bronx and other NYC scenes, but this major point of contention will be discussed later. Latin American musical and dance styles have also been discussed as foundational to Hip Hop and rap, but this too is a point of contention and will be discussed later. Initially, rap authenticity was tied to a scene's relationship with South Bronx or NYC creation hubs. Toop's *Rap Attack*, for example, lists managers of the first four major rap labels as persons who "had all been involved in the New York music scene since the 1950s."[78] This included the following managers (and record labels): "Sylvia Robinson (Sugarhill); Bobby Robinson (Enjoy); Danny Robinson (Holiday); and Paul Winley (Winley)."[79] Over time, this rap authenticity was extended from being only the Bronx to only NYC to only the East Coast to only the East Coast and LA. The Caribbean and Latin American connections and expansion of authentic rap styles are discussed in the foundation and emergence sections below.

Foundation

There are three major points of contention with regard to rap's foundation. Each involves the recognition of contributions to its foundation, but the claims come from rap's early history, its development, and its fiftieth anniversary celebration. The first version of the foundation story is that Black Americans were the main (and solo) drivers of rap's foundation. This claim has been read through original work or revisions of work from Toop, Hebdige, and Hager (all of whom wrote at the time of rap's NYC emergence). Some of the more recent and prominent voices presenting this claim include Said and Nasheed, although there have been others who have made similar claims or who have (intentionally or unintentionally) presented research in support of similar claims. The second version of the foundation story is that Black Caribbean music and culture was essential to rap's founding (including the rich background predating Kool Herc's party). Chang, Rose, Perry, Connell, Bradley, and Keyes present scholarship that recognizes the contributions of Black Caribbeans as essential to the foundation of rap. The third version of the foundation story is that Latin American music and culture (particularly Puerto Rican music and culture) was important to the beginning of Hip Hop (well before Kool Herc's party). Perkins, Spady, and Saucier present scholarship that recognizes Latin American contributions as essential to the foundation of rap.

Black American Foundations

The first foundation story has become a renewed point of emphasis and must be taken seriously. This point seeks to emphasize rap and Hip Hop as a Black American creation at its foundation. Sometimes this argument will start before the 1970s and include non-Bronx geographies. There are two major examples of this argument, one provided by Said and another provided by Nasheed.[80] Said's points are released and in writing; Nasheed's points are (at the time of publication) still in Kickstarter form. Part of Said's aim is in deeply troubling connections between rap and Jamaican dub. Taking issue with an original account of the connections in Hebdige's *Cut N Mix*, Said wholeheartedly rejects the influence of reggae on Hip Hop.[81] Noting Hebdige's "misreading" of Kool Herc's words, Said makes it a mission to expose the connection between reggae and Hip Hop as myth.[82] Said centers on Chang's work as responsible for further popularizing or spreading the "myth" of the reggae and rap connection.[83] Yet, ultimately, Said concedes parallels exist between reggae and rap with "sonic priorities" and a "focus on rhythm and groove."[84]

Nasheed's work is far more controversial, and by design, as it is meant to provoke to gain views, donations, and support. Nasheed's documentary *Microphone Check* has the intent of "dispelling the myths once and for all."[85] Promotion for the film features a set of hashtags related to the fiftieth anniversary of Hip Hop, and there are users in Facebook groups stirring the controversy over Caribbean and Latinx contributions in Hip Hop around the key funding deadlines for the documentary. The release promises to be "a documentary revealing the untold history of hip hop, dispelling misconceptions, and shedding light on its true creators." What is most intriguing about the Nasheed's work is that artists Grandmaster Caz, Melle Mel, MC Sha-Rock, Busy Bee, and others (such as graffiti artist Cornbread and breaking legend A1 B-Boy Sasa) go on camera and attest to Hip Hop as a Black American creation.

What is often implied or meant to be implied by the types of arguments offered by Said, Nasheed, and others is that Hip Hop started *solely* as a Black American creation—without major contributions from other groups and that foundation stories that emphasize contributions from Black Caribbeans or Latin Americans are incorrect, inauthentic, or both. This argument is not new. It usually involves the Mills Brothers, Cab Calloway, or The Jubalaires inventing rap in some way and as early as the 1930s. Even authors not dwelling in this space show links between Black American arts of the past and rap. For example, Keyes shows a certain link between rap and early jive talk in "quasi-narrative sections" of jazz bandleaders such as Cab Calloway, Duke Ellington, Count Basie, and Louis Jordan.[86] Perkins also shows Cab Calloway as a sort of grandfather of rap music through his "jive scat."[87] This Black American origin story also connects Hip Hop and rapping to Black American DJ techniques such as "talking through" and "riding gain," or talking over records and lowing volume to talk over records.[88] Perkins shows Black disc jockeys during the 1940s, 1950s, and 1960s "engaged in intense verbal competitions to ensure and protect their market shares."[89] "Jocko Henderson, Pigmeat Markham, Gil Scott-Heron, and Rudy Ray Moore" are also mentioned as Black American artists using spoken word techniques over sound before rap emerged.

For Hip Hop DJing, those wishing to establish a Black American–only narrative often mention Pete DJ Jones or Disco Mario King, as both were born in North Carolina and participated in the NYC foundation of Hip Hop. Disco Mario King was likely DJing parties that were similar to Kool Herc's 1973 event, but perhaps two years before Herc's party. Disco Mario King may have also loaned equipment to Bambaataa for his first gigs. DJ John Brown influenced a style similar to Hip Hop DJing as early as 1969 (five years before Herc's party). During rap's emergence, Toop mentions what has become a point of contention, that most rappers "will tell you that they either disliked reggae or were only vaguely aware of it" in the early to mid-1970s.[90] The real contention is over the amount of value placed on reggae in Hip Hop and rap roots. While some say dub was an overwhelming influence on rap (with other influences including soul, R&B, and rock), others maintain that the contribution of dub and these other musics to rap have been overstated.

With regard to rapping, Coke La Rock or Keith Cowboy are usually acknowledged as the first rappers, and both are Black Americans. Even in breaking, some have emphasized Black American contributions. Aprahamian's work on the South Bronx concerns the "invisibility" of "breaking's African American founders" and emphasizes that there was no cross-fertilization or association with Puerto Rican youth at the time: "On the contrary, in its first decade of existence, the dance was an exclusively African American practice."[91] In advertising the *Microphone Check* film, the provocation is that the first breaker, first DJ (through his daughter's account), first male rapper, first female rapper, and first writer were all Black Americans. The documentary uses this evidence in an effort to establish Hip Hop's foundation as a unique Black American contribution (with overemphasized Caribbean and Latinx contributions).

Black Caribbean Contributions

The other side of this debate, one that sees contributions beyond Black American culture as foundational to Hip Hop, is extremely strong. The first point to this debate is in Jamaican dub influencing rap. Given the similarities between dub and rap in sound systems, lyrical delivery, and instrumentalized format, some have seen the two musics as interrelated. Chang writes about reggae as "rap music's elder kin."[92] Keyes adds, "The link between the Bronx and Kingston is substantial, though in general it has been unmentioned or simply glossed over in previous works on rap music and hip-hop culture."[93] Rap and reggae grew out of similar environments of conflict between Black youth and the state, as reggae grew out of a time of "growing dissatisfaction and joblessness," "to deal directly with the problems of race and class," and "to resurrect the African heritage."[94] So, as Cobb insists, when Black and Caribbean Americans "found themselves building a new culture up in the South Bronx in 1974," they were able to find shared meaning in "centuries of collective history" as they "had come from the same boat, having merely departed at different stops."[95] Examples of this shared Black American and Black Caribbean heritage include the traditionally cited founding fathers of Hip Hop DJing: Herc (Jamaican descent), Bambaataa (Jamaican descent) and Flash (Barbadian decent).[96]

Furthermore, many MCs, such as Notorious B.I.G., Busta Rhymes, Doug E. Fresh, Heavy D, Pete Rock, and Slick Rick have direct Jamaican roots. Even if one finds rap's foundation unrelated to reggae, later rappers began to blend rap and reggae into a style that has continued throughout rap's development. From Brooklyn to LA to USVI, one can find blended English and Patois, Caribbean influences, and West African–rooted music.

Perry writes, "The most powerful critiques of the construction of hip hop as black American music have come from people who understand how critical the influences of the English-speaking Caribbean have been, in particular in the early days of hip hop formation and in the creation of DJ technique."[97] The sound system clashing, summer splash, dancehall, dub, and even soca elements seem to be strong influences on the soundscape of rap. Perry finds that the DJ techniques of Hip Hop were "influenced by a form of Jamaican deejaying," the raps impacted by the Black Jamaican outlaw, and musical compositions influenced by the global popularity of reggae compositions from the days of Bob Marley and Stevie Wonder (who appropriated reggae compositions in the late 1970s).[98] Perry adds that "it was the Jamaican deejays who first turned chanting/toasting/scatting into a commercial musical form that stood on its own and pushed all accompaniment into the background."[99] Keyes adds that dub's "musical collages," "various musical motifs," and heavy bass sounds all laid the "musical foundation" for US rap.[100] In other words, the concept of a rap instrumental or a beat to put lyrics and other sounds over is rooted in dub's innovations.

Additionally, the Black American foundation story has ascriptive issues when excluding Black Caribbean contributions. Mainly, it would be hard to distinguish Black Americans from Black people from the Caribbean or Latin America (legally or visually). While participating in Hip Hop events, how would someone visually distinguish between a Black person from the US, the Caribbean, or Latin America? With migration to the US, Blacks from the Caribbean or Latin America would often be considered Black on US censuses (especially until 1990). How would US census workers (who were often told to ascriptively assign a race to survey takers) distinguish between a Black person from America, the Caribbean, or Latin America?

Toop, Hager, and Said are clear that reggae was not part of the consciousness of early Hip Hop DJ. Hebdige's correction, over a misunderstanding of Herc, also works to lessen the reggae and rap connection. Yet, Toop also writes that the first rap records were just "the tip of an iceberg" to a larger movement of Hip Hop, which was under the surface, and beneath the Hip Hop level was another level further under surface with "a vast expanse of sources reaching back to West Africa."[101] Connell adds that "like so many other musical genres," Hip Hop (or rap) "emerged from a fusion of elements brought by migrants (in this case from the Caribbean to the US) with local musical forms of residents of deprived inner-city neighborhoods."[102] Or, as Perkins expresses, "the Latin/Jamaican lineage reveals more about the cultural continuities of the slave experience and its consequences than it does about the regional, linguistic, and cultural differences of the slaves' descendants."[103] This rap lineage stretches deep, including New World origins in "mixed traditions" of "African American spoken word practices such as the toast and the dozens as well as musical traditions like Jamaican dub and southern blues."[104]

Latinx Contributions

The side of the debate that sees Hip Hop's foundation beyond Black American culture is also highly related to early Latinx contributions. For early or fairly early Latinx musical contributions to Hip Hop and rap, one could see DJ Charlie Chase (Cold Crush Brothers), DJ Disco Wiz, Pumpkin, Rock Steady Crew, Devastating Tito, Prince Whipper Whip, The Mean Machine, The Real Roxanne, Prince Markie Dee, or Mr. Magic. The Rock Steady Crew, a breaking and musical crew, consisted of four members of Latinx descent—Crazy Legs, Baby Love, Buck 4, and Kuriaki.[105] Ruby Dee of the Fantastic 5 (and Fantastic Freaks) announced his Latin American heritage when starting his rhyme: "Well, Ruby Dee is my name, and I'm a Puerto Rican / You might think I'm Black by the way I'm speakin'."[106] In B-boying and breaking, Shabba-Doo, New York City Breakers, Rock Steady Crew, Dancin' Doug (who was around Kool Herc), and Spy (a B-Boy from Puerto Rico) also made significant contributions. Additionally, moves such as the uprock and powermove have distinct capoeira influences (which is a Latinx form of martial arts). Breaking has elements of *bomba* and *plena* as well. Even in tagging or graffiti, Tracy 168, Lee Quiñones, Lady Pink, and CRASH could be cited as early Latinx Hip Hop artists.

Puerto Rican participation in the early waves of Hip Hop and rap was apparent in the South Bronx and Harlem. Later, in the early 1990s, the rise of *reggaeton* reinvigorated culture both on the island and in the US, and *reggaeton* is deeply rooted in interaction between Caribbean and Central American peoples—specifically Jamaican immigrants in Panama. Connell observes that many "Jamaicans came to Panama as workers on the canal construction project" at the start of the twentieth century and "brought their music with them."[107] Spady adds, "Reggaeton is also Afrodiasporic at its core, combining Spanish Rap, Dancehall, Reggae, African dance rhythms, and the energetic force of African American rap."[108]

The historical record of show tapes, flyers, and other materials tends to show Black American, Caribbean, and Latin American influences during rap's inception. Even other world influences—including European influences—have been integral to rap's development. The Black American–only foundation story can cite compelling examples, but there are many contributions made by people who are not Black American. For example, what do we make of Walter Gibbons, a disco DJ who was White, working on "seamlessly extending breaks in the early 1970s."[109] As one of the first DJs able to seamlessly mix records, he feared his music would be rejected by his audience—which happened to be largely White and gay. While certainly a Black American–led artform, Hip Hop's foundation likely includes groups beyond Black Americans.

There are many key questions related to foundation: Are Black American contributions to the foundation of Hip Hop and rap underemphasized? Are Caribbean contributions overstated? Are Latinx contributions overstated? These are the major questions being raised around Hip Hop's fiftieth anniversary. While energy could be better spent on making Hip Hop better, it is very important to listen to stories of founders and those at the construction era of Hip Hop. If founders did not see Caribbean or Latinx contributions to Hip Hop, it is important to take that seriously. But this also leads to some questions—some about who was there and others about how those providing these accounts were able to distinguish between Black American, Caribbean, and Latinx identities. Would it be by familiarity (i.e., knowing everyone's background in the space)? Would it be by ascriptive qualities such as skin color and hair texture? Would it be by accent while speaking or rapping? Also, when Black Caribbeans migrated to the US and gained citizenship, would they be counted as Black Americans? These might be important questions for future research on the eras between 1920 and 1973 and from 1973 to 1979.

Rap's Musical and Narrative Development

Rap has both musical and narrative components. In fact, rap is said to be "distinct from most other genres of popular music in that it originated as much from speech as from song."[110] Meanwhile, as Krims argues, rap's "musical poetics" (and its musical organization) "must be taken seriously, because they are taken seriously by many people in the course of its production and consumption."[111] As a core definition offered by Bennett, "rap is a narrative form of vocal delivery which is spoken in a rhythmic patois over a continuous backbeat, the rhythms of the voice and the beat working together."[112] Diallo describes rapping as an "act of reciting elaborate rhymes over a melodic and rhythmical loop."[113] The narrative, vocal delivery, and continuous beat are all essential in defining rap.

While there is tremendous nuance and disagreement about the early Hip Hop era and rap's evolution from it, there are a few commonly held facts. One is that between 1973 and 1979, DJing and other elements of Hip Hop remained more integral than rap, and it was not until the late 1970s and early 1980s that rappers (or MCs) began to be the most popular element of Hip Hop. This transformation, largely occurring in South Bronx and Harlem, can be seen in the film *Wild Style*, as the story evolves from a DJ creating breakbeats (Grandmaster Flash) to crews of rappers battling without a DJ (the Cold Crush Brothers versus the Fantastic Freaks) to duos of rappers at the musical forefront (Double Trouble) to a single MC with stage props (Busy Bee).[114] Pough sees this change in *Wild Style*, astutely noting that by the film's end, "graffiti provides the backdrop and rap takes center stage," reading the film to suggest that "it is the rap element" of Hip Hop that "can take the culture to the level of worldwide success."[115]

Musical Development

Rap's core musical roots are in the developments of "rhyming, scratching, and the use of breakbeats," and "the work of Pigmeat Markham, James Brown, Amiri Baraka, and Gil Scott-Heron." DJ Kool Herc's sister's party at 1520 Sedgwick Avenue in the South Bronx on August 13, 1973, is the traditional date given for the birth of Hip Hop.

The time between 1973 and 1980 would be key for rap music development.[116] In rap's infancy, Keyes noted that most rappers still preferred to perform with a DJ "spinning and mixing records as accompaniment."[117] In fact, Barone explains rapping was "coined as an accompaniment to DJs" as "MCs would shout catchphrases and rhymes in order to hype-up audiences and fuel the dance."[118] In mid-1970s reggae terms, this would have been known as an MC coming to "nice up" the dance by getting the dance started with nice, positive energy. In fact, such DJing in South Bronx and other NYC locations likely "provided the context for the different elements and youth practitioners" of Hip Hop to assemble "as a single cultural scene."[119] Terminology for an "MC" evolved into the commonly used term "rapper," largely without the input of original creators. Diallo highlights "widespread use of the term 'MC' to designate the first live performers who used rhyming on the microphone to supplement the mixes of the DJs."[120] From 1977 to 1979, "MC" was predominately used to described what was occurring on the scene, and "'rapping' was used to describe what jive talking DJs were doing to get the dancers to participate in the performance."[121]

The shift and solidification of the term "rap" was led by outlets "interested in profit and use of rap music, rather than the culture itself, such as radio, the new media, the recording industry, and academia."[122] Diallo finds that the term "rap" was not mentioned once in party tapes recorded after 1977 and before 1979, and that on "hundreds of existing flyers" from 1974 to 1979, "'MC' is the term in use."[123] Early MCs also had a "persistent concern" of establishing "a dynamic relationship with their audience."[124] Music was mostly listened to in a live format at the time.[125] Meanwhile, Samuels finds this early rap to reflect funk and disco musics and early rappers to be "unsophisticated about image and presentation."[126] Use of the term "rapper," first seen in 1978, increased in 1979 when "rap music gradually shifted from live performance to studio recorded performance and supporting DJs and hyping the crowd was no longer the primary function of MCs."[127]

As rap progressed, there was an overall growth of multimember groups, then a rise of duos and solo rappers.[128] MCs began to "stray from the ebullient rapping style of the early years and explored new options in terms of flow, of rhyming patterns, and of cadences."[129] On stage, Diallo shows rappers began using backup MCs and other performers (in addition to continued used of DJs) to help rappers "reinforce some of the points" they were trying to make in lyrics or to "express some critical ideas more forcefully."[130] He also explains techniques such as the reoccurring "use of polyphony interjections" (such as "uh," "yeah," or "let's go") as a means of bringing the "live feel" and "physicality" of stage shows to rap's studio performances. Ultimately, this was intended to give the "impression of it being spontaneous or unrehearsed."[131] There were tremendous advancements made by T LA Rock and Rakim in delivery and rhyming techniques. Subject matter also developed as "rappers also began pushing past the once-dominant party rhymes, boasts, and chants with intricate storytelling, complex wordplay, and sociopolitical consciousness."[132] Rap also has developmental roots in the cipher, which Perry describes as "a privileged outlaw space," as "those inside the cipher are central, so it claims an insider rather than outsider consciousness."[133]

Narrative Development

Rap's narrative is driven by poetry, and Adam Bradley shows that as "public art," rappers could be "our greatest public poets, extending a tradition of lyricism that spans continents and stretches back thousands of years."[134] The combination of rapping and backbeat is at the core of rap's rhythm, which is created through a "voice and a beat" forming a "patterned verbal expression."[135] Keyes writes about rapping becoming the highlight of Hip Hop performance, using "conversational folklore" and the "artistic usage of language" in Black communication areas such as folk preaching, other narrative forms, and Black talk.[136] Keyes finds rap performances to be participatory in nature, starting with song introductions, stating,

> In many instances, a rapper's salutation to the audience is not formulaic, unlike the narrative rhyme section. The introduction is crucial and is spontaneously created by the rapper according to the audience's mood. Audience inter-play becomes essential in the presentation of the main text.[137]

This type of interaction often develops into a call-and-response format, or an "an interactive network between performer and auditor."[138] From there, techniques such as signifying, or taking on double entendres and hidden meanings, are also used.[139] A list of tonal semantics are employed by many rappers as well, and this involves "song/speech, repetition and alliteration, intonational contouring, and rhyme," in addition to "paralinguistic features" such as pitch, tempo, and other vocal qualities.[140]

Smitherman sees forms of narrative expression in rap through exaggerated language, mimicry, proverbial statement, punning, spontaneity, image-making, braggadocio, indirection, and tonal semantics.[141] While many of these involve narrative, tonal semantics also includes musical elements related to tone. Smitherman explains that "verbal power can be achieved through the use of words and phrases carefully chosen for sound effects," and elaborates thus:

> In using the semantics of tone, the voice is employed like a musical instrument, with improvisation, riffs, and all kinds of playing between the notes. This rhythmic pattern becomes a kind of acoustical, phonetic alphabet and gives black speech its songified or musical quality. Black rappers use word sound to tap their listeners' souls and inner beings in the same way that the musician uses the symbolic language of music to strike inward responsive chords in his listeners' hearts.[142]

These tonal semantics are also linked to narrative or storytelling. Bradley details the mechanics of rap, focusing on six elements: rhythm, rhyme, wordplay, style, storytelling, and signifying.[143] The overall message is created through voice and storytelling, as it is the "governing authorial intelligence of a narrative."[144] In addition, although "the MCs and speakers" may seem to be the same entity, it is important to remember that rap is a performance art and "a blend of fact and fantasy, narrative and drama expressed in storytelling."[145] Rap narratives can also be understood in scientific terms, with lyrics detailing "vivid and accurate descriptions of urban lives," sometimes engaging "in the same practices revered among biologists" when conducting groundbreaking research.[146] Emdin compares these practices to Kohler's analysis of "biologists who cross the lab-field border."[147] Narrative is also connected to fashion. Keyes notes rap's early fashions, with the majority of rappers wearing street clothes such as "high top tennis shoes, black leather jackets, pre-washed blue jeans, spiked wrist bands, bandannas, pierced-ear ring(s), and gloves with cut-out fingertips."[148]

Poetry is also integral to rap storytelling. Adam Bradley writes, "Rap is poetry, but its popularity relies in part on people not recognizing it as such."[149] By looking at flow, rhyme, and wordplay, Cobb is able to highlight rap storytelling as an innovation. With flow, the goal is to be similar to fluid or liquid. He explains, "Water and blood flow, liquids take the shape of their vessels—in this case, the vessel is the particular beat composition that the MC is rhyming to."[150] Rhyming in rap is built off of rhyming in poetry and "consists of the repetition of the last stressed vowel sound and all the sounds following that vowel sound."[151] Bradley explains rhyming works with expectations and novelty as "all rhyme relies on the innate human impulse to identify patterns and to anticipate what will follow."[152] Another important concept is wordplay, which describes "the array of techniques MCs have developed over the years to do things with words." This can range from "common techniques like metaphors and similes to more obscure techniques" and can involve "transferring, exchanging, and transforming meaning from one word to another."[153]

Developing Local Rap Styles and Genres

Regional and local rap styles emerged over time, and rap's audience diversified. Rap developed from Bronx clubs to "small labels in Harlem and New Jersey," and began growing a more diverse audience and new West Coast artists and groups such as 2Pac, Ice Cube, and N.W.A.[154] While explanations for this diffusion of rap are varied, one reason given is that many of the newly emerging sites of rap had similar social environments as earlier sites. Toop's *Rap Attack 2* warns of the palpable intensity in many American cities, advising,

> There are places—Southcentral Los Angeles, Miami's Overtown, Chicago's Cabrini Green, north Philadelphia, southeast Washington D.C., whole areas of New York City and Detroit—where you could touch this intensity but if you had the choice you would walk away. Those unable to walk away, the endangered species, are not listening to New Age music to calm themselves down; they are listening to Ice Cube and Public Enemy.[155]

There are a few key observations about this quote. First, it proves to be an accurate prediction of how the music would diffuse, accurately naming future cities where rap would take hold. Second, while Toop mentions "whole areas" of some cities as "intense," his analysis also highlights sections, sides, and neighborhoods as "intense." This neighborhood level of detail connects to the concept of internal colonization and is something that academic scholars are just beginning to better understand and analyze. Toop's quote is from 1994. Wilkins's *Welcome 2 Houston* was published in 2023 and is really one of the first thorough analyses to cover rap scenes at a neighborhood level.[156] It took almost thirty years to return to the level of detail suggested by Toop's analysis. The neighborhood (or even local) level is important for understanding the new rap styles that emerge as well.

New rap styles contribute to changes in rap as a genre. As Holt shows, "genre is a fundamental structuring force in musical life." Among other things, it helps influence how we "think comparatively about music."[157] Areas such as "emergence and basic operations," "networks and collectives," and conventions such as "codes, values, and practices" are important elements in genre development.[158] Lena and Peterson examine four types of genre formations: avant-garde, scene-based, industry-based, and traditionalist. Avant-garde are very small and insular. Scene-based are locational and include arts, fans, and record labels. Industry-based is when the "primary organizational form is the industrial corporation."[159] Finally, the traditionalist formation works to "preserve a genre's musical heritage and inculcate the rising generation of devotees in the performance techniques, history, and rituals of the genre."[160]

Klement and Strambach study genre emergence and diversification of general music scenes.[161] They find "city-related tags (e.g., memphis rap, seattle, south london) used by more than 1000 users" in their sample.[162] Klement and Strambach find 118 new genres in their database search between 1970 and 2009, and this is accounted in their outstanding "Table 1. New music genres by the first year of appearance in the database."[163] From 1970 to 1974, there were fifteen new genres, with none related to rap. From 1975 to 1980, there were thirty-two new genres, with none related to rap. From 1980 to 1984, there were twenty-three new genres including gangsta rap and West Coast rap. From 1985 to 1989, there were twenty-six new genres including Dirty South, East Coast rap, G-funk, jazz hop, Memphis rap, rapcore, Southern rap, underground (Hip Hop), and underground rap. From 1990 to 1994, 1995 to 1999, and 2000 to 2004, they found a total of nineteen new genres. None of these genres were related to rap. Then, from 2005 to 2009, they found three new genres, with trap music being related to rap. This gives clues to the diversification of rap's creators and audience. The main diversification of new rap styles (or genres) seems to have occurred between 1980 and 1989, with the next new rap genre not arising until the period between 2005 and 2009. This means that the creation of regional and local rap styles began to occur fairly soon after the birth of commercial rap. Later, there were other developments such as chopper flow and triplicate flow. Recently, among the newer styles such as trap, mumble rap, and cloud rap, triplet flow became a prominently emphasized form.[164] Mumble rap "rose to prominence" in 2010 and "was more about an overall vibe than digestible lyrics."[165]

Connectivity of Local Scenes

Rap has been deeply tied to Black music-making, and early studies of rap observed the Black musician as a provider of a "kind of standard" in the Black community, and since the music preserves Africanist tradition and "speaks to the uniqueness of black, cultural sensibility, it is only logical for musicians to be elevated to the position of cultural heroes."[166] Capitalism helps spread rap from the local scene to global audiences, as Adam Bradley contends: "Thanks to the engines of global commerce, rap is now the most widely disseminated poetry in the history of the world."[167] Yet, as Perry shows, although rap is "disseminated through record companies and radio stations far more than through local ventures," it still "maintains a space of intellectual communication existing beyond the institutions of production and transmission."[168]

Rapping in the US started as a way to link songs through speech, as Barone shows: "Rap started as live 'spice' to DJ performances but acquired prominence; by the late 1970s, it had become the core musical element in hip-hop."[169] Rap then began to connect Hip Hop scenes, and this connectivity is apparent from the earliest NYC scenes well into the beginnings of Philadelphia, New Jersey, Boston, and LA scenes. Later, additional scenes in the West, the South, and the Midwest become substantial sites of US rap. Dimitriadis shows how scenes in the South have been "reclaiming" Hip Hop and returning it "to its roots in live, social interaction," how this music is "often circulated by way of self-produced mixtapes," and thus "operating outside of the dominant commodity forms."[170] Essentially, the South has created alternative models for reclaiming Hip Hop and making a profit from it.[171] Some scenes in the South faced early and continued challenges to its music's authenticity, similar to scenes in the West and the Northeast during their respective emergences. Historically, each scene beyond South Bronx faced some direct challenge around authenticity to Hip Hop. Regina Bradley contends that certain "topophobias" have developed in rap. Toward the South, she argues, "The topophobia … was not a reaction to the music, but an anxiety about the concept of a place where the music originated" and "the lack of familiarity or blatant refusal to update" the South's "creative role in Hip Hop."[172] Arguably, a similar "topophobia" grew in regard to the earliest West Coast records, especially those created outside of the LA region. Yet, it is now clear that rappers in the East, West, South, and Midwest were facing similar social conditions, and rap was seen as a way of transforming these conditions.

Conclusion

This chapter explored rap's evolutionary growth on twenty-five US rap scenes. The chapter analyzed the origins, foundation, musical and narrative parts of rap, the development of local rap styles and genres, and the connectivity of local scenes.

6

Technology

Introduction

Philadelphia rapper Bahamadia's "Spontaneity" (Figure 8) is a perfect introduction to the use of technology in rap:

The monstrous bass beneath my pace be like Morse Code / Slash, beep, slash, beep, scanners / Zero in to the system in your jeeps.[1]

Bahamadia's mentioning of bass, Morse Code, and scanners (as she voices repeated and patterned "slash" and "beep" sounds in the background) explains how her music is designed to fit into the listener's jeep (with the bass heavy car audio system). Bahamadia draws on influences such as Lady B, Salt-N-Pepa, and Queen Latifah. Iandoli describes Bahamadia's voice as "gruff yet slick," helping create "her own lane" on the Philadelphia scene.[2] Bahamadia also clearly uses technology as a theme in the lyrics above, and DJ and producer uses of technology are major factors for the growth of local rap scenes. As discussed in the Introduction to *American Rap Scenes*, technology plays a key role in helping shape rap as a commercial product—both in the form of live shows and in the form of physical and digital media.

DJs create new sounds through manipulation, and producers create instrumental beats by transforming raw sounds and samples. A DJ's core role is usually in the manipulation of two spinning discs or sound sources into a new mix—sometimes blending the songs together into a single mix and sometimes using the equipment to seamlessly transition from one song to another. Other DJs, specialists known as turntablists, focus on scratching, beat juggling, and other techniques. Traditionally, DJs have used vinyl records, CDs, or digital files (such as .mp3, .mp4, .wav, or .aiff) as primary audio sources. Song selection and crowd control are also important, as Perry adds that a DJ responds to a crowd and its "styles, professions, ages, social economic class, and ethnicities" to figure out what will make the crowd dance.[3] Or, as Harris and colleagues write, DJs manipulate "time and space to find the best rhythm that many people can share communally."[4]

Producers use samples, live instruments, and electronic equipment to turn raw sounds into a background instrumental (or beat) to which rappers later rhyme over. As Hip Hop's "original instrument," the turntable has driven rap production for years.[5] The Technics SL-1200 turntable and its variations link the DJ and production worlds.

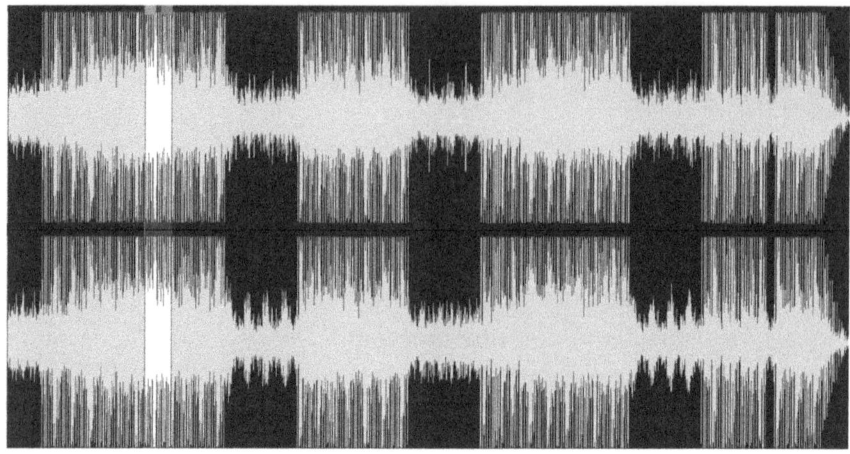

Figure 8 Bahamadia "Spontaneity" Akai WAV snapshot with quoted material highlighted.

Rap production and sampling exist between two interrelated forms of media and instruments—analog and digital. Music production console (MPC) technology has been fundamental to the development of rap since the golden age. Changes in MPC, computing, and other technology led to changes in techniques, sounds, styles, and subgenres.[6] MPC and other samplers also led to changes in digital sampling, which Katz explains as "a type of computer synthesis in which sound is rendered into data, data that in turn comprise instructions for reconstructing that sound."[7] The clear advantage is that once sound is digitized into data, it "can be manipulated in a variety of ways down to the smallest details."[8] Perry adds, "An excellent producer puts together a multilayered web of sounds using rhythms, beats, and noise."[9] Bell writes that the "concept of using the studio as a musical instrument" is about "samples in synthesis," and that "what was first done with turntables, and second with samplers, is now done with laptops, tablets, and smart phones."[10] Perone points to further changes after 2020 and COVID-19 policy:

> The recent lockdowns, stay-at-home orders, and so on, associated with the COVID-19 pandemic, have also helped to expose more of us around the world to some technologies and music-sharing and music-collaboration applications that, although some may have been around for several years, suddenly became commonplace in the year 2020.[11]

With producer technology, rap scenes begin to extend beyond commercial studios, clubs, and radio stations and into bedroom studios. Technology has played a part in both live and studio performances by helping change what is possible to perform live or capture in the studio.

Overall, technology helps build local rap scenes (through local innovations and through local creators applying innovations developed elsewhere to their local scenes). Technology helps create connections between local scenes, styles, and sounds (through the contributions and relocations of DJ and producers). Technology also helps create scenes beyond a local or regional focus (such as scenes with more domestic, international, or even virtual reaches). However, the relationship of technology with local scenes differs slightly from the types of relationships explored in the previous chapters (Geography, Migration, Movement, and Music). The previous factors are more attached to place: Geography is based on local setting; Migration is based on human movement to and from locations; Movement is based on political activity in a location; and Music is based on rap's development on a locale. Thus, the Technology chapter departs slightly from the ultra-geographic focus of prior chapters. Ultimately, technology is explored as a tool in the development and dissemination of rap and is considered to work in both local and translocal ways. Meanwhile, changes in technology (and its uses) are explored as driving forces to the changes in rap's style and sound development.

This chapter explores the development of production styles on US rap scenes, discussing specific producers, their styles and technological innovations, and their relationship to other local, regional, domestic, and international rap scenes. The chapter also focuses on technological development related to DJing and production, DIY, manufacturing and distribution, and Music 3.0.

Development of Production Styles on Local US Rap Scenes

East Coast

East Coast sites such as South Bronx, Manhattan, Queens, Long Island, Philadelphia, and others played a large role in early rap production. These scenes had some of the earliest DJs who then led rap's development into more advanced turntable and sampling techniques, as well as rap's first radio shows and airplay. In short, these early DJs turned into some of the first rap producers. Some studio bands and record executives were also integral to rap's early production history. Early South Bronx DJs dealt with a tension between postindustrial decay and rising technology, according to Rose. The decay was led by government greed to "reclaim and rebuild downtown business and tourist zones with municipal and federal subsidies," and this "exacerbated the already widening gap between classes and races."[12] Robert Moses's expressway construction helped create a trend of housing vacancies. The Bronx homeowners who committed arson to collect insurance payouts also increased vacancies. On July 14, 1977, there was a power outage that "blacked out New York, and hundreds of stores were looted and vandalized."[13] Hager claims that "almost immediately" there were "reports of looting, arson, and robbery, most of which came from the ghetto areas of Bedford-Stuyvesant, Brownsville, Harlem, and the South Bronx" and that there were three thousand arrests in twenty-four hours.[14] Abrams explains, "While most sought food and domestic necessities, some trained their attention on electronics stores, breaking down doors and snatching equipment."[15]

Toop claims that prior to 1979, Hip Hop was "transmitted via cassette tapes" with Grandmaster Flash's tapes "reputed to have sold … for a dollar per minute of tape."[16] Perkins calls this early distribution of rap via audio cassette tape "the most democratic of technologies."[17] Flash's innovations are legendary, as Toop also documents his experimentation around an electrical "double throw switch," with Flash using crazy glue to attach the switch to a mixer, amplifier, and headphone and jumping for joy when his invention worked.[18] Another Bronx invention occurred when Grand Wizzard Theodore's mom knocked on his door to complain about the noise coming from his room when he was DJing, and "not wanting to lose his place in the song," he pulled the record back and discovered scratching.[19] Ewoodzie's study of the Bronx from 1975 to 1979 provides a closer look at the change from the DJ to the MC as the lead figure in rap performance.[20] Rose also gives particular attention to the early transformation of "commodities" into cultural expression.[21] She reads the names of early participants as a "form of reinvention and self-definition"—while DJ names "fuse technology with mastery and style," rapper names "suggest street smarts, coolness, power, and supremacy."[22] In addition, crews began to "claim turf and gain local status by developing new styles."[23] Said sees beatmaking as a sort of reconstruction, arguing that "producers rebuilt South Bronx after the 'South Bronx Disaster'" of the 1960s and 1970s (referring to the social conditions).[24] Many Bronx DJs and producers became integral to other scenes. For example, The 45 King is also known for producing New Jersey rapper Queen Latifah's music.

Manhattan's rap producers are also linked to other scenes. The Heatmakerz were originally from Kingston, Jamaica, before moving to NYC. Many artists, such as Just Blaze, are also associated with the nearby New Jersey scene. 88-Keys is named for his skill on the Ensoniq ASR-10 keyboard. By the end of the 1980s, Paul C. had developed production styles and techniques that predated Detroit legend J Dilla's styles. However, Paul C. was killed in 1989 at the age of twenty-four. Queens emerged as a crucial East Coast and NYC center of rap production in the 1980s. Queens native Marley Marl is known as the first rap producer to sample records. He accidently discovered rap sampling during a session for Captain Rock's "Cosmic Blast" at Unique Studios in NYC, when a snare drum went through as a sample, instead of the voice that he was trying to sample.[25] Marley Marl found that he could create new drum sounds from old records.[26] Abrams details a story of Brooklyn-rapper Masta Ace winning a prize for recording time with Marley Marl, being given a studio phone number to schedule the recording session, and constantly calling the studio phone number to schedule the promised session. The studio doubled as Marley Marl's sister's apartment. Apparently, Masta Ace called so many times, that Marley Marl's sister felt bad for him and intervened by asking Marley Marl to respond to Masta Ace's many calls.[27]

Marley Marl also impacted rap's move to radio. Klaess shows how Mr. Magic and Marley Marl combined studio and radio expertise to realize "new combinations of recorded sound."[28] Their radio show helped define rap's sound during a critical moment in its development and "their efforts, selecting, mixing, and presenting rap music helped a generation of listeners hear new possibilities for recorded sound."[29] During the time, and certainly thereafter, DJs began using radio to develop new approaches to beat production; shortly after, Marley Marl, Hank Shocklee, and others used radio as a platform to try new ideas.[30] Klaess's study of the era shows the radio station as a "sonic laboratory" in which listeners could hear the evolution of rap in real time, "changing imperceptibly but indelibly week to week."[31] The radio was a place where one could "tinker" and "invent," but the ability to perform the same maneuvers in front of crowds during live performances was still vital. Marley Marl's contemporaries Chuck D and DJ Red Alert, for example, recorded live performances outside of the radio studio and then brought the tapes to be prepared for broadcast (in the early 1980s).[32] Queens, Long Island, and NYC scenes are also linked through Marley Marl and DJ Red Alert. Also from Queens, Larry Smith and Salaam Remi have been known for their roots in other NYC and New Jersey scenes, respectively. Long Island's Doctor Dré was the Beastie Boys' DJ and taught Rick Rubin how to program a Roland TR-808 drum machine. Mathematics has been associated with Staten Island's Wu-Tang Clan. Ty Fyffe has LA and Detroit connections.

Brooklyn's DJ tradition is rich and starts as early as 1959. In 1959, Big John Ashby "becomes a mobile DJ who plays records at basement parties"; in 1969, "Grandmaster Flowers opens for James Brown in South Bronx's Yankee Stadium"; and in 1971, "Brooklyn DJ Ras Maboya receives an invitation to perform in London."[33] Brooklyn producer Oddisee is also associated with the DMV scene. In Staten Island, the business "genius of RZA," according to Cobb, "was in conceiving of a group that was *intended* to split up."[34] The Wu-Tang Clan (and its nine members, forty or so affiliated solo artists, and twelve affiliated groups) has been a major influence on global rap. The nine Wu-Tang Clan members also help shape rap in significant ways as solo artists. In 2019, Staten Island's Park Hill neighborhood was renamed "Wu-Tang Clan District" in honor of the group's legacy and influence. Meanwhile, RZA's production legacy is comparable to producers such as Diamond D (South Bronx), Dr. Dre (LA), J Dilla (Detroit), Pharrell Williams (Virginia Beach), and Timbaland (Norfolk). With NYC production, some producers are also considered NYC-located, which can also include the Bronx, Brooklyn, Harlem, Queens, or Staten Island.

Long Island, in addition, greatly influences NYC and East Coast rap production. Coleman explains that Long Island was not only "close enough to have contact" with Hip Hop at its beginnings but also "far enough away from the urban congestion and stress."[35] This geographic position has been discussed as a direct factor on local musical content. De La Soul was located twenty miles east of Manhattan, and other groups have remarked on how they were able to practice their musical skill in basements. This analysis points to additional space in Long Island homes (e.g., basements, backyards, additional rooms) as a factor in the development of rap and production on the scene. Long Island youth practicing in basement and bedroom studios may have led to some of the incredible advances in rhyme patterns, flows, and musical production techniques. Long Island youth played a large role in creating rap's second-generation sound. Barone notes that Public Enemy transformed Hip Hop "into multimedia warfare" and, along with Eric B & Rakim and De La Soul, would come to "represent the musical soul of late 1980s East Coast hip-hop."[36] De La Soul's music was largely produced by Prince Paul, a formative figure in the sampling era.

Philadelphia's DJ and production also contributed to the early development of the East Coast. Philadelphia DJs invented new styles of battling, new turntable layouts, and new recording techniques. Women DJs, producers, and MCs were also featured earlier and more substantially than many other scenes. There are some additional cross-scene connections. DJ Royal Rocker connected Philadelphia and Camden. Jahlil Beats has also been associated with the NYC scene. Diplo has also been associated with the Florida scene. Members of the group OuterSpace are of Puerto Rican descent. Other East Coast sites also developed production influence. In Newark, Afrika Islam's radio show on WHBI was a big part of Hip Hop's growth. Additionally, George Clinton has origins in Newark, has been sampled often in rap songs, and has been listed as a producer on rap songs—all of which show the funk musician's influence on rap production.

Boston's scene was one of the first scenes outside of the NYC and Philadelphia area to produce rap. Boston was integral in radio and print dissemination of rap culture, through college radio and *The Source* magazine, respectively. In the 1980s and early 1990s, there were challenges to rap being heard above the city's thriving rock music scene (e.g., Aerosmith, The Cars, and Pixies) and its popular R&B scene (e.g., New Edition and Bel Biv DeVoe). Boston producers with links to other scenes include Statik Selektah with NYC, Bay Area, and New Orleans production. Other artists such as Sage Francis and Edan have developed Boston followings as well as followings in their origin scenes of Providence, RI, and DMV, respectively.

West Coast and Northwest

West Coast rap production has been led by scenes such as LA, the San Francisco Bay Area, Seattle, and Portland. Some of the styles developed in LA and Compton occurred early on the West Coast and became major influences on other regional scenes. Regarding the LA scene, Cross observes,

> In LA rhymin' developed quickly in school yards, on buses and in lunch rooms with young MCs (masters of ceremonies) battling each other (challenging each other to rhyme better). Early battles in LA consisted of MCs rhyming over Sugarhill/Enjoy or Uni instrumental tracks in the same meter as the rhymers whose tracks they were, but changing the words in ways that described local situations or altered the meaning of the original in humorous ways—in much the same way as Toddy Tee and Mixmaster Spade's tapes were constructed.[37]

Scholars have questioned if the East Coast influence on LA's rap development has been overstated. Viator maintains the "Bronx West story" or the concept that "the burst of B-boy activity in Los Angeles that caught the attention of artists, writers, and entrepreneurs of the period was assessed as a derivative novelty, explained simply by the westward dissemination of New York ideas."[38] Viator shows that in LA, "communal crews worked together to pool their resources to book event spaces, hire security, recruit talent, purchase new records, and promote dances."[39] The early LA scene developed as "mobile DJ sound systems emerged as cultural trailblazers, laying the groundwork for a thriving independent music recording industry and eventually the ascendancy of West Coast rap." Viator mentioned that young Black mobile DJs and entrepreneurs (including people such as Mixmaster Spade, Lonzo, Dr. Dre, and Eazy-E) "were the architects of a do-it-yourself dance culture based not on traditional, brick-and-mortar nightclubs or on the patronage of label A&Rs and white bohemians."[40] These mostly Black-owned and Black-run "entertainment businesses relied instead upon borrowed and rented spaces that dotted the urban-suburban landscape of Los Angeles."[41] Local DJs and producers also sold dubbed cassette tapes, "which ultimately netted them more cash than did their modest mobile events" and helped them "earn the local stardom they sought."[42] The Macola Record Company also began to provide "affordable access to vinyl pressing machinery."[43]

According to Guerra and Alberto, this local development of rap occurred alongside "the closure of most factories in the automobile, rubber, steel and aircraft industry," which were a "steady source of jobs" for Black men in South LA.[44] Overall, this caused changes in the locale, as "economic restructuring and deindustrialization increased suburban capital flight and the systemic pauperization of the inner city."[45] Quinn shows that the gangster rap style from LA "finally broke nationally in 1989, establishing a new localized industrial infrastructure and rap subgenre."[46] Quinn posits technology at the center of a "coalescing" of the Compton, South Central, and Long Beach scenes and credits "the radio station, clubs, and famed swap meet, the extraordinary creative talents of Dr. Dre and Ice Cube, the proximity of entertainment industry apparatus, the availability of entrepreneurial capital, along with the extreme lived experiences associated with gang and drug culture" as major factors on LA's rap development.[47]

As the US entertainment capital, LA connects to many other scenes, and producers from other locations relocate to be closer to the work opportunities available in LA. There are producers with multiple scene connections, such as producer E-Swift (Columbus, GA, and raised in Toledo, OH). There are multiple Houston links, such as Crazy Toones and WC. D.O.C. is originally from Dallas. Some producers were born on the East Coast or traveled through multiple cities to LA. DJ Muggs moved to LA at the age of fourteen. Producer Johnny "J" is originally from Ciudad Juárez, Mexico. Geographically, LA's scene is expansive, including producers located in Oxnard, Fontana, and Bakersfield. Similar to the NYC scene, some LA producers are simply associated with the California scene, which might include LA, the Bay Area, San Jose, San Diego, or anywhere in between.

The San Francisco Bay is another area where rap production developed fairly early on the West Coast. Known as the "Silicon Valley," the area has been at the center of technology in the US since at least the 1960s. This technological innovation has been important to rap on the scene. Then, as Chang argues, Bay Area college campuses became the "hub of the local underground" with grassroots groups consolidating local scenes.[48] In the mid-1980s, four Bay Area radio stations (KPOO, KZSU, KUSF, and KALX) were transformed because KMEL "desperately needed street credibility" and recruited locally established DJs around 1988. The media conglomeration helped local DJs launch the careers of 2Pac, MC Hammer,

Digital Underground, Too $hort, and Eazy-E, and the Bay Area became the number two rap market in the country. In 1992, there was a duel between KMEL and emerging newcomer KYLD; the latter was focused on breaking new records on DJ mixshows.[49] Although rapping in Richmond, CA, 2Pac's early production included Queens producers Stretch and Live Squad. Vallejo, CA's Coolio Da Unda Dogg, and Droop-E. are also legendary producers on the scene. Chief Xcel's origins are in Sacramento, with additional work in the Bay Area and LA. Producers have also emerged from Fairfield and Santa Rosa. Some San Francisco producers also have Atlanta, NYC, or New Orleans connections and roots.

Seattle is another early contributor to West Coast style formation. Seattle's development of digital technologies, especially around personal computing, software, sound design, and car audio, has been central in shaping Seattle's sound and reputation. Some of the scene's early independent producers are featured in Schloss's *Making Beats*.[50] Schloss focuses on rap producers and the technologies of beatmaking (such as MPCs).[51] Many of Schloss's participants were producers from the Seattle area ("B-Mello, Jake One, King Otto, Kylea, Mr. Supreme Negus I, Samson S., Strath Shepard, Specs, DJ Top Spin, Vitamin D, and Wordsayer").[52] It is clear from Schloss's interviews and overall account just how advanced rap production had gotten in Seattle by the 1990s.[53] With regard to local producers and migration, Onry Ozzborn and Sleep, from Seattle and Portland, respectively, are linked to New Mexico.

Midwest and North

In the Midwest and North, Chicago, St. Louis, Minneapolis, and Detroit stand out as major contributors to new rap styles. Chicago's scene has a long history of underground rap production, yet drill styles have grown into one of the most well-known Chicago specializations. Regarding Chicago drill music and drillers, Stuart asks, "How do people with less economic and social capital build micro-celebrity? How do they create and cultivate a self-brand that is compelling enough to stand out in the attention economy?"[54] Kanye West (Chicago's most well-known producer) has also been associated with Atlanta (through birth), New Jersey and NYC (during his move to the Jersey City area and tremendous production output there), and LA. This is in addition to the other US and global scenes his production and rapping have impacted. Other Midwest and North scenes have also influenced rap production. St. Louis led developments into Hip Hop radio and features producers who have influenced rap overall (The Trak Starz) and more recent producers such as Metro Boomin and Zado. Meanwhile, in Minneapolis, Travis "Travitron" Lee is a scene forerunner, moving from "from Brooklyn to Minneapolis to attend the University of Minnesota."[55] Rhymesayers Entertainment has been a major force on the scene. Micranots, started in Minneapolis, relocated to Atlanta in 1994. In Detroit, early techno and funk sounds have been major influences on rap production. Detroit producers are also connected to other scenes. Spyder D is originally from NYC. Athletic Mic League (Ann Arbor artists) are also associated with Detroit. Apollo Brown is from the nearby Grand Rapids scene. In terms of migration, Luis Resto is of Puerto Rican descent. Many producers from Detroit have influenced other scenes, such as J Dilla and Black Milk.

South and Contested Islands

The South's regional production has been led by the Houston, New Orleans, Memphis, Atlanta, and Miami scenes. Other scenes in Hampton, DC, and Baltimore also greatly influence rap production. It is important to note that regional production in the West and South were the first major breaks from NYC production. Barone examines regional sound innovation and development, finding that the West Coast "produced sonic innovation, particularly visible by the turn of the decade." Dr. Dre also "invented g-funk," a "new style of beats based on mellow samples from funk bands such as Parliament and Funkadelic."[56] At the end of the 1990s, the South was in a position to make an impact on the US market, "as gangsta rap and the West Coast-East Coast confrontation had lost momentum, allowing for the emergence of a diverse array of rap subgenres that had been spawning underground during the decade."[57] Some of these regional styles were in the South, with "the appearance of a third main element in the country's hip-hop map" and "the styles and cluster of scenes known as Dirty South" featured several signature musical sound innovations including bounce, bass, and chopped and screwed.[58]

Houston artists and executives such as DJ Screw, J. Prince, and Tony Draper led the entrepreneurial nature of Houston rap. DJ Screw, according to Long, "paved the way for Houston Hip Hop entrepreneurs to make a significant living within the neighborhoods that had been systematically oppressed without having to fit into and create work and success within the mainstream, White-dominated culture."[59] Thus, Long shows, "Screw's contribution, via rap music, gave Houstonians a style that they could capitalize on, and everyone in the city who followed Hip Hop understood."[60] Houston production grew to be incredibly unique, as described by a University of Houston Libraries DJ Screw photography and memorabilia collection:

> By the early nineties, he had begun slowing down the music on his tapes to a hypnotic crawl and emphasizing certain words and phrases by repeating them manually. Screw sold these "chopped and screwed" mixtapes directly to eager fans. Friends and local rappers began ordering personal tapes from Screw, and he invited the rappers to freestyle, or improvise, over beats at the beginning and end of the tapes. Over time, the rappers themselves developed followings and many released successful independent solo albums.[61]

This DJ Screw archive features photos, rap lyric pages, setlists for mixtapes, and flyers. Houston's rap is interconnected with other scenes in the South, such as other scenes in Texas and scenes in New Orleans and Atlanta. Meanwhile, Rap-a-Lot Records (owned by J. Prince and Cliff Blodget) also had releases in the West (such as the Bay Area). Compared to Houston rap, New Orleans rap features much faster sounds. 10th Ward Buck announces, "Everybody else's music is slow. Our BPMs in bounce go from 90 to 110, and it's getting faster."[62] 10th Ward Buck also notes that current rap is at 50 or 60 BPM "and they slow it down when they rap."[63] Master P's business acumen is also important to New Orleans rap. He bargained for his No Limit Records to retain "complete ownership of their master recordings and 85 percent of their record sales, paying Priority Records 15 percent for pressing and distributing records."[64]

With regard to Memphis, Coughlan-Allen notes a relationship between low-fi recordings, "rip tapes," and archived Memphis raps in online virtual spaces.[65] Coughlan-Allen finds "digitized Memphis rap cassette recordings or *tape rips* are now publicly available for a global audience to experience and interpret" and can be seen as "time capsules carrying an image of Memphis."[66] Coughlan-Allen shows these lo-fi recordings can "offer an uncanny, distorted, and noisy version of events," and in the case of Memphis rap, some of these recordings featured lo-fi production due to the samples used, DIY techniques, and equipment and knowledge that sometimes ran counter to industry standards.[67] The soundscape was often created using "digital rhythm composers such as the BOSS DR660 ... and the BOSS DR-5," samples from "Stax soul, funk, and horror film soundtracks," and "hooks sampled from other Memphis rap tapes."[68] These samples (sometimes drawn from VHS or cassette tapes) were paired with equipment that was more readily accessible than industry standard and with recording techniques that were more about survival than best practices.

This created a "Memphis" sound that could result in a "tape hiss" or with a magnetic tape sound. Furthermore, these tapes were often bootlegged (making a copy of a copy) before being transferred to online websites and forums. During these transfer processes—especially from analog tapes to digital files—it became unclear "which perfections were part of the original and which have been introduced" during the transfer process.[69] Coughlan-Allen's ultimate "aim is to demonstrate and question how areas of online discourse in the Memphis rap mediascape might curate the construction of an imagined Memphis."[70] This inquiry connects Memphis rap technology, the low-fi sound, and the move from a local scene specialization to a worldwide (and sometimes virtual) audience.[71]

In Atlanta, Balaji claims that Gorilla Zoe and other rappers must work to get past "critical gatekeepers before they are viewed as legitimate for wider consumption" and that these gatekeepers include "media managers, street teams, strip club DJs, and local radio hosts/program directors."[72] Also in Atlanta, Lex Luger has a Suffolk, VA, connection. El-P (from NYC) produced for Killer Mike and produced for his duo with Killer Mike (Run the Jewels)—creating a new type of Atlanta sound. Don Cannon is originally from Philadelphia. Young Nudy is of Jamaican descent. In Miami, Infamous is a DJ titleholder in many events. There are DJs and producers from Orlando that influence the Miami scene (such as DJ Magic Mike and Kane Beatz). Mr. Mixx had roots in Santa Ana, CA, prior to the Miami scene. Additionally, pirate radio has been used as a form of resistance in Miami. This entails the use of technology to independently broadcast music on unauthorized airwaves.

Located in the US Mid-Atlantic region, Virginia Beach (and the nearby area) ushered in phenomenal advancements in rap production, and then some producers from the scene begin to link with other popular musics. Teddy Riley moved his studio to the scene, and Devante Swing ran a studio in Rochester, NY, with some key artists from the Virginia Beach area as the features.[73] Teddy Riley, brought to the scene by Greekfest in 1988, decided to move his studio to Virginia Beach. "Future Records Recording Studio" then "became a haven for up and coming rappers and producers," and Timbaland, Pharrell, Chad Hugo, and The Clipse have all credited their time in the studio as essential to their development.[74] Devante Swing's plan to record in a Rochester studio called the "Bassment" was important in creating production styles and sounds that would grow into the Virginia Beach standard. Jodeci, 702, Ginuwine, SWV, and Tweet (who is from Rochester) featured such production. Devante Swing's plan was to create a studio experience around a dozen feature artists, forming an "aspiring-artist colony."[75] This plan, while different in background and scope, seems to carry a vision of collective and individual success similar to RZA's five-year plan in Staten Island. The Devante Swing plan proved to be wildly successful. Timbaland and Missy Elliot assisted in production for Aaliyah and Tweet. Later, Timbaland helped with production for Nelly Furtado and Justin Timberlake. Thus, Teddy Riley and Devante Swing seem important in the training of Timbaland.

Pharrell and The Neptunes also became large producers from the Virginia Beach area. Nottz, Bink, and Timbaland, all from Norfolk, created signature sounds. Missy Elliot is from nearby Portsmouth. Danjahandz is also from Virginia Beach. Over time, Timbaland worked in multiple avenues of rap—as a DJ, producer, group member, and rapper. There was even a group led by Timbaland called "Surround by Idiots," that featured Pharrell and Magoo. Additionally, many Virginia Beach area producers have impacted many different styles of music—from rap styles to other popular music styles—at national and global levels. Additionally, the scene features some of the first widely successful producer-rappers and producer-rapper-fashion icons. Timbaland and Missy Elliot are among some of the first producer-rappers. Missy Elliot and Pharrell have key work related to the fashion industry. Timbaland has also greatly influenced beatmaking's aesthetic culture.

DC is also located in the US Mid-Atlantic region, and its go-go music has been described as hard to transfer to media formats such as vinyl, CD, and tape because of the live instruments and venue types, drumming styles, and types of crowd participation. Elements of go-go can be heard in some music from Baltimore as well. On "Contested Islands" such as Hawaii, one of the key questions about the development of rap is related to access to technology, music, and communication systems. In Honolulu, the cost and availability of products is different than on the mainland. The scene's production also grows with the spread of high-speed internet. In Puerto Rico and the USVI, there has been travel and influence among producers on scene. The San Juan scene has been especially influential in the rise of *reggaeton* styles. Tony Touch influences music on the Puerto Rico and Brooklyn scenes. Verse Simmonds is an LA producer but is originally from Puerto Rico, the Virgin Islands, and Fort Lauderdale.

Themes in Local Rap Technology

Technologies of Rap Production

DJing and Manipulation of Source Material

Since the late 1970s, a typical, professional DJ system has often included some variation of two turntables, a mixer with a crossfader, a set of headphones, a set of speakers, and a microphone. The two turntables act as control devices, controlling the playback location of multimedia content and its playback speed ("pitch"). The mixer (and, in particular, the crossfader component at the bottom center of the mixer) has two main functions. First, the mixer's crossfader is used select the multimedia content that will be output to the main speakers (to the audience). Second, the mixer is also used for DJs to "cue" music. With cueing, DJs use headphones or monitor speakers to preview possible content to be scratched, blended, or mixed with the multimedia content currently being output to the main speakers. The microphone is often used to introduce multimedia content, make announcements, or for spoken word over audio (i.e., rapping).

DJing often involves controlling real or virtual spinning devices. Origin DJs took "drums and accompanying bass lines of the songs," breakdowns, or breaks of original records and manipulated this content into new loops that people could dance to and rhyme over.[76] Exarchos shows that DJs use "multiple phonographic segments that are then cut, manipulated and juxtaposed."[77] Baker puts it differently: "Instead of listening to the sound of an entire record, DJs decided to clip the seconds of worthwhile sound" by using copies of the "same disc on separate turntables" and moving between the devices in "DJ-orchestrated patterns, creating thereby a worthwhile sound."[78] In the process, DJs have been "manipulating prerecorded music" and manipulating other audio equipment, and this process "has birthed the subcultures of turntablism."[79] DJing also birthed modern rap production. When South Bronx's Grandmaster Flash was inventing the "clock theory" of reading records, he was actually ahead of the "use of drum machines in making rap records."[80] He also foreshadowed the future of visually editing sounds by marking records with a grease pencil or crayon. Over time, DJ culture grew with the "discipline of turntablism" and events such as the DMC World DJ Championships, where DJs from all over the world gathered to battle. Barone explains that "turntablism itself relentlessly changed as new techniques and new technologies (such as digital turntables) emerged."[81] Bass and vinyl are central to this technology too, as Milano writes that by the mid-1980s, "the twelve-inch rap and disco single was proving just how much loud bass could be captured on a vinyl slab."[82]

As a formative work on DJ evolution in the US, Katz makes three vital claims. First, he claims that DJs "*re-created*" the turntable into more than a "playback device."[83] Second, he shows DJs used this creation as a "means for manipulating sound."[84] Third, he shows how DJs saw the turntable as an "instrument of infinite possibilities."[85] Other authors have also analyzed the turntable as a musical instrument. Souvignier traces the "evolution of the turntable" as it grew "from a consumer playback device into a professional musical instrument."[86] The argument here is that "when the turntable became obsolete, the DJ rescued it, and transformed it from a consumer entertainment device into a professional audio tool."[87] The Technics SL-1200, the feature device for Technics, only saw "one update per decade" since 1978.[88] Souvignier centers on turntable anatomy in very detailed and specific ways.[89] Using source interviews from DJs such as the San Francisco Bay Area's Q-Bert and South Bronx's Grand Wizzard Theodore, Souvignier documents the history of DJing in the US—from its earliest forms before Hip Hop, through the invention of Hip Hop DJing, and into new CD deck and production technologies.[90] The key contribution is in recognizing the ways DJs "bend the equipment to their will, altering existing sounds and producing a wide range of new ones."[91]

DJing was influenced by technological change and labor, as Rose shows: "Early Puerto Rican, Afro-Caribbean, and black American hip hop artists transformed obsolete vocational skills from marginal occupations into the raw materials for creativity and resistance."[92] This was part of bigger shifts, as "large-scale restructuring of the workplace and job market has had its effect upon most facets of everyday life. It has placed additional pressures on local, community-based networks of communication, and has whittled down already limited prospects for social mobility."[93] Barone sees the use of DJ technology (and its aims at "flow, layering, disruption, and repetition") as "a symbolic language that reconstructs Black cultures and communities."[94] Yet, when rap initially gained attention in NYC, DJs were quickly threatened with their talents becoming obsolete in the studio and only as background performers at shows. Barone shows that Hip Hop transformed into "a record-driven commodity" and "marginalized the importance of DJs," who were initially less important in studio performances than in live ones.[95] Then, as Hager claims, "when emcee groups realized they were the primary reason why many people were coming to hip hop parties, they demanded more money from their deejays, which led to arguments and eventual breakups."[96]

Meanwhile, as Nava explains, DJs found their role in rap's backbeat—as DJs and producers, who have "made beat-making their primary reason for being—digging in crates for forgotten breaks, excavating buried treasures of sound, looting old LPs, and looking around street corners for the right sonic boom, din, and clamor to characterize life in urban America."[97] Perry adds that Hip Hop "engages in the insertion of local knowledge and culture into production and yet also uses replication" and explains that "it reuses commodities, records on wax, and makes them local and new by putting them into a musical collage via sampling or riffing."[98]

More recently, DJs have moved to equipment that requires a laptop and that is connected to a device used to emulate vinyl (known as digital vinyl systems or DVS), to other emulation equipment, or to controllers that are designed to be both mixers and control devices for two to four virtual turntable "decks." This change in DJ systems is reflected in the 2024 Global DJ Census, which surveyed over fifteen thousand DJs.[99] Although the survey is most likely not a scientific survey (given the respondent pool, commercial sponsors, and raffle prizes given to participants), the census is likely the most thorough survey of current DJs. It is also a global survey of DJs of all formats, which differs from the *American Rap Scenes* focus on technology use in the manipulation and production of US rap. The audience for the survey was "primarily hobby DJs," and the survey was offered to 37,000 students, 150,000 DJs on their "private email list," and the "wider 2.5 million" people who visit their websites and social media.[100] The information was gathered to (1) serve their "students, subscribers, readers and viewers in the year ahead", (2) "share with the DJ industry and the wider DJing world" insight about the practice of DJing and production, and (3) for general information for DJs.[101] There were 40 questions asked, and the questions received between 4,776 and 16,706 respondents. The average number of responses to the questions was 13,642. There were five categories: demographic information, DJ type and experience, DJ setup, musical styles and sources of music, and social media.[102] Majority responses from the survey are noted below as well as their percentages (rounded to the nearest percentage).

In terms of demographic information, the majority of respondents were as follows: between the ages of forty-five and fifty-four (32 percent); male (92 percent); from the US (33 percent); earning an annual income between $25,000 and $50,000 (24 percent); earning a DJ income of 0 percent of their annual income (41 percent); and receiving currency in US dollars (35 percent).[103] In terms of DJ type and experience, the majority of respondents were as follows: DJs for over ten years (54 percent); playing in public regularly (27 percent); bedroom/hobbyist DJs (22 percent); aspiring to be touring DJs (21 percent); not livestreaming DJ sets (49 percent); "streaming from a laptop or computer separate" from their DJ setup (if livestreaming) (46 percent); using Twitch (if livestreaming) (45 percent); "confident, but still learning" (in terms of self-described skill level) (57 percent); not producing their own music (but wanting to do so) (36 percent); and using Ableton Live (if producing their own music) (36 percent).[104]

In terms of DJ setup, the majority of respondents were as follows: using a controller and laptop as a main DJ setup (57 percent); using Pioneer DJ as a "main brand of hardware" (56 percent); owners of other Pioneer DJ equipment (31 percent); using a setup that cost between $1500 and $3000 (26 percent); planning to upgrade in the next twelve months (63 percent); happy with their current setup (as a reason not to upgrade) (50 percent); seeking to upgrade to Pioneer DJ (if looking to upgrade) (53 percent); playing at venues without provided equipment (37 percent); most excited by technological developments in real-time "stem DJing features" (51 percent); envisioning the "Pioneer DJ system (2 x CDJ-3000 players & 1 x DJM-A9 mixer)" as the ideal DJ system if money were not an object (57 percent); using Windows desktop or laptop computers (55 percent); choosing DJ gear based on quality and durability (66 percent); and using Rekordbox (31 percent).[105]

In terms of musical styles and sources of music, the majority of respondents were as follows: DJing mostly "open format" or "multi-genre" (57 percent); DJing mostly house music (when DJing only one genre); DJing house as a secondary or other genre (55 percent); buyers of music from online stores (66 percent); using Beatport as a current or regular download source (62 percent); using a "streaming music service" (74 percent); subscribers of Spotify (66 percent); not subscribers to DJ download pools (69 percent); and subscribers of BPM Supreme (if subscribers of a download pool) (39 percent).[106] In terms of social media, the majority of respondents were as follows: regular users of Instagram (68 percent); using WhatsApp as a favorite "method of communication" (30 percent); and using email as another form of communication method (49 percent).[107] As a whole, this survey shows a skilled hobbyist DJ community mostly based in bedroom and studio environments but with aspirations of playing more live shows, going on tour, and further developing their equipment and sound.

Production and Transformation of Source Material

Rap production is driven by inventions in sampling, and Queens' Marley Marl is the inventor of modern sampling. In the mid-1980s, Marley Marl was in a full radio studio, but Patrin shows producers of the late 1980s and early 1990s began using "more inexpensive home studio options based around equipment like the E-mu SP-1200."[108] Bell recognizes this type of home studio as a new form or musical instrument, showing that Mantronix's *The Album* was recorded in a studio in NYC's Chelsea Hotel, Marley Marl worked out of his sister's Queensbridge apartment, and LL Cool J's "I Need a Beat" was made in Rick Rubin's New York University dorm room.[109] Perry notes that beatboxing was popular before these "expensive drum machines became readily available to the average young person wanting to rhyme."[110] Once affordable, DJs began using machines such as the E-mu Emulator II and the Ensoniq Mirage to apply Marley Marl's sampling techniques, as Exarchos explains:

> The significance of this discovery—and Marl's influence on a genealogy of producers associated with Boom Bap, such as DJ Premier, Pete Rock, Q-Tip, RZA, Prince Paul, DJ Shadow, J Dilla and Madlib—is that it empowered rap producers to transition from "surface manipulators" (users of drum loops or breaks referential to a turntable affordance) to drum "scientists": samplist-programmers who could come up with new patterns altogether, layer multiple drum sounds upon one another and create original rhythms out of minimal sonic segments from the past.[111]

By the late 1980s, parts of rap's production process could be automated using tools such as synthesizers, drum machines, digital audio tapes, and early software programs.

Transformation of samples has also been central to rap production, although some rap production is not dependent on samples. By transforming samples of original source material into a distinctly new instrumental (or beat), rap producers seek to meet a legal threshold of "transforming" original source material enough to be able to "legally" use the material under "fair use." Stim, a leading attorney on transformation, writes that this "relatively new" transformation doctrine is related to the application of one of the four factors of "fair use" and that it "emphasized that the most important aspect of the fair use analysis was whether the purpose and character of the use was 'transformative.'"[112] By transformative, there are two main questions. First: "Has the material taken from the original work been transformed by adding new expression or meaning?"; Second: "Was value added to the original by creating new information, new aesthetics, new insights, and understandings?"[113]

Sampling is often associated with the SP-12 or SP-1200. The SP-12 could sample 1.2 seconds of material and was largely adopted by rap producers in the mid- to late 1980s. Overall, Harkins and Prior claim that "falling costs" of equipment and recording advances paid to producers were factors in the growth of SP-12 use and that unsigned artists also tried to access the new technology by saving "money from part-time jobs," through "gifts and second-hand equipment from family members," or through "credit facilities."[114] Writing about the SP-12 and other equipment, Harkins and Prior explain, "We need to know who had access to these technologies and how affordable they were. The introduction of new sampling products by companies such as E-mu as well as Ensoniq, Akai, and Casio resulted in lower prices."[115] Regarding the early South Bronx scene, Harkins and Prior argue, "It is impossible to know *how many* SP-12s existed in the Bronx at this time," noting research suggesting that "they were scarce" as producers "borrowed them from owners who were well connected and therefore rich in social capital."[116] The SP-1200 could sample 2.5 seconds of a recording, and it was accessible, approachable, and unbreakable enough to become a production staple. Innovations were created on the device, as Harkins and Prior discuss: "Hank Shocklee, of Public Enemy's Bomb Squad, often sampled the sounds of preexisting recordings at the wrong speed. LPs designed to be played at 33 1/3 rpm were played at 45 rpm so that a longer excerpt could be sampled. The pitch of the sampled recording was then shifted downwards afterward."[117] This technique is still regularly used in sampling, although some of the original innovators have retroactively discussed the sound quality degradation caused by its use. The E-mu Emulator is seen as the first pure sampler, as it had the "ability to store, manipulate, and play back any sound" stored on it, and operating the device required no prior musical knowledge or experience.[118] George's account of this device was that "to make it work, you just had to know how to push the buttons."[119] Today, there is a "growing literature" on music production around Akai's "range of MPCs."[120]

The importance of sampler, synthesizer, and production technology lies in the equipment's ability to help democratize the music making process. In fact, Harkins and Prior show that synthesizer creator Robert Moog used "the term democratization when explaining how the price of microprocessor-controlled synthesizers had decreased over the last ten years, were now available in a larger number of retail outlets, and were owned by many more musicians."[121] Exarchos details that later MPCs "enter the historical timeline" and begin "replacing E-mus as preferred weapons" of DJs due to the MPC technology's "unique swing quantization parameter, the higher bit-depth resolution, the touch-sensitive drum pads of the physical interface and the internal mixing functionality."[122] Exarchos also offers tables and figures showing the use of MPC technology alongside the development of rap. One such table offers a "mapping of boom bap stylizations against MPC affordances and limitations."[123] This boom bap aesthetic was "an onomatopoeic celebration of the prominence of sampled drum sounds programmed over sparse and heavily syncopated instrumentation."[124] Specifically, it references the "sound of a loud kick drum ('boom') and hard-hitting snare ('bap') exposed over typically sparse, sample-based instrumental production."[125] Meanwhile, Exarchos also offers figures of timelines and schematic depictions. One figure maps a timeline of Hip Hop eras "against E-mu and Akai products," another example shows the characteristics of "seminal releases" and their subgenres, and another figure offers a "schematic representation of technical characteristics of the MPC range mapped against workflow affordances and sonic signature categorizations."[126] Pelleter adds that the main selling point to Akai hardware has been the "influential design of the 4×4-pad interface," using the Akai MPC 60 as a core example.[127]

During this democratization of sampling technology, makers of products such as the SP-1200 were not particularly happy about its prevalent use in rap production and "eventually discontinued it in 1990."[128] Yet, other companies, such as Akai (with their MPC models), embraced the culture and built products to meet the culture's needs. Much of Schloss's *Making Beats* revolves around the early 1990s, which included MPC technology. Although presenting Seattle as an example, Schloss's analysis helps explain beatmaking culture in general. There are discussions of RZA's use of MPC (and other) technology, sections on radio and other audience elements, and additional contextualization of the ethnography of beatmaking. A key discussion involves sampling ethics, secrecy, and other codes known to beatmakers. Yet, the driving force to this narrative is in the ways local producers have applied MPC and other technologies. Eventually, by the 2000s, beats could be made on computers and even on video game consoles. An example is Sony PlayStation's *Music 2000*, as grime producers used this software, other software, and hardware such as "Fruity Loops, Cubase, Mario Paint, and secondhand PCs" to make music.[129] Exarchos sees the MPC as a digital instrument, noting:

> The latest incarnation of the MPC range (MPCX) seems to be acknowledging the methodological alternatives contemporary producers practice, retaining the interface, operating system and workflow affordances that powered Golden Era aesthetics, while maximizing the potential for recording new music directly into its interface and leveraging interaction with synthesized music forms (exemplified by direct inputs for live instruments, CV outputs for analogue synth control, pre-loaded Trap and EDM sound libraries, and a 'controller' mode for working with a computer).[130]

This certainly brings about changes in techniques. Perone observes that vast developments in synthesizers, digital audio, and MIDI technology in the 1980s and 1990s led to more advanced home studios and more "computer-based multi-track recording" options.[131]

DIY

DIY (do-it-yourself) can be seen as a form of resistance in itself. With DIY, economically, local rap artists started trends toward self-ownership. Forman writes, "By forming self-owned labels and publishing companies and establishing themselves as autonomous corporate entities, forward-thinking rap artists were also able to maintain greater creative control over their production while ensuring increasing returns on their sales."[132] Cross adds that Hip Hop has "simultaneously acted as a continuum to earlier traditions and as a kind of DIY response to new technological possibilities opening up through the advance of microelectronics.[133] With sampling and sequencing technology options increasingly available, production ultimately got less expensive.[134] This created new opportunities for DIY artists, who have been described by den Drijver and Hitters as "musicians who want control over the production, promotion and distribution processes of their music." DIY is typically separate from major label networks, involving an "expression of symbolic resistance against the capitalist discourse within the mainstream music industry."[135]

Fonseca shows how early rap labels were driven by DIY production and releases, as "most early labels got their start when rappers and producers used glorified home studios to record music CDs, which were then sold out of their car trunks."[136] Forman noted that an "explosion of localized production centers and regionally influential producers and artists" had altered the Hip Hop map "throughout North America."[137] This economic empowerment did not end with music, as rappers also began to "incorporate themselves as localized businesses (often buying or starting companies unrelated to the music industry in their local neighborhoods, such as auto customizing and repair shops) and to employ friends, family members and members of their wider neighborhoods."[138] Barone finds that the "surge of such a diversity and quantity of rap music is rooted in the conditions of its production" and that it is "easier and handier to produce a rap track (or an electronic music track) than a song based on 'classic', non-digital instruments." Essentially, rap "can be created in a bedroom using only a digital audio workstation, an interface and a microphone."[139] Bell describes a type of industry standard recording software that can be used in professional, home, or bedroom studios: Consider the case of Pro Tools—the industry standard program in professional recording and its adherence to tape metaphors in its design. Conceptually, it is quite similar to the tape recorder; instead of storing tracks to tape, they are saved to a computer's memory." However, the tape recorder and Pro Tools (DAW) technologies differ greatly when it comes to "editing capabilities"—as Pro Tools and digital audio do not "degenerate with every passing play like that of a tape."[140]

As Rose finds, rap prioritized "voices from the margins of urban America," and "like all contemporary voices, the rapper's voice [was] imbedded in powerful and dominant technological, industrial, and ideological institutions."[141] Additionally, she explains that rap producers have been using "digital imagination" and sampling technology to transform post–World War II developments in jazz, blues, and R&B into Hip Hop expressions as an extension of "African-American oral, poetic, and protest traditions."[142] The technological advancements in rap are often born out of "absolute necessity," as Harris and colleagues find the use of "some of the most innovative technologies amid dispossession and destruction."[143] DIY is also related to terms such as "democracy," "democratization," and "digitalization." These terms, as Harkins and Prior explain, "identify technology-led shifts in music making—where the 'digital' becomes a short-hand for a flattening of hierarchical structures of genre, access, and production—elides socio-musical change as an uneven and gradual process."[144] Yet, as Perry notes, this type of "speak your piece" democracy is contrasted with the competitiveness of "be the best MC" that exists in Hip Hop.[145] Kabongo, Arthur, and Paige have used DIY music for teaching to "remove barriers to entry," to "recognize art as scholarship," to "learn by doing," and to have fun.[146] This DIY "pedagogical model" is designed to "foster a sense of community among artists, fans, and scholars."[147]

Technologies of Manufacturing and Distribution

Hip Hop, what Asante describes as the "cultural expression of young Black America," is largely disseminated outside of the control of young Black America.[148] Ogbar adds, "Corporate America has generally been unable to market break dancing and graffiti art, both of which fell outside the confines of an easily commodified art. The music, which has been the centerpiece of the culture, was easily marketed throughout the 1980s and 1990s."[149] Local, underground rap scenes and markets are important, as Gebesmair writes that:

> almost all national markets except for some Asian countries are dominated by the big four: Universal, Sony BMG, EMI and Warner. They share about 80 per cent of the global market with recorded music. Radio and TV markets show similar degrees of concentration, although in many countries the corporate power is balanced by public broadcasting which is committed not just to profit, but also to public values.[150]

DIY and Music 3.0 technologies offer possibilities to change some of this. Weheliye shows that "sound recording and reproduction technology have afforded black cultural producers and consumers different means of staging time, space, and community in relation to their shifting subjectivity in the modern world."[151] As Drijver and Hitters note, DIY can offer "symbolic resistance, as well as alternative and collectivist business operations … to counter the commercial music industry."[152] Much of rap's development happens at an underground production level because "genres unknown or less popular, are deemed unsuitable for major record labels."[153] Rabaka describes major rap artist use of the "mixtape format" between 2002 and 2009 to "release either more decadent or more politically charged music that their more 'mainstream' and pop chart-obsessed record labels have either passed on or do not want to be linked to."[154]

Overall, the DIY ethos is also closely tied to local rap production. Forman finds that it has been a necessity to retain close ties to the locale:

> The requirement of maintaining strong local allegiances is a standard practice in hip hop that continues to mystify many critics of the rap genre. It is, therefore, imperative to recognise and understand the processes that are at work and to acknowledge that there are different messages being communicated to listeners who occupy different spaces and places and who identify with space or place according to different values of scale.[155]

Independent- or industry-label ownership is another factor to explore. Lena addresses an important set of differences between independent products and the corporate industry:

> There is a link between the context of production and the content of rap music singles. This research finds that when independent labels owned most of the charted singles, lyrics emphasized features of the local environment and hostility to corporate music production and values. In contrast, the major-label dominated market featured lyrics blending "street" credibility and commercial success in the "hustler" protagonist.[156]

Another major change in music distribution was led by unauthorized downloads, digital files, and streaming services. Mass unauthorized downloads started as early as 1999 through Napster, digital files could be purchased on the iTunes Store by 2003, and major streaming services started between 2000 and 2006. In 2006, Katel found that rap sales in the US accounted for only 11.4 percent of all music, trailing rock and country, but that the sales figures did not include "illegally downloaded computer files," which Katel argues contributed to Hip Hop's "overwhelming popularity."[157]

Digital Audio Workstation (DAW) technology, while related to MPC and production technology, has also grown to include tools that can help users directly release the "mixdown" in the program to streaming services. Even Final Cut Pro—a video workstation—allows users to post "mixdowns" directly to web and streaming serives. Strachan sees current DAW technology as the product of several different moments—with important eras from the 1950s to the 1970s, the 1980s to the mid-1990s, and the years thereafter. In the 1950s to the 1970s, there were "collaborative experiments involving scientists and musicians in the foundational days of mainframe computing."[158] From the 1980s to the mid-1990s, there was a "rapid digitalization of analogue instrumentation and studio technology and a resultant progression in common practices in composition, recording, sampling and sequencing across a broad-ranging context of music making and music production."[159] Since the mid-1990s, several "strains stemming from earlier patterns of digitization converge upon the singular site of the personal computer."[160] There has been subsequent development around teaching DAW techniques, as Strachan discusses a "democratization of knowledge" in YouTube video tutorials for DAWs such as Pro Tools, Logic Pro, Abelton, and FL Studio.[161] This has led to a "democratization of distribution and promotion" on online platforms:

> The technical ability to distribute information and digitize cultural products at little cost to a potentially global audience has been at the heart of the celebratory reception of digital technologies. The democratization of distribution argument suggests an open field in which audiences are available easily and readily for anyone who produces music. Online platforms such as SoundCloud, YouTube, iTunes, and Bandcamp act as global aggregators, central nodal points through which cultural producers can reach worldwide audiences.[162]

Wilkins mentions the prevalence of Bandcamp, Datpiff, and mixtapes in the example of Houston rap.[163] Each of these had a role in creating Music 3.0 and a certain democratization.

Technologies of Music 3.0

Today's music industry is different from the industry in 2006 and perhaps different from the music industry in 2020. Oswinski describes social media changes and applications for artists: "The music business truly changed forever around 2010 with the inception of the fifth generation of the music business called *Music 3.0*. It's a world where for the first time an artist could communicate, interact, market and sell directly to her audience, and they could communicate right back."[164] The structure of Music 3.0 changes Music 2.0, as "record label middlemen were now cut out of the loop."[165] Coddington notes changes brought about by websites and services such as "Last.fm (2002), the iTunes Store (2003), MySpace (2003), Pandora (2005), YouTube (2005), SoundCloud (2007), Bandcamp (2007), Amazon Music (2007), Deezer (2007), Spotify (2008), Tidal (2014), Apple Music (2015), and TikTok (2017)."[166] Specifically, these websites and services have worked to reduce radio's audience. Katz lists major streaming services founded between 2000 and 2015, including Pandora, Spotify, SoundCloud, iHeartRadio, and Apple Music, noting that Spotify and SoundCloud were founded in Sweden while the others were founded in the US.[167]

Straw illustrates that this new industry is consumer-driven: "Musical recordings now pass through convoluted media chains which begin with the exposure of songs in public places like restaurants, the immediate use by customers of smartphone-based music-recognition apps like *Shazam* to identify them, and subsequent replays on *YouTube* or streaming services such as *Spotify*."[168] Perone adds that these streaming and internet radio options can bring the consumer "a curated listening experience while also providing access to music that a listener otherwise might never have experienced."[169] Music 3.0 also includes newly emerging artificial intelligence (AI) raps. This trend has been shared on social media, and some of it is user-generated through ChatGPT or other systems. In recent examples, AI has been used to create songs with artists who are no longer living, to create AI blends (such as an AI Kanye West rapping over Dr. Dre's "Still D.R.E." instrumental), and for many more applications. The question posed during the Kanye West/Dr. Dre AI combo was, "As we enter an era in which you can effectively make anyone sing any song—which combos do you want to see?"[170] In addition, HKA, known as the first AI or virtual rapper to be signed by a major label, is also a sign of the growing impact of AI on production.[171]

Music 3.0 has altered the production process for artists, producers, and labels. A contemporary production process would include about seven multimedia steps: sourcing samples, sampling sources, sequencing songs, layering songs, album or song construction, audio editing and finishing, and video capture, editing, and finishing. Prior to Music 3.0, much of this process was done before release and, arguably, mostly readied as a whole (with the exception of music videos). With Music 3.0, elements of this process can be released, shared, and even made to be collaborative with fans and other artists. Overall, Music 3.0 impacted how and where consumers could listen to music, and this likely started in Music 2.0—with the advent of digital technology and .mp3 files. Bloustien, Peters, and Luckman discuss MP3 players as the "end of the set order list of the album" as "each user becomes more and more" their own DJ—allowing them to customize their "aural space and experience."[172] Yet, others show that physical formats are still somewhat in demand. Sax explains that when "surrounded by digital" from day to day, we begin to seek out "experiences that are more tactile and human-centric" and interactions with "goods and services" related to our senses.[173] Sax also proclaims that vinyl never really went away and that "billions and billions" of records "hibernated in shelves, crates, and boxes in record stores, flea markets, and basements" during the time that vinyl was thought to be relegated to DJ and producer subcultures.[174] The internet has also opened markets for buying and selling vinyl, and events such as Record Store Day (RSD) have helped vinyl's consumer resurgence.[175]

Manipulation of sources and transformation of samples have been central to DJing and rap production. Technology plays a big role in helping make this process possible. The turntablist style and use of samples from records—both integral to rap's growth— were enabled by the availability of industry-standard equipment such as the Technics SL-1200 direct-drive turntable and the affordable Akai S900 sampler. Overall, as Patrin shows, sampling has many influences: "Sampling was built off word of mouth, broken secrets, technological experiments, fierce competition, artful introspection, happy accidents, memetic replication, strokes of good luck, DIY necessity, collector impulse, and unbridled fandom."[176] Yet, Perry shows that rap has never been considered "musician's music," partly because of "desegregation in some communities and school cutbacks in others."[177] She argues that there was a "loss of ritualized formal space for instrument learning and practice" for Black children.[178] Although not considered "musician's music" to some, Travis Jr. shows that DJs "have always been immersed in technology, using turntables, faders, drum machines, and now DAW software and computers, among other things to create music."[179] Some DJs have moved toward video DJing—or VJing. Meanwhile, some producers also use instruments (both traditional and digital/electronic) in their creations.

Conclusion

DJ and production technologies are factors in the growth of local rap scenes in the US. While some of the producers discussed in this chapter are more locale-specific, others have formed wide-ranging styles and technological innovations leading to connections to other local rap scenes and regional, domestic, and international rap scenes.

7

More Scenes

Introduction

On "Everybody Rise" (Figure 9), Busta Rhymes calls upon twenty-eight rap scenes to surface, ascend, or rise up:

New York, Jersey, Philly, B-more, D.C. / Virginia, Atlanta, everybody rise! Come on!
N.C., L.A., Texas, Detroit, Chicago, Miami / N.O., Cleveland, rise! Come on!
Denver, Boston, Nashville, Seattle, Albany / Kansas City, everybody rise! Come on!
Buffalo, St. Louis, New Haven, Kentucky / Oakland, Phoenix, Vegas, everybody rise!
Come on![1]

Busta Rhymes (a rapper with origins on the Long Island and Brooklyn scenes) mentions about fifteen locations in his raps that also appear in *American Rap Scenes*. Yet, more important to this chapter's analysis is the fact that Busta Rhymes mentions an additional twelve locations *not* covered in *American Rap Scenes*, including the following: Virginia; North Carolina ("N.C."); Texas; Cleveland, OH; Denver, CO; Nashville, TN; Albany, NY; Kansas City, MO; Buffalo, NY; New Haven, CT; Phoenix, AZ; and Las Vegas, NV.

While Busta Rhymes's raps above are limited to cities within the US, Spady explains the concept of Hip Hop Nation through a plethora of US and Global scenes:

Hip Hop Culture—and the sense of belonging to a Hip Hop Nation—serves as a groundation and cohesive force for youth worldwide, a sight for them to fashion and express their identities, languages, styles, and both physical and political stances. Since its inception in the 1970s, members of this "nation without borders" have recognized the desirability of change based in human self and group emancipation. Members of this vast body can be found in Philly, East Palo Alto, San Juan, Brooklyn, Chicago, the Bronx, Miami, Mexico City, Cairo, Johannesburg, Algiers, Marseille, Dakar, Bordeaux, Berlin, Oakland, Sao Paulo, Ramallah, Newark, Havana, Miami, Milan, New Orleans, Los Angeles, Toronto, Kingston, New Haven, Auckland, Shaolin, Tokyo, London, Washington DC, Memphis, Atlanta, Nairobi, Dar Es Salam, Sydney, Harlem and Paris.[2]

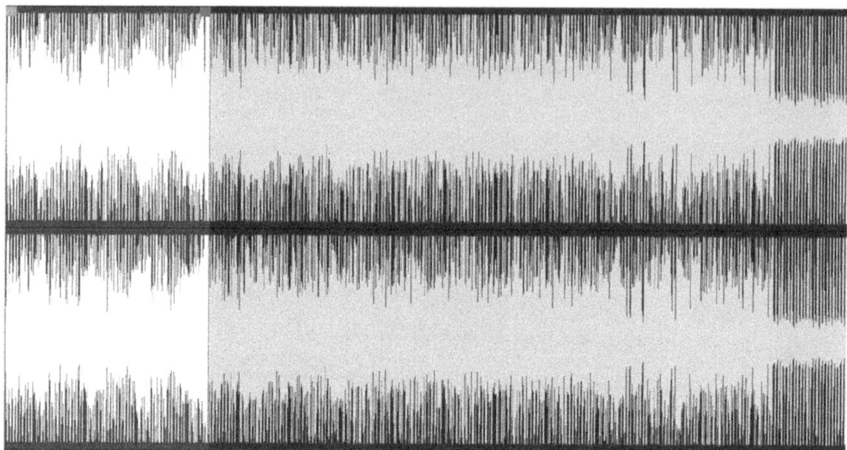

Figure 9 Busta Rhymes "Everybody Rise" Akai WAV snapshot with quoted material highlighted.

Spady's analysis highlights many US, North American, and global scenes, mentioning thirty-nine scenes, and fifteen of the scenes appear in *American Rap Scenes*. This leaves twenty-four additional scenes that were outside the scope of *American Rap Scenes*, including the following: East Palo Alto, CA; Mexico City, Mexico; Cairo, Egypt; Johannesburg, South Africa; Algiers, Algeria; Marseille, France; Dakar, Senegal; Bordeaux, France; Berlin, Germany; São Paulo, Brazil; Ramallah, Palestine; Havana, Cuba; Milan, Italy; New Haven, CT; Auckland, New Zealand; Shaolin, China; London, UK; Nairobi, Kenya; Dar Es Salam, Tanzania; and Sydney, Australia. With the exception of East Palo Alto and New Haven, the remaining scenes above are located outside of the US—and many are located outside of North America. Each of the rap scenes mentioned by Busta Rhymes and Spady could be explored in terms of factors such as geography, migration, identity-based movements, prior musics, and technology. Spady's quote also helps readers imagine additional rap scenes in location-based, global, or glocal (combining local and global) ways.

Peterson and Bennett write about three music scene types: local, translocal, and virtual. Local scenes are "clustered around a specific geographic focus," translocal scenes are "widely scattered local scenes drawn into regular communication around a distinctive form of music and lifestyle," and virtual scenes are ones in which "people scattered across great physical spaces create the sense of scene via fanzines and, increasingly, through the internet."[3] Local scenes are absolutely foundational when one considers that the following: "Initial academic work on popular-music scenes considered the relationship between local music-making processes and the everyday life of specific communities, where the forms of music in question were seen as imbedded in long-standing local cultures."[4] Translocal scenes "focus on a particular kind of music" but are in "regular contact with similar local scenes in distant places" by way of exchanging "recordings, bands, fans, and fanzines."[5] Virtual scenes are similar to translocal scenes; however, participants in virtual scenes are "widely separated geographically" but "come together in a single scene-making conversation via the internet."[6]

The topic of "more scenes" matters, as there will likely be more rap scenes created in urban sites throughout the US and the world. The increasing economic divide between the Global North and Global South will likely continue the use of rap as a vehicle of expression and social protest in the future. Also, the same environmental factors that produce mass migration of peoples to new urban places will likely produce new musics and new cultures. Additionally, alongside COVID-19 lockdowns in the US and other nations, producer technology made big leaps and became more user-friendly and affordable. Meanwhile, there were more tools available to help new users (and legacy users) learn and train on the technological devices related to music production.

More US Scenes

It is important to acknowledge that the twenty-five scenes covered in this book offer a limited view of rap in America. While the scenes were selected to cover a representative portion of US rap, the twenty-five scenes in the book do not represent all (or even most) of the rap scenes in America.

Geography

Some additional scenes important to explaining rap in America include the following: Birmingham and Huntsville, AL; Anchorage, AK; Phoenix and Tucson, AZ; Little Rock, AR; Fresno, Sacramento, and San Diego, CA; Denver, CO; New Haven, CT; Jacksonville, Orlando, Tallahassee, and Tampa, FL; Augusta, GA; Indianapolis, IN; Kansas City, KS; Lexington and Louisville, KY; Baton Rouge, LA; Flint and Lansing, MI; Jackson, MS; Omaha, NE; Las Vegas, NV; Albuquerque, NM; Albany, Buffalo, Rochester, Syracuse, and Yonkers, NY; Charlotte, Durham, and Raleigh, NC; Akron, Cincinnati, Cleveland, Columbus, Dayton, and Toledo, OH; Oklahoma City and Tulsa, OK; Allentown and Pittsburgh, PA; Providence, RI; Charleston, Columbia, and Greenville, SC; Nashville, TN; Austin, Dallas, El Paso, and San Antonio, TX; Salt Lake City, UT; Alexandria and Richmond, VA; Spokane and Tacoma, WA; and Milwaukee, WI. Additionally, some states could also be examined as scenes of rap production, such as Alabama, Alaska, Connecticut, Florida, Kentucky, North Carolina, Mississippi, Texas, and South Carolina.

Several rappers and groups also emerge from scenes that are not attached to major cities, including groups formed at colleges such as Virginia State University (Das EFX) and Western Kentucky University (Nappy Roots). Questions about what constitutes being "from" a scene are also important. Questions about smaller (and sometimes suburban scenes) around major cities are also important. Are they part of their own scene or part of the larger city's scene? Is College Park grouped with the Atlanta scene? Is Milledgeville, GA, grouped with the Atlanta scene? Is Port Arthur grouped with the Houston scene? Is Pacoima grouped with the LA scene? Is Morrisville grouped with the Philadelphia scene? In the current study, generally rappers who had performance or studio origins in or near major scenes were grouped with artists from the related major metropolitan scene. However, this metropolitan grouping does tend to miss more rural scenes and themes—such as themes in Lil Nas X's work (which is grouped with the Atlanta scene), themes contained on Beyoncé's *Cowboy Carter* album, and themes from Shaboozey's songs.[7] Overall, these types of rural scenes and themes are slightly beyond the boundaries of the *American Rap Scenes* inquiry.

US local rap scenes are both independent and interdependent. In a study of Houston, Faniel writes of the real importance of recognizing local scenes:

> By not giving Houston hip-hop culture the attention it deserves, one generalizes hip-hop cultural development by assuming that hip-hop in Houston developed in the same way it did in other sites, ignores the contribution that hip-hoppers in Houston made to the broader culture and misses how Houstonians specifically participated in the hip-hop culture that came from New York and how they adapted hip-hop to fit their needs.[8]

This seems true of additional scenes in the US and elsewhere.

Migration

Migrationally, a starting point for additional scene exploration would be the sites along three main tributaries of Black migration in the US. Even the "Contested Islands" of Hawai'i, Puerto Rico, and the USVI offer layers beyond what can be examined with a US-only focus. DC and the associated call for statehood as "New Columbia" is also slightly beyond a US-only focus, as DC is not treated similarly (or equally) to the fifty US states. Hip Hop and rap dealing in US colonization and the Middle Passage also require additional tools to fully understand the messaging, and these tools would entail a North American or global framework. US slavery is a prime example of this, as many Black Americans have ancestors that traveled through the Caribbean en route to the US.

Movement

There is also social movement chapter history on sites slightly beyond the scope of the twenty-five scenes analyzed in the book. For example, there were Brown Beret chapters in locations near the scenes in this book. There were multiple Bay Area chapters (Berkeley, Palo Alto, Richmond, Santa Clara, Stockton, and Richmond), and there were chapters in the LA area (Ventura and Oxnard). For May 1970 activity, there were additional actions on sites near scenes covered in this book, such as Philadelphia (Villanova); Newark (South Orange); Boston (Cambridge, MA, with two direct actions); Oakland (Berkeley, Santa Cruz, and Stockton); San Francisco (Palo Alto); Chicago (Evanston); and Detroit (Ann Arbor and Ypsilanti).

Music

For East Coast scenes, there are many important artists and groups that are beyond the scope of the twenty-five sites explored. A few examples include Brand Nubian (New Rochelle, NY); Heavy D (Mount Vernon, NY); DMX (Yonkers, NY); Das EFX (Brooklyn via Petersburg, VA, at Virginia State University); and Apathy (Willimantic, CT). Additionally, Harlem DJ Red Alert was born in Antigua, West Indies, and came to influence the NYC scene—creating connections between Long Island, Queens, and New Jersey artists and groups. Pittsburgh, PA, producer ID Labs is also important to mention, as is Pittsburgh as a rap scene.

On the West Coast, there are some additional connections to other rap scenes. Rapper Xzibit emerges from LA, but via Detroit, and Albuquerque. Fashawn is from Fresno, which is not LA or the Bay Area. Rapper Larry June is from San Francisco but also has roots in Atlanta (during childhood summers). The Bay Area contains cities such as San Jose, Milpitas, East Palo Alto, and Santa Cruz that are not part of the core analysis of Oakland, East Bay, or San Francisco. Early San Jose artist, duo, and group examples include Chris & Ray, MC Twist & The Def Squad, and Charizma & Peanut Butter Wolf. Sacramento's scene also deserves thorough discussion. Sacramento is geographically close to the Bay Area scene, and artists such as Mac Dre have been part of both scenes. There is evidence of a very early rap scene with artists such as M.J. Freeze.

Locations in Ohio, Wisconsin, Kentucky, and Iowa are also part of rap in America. Kenny P emerges out of Cincinnati as one of the first local rap artists to release an independent album. DJ Hi-Tek, a highly respected DJ and producer, is also from Cincinnati. There are several artists from Columbus, such as DJ/producer RJD2. However, the largest Ohio omission is Cleveland, hometown of Bone Thugs-N-Harmony, a group of five rappers discovered by Compton legend Eazy-E. The group's members (Bizzy Bone, Wish Bone, Layzie Bone, Krayzie Bone, and Flesh-n-Bone) have also released solo, joint, and compilation albums. The Milwaukee scene and its "lowend" rap style should be further explored. It is in close proximity to the Chicago scene but has emerged with its own unique sound. Rico Love emerges from Milwaukee via Harlem and Atlanta. Rappers from the group Kidz in the Hall have both Chicago and New Jersey links. There are other artists outside of major Midwest scenes or with links to other scenes. Bangladesh is a popular producer from Des Moines. Lizzo emerges from Minnesota but with close links to both the Detroit and Houston scenes before her emergence. Louisville features producer Static Major. Bowling Green, KY, features the group Nappy Roots, who met at Western Kentucky University.

In the South and "Contested Islands," there are areas missed in Southeast, mid-Atlantic, and Deep South regions. In North Carolina, Fayetteville native J. Cole is a key artist missing from the analysis of the twenty-five sites. Durham also represents a very strong scene, with producers such as 9th Wonder (who is also a college professor at North Carolina State University) and Khyrsis. The group Little Brother (Phonte, Big Pooh, and 9th Wonder) is rooted in Durham as well. Rhapsody is also from North Carolina, and she is an important woman rapper with complex rhymes and a large following. Addtionally, South Carolina has a great deal of rap and related production. For example, Speaker Knockerz (a producer) was originally from the Bronx before emerging in Columbia, SC. For Virginia, although both the DMV and Hampton areas are covered in *American Rap Scenes*, there are many scenes—urban, suburban, and rural—left uncovered.

Florida also presents challenges because there are many scenes located beyond the Miami area. Even the Miami area presents challenges, as the "Miami scene" exists beyond its city limits. Orlando has also been important since at least DJ Magic Mike, and production teams such as the Nasty Beatmakers continue Orlando's legacy. Currently, there are South Florida rappers from Broward County and Palm Beach, who have emerged somewhat independently from the Miami scene. Bhad Bhabie is also from a city near Miami, and Iggy Azalea has Miami roots (as well as Houston, Atlanta, and LA roots) since moving from Sydney, Australia. Rapper Khia has Tampa origins, moving from Philadelphia as a youth and living in Honolulu before moving back to Tampa to start her rap career. Tampa is also where the J.U.S.T.I.C.E. League formed; Tampa features producer Celph Titled as well.

Texas presents similar challenges as Florida, as both are sometimes considered regions having rap styles of their own. The twenty-five scenes in this book do not account for a united "Texas sound" or for individual rap scenes in Dallas, San Antonio, Austin, Fort Worth, or El Paso. Underground Kingz (UGK), a duo from Port Arthur, TX, is often considered under the Houston scene, which is a very limited scope of their origins. The political, economic, and social reality of Port Arthur is distinct from Houston in some significant ways. Other Texas scenes also appear to have popular and influential rappers. Gensu Dean, Asian Da Brat, and Cuban Doll are from Dallas, and S1 (Symbolic One) is from Waco.

There are two additional points about the South to be made here. First, the Deep South's scenes such as Jackson and Meridian, MS, are missed in *American Rap Scenes*. David Banner is from Jackson, and Big K.R.I.T. is from Meridian. Their work is very important, offering perspectives slightly different than other scenes in the South and urban North. Second, there are additional scenes missed in the Deep South, especially when looking at cities with populations between two hundred thousand and four hundred thousand. Augusta, GA, is important for rural blues, which is a musical form important to rap's soundscape. Augusta is also where soul, R&B, and funk legend James Brown emerged. James Brown became the most sampled musician in rap's history. As David Banner mentions, "James Brown from Georgia was rapping before rap was rap."[9]

Technology

There are many producers from site locations that are nearby (but not within) the sites covered in this book. Some producers migrate from one US scene to another. Other producers have immigrated to the US. Producers also make instrumentals (or beats) for artists from regions and locales outside of their own home scene. Technology also links smaller scenes together. A microscene, as defined by Grazian, involves "small groups of digitally networked participants of young adults that perform and consume niche subgenres of alternative popular music, particularly variants of indie, rock, experimental, and underground hip-hop."[10] The microscene is distinct from the scene level in three significant ways. Microscenes tend toward "spatial *decentralization* within cities, appearing sporadically," tend to be "DIY-*based* and created almost entirely *outside* the context of (and often in defiant opposition to) the dominant music industry," and tend to be "more oriented toward *local* cultural dynamics and processes, attendant to issues specific to their own provincial social worlds."[11] Many of the scenes in *American Rap Scenes* meet Grazian's description above; however, it is likely that there are additional microscenes in the US and beyond.

Worldwide Scenes

The US scenes in this study also represent a limited view of North American and global scenes. As Harris and colleagues observe, "a lot of Hip Hop written in the US is too US centric and does not account for Hip Hop around the world or the subfield of global Hip Hop studies."[12] Toop writes that the first rap records were just "the tip of an iceberg" to a larger movement of Hip Hop, which was under the surface, and beneath the Hip Hop level was another level further under the surface, "with a vast expanse of sources reaching back to West Africa."[13] The mixture of West African and Caribbean themes and Black American migration led to substantial developments in Hip Hop at the origin stage in the mid- to late 1970s South Bronx and other NYC boroughs. Saucier studies Hip Hop on the African continent and sees a full-circle development, from "the original side of the drum and dance" from which Hip Hop originated.[14] Bradley writes that rap's New World origins included the "mixed traditions" of "African American spoken word practices like the toast and the dozens as well as musical traditions such as Jamaican dub and southern blues."[15]

A central argument to this book is that scenes located outside of the US are also important sites for rap production for the US and elsewhere. Scenes in North America, such as Kingston, Jamaica, and Toronto, Canada, are both *influenced* by US rap and have an *influence* on US rap. Kingston is a vital scene, as its dub music is often considered a major influence on the South Bronx Hip Hop scene, especially in the areas of DJing (sound systems) and rapping (toasting). Recently, some scholars have questioned this connection and, in some cases, almost in its entirety. However, it is clear that Kingston had some influence on rap's beginnings in the South Bronx—even if considered a minimal influence by some experts. By the 2000s, Kingston also grew into an important participant in rap development.

Toronto is another North American scene with a strong relationship to US rap. Toronto's total geographical area is similar to San Francisco or Chicago, and Toronto's population is similar to Chicago or Brooklyn. Toronto also has a large metro area, which is similar to some US sites. Toronto had at least one SNCC organization or action. The deep connections to reggae music and Caribbean culture have been noted as different from US rap. As Haines explains, "the traditionally stronger influence of reggae music and Caribbean language" is "due to large Jamaican communities" in Toronto and Montreal.[16] There are Toronto producer links to US scenes covered in this book. There are links to Queens with Sir Scratch, Main Source, and K-Cut. Marco Polo has ties to NYC's scene. Murda Beatz has produced for Chicago and Atlanta scenes. Freaky Flow has links to LA and Philadelphia. Boi-1-da was born in Kingston before migrating to the Toronto area.

The reason Kingston, Toronto, and other locations share roots with the rap scenes discussed in this book lies in their relationship to the African Diaspora. Overall, understanding Hip Hop's origins in West Africa helps us better understand Hip Hop locationally and historically. Hayes's explanation of the link to the past is telling: "The African past is essential to African American Studies. Retrieving, recapturing, and rehabilitating the African history before the coming of the European links African-descended Americans to a human, geographical, temporal, and intellectual context beyond the confines of brutal enslavement and cultural domination in the Americas."[17] Lipsitz declares that the links between people of African descent have implications for political power, stating, "The 'diasporic intimacy' linking cultural production and reception among people of African descent in the Caribbean, the US, Europe, and Africa has resulted in a cultural formation with extraordinary political implications."[18] As Weheliye observes, a "diasporic citizenship" is even embraced by groups such as New Jersey's Fugees, by "coarticulating the national and transnational instead of playing a zero-sum game with political identification."[19]

Geography

North American scenes (outside of the US) were well beyond the scope of this book's analysis. However, there are some important sites to be considered. In Canada, and in addition to Toronto, Vancouver, Montreal, and Ottawa scenes also seem important. In Cuba, scenes in Havana and Santa Domingo warrant analysis. Scenes in Port-au-Prince, Haiti, Kingston, Jamaica, and Mexico City, Mexico, also help explain rap and its many North American forms. Floyd finds music of the circum-Caribbean region, "which includes the West Indies and South America," to be important in "any attempt to bridge the gap between the musics of Africa" and the US.[20] Referring to Toronto, Stewart and Scobie observe a continuation of a "diasporic dialogue" crossing over from the US into Canada in the mid-1980s and then "adopted by a number of young musicians in Toronto whose cultural ancestry was rooted in the African diaspora and, more specifically, in West Indian and Caribbean communities."[21] For example, Michie Mee regularly switched from "Standard Canadian English and Jamaican Patois," and this is explained as another "example of code-switching in the construction and performance of a hybridized Jamaican Canadian identity."[22] An analysis that does not take Toronto seriously also misses important artists such as k-os and Drake. An analysis of the Toronto rap scene is also needed to fully contextualize the 2024 rap battle between Kendrick Lamar and Drake, but it seems as if one factor in Kendrick

Lamar's success in the battle was in rooting the song "Not Like Us" in long-standing Compton and West Coast themes. While Drake's battle responses did not seem to overtly call upon the Toronto rap scene, the scene is still very rich and should be further analyzed.

These sites (and many other sites) are essential to the development of rap and to the body of Hip Hop, and future attention should be given to these and other scenes. Attention should also be given to local rap in Africa, Central and South America, Europe, Asia, and Australia. Mitchell's work highlights local scenes from "most of Europe, Anglophone and Francophone Canada, Japan, Korea, and Australasia."[23] In Europe, George notes French rap as different from Danish or Swedish rap (where English is used) "because the sentence structure of their native tongues doesn't work well for rap."[24] Barone adds that "francophone rap is the second biggest niche" in global Hip Hop music.[25] There are also growing studies of rap in Africa, such as Gooding's analysis of rap on the continent, which lists five regions of the African continent—grouping its sovereign countries: Northern Africa (7); Western Africa (17); Eastern Africa (22); Middle Africa (i.e., "Central" Africa) (9); and Southern Africa (5).[26] Gooding's "Chapter 5: Sound Reasoning" samples the history of Hip Hop and rap in each country from the regions listed above.[27] It is incredibly rich work on the topic.

Migration

Rap is clearly the product of Black migration. Connell contends that "like so many other musical genres," Hip Hop (or rap) "emerged from a fusion of elements brought by migrants (in this case from the Caribbean to the US) with local musical forms of residents of deprived inner-city neighborhoods."[28] Migration is essential within the Americas, as seen in the cases of Caribbean and Latin American migration. Such migration led to Puerto Rican participation in the construction of Hip Hop and rap. Later, in the early 1990s, *reggaeton* reinvigorated culture both on the island and in the US. *Reggaeton*'s roots "can be traced back to interactions between the Caribbean and Central America and specifically Jamaican immigrants living in Panama." Connell conveys that many "Jamaicans came to Panama as workers on the canal construction project" at the beginning of the twentieth century and "brought their music with them."[29] Aparicio, Jáquez, and Cepeda characterize these types of trends under the concept of "musical migrations," which "foregrounds the processes of dislocation, transformation, and mediation, that characterize musical structures, productions, and performances as they cross national and cultural borders and transform their meanings from one historical period to another."[30]

Migration is also an important area for global rap scenes, and special attention should be paid to connections between rap's foundation and its West African origins and roots. There is also an interplay between the migration destination and the former country, as Barone tells how a "great presence of Senegalese immigrants in New York in the 1980s fostered the circulation of the culture and informed the first local hip-hop generation."[31] Furthermore, migration highlights ways in which parents seek out better outcomes for their children and ways in which children find new identities that are both similar and dissimilar to previous generations. Buckingham and de Block find that children are using media, "particularly new media, to reaffirm their 'local' domestic identities as members of particular communities, nations, transnational or ethnic groups."[32] These migrations tell us about the nature of movements, including musical participation on route to collective empowerment ranging from playing music as a form of self or group empowerment to using music to convince people to alter their activity in society. Musical participation can lead to collective empowerment, new communities, and new local power bases starting with the mere act of playing or creating music.

Movement

Politically, much of reggae's beginnings are in Rastafari teachings, which were influenced by Jamaican-born Marcus Garvey's Black Star Line (created while in Harlem), which was "a commercial shipping line formed to assist in the repatriation of the Black diaspora to Africa."[33] Later, as Meek writes, "in 1968, Black Power swept across the Caribbean. The immediate trigger was a riot in Jamaica following the banning from the island of Black Power activist and scholar Walter Rodney."[34] Meeks notes that "by design Black Power in Jamaica was decentralized, multipolar, and community based."[35] This history had an impact on recordings from Kingston. Borthwick describes the content of Kingston roots recordings: "In particular, most roots recordings had a focus on sufferation, struggle and liberation, although the route to liberation was contested, especially around whether a 'repatriation of the mind' and a spiritual liberation in Jamaica should take precedence over the struggle for physical repatriation to Africa."[36] As Kaltmeier and Raussert add, reggae began in "response to British colonialism and drew inspiration and guidance form the pan-Africanist visions of the Jamaican pan-Africanist Marcus Garvey."[37]

Also, politically, it is important to note one unconventional factor for rap's growth on Toronto's rap scene. Stewart and Scobie show that the "push for increased airplay" of Hip Hop, reggae, and R&B "was part of a larger movement in the 1980s and 1990s aimed at increasing commercial recognition of, and support for, Afrological musics in Canada."[38] Another very important aspect of Toronto's rap scene is the role of women. Stewart and Scobie note, "Dancehall fashion and beauty standards oppose Eurocentric norms concerning femininity and female sexuality, providing instead a space in which women can assert themselves through bodily and satirical decisions."[39]

Barone's analysis is also helpful when looking at international movements beyond North America, writing, "The political significance of rap in the 2010s has an obvious source in the Middle East and North Africa: the cases of Senegal and Burkina Faso were indeed inspired by the Arab Spring protests inaugurating the decade."[40] Additionally, from 1998 to 2010, there was a collective of "freedom fighters" called the Black August Hip-Hop Project, representing productions from NY, Cuba, and South Africa.[41] Even the origins of the Universal Zulu Nation (UZN) were also international, as Fernandes claims the UZN "drew on the mythology of anticolonial South African warriors to redirect the energies of inner-city gang youth."[42]

Music

In Kingston, Power and Hallencreutz estimate that roughly two thousand (single artists or groups) with either a history of popular music, sales, or chart success (international or Jamaican) "currently reside or have their origins in Kingston."[43] Discussing Penthouse Studio in Kingston, Borthwick finds a roster of "more than 280 artists" including "Capelton, Jah Cure, Elephant Man, Freddie McGregor, Morgan Heritage, Frankie Paul, Queen Ifrica, Lady Saw, Tony Rebel, Taurus Riley, Sanchez, Richie Spice, Tanya Stephens and Wayne Wonder."[44]

Charry adds much to this conversation about music with an analysis of African nations. *Hip Hop Africa* is essentially a comparison of rap scenes in Algeria, Côte d'Ivoire, Ghana, Kenya, Malawi, Mali, Nigeria, Senegal, South Africa, and Tanzania.[45] Charry notes that "African rap artists get little international respect" and that African Hip Hop has "reached a maturity and urgency."[46] He details the African origins of Hip Hop, the French connections, and then the 1990s and 2000s scenes.[47]

Technology

Similar to some foundational scratch and sampling techniques being discovered by "accident," dub was also an accident of invention. According to Bell, Ruddy Redwood was working at Treasure Isle studio when engineer Byron Smith "failed to add in the vocal to the instrumental at the right time when cutting the record."[48] Redwood cut the record anyways, and dub was officially created.[49] For those who see rap's soundscape related to dub, the relationship would begin in the "studio producer," "sound system selectors," and the emergence of "dub plates" in 1967. Chang claims, "Early on, selectors made frequent trips to America to secure obscure exclusives. As the Jamaican music industry expanded during the sixties, sound systems began to record local artists' songs onto exclusive acetates or 'dubplates.' "[50] Dub's development was central to Jamaican electoral politics, especially as a source of political information. In addition to the dub sound, reggae provided one of the first sampled records when The Harry J All Stars' "Liquidator" from 1969 was used for the instrumental for the Staple Singers' "I'll Take You There" in 1972. The Staple Singers' sample was later used in Big Daddy Kane's "I'll Take You There" in 1988. The production scene in Kingston is very different compared to most US sites. Power and Hallencreutz argue Kingston is an independent music production center, as "the global majors have almost no direct presence or role," and it is instead run by largely fragmented, small-scale A&R and "original-creation-driven-firms."[51]

Overall, technology seems to be a driver of global Hip Hop, as Mitchell finds that "rap and hip-hop outside the USA reveal the workings of popular music as a culture industry, driven as much by local artists and their fans, as by the demands of global capitalism and U.S. cultural domination."[52]

Virtual Scenes

Virtual Scenes existed long before Music 3.0, yet Music 3.0 creates new opportunities for rappers and producers to exist mainly in virtual spaces. Today, these virtual spaces could be key social media sites, blogs, message boards, artist websites, and other networks. As of 2020, Oswinski finds the largest social media sites to be Facebook, YouTube, WhatsApp, Messenger, WeChat, Instagram, QQ, Timber, Qzone, TikTok, Sina Weibo, Twitter, Reddit, Baidu Tieba, LinkedIn, Viber, Snapchat, Pinterest, Line, and Telegram.[53] At the time, Facebook had 2.23 billion users, YouTube had 1.9 billion users, and WhatsApp had 1.5 billion users.[54]

Also, with Music 3.0, it is hard to separate the music-making and social media processes. Kruse sees scenes as both local formations and social networks, or as "geographical sites of local music practice and the economic and social networks in which participants are involved."[55] The rise of the internet at the scene level has allowed for online dissemination of independent music, as "people can connect easily across localities, regions, countries, and continents."[56] The internet has increased as a key factor in the "production, promotion, dissemination, and consumption of independent music."[57] There may also be "commonalities of collective positions among local subcultural groups within a nation and across states."[58] Translocal analysis can also link local and virtual scenes. Baptist uses the term "translocal" to refer to "a geographically specific network, which exports a local context and production, binding itself to the experiences of supporters globally via music and social media."[59] Lane also mentions interaction between physical and virtual sites, arguing "that street life is characterized by its flow online and offline."[60]

The Twenty-Five Scenes

Why *those* twenty-five rap music scenes? or Why *twenty-five* cities? These questions were quite common over the course of writing the book. The twenty-five cities are based on prior research about regional and local growth of rap in general and specific analyses of the South Bronx, LA, New Orleans, Houston, Seattle, San Francisco Bay Area, and Atlanta scenes.[61] The local scenes were selected with the aim of capturing most major US rap genres, subgenres, and micro-subgenres. The mapping of twenty-five US cities is a modification of the framework used in Hess's *Hip Hop in America*. Hess's edited volume groups twenty-one local scenes by region (East Coast, West Coast, Midwest, and South). Within each region, cities are listed (roughly) in order of their scene's popular emergence. Additionally, many of the sites have relationships to larger metro areas. Some sites neighbor other states or nations, and many of the sites feature major waterways, railways, and highways.

Many of the twenty-five sites also have a history of Black migration and radical, Black social movement activity. Many sites had a BPPSD chapter, before facing post-industrialization and local manifestations of wars on crime, poverty, and drugs. Finally, twenty-five scenes allowed for a finite study domain and was useful to sort, classify, and organize data for the book (both physical and digital data).

There were five main impetus points for this book. Discussing these starting points might be helpful when thinking about additional scenes beyond the scope of this book. *American Rap Scenes* began with five main reasons or very strong points of evidence— leading to further inquiry and study. These points included the following:

Impetus 1: Prior Research Findings
Impetus 2: Cities of Black, Latinx, and Caribbean Migration
Impetus 3: Political, Radical, and Militant Movement Chapter History
Impetus 4: Changes in Production and DJ Technologies
Impetus 5: Project Feedback

These five main areas are discussed below.

Impetus 1: Prior Research Findings

The first impetus for this book was the growth of local and regional research on rap. There have also been great developments in ethnographic methods related to local rap scenes.[62] This ethnographic research has continued to evolve into deepened analyses of local scenes and musical content—often longitudinal in approach, with examples from local scenes such as New Orleans, Houston, Oakland, and Seattle.[63]

My study of the Oakland and San Francisco Bay Area compared local sources to a "control group" of Billboard sources on the basis of political content, by selecting top album or song releases on Billboard charts at the time of local (Oakland, East Bay, or San Francisco) album or song releases. When examining political content of Billboard sources, several cities from this control group had high levels of political content as measured against the BPPSD framework.[64] These cities included "Queens, Brooklyn, Philadelphia, Compton, South Central Los Angeles, Atlanta, Houston, Memphis, New Orleans, and Chicago."[65] I argued that a deeper analysis into any of these scenes would likely yield "very high levels of political content."[66] *American Rap Scenes* expands the analysis beyond a political inquiry (from settings, representatives, movements, rap narratives, and impact) to a wider scope of geography, migration, movements, musicology, and technology. These five themes should help add precision to the study of underground rap scenes.

Table 9 shows the locations of my control group in *Rap and Politics* that had elements of militant and/or anti-statist imagery, internal colonization framework, or warfare framework similar to the themes used in BPPSD media.

American Rap Scenes grows out of this evidence and explores whether these rap scenes have had a "major influence on rap music evolution in the US."[108]

Impetus 2: Cities of Black, Latinx, and Caribbean Migration

The second impetus for this book is in the evidence of these cities as sites of Black, Latinx, and Caribbean migration. Studies of US growth and population change highlight distinct population patterns. Dilworth, one of the most comprehensive

Table 9 Rap and Politics Control Group with BPPSD Rhetoric as Measured by Rap and Politics.

Scene	Artist – Product (Citation)
Bronx	• Terror Squad - "Lean Back"[67] • Fat Joe - "Make It Rain"[68]
Queens	• Onyx - *Bacdafucup*[69] • Mobb Deep - *The Infamous*[70] • Nas - *It Was Written*[71]
Brooklyn	• Junior M.A.F.I.A. - *Conspiracy*[72] • Smif-N-Wessun - *Dah Shinin*[73] • Notorious B.I.G. - *Life After Death*[74] • Jay-Z - *Vol. 2 … Hard Knock Life*[75] • Jay-Z - "Empire State of Mind"[76]
Staten Island	• GZA - *Liquid Swords*[77]
Long Island	• Public Enemy - *Apocalypse 91…The Enemy Strikes Black*[78] • EPMD - *Business as Usual*[79] • Public Enemy - *Greatest Misses*[80] • Product G&B - "Maria, Maria" (featuring Carlos Santana)[81]
Barranquilla, Colombia (Newark via Haiti and Brooklyn feature)	• Shakira - "Hips Don't Lie" (featuring Wyclef)[82]
LA	• Ice-T - *Power*[83] • Cypress Hill - *Cypress Hill*[84] • Ice Cube - *Death Certificate*[85] • Eazy-E - *It's On (Dr. Dre 187um) Killa*[86] • Snoop Doggy Dogg - *Doggystyle*[87] • Cypress Hill - *Black Sunday*[88] • *Dangerous Minds Soundtrack* (Coolio's "Gangsta's Paradise")[89] • Mack 10 - *Mack 10*[90] • Snoop Dogg - "I Wanna Rock"[91]
Terrell, TX (Chicago feature)	• Jamie Foxx - "DJ Play a Love Song" (featuring Twista)[92]
Detroit	• Boss - *Born Gangstaz*[93] • Eminem - "Lose Yourself"[94]
Houston	• Scarface - *The Untouchable*[95]
Houston (Cleveland feature)	• Chamillionaire and Krayzie Bone - "Ridin' "[96]
New Orleans	• Hot Boys - *Guerrilla Warfare*[97]
Memphis	• Eightball and MJG - *On Top of the World*[98]
Atlanta	• Goodie Mob - *Soul Food*[99] • OutKast - *ATLiens*[100] • OutKast - *Stankonia*[101] • Purple Ribbon All-Stars - "Kryptonite (I'm On It)"[102] • Yung Joc - "It's Going Down"[103] • Young Dro - "Shoulder Lean"[104] • Young Jeezy - "Lose My Mind"[105] • T.I. - "Live Your Life"[106]
Miami	• Rick Ross - "The Boss"[107]

examples, features a methodology that involves selecting cities using the ten most populous cities during a given decennial census.[109] In the years after 1870, slightly over 75 percent of the cities examined by Dilworth are also one of the twenty-five scenes examined in *American Rap Scenes*. Over census years 1870, 1890, 1920, 1940, 1950, 1980, and 2010, a city discussed in *American Rap Scenes* is on the most populous cities list fifty-three of seventy times. While this is a snapshot, even the historical range is telling—from 1870 to 2010—with Dilworth looking at a census at least every thirty years. The historical data is actually worth a breakdown by year (with the ratio of sites in *American Rap Scenes* to Dilworth city coverage): 1870 (8/10), 1890 (7/10), 1920 (8/10), 1940 (9/10), 1950 (8/10), 1980 (7/10), and 2010 (6/10). Dilworth's US foreign-born population charts were also influential and spurred an initial interest in immigration and migration as factors.

For cities prior to 1870, Dilworth features sections on "Cities and APD (1776–1854)," "Cities in the Early Republic (1790–1828)," and "Cities in the Age of Jackson (1828–1854)." In these early eras, New York, Philadelphia, Boston, Baltimore, New Orleans, and DC are also among the most populous cities in the US. Dilworth also notes that NYC and Philadelphia have had numerous changes in city structures, NYC by consolidation and Philadelphia by annexation. Dilworth's findings and approach led to the current book's inquiry into census data around population and migration on the twenty-five sites. Dilworth's study also confirmed the changing racial and ethnic population of the sites—first by foreign-born populations of Whites, then by Black migration, and then by immigrants from other global sites.

Impetus 3: Political, Radical, and Militant Movement Chapter History

The third impetus for this book is in the local chapter history of the BPPSD. Many of the sites in this book had BPPSD activity and other groups with radical chapter histories. This led to an inquiry into Black Arts, Latinx, and Women's movements. The BPPSD was part of a larger conversation around Black leadership, rising expectations, and the limits of Black mayors in some mid-size and large US cities from the late 1960s through the 1970s. The Panthers also discussed the relationship between US imperialism, colonization, and slavery. The Panthers also proudly documented their chapter history.[110]

The following sites with Panther chapters overlap with scenes in this book: the Bronx; Harlem; Jamaica (Queens); Brooklyn; Philadelphia; Newark; Boston; LA; Oakland; Seattle; Chicago, Minneapolis; Detroit; Houston; New Orleans; Memphis; Atlanta; and DC. Thus, seventeen of twenty-five sites from this book had at least one Panther chapter. In the cases of Newark, LA, the San Francisco Bay Area, Seattle, and DC, there were also Panther chapters in nearby areas or cities. Additional BPPSD chapters were in Northern New Jersey, which would be near Newark. Portland and Baltimore BPPSD chapters were near Seattle and DC chapters, respectively. There were also two chapter sites in Oakland—one in West Oakland and one in East Oakland.

In fact, the only sites in this book that appeared *not* to have a local BPPSD chapter are Staten Island, San Jose, Gary, St. Louis, St. Paul, Miami, Hampton, Hawai'i, San

Juan, Puerto Rico, and Saint Thomas. There were BPPSD locations such as Nassau and Suffolk Counties in New York that would cover Long Island. Gary's closest chapter would be Chicago, and St. Paul's closest chapter would be Minneapolis. Even St. Louis had a neighboring East St. Louis, IL, BPPSD chapter. This significant overlap between Panther chapter history and the emergence of rap from these scenes began an inquiry involving wider questions about how Black Power and rap movements might be connected in the US.

Impetus 4: Changes in Production and DJ Technologies

The fourth impetus for this book is around technological advancements leading to the development of new rap styles and production. This is especially true of recent advancements in music production console (MPC) and MIDI (Musical Instrument Digital Interface) production center technology. These resources have been used by rap producers to transform musical samples and instruments into new instrumentals (or beats). Since 2020, there have been key advances in MPC, MIDI, and other home studio technologies—particularly with all-in-one studio devices. With these devices, a producer can make entire songs—from ideas to beats to songs with vocals—with one device. The Akai Live II also features a speaker and battery. Moreover, it is easier to learn how to use these devices. Resources to learn the Akai MPC Series devices (e.g., MPC X, Live II, and ONE) include YouTube videos, equipment instruction manuals, or training literature (such as the "MPC Bible").[111] There have also been significant changes around DJ emulation technology.

Impetus 5: Project Feedback

The fifth impetus for this book is related to two different types of feedback (one type of feedback from coursework, presentations, and workshops with students, experts, and the general public—and the other type of feedback from reviews of prior research, submissions to grants, and other proposals). The core material from this book has been presented to students, which has helped in forming better questions and better foci. Additionally, the book benefited tremendously from practitioner and expert feedback. This peer feedback from prior studies, grants, and proposals helped sharpen and better explain the study.

Conclusion

American Rap Scenes is limited to twenty-five scenes. This chapter identifies additional US, world, and virtual sites. These additional sites have rap scenes, artists, and groups that warrant further analysis.

Conclusion

Introduction

MF Grimm's "Stable" (Figure 10) begins with an introduction between two speakers: Man #1 and Man #2.

> [Man #1, Calling for Jet Jaguar]
> *"Jet Jaguar, come down! / Jet Jaguar, come down!"*
> [Man #1, Speaking to Man #2]
> *"He's programmed himself for survival. / I built that into him, he's on his own."*
> [Man #2, Speaking to Man #1]
> *"You sure? / You mean he'll simply operate on his own from now on? / Without further orders from you?"*[1]

This conversation on NYC rapper MF Grimm's "Stable" revolves around a robot named Jet Jaguar, created by Man #1. After he calls Jet Jaguar to "come down" for the second time, he mentions to Man #2 that Jet Jaguar has "programmed himself for survival." At this explanation, Man #2 is astounded and asks (in disbelief) whether the machine can operate on his own without receiving new instructions from his creator. Jet Jaguar is an outstanding metaphor for rap development. Once rap was created and reached listeners outside of the original culture, rap began to be influenced by those outside its original founders or creators. An example of this can be seen in The Sugarhill Gang's "Rapper's Delight." The song was out of the hands of rap's Bronx creators, as was rap's emergence in New Jersey, Boston, LA, Chicago, Miami, San Juan, and everywhere else rap has been created. Similar to MF Grimm's song opening above, rap has also been programmed for survival. In its live and studio performances, it leaves records of scenes and helps marginalized voices survive.

The exploration in *American Rap Scenes* should ready those interested in forming a deeper, historical, or method-driven examination of rap's local development. The book also helps in identifying established and under-explored local rap scenes. Woo, Rennie, and Poyntz find scenes to be part of the "social imaginary of urban life," writing,

> Scenes are set within the fabric of everyday life but also function as an imagined alternative to the ordinary, work-a-day world. They can be utopian in moments,

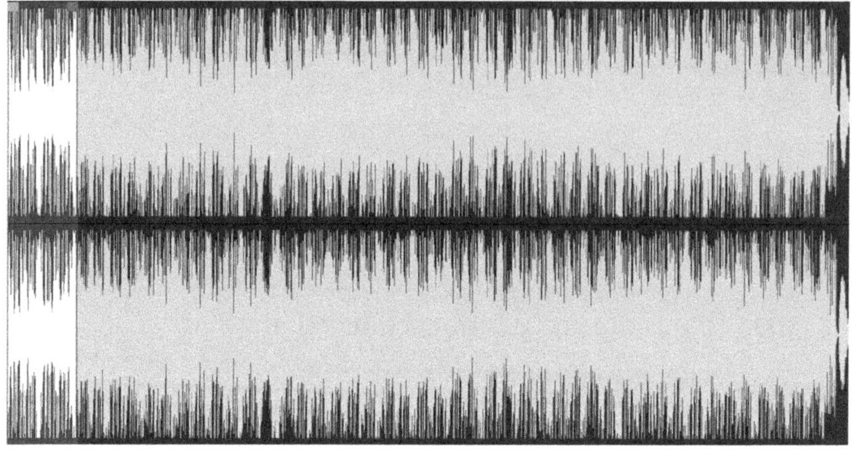

Figure 10 MF Grimm's "Stable" Akai WAV snapshot with quoted material highlighted.

especially when scenes allow otherwise ignored or disappeared communities and subjects to find a home, but problems of institutionalization and coordination often push back against utopian aspirations. A scene may endure in one form or another for many years or it might quickly give way to the next big thing or hip neighbourhood.[2]

The rap scenes in this book have helped people, who would have otherwise been ignored, reach outside listeners. Many scenes in this book have been long-standing. Many scenes have been active for at least twenty years, with Bronx origin and nearby NYC scenes being active for over fifty years. There is a volume of sources on these local scenes. By focusing on community-specific sources, future research can help answer critical questions about identity and inequality on US, global, and virtual scenes. This Conclusion summarizes the findings in *American Rap Scenes* and explains why future research into rap's relationship to place, identity, power, social change, media, technology, and methods remains important.

Summary of Findings

American Rap Scenes focuses on local rap scenes, hoping to achieve additional clarity and precision when speaking about the comparative local geographic, political, economic, and social conditions. *American Rap Scenes* surveys twenty-five local rap scenes, looking at geography, migration, social movements, prior musics, and technology as factors. This survey includes the following US scenes: South Bronx; Manhattan and Harlem; Queens; Brooklyn; Staten Island; Hempstead; Philadelphia; Newark and Jersey City; Boston; Los Angeles and Compton; Oakland and the San Francisco Bay Area; Seattle and Portland; Chicago and Gary; St. Louis; Minneapolis;

Detroit; Houston; New Orleans; Memphis; Atlanta; Miami; Hampton; Washington, DC and Baltimore; Honolulu; and San Juan and Saint Thomas.

Geography

When looking at geography on scenes, the null hypothesis would likely follow the null hypothesis for most spatial patterns—that all geographic "features" are randomly distributed across the study area. Yet, regions and sites obviously carry physical and cultural characteristics that are connected through place. Additionally, locations can help create a sense of place, which can include personal or group attachments to a location. Even more, Tobin's Law of Geography holds that "features" in close proximity to other features tend to be more similar to one another.

There were some challenges and issues in working with geographic data for *American Rap Scenes*. While a scene might be a site, city, or region, data is usually collected at the city, county, state, or national level in the US. This means that a musical scene may not overlap with available data. Much of the data used in this book relies on the city or county level, but in the case of Louisiana, the term "parish" has been used; in the cases of Maryland and Missouri, the term "independent cities" has been used; and in the case of Puerto Rico, the term "municipios" has been used.[3] There were issues in getting comparable data from locations such as Hawai'i, Puerto Rico, and Brooklyn. The US census has used different data instruments for Hawai'i, DC, Puerto Rico, and the USVI. Also, in the cases of Hawai'i, Puerto Rico, and the USVI, different authorities collected data before the US began collecting its data. Scenes as metro areas also present a challenge, as metro areas are porous and can be quite large. As Enos shows in the examples of Chicago and New York, "the metropolitan area consists of much more than the diverse big city we might picture at first." In the example of Chicago, the metropolitan area known as Chicagoland "covers eight counties, stretching far into suburban and rural Illinois."[4] This area would also cover portions of Wisconsin and Indiana.

Other geography and placemaking questions remain, such as: Do scenes have a geographical epicenter? What role does geography play in the development local rap's musical content?

Migration

Migration seems phenomenally important, as rap is driven by migratory patterns of West African peoples. As Bradley explains, over centuries of time, Black "expressive culture has developed a tradition" of signifying as "a rhetorical practice that involves repetition and difference, besting and boasting," which has roots stretching back "through slavery and back to West Africa."[5] For migrations, the book uses US decennial census data to examine trends. The census is ordered in Article I, Section 2 of the US constitution but has been applied differently over time to US territories. Furthermore, the book focuses on site changes in total population and Black and Latinx percentages. There are issues with the comparability of this data, as the definitions of Black and Latinx have changed over time. Additionally, a more thorough examination of these sites would look into US census data related to sex, Whites, First Nations, Asian Americans, families, children, household population, income, and poverty measurements. Remaining migration and identity questions include the following: Which groups entered the location? How did they enter and under what conditions? What were their political, economic, and social experiences? How did they respond to these experiences?

Movement

Rap and Hip Hop provide avenues for expression within what Hager calls the "most imaginative leap forward since the sixties," and these subcultures "play an important role in society, since they provide the experimental laboratory where new cultural concepts can be tested free from restrictions."[6] Rap impacts both micro and macro politics. Shabazz writes that artists, groups, and directors such as Ice Cube, Public Enemy, Professor Griff, Sista Souljah, 2 Live Crew, Spike Lee, N.W.A., The Concept, Ice-T, and X-Clan are "not public office holders, but they carry more political clout than a lot of politicians occupying a seat on Capitol Hill."[7] Osumare shows that the Hip Hop Nation "could become more than rap rhetoric" and could move into making a "cultural and economic impact and envisioning itself as a power bloc to be reckoned with politically."[8]

Over time, rap grew into a form of representation for some communities. In a study described as a "side-by-side comparison of the development of reality rap (and what some would call gangster rap … against the development of reality media (news, TV, entertainment, web) coverage," Harvey shows that rap can be compared to a growing form of user-generated messaging and coverage.[9] Harvey even writes about the Watts Riot as "a reality rap validation," when an 81-second video "verified the street reporting of N.W.A. and Ice Cube and cast the growing faction of reality rappers not merely as angry young Black men but as street prophets."[10] Remaining social movement questions include the following: What role does identity play in local rap's development of political content? What types of government and representation structures do migrants and immigrants enter on these sites?

Music

Baptist highlights the political function of rap on local scenes when writing that "rap allows Black people to erect sonic safe spaces where they can produce and share their inner-most feelings about the Black condition to all who will listen."[11] These sonic safe spaces can be used to point out discrepancies between their day-to-day lives and the experiences of others. These discrepancies can be pointed out to others on the scene (both rap participants and nonparticipants) and to listeners beyond local scenes and at regional, domestic, and international levels. As Bynoe underscores, "Rap is American, but with a defiant shout. The sexism, violence, and nihilism that are depicted in rap music are that which exist in this country."[12] As long as these social ills exist, rap will likely exist. This is in addition to the possibility that if these social ills cease to exist, rap still might persist as "party music."

Remaining music questions include the following: What is the musical background to US scenes prior to 1980? Which subgenres and micro-subgenres of rap emerge on scenes? What is the relationship between rap and other popular musics on scenes? Who are the most important rap artists associated with local scenes?

Technology

Manipulation of sound by DJs was a key element to rap's beginnings. Schloss reminds readers that Hip Hop "existed as a culture and performance context for at least five (1974–1979) years before it became a genre of popular music."[13] This definition period at "ground zero" shows the evolution of rap's growth into a product. Schloss also shows the role and growth of the industry, MCing, and Black and Puerto Rican contributors.[14] Adam de Paor-Evans has attached Hip Hop's DIY technological innovation with identity, emphasizing that Hip Hop's heritage rooted in "African-American, Jamaican, and Latinx diasporas" actually "fueled its pioneering creative and cultural drive."[15]

As noted in this book's Introduction, there are many issues with musical examination—especially related to samples, fair use, and transformation. DJs and producers have traditionally been secretive with regard to their sources for samples, especially when engaging outside communities. While it might be important to write about a sample's source to better contextualize a song's meaning, presenting a source can also expose artists, producers, and labels to legal issues. This is especially true of writing about sources that use "stabs" (short seconds of sounds) or in cases in which the sample has been wholeheartedly transformed.

Remaining technology questions include the following: How do rap producers transform preexisting texts and themes to create new instrumentals (or beats)? What are the major innovations and changes in rap production on local scenes? What are the major technologies used in the production of music on local scenes?

Applications to Topical Studies

This book's findings have implications for several topical areas (and fields) such as

1. Place (geography; urban politics; urban sociology; and local government and politics)
2. Identity (migration/immigration; group identities; race and ethnicity; gender; sexuality; and class and inequality)
3. Power (political/social thought; political socialization; mass communication/public opinion; and collective behavior/social movements)
4. Social change (cultural sociology; socialization; and community and urban dynamics)
5. Media (communication; discourse analysis; art/music; and film analysis)
6. Technology (production, communication, and information technologies)
7. Methodology (ethnography; anthropology; mixed-methods; and qualitative methodology)

This list does not exhaust the possible areas of inquiry about rap. Rap and Hip Hop research is incredibly interdisciplinary; however, many academic disciplines carry some requirement of a core methodological approach (whether formal or informal). Holt shows that there is an "irony in the marginality of ethnography in hip-hop scholarship," as "the very scholars working to give voice to hip-hop communities in some ways centralize methodologies that perpetuate their voicelessness."[16] Harris and colleagues find that Hip Hop studies has had five clearly definable subfields since 2004: "Hip Hop based education (HHBE), global Hip Hop studies, religion and Hip Hop Studies, Hip Hop feminism, Hip Hop dance studies, and Hip Hop linguistics."[17] Such subfields might be more liberating than traditional academic fields and subfields, as scholars seek to build more representative Hip Hop methodologies.

Place

Overall, the focus on place creates opportunities for more accurate comparisons of rap between cities, regions, and nations. Meanwhile, the use of community-informed sources to focus *on* and engage *with* music, art, and other materials actually circulated on local scenes will assist local communities, archivists, and others in creating more careful studies.

In terms of place, many local artists offer deep critiques of their local conditions and attempt to offer systemic explanations for the conditions. Sometimes, local artists are able to contextualize current conditions within other local or global historical eras. The relationship between geography, placemaking, and migration also needs to be further explored. In the US, there are issues related to land and Indigenous people and issues related to colonialism, slavery, Reconstruction, and Great Migrations.

Identity

Hip Hop Nation language and theory and internal colonization framework were also important parts of the identity expressions covered in this book. Internal colonization framework was developed from Indigenous understandings of land removal, Latin American dependence theory, and radical Black politics. Meanwhile, the concept of Hip Hop constitutes an identity that both engages and goes beyond nation. Hip Hop even extends beyond space and time, according to some artists and scholars. It is also clear that Hip Hop has created an identity area (or even a social movement) that could be articulated as a Hip Hop Nation.

Power

Identity politics were a driving force in this book. For many sites in the book, the increasingly radical politics were responses to democratic systems that were unable (or unwilling) to fully accommodate the needs and interests of identity groups who were outside of power. Thus, these social movements were formed to put pressure on the political system. Gaines adds that "the stories and narratives of the oppressed are extremely relevant and very necessary. Communicating the everyday realities of such groups could lead to serious conversations around solutions, could make space for prevention of such oppressions, or could encourage the much-needed discussions of resistances required for the subjugated."[18] With respect to women and Hip Hop, Pough shows that their contribution "has been lost, or rather erased," and some Hip Hop historians seem to write as if "there were no significant women" in Hip Hop history.[19] Clearly, there is room for additional exploration of identity in Hip Hop.

Of course, race and Blackness are essential subjects of this book, as some rappers stress a history of Black struggle in America dating as far back as North American colonization, throughout US slavery and its aftermath, into generational poverty, and into the experience felt in their daily lives. Ethnicity is also discussed in the book, and throughout rap's development, intersectional critiques in areas such as ethnicity, gender, and social class have also been common parts of rap and its journalistic and academic study. Overall, rap's power to expose shortcomings within the American system is likely one of the reasons it has been such a big part of the day-to-day lives of many Black, Latinx, and minoritized youth in US cities.

Class

Admittedly, class analysis in *American Rap Scenes* could be augmented. Hip Hop's relationship to class identity is complex. Many times, race (or ethnicity) can be a simple stand-in for race. Johnson describes the complexity of looking at class consciousness in early Hip Hop, as rap artists "playfully engaged, criticized and embraced bourgeois norms, high fashion, and consumer culture," while coming from working-class or impoverished roots.[20]

There is also a thesis that the urban environment—or site—might have more to do with uniting the Hip Hop Nation than race. Writing about "the hood" as the "capital of both a new American art form and a new social identity," Jones explains,

> They challenged not political order but cultural order, through forms of dress, music, and language, which flies in the face of mainstream values and the values of middle blacks as well. During this rebellion of music, dance, and dress they seek to emancipate themselves—or at least create a sense of independence and freedom. Identity in the past was associated with national categories of race. Identity has become local, defined less by race than by whether or not you are from the hood.[21]

Jones also comments on a class distinction growing within the Black community:

> There was a time in America when all black people regardless of class status had to occupy the same physical space ... But when people with the proper resources could move to other places, the only people remaining were those who could not afford to move. This is the point at which a purely black community ceases to exist, at least in a physical, racially exclusive sense.[22]

These analyses show that class consciousness should be considered in addition to race and ethnicity.

Social Change

Rap is related to the day-to-day reality and dreams of urban America. Rose notes, "Rap music and hip hop culture are cultural, political, and commercial forms, and for many young people they are the primary cultural, sonic, and linguistic windows on the world."[23] Perry adds,

> The duality of the black everyman/rap star is, of course, in large part born of the reality that many MCs morphed from being regular brothers in the hood into celebrities. Through excellence and personal narrative, they wish to represent for the people and environment they call home, but they also want to provide a more general story of black urban youth in the US. Moreover, they recognize that regardless of their growing fame and fortunes, they still cannot escape the vicissitudes of American racism.[24]

The duality between this day-to-day local struggle and "rap star" representation should be further explored.

Media and Technology

New studies are needed to better understand evolving rap production styles, innovations, and techniques. Analysis of music by key, beats per minute, and other factors also seem especially promising for future research. Analysis of song layers and sequences would also push research forward. Analysis of local scenes requires some level of archival interest as many local scenes feature music that is not available to stream or for purchase. As Persello urges, documentation is essential for subcultures, as the original sources "are going to be lost soon":

> Subcultures have always produced a huge amount of subcultural documents, fanzines, records, events and radio programs, political action: many of these documents are lost forever, and others are going to be lost soon, but there are also interesting examples of preservation. There are plenty of private collections and some of them are open to the public; some subculture groupings have already started small-scale archives, some libraries collect materials in their local history repositories, some art galleries organize exhibitions.[25]

Persello continues, "The archiving of subcultural objects is urgent because they are precious and fragile documents of capital interest for the research, but the lack of field definition jeopardizes their quality."[26] Archival research of local rap scenes could be important for both ethnography and ethnomusicology. Vallier identifies different types of archivists: community nonprofits and performers, recording engineers and for-profit, collectors and fans, and community archivists.[27] These types of archives could be used to better document rap's history at the local scene level.

Methodology

Ethnographic approaches should be considered starting points for building better methods to further understand local scenes. Ethnographers have used observation-based approaches (participant–observer or cultural anthropologist) and activity-based approaches (involved–observer and active–participant) to better understand local scenes. Morgan's study of LA rap offers a great example of the development of an ethnographic approach by offering different types of data sources. These include interviews with performers, examinations of performers' work, personal observations, videotaped performances, ethnographic interviews, formal interviews, analyses of conversations, letters, and interviews from sources such as Hip Hop "magazines, rap sheets, radio and video programs, call-in shows, and playlists."[28] Her study is also based on twenty years of observation "in schools, at work, at play, in underground venues, at open mic-session and at concerts and rap contests throughout the US."[29] She also compared LA's scene to prior research on "Philadelphia, New York, Chicago, Atlanta, Boston, and parts of Alabama and Mississippi."[30]

Meanwhile, Harkness's study of Chicago also presents a robust method, stating, "This six-year study utilized traditional qualitative methods such as participant observation and in-depth interviews, as well as methods drawn from visual sociology. The fieldwork consisted of attending more than 500 live performances, observing home-studio recording sessions, listening to radio broadcasts, and attending poetry slams, rap battles, and breakdance competitions."[31] My study of the Oakland and San Francisco Bay Area uses an ethnographic method largely built from community requests written on clipboards at live shows, which was then converted into a study of five hundred newsletter, album, and song sources.[32]

Harris and colleagues feature an "ancestral call" to "Hip Hop scholars" and explain, "Answering this call pragmatically looks like building on the field, developing new and innovative research methods, and engaging with all the elements of Hip Hop."[33] This could be very interdisciplinary in approach while still respecting disciplinary areas "such as religion, education, politics, literature, gender, activism, philosophy, sociology, anthropology, communication, rhetoric, culture, critical race theory, missiology, law and psychology."[34] These field methodologies could include quantitative, qualitative, ethnographic, or mixed-method study approaches.

Future Directions and Questions

There are two main suggestions for future directions. First, when possible, rap should be contextualized with regard to the scene from which it emanated. In other words, rap should be explained at a local level, or the reasons why it is not considered at a local level should be made explicit. Second, when possible, local rap scenes should be contextualized with consideration to long-standing factors on the scene. Migration and mobility should also be considered. These seem essential to a rap scenes analysis. There are also four areas of recommended study, including developing studies of the following: (1) the twenty-five scenes in this book; (2) additional North American and global locations; (3) virtual scenes and Music 3.0; and (4) other music scenes and the factors that produce them.

Conclusion

American Rap Scenes shows that the development (emergence, persistence, and legacy) of rap on twenty-five US scenes has been influenced by the common factors of geography, migration, movement, prior musics, and technology. The twenty-five rap scenes covered in this book are also connected to scenes on other US, global, and virtual sites.

The evidence from *American Rap Scenes* shows that these twenty-five scenes deserve further exploration and that there are additional rap scenes in the US and around the world that commonly use rap as a form of resistance. Additional scenes and factors should be explored at the local level, as it is a careful layer of analysis and an essential tool in understanding rap as an aspect of global Hip Hop culture.

By centering on rap's local emergences at the scene level, future researchers will be able to document a culture of resistance and help others form better comparisons and connectivity between local, regional, national, and global rap cultures. *American Rap Scenes* urges qualified artists, scholars, teachers, community leaders, and the public to form deeper, more historical, and more method-driven examinations of local rap scenes before the moment or source material is lost forever.

Appendix A

Technical Appendix

Introduction

Scoping Review Design

American Rap Scenes was designed as a scoping review. The book surveys ten database and source types:

Scopus
Web of Science/Clarivate
DOAJ
JSTOR
World Cat
ProQuest (Dissertation and Thesis)
Google Scholar (Grey literature)
Bibliographical Guides
References Guides
Canonical and Current Material

The first five are research databases, the next two are dissertation and grey literature databases, and the final three are based on prior research on the topic. Grey literature is characterized as material that includes the following: traditional literature such as peer-reviewed articles and books; dissertations, theses, conference papers; and other materials published in non-traditional avenues.[1]

Source relevancy was determined by a framework with four bounds or sides. The source abstract needed to be relevant in terms of locality, to the US, one of the scenes by name, and in terms of rap. The four sides of this framework would be: local AND US AND [topic/city] AND rap music. Searches for topics were conducted for print, eBook, article, chapter, and print journal sources:

"local AND rap AND music AND [factor]"

For factors, there were five searches: geography, migration, movements, musicology, and technology. This meant performing the following searches in databases:

"local AND rap AND music AND geography"
"local AND rap AND music AND migration"
"local AND rap AND music AND movements"
"local AND rap AND music AND musicology"
"local AND rap AND music AND technology"

For sites, there were twenty-five searches. The following search technique was used:

"rap AND music AND [site name]"

The following terms were used for scenes: bronx, harlem, queens, brooklyn, staten, long island, philadelphia, newark, boston, angeles, oakland, seattle, chicago, louis, minneapolis, detroit, toronto, houston, atlanta, orleans, memphis, hampton, baltimore, honolulu, miami, and puerto. Note that only twenty-five sites (of about thirty-five) were in the search, and some search terminology was not ideal to capture the most information about some rap scenes. Most of the searches were performed between April 15 and April 20, 2023. Toronto and Kingston were originally part of this search. Based on anonymous peer feedback, the focus was changed to the US. So there was an additional search completed for Hempstead and Hampton between September 17 and September 20, 2023.

Table 10 shows the results of the topical search by database. There were 807 results, and 56 results were found to be relevant to the study, a rate of 6.94 percent. The topical results were as follows: Musicology (20.93 percent, 9, n=43); Geography (16.96 percent, 19, n=112); and Technology (4.31 percent, 24, n=557). Movements (2.74 percent, 2, n=73) and Migration (9.09 percent, 2, n=22) did not return significant results. The database results were as follows: Scopus (19.51 percent, 8, n=41); WoS (13.33 percent, 4, n=30); and World Cat (5.91 percent, 43, n=727). JSTOR only returned one article (which was relevant), and DOAJ returned eight articles, with none of them relevant to this study.

Table 11 shows the results of the topical searches in ProQuest and Google Scholar. Ranking by most results, the following was found: Movements (542,000 dissertations and theses, 99,900 grey literature entries); Migration (148,000 dissertations and theses, 41,200 grey literature entries); Technology (26,000 dissertations and theses, 92,000 grey literature entries); Geography (15,400 dissertations and theses, 58,800 grey literature entries); and Musicology (2,300 dissertation and theses, 13,400 grey literature entries).

Table 12 shows that there was a total of 2,397 locational items accessed, and 195 were found to be relevant (8.14 percent). For locational searches, the following were the highest rates of relevancy: Harlem (39.53 percent, 17, n=43); Puerto Rico (21.43 percent, 12, n=56); Oakland (17.95 percent, 7, n=39); Atlanta (17.78 percent, 16, n=90); Detroit

Table 10 Results of Topical Search by Database.

	Geography Relevant	Geography Total	Migration Relevant	Migration Total	Movements Relevant	Movements Total	Musicology Relevant	Musicology Total	Technology Relevant	Technology Total	Total	Total (Relevant)	Percentage Relevant
Scopus	3	6	1	5	1	18	1	1	2	11	41	8	19.51%
Web of Science/ Clarivate (Core)	1	1	0	5	0	18	0	0	3	6	30	4	13.33%
DOAJ	0	0	0	0	0	8	0	0	0	0	8	0	0.00%
Jstor	1	1	0	0	0	0	0	0	0	0	1	1	100.00%
World Cat	14	104	1	12	1	29	8	42	19	540	727	43	5.91%
Total	19	112	2	22	2	73	9	43	24	557	807	56	6.94%
Percentage Relevant		16.96%		9.09%		2.74%		20.93%		4.31%			

Table 11 Topical Searches of Theses and Gray Literature.

	Geography	Migration	Movements	Musicology	Technology	Total
ProQuest (Dissertation and Thesis) *K	15.4	148	542	2.3	26	733.7
Google Scholar (Grey literature) *K	52.8	41.2	99.9	13.1	92.2	299.2
ProQuest and Google Scholar *K	68.2	189.2	641.9	15.4	118.2	1032.9

(17.24 percent, 10, n=58); Miami (17.24 percent, 10, n=58); Houston (17.11 percent, 13, n=76); and Bronx (17.07 percent, 14, n=82).

No other scenes had relevancies above 15 percent. Chicago and LA returned many results. Chicago had 247 results, but only 16 were found to be relevant (6.48 percent). LA was similar with 233 results, but only 26 were found to be relevant (11.16 percent). The results by database were as follows: JSTOR (73.53 percent, 25, n=34); Scopus (51.19 percent, 43, n=84); DOAJ (40.91 percent, 9, n=22); WoS (10.78 percent, 18, n=167); and World Cat (4.78 percent, 100, n=2090). These results are also an indication of how well the search terms functioned. The searches for Hampton, Long Island, Seattle, Philadelphia, and St. Louis yielded low relevancy rates for results.

Table 13 shows the results of locational searches in ProQuest and Google Scholar. There was a total of 1,114,200 items found, which included 307,100 dissertations and theses and 835,100 grey literature entries. Sites with over 100,000 total included Chicago (140,000) and Boston (100,000). Sites with over 75,000 included St. Louis (86,000) and Philadelphia (75,700). Queens returned 52,600 results. Baltimore returned 46,000 results. It was surprising that Memphis returned relatively few results, with 4,000 ProQuest dissertations and theses and 12,800 grey literature hits. However, it is less surprising that Honolulu returned relatively few results, with 2,700 dissertations and theses and 5,600 Google scholar results. Staten Island, Newark, and Hampton also returned fewer results than other site searches. Many databases would not allow a two-character search of "LI," so the term "Long Island" was used instead. This is the only instance of two terms being used for a site in searches.

Methodology and Known Issues

There are several known issues related to method. The data was not cleaned (by compiling results into one common database), so there are duplicate results analyzed. When testing the method, there was a lack of tools to compile the different databases into one program. In fact, many searches could only be performed online at the database URL. Additionally, costs began to rise when performing searches beyond the selected databases.

There were thirty searches performed (five for factors, twenty-five for locations). There are about thirty-five cities or sites, so ten cities or sites were not part of the search.

Table 12 Locational Searches by Database.

Search Term	Scopus	Scopus	WoS	WoS	DOAJ	DOAJ	Jstor	Jstor	World Cat	World Cat	Total (Assessed)	Total (Relevant)	Percentage Relevant
1 – Bronx	2	8	3	9	0	2	2	2	7	61	82	14	17.07%
2 – Harlem	0	0	0	3	1	1	1	3	15	36	43	17	39.53%
3 – Queens	2	3	0	4	0	0	0	0	2	101	108	4	3.70%
4 – Brooklyn	2	4	0	1	0	0	1	1	3	44	50	6	12.00%
5 – Staten	0	0	0	0	0	0	0	0	1	7	7	1	14.29%
6 – Long Island	0	0	0	4	0	0	0	0	4	344	348	4	1.15%
7 – Philadelphia	0	0	0	9	0	1	0	0	3	100	110	3	2.73%
8 – Newark	0	0	1	7	0	0	0	0	1	17	24	2	8.33%
9 – Boston	1	2	1	17	0	0	0	0	3	138	157	5	3.18%
10 – Angeles	11	19	5	26	0	1	4	5	6	182	233	26	11.16%
11 – Oakland	2	2	1	6	0	0	0	0	4	31	39	7	17.95%
12 – Seattle	0	1	0	4	0	0	0	0	1	64	69	1	1.45%
13 – Chicago	4	10	3	18	0	1	2	3	7	215	247	16	6.48%
14 – Louis	1	2	0	4	0	1	0	0	2	100	107	3	2.80%
15 – Minneapolis	1	1	0	7	1	1	0	0	2	90	99	4	4.04%
16 – Detroit	3	7	3	4	0	0	0	1	4	46	58	10	17.24%
17 – Houston	2	6	0	3	0	1	2	3	9	63	76	13	17.11%
18 – Orleans	3	4	0	5	1	3	6	6	3	81	99	13	13.13%
19 – Memphis	0	2	0	3	1	2	0	2	3	20	29	4	13.79%
20 – Atlanta	4	4	1	16	2	2	4	4	5	64	90	16	17.78%
21 – Miami	1	2	0	5	1	1	2	3	6	47	58	10	17.24%
22 – Hampton	0	0	0	1	0	0	0	0	1	116	117	1	0.85%
23 – Baltimore	0	0	0	7	0	1	0	0	2	59	67	2	2.99%
24 – Honolulu	0	0	0	3	0	0	0	0	1	21	24	1	4.17%
25 – Puerto	4	7	0	1	2	4	1	1	5	43	56	12	21.43%
Total	43	84	18	167	9	22	25	34	100	2090	2397	195	8.14%
Percentage Relevant		51.19%		10.78%		40.91%		73.53%		4.78%		8.14%	

Additionally, almost all searches were performed using one word, and some locations are not one word. The search also considered abstracts, titles, and keywords, which limited returns from databases that only presented a full text search option. According to JSTOR, at the time of the search, only about 10 percent of their articles had abstracts, so JSTOR urged researchers to search through full text. Other databases had abstract-only searches.

For search terms, there are also several issues to be discussed. The search uses "rap," even while "Hip Hop" would return far more results, and the search uses "local" when its omission would return far more results. Many of the terms "geography," "migration," "movements," "musicology," and "technology" would have returned far more results if they had been modified or changed in some way.

Chapter 3: Migration

Use of Census Data

Several census documents were tremendously helpful to this study. Much of the primary data related to population change and racial and ethnic composition on city sites is drawn from census publications.[2] Much of the US Census data used for population, race, and ethnicity was informed by the work of Gibson and Jung. One particular study was very important to *American Rap Scenes*: Gibson and Jung's working paper entitled "Historical Census Statistics on Population Totals by Race, 1790 to 1990, and by Hispanic Origin, 1970 to 1990, for Large Cities and Other Urban Places in the US." This document contains data from 1790 to 1990 for all major US cities. In addition, some data were formed from other US Census, county, and state data. Typically, government websites at the local, county, or national level were taken as trusted resources.

There are some issues with use of race and ethnicity data, as there are changes in the questions asked of census interviewees. These are important when trying to understand the data, as only data from 1790 to 1990 can be used comparatively for race and only data from 1970 to 1990 can be used comparatively for ethnicity. Even that data use has potential issues when used comparatively. Additionally, since 2000, the census has considered two or more races and has considered ethnicity in new ways. At the time of this writing, the US Census was seeking expert feedback on whether to combine race and ethnicity into one question type.

The formula used for population percentage change was:

(New value – old value) / old value.

For total population, the data is explained in three stages: 1850 to 1900, 1900 to 1950, and from 1950 to 2020. This is because of the nature of population change, changes in collection, and the emergence of new data. By 1910, more locations were reporting population data, and by 1950, there was increased interest in measuring the population

Table 13 Locational Searches of Theses and Gray Literature.

Search Term(s)	ProQuest (k)	Google Scholar (k)	ProQuest and Google Scholar Total (k)
1 – Bronx	4.5	17.7	22.2
2 – Harlem	7.7	22.3	30
3 – Queens	18.5	34.1	52.6
4 – Brooklyn	9.1	27.5	36.6
5 – Staten	1.3	4.1	5.4
6 – Long Island	15.4	63.6	79
7 – Philadelphia	22.8	52.9	75.7
8 – Newark	4.4	9.3	13.7
9 – Boston	30.4	71.8	102.2
10 – Angeles	22.5	71	93.5
11 – Oakland	6.1	15.2	21.3
12 – Seattle	9.9	23.7	33.6
13 – Chicago	33	107	140
14 – Louis	20.2	66.2	86.4
15 – Minneapolis	16.1	33.7	49.8
16 – Detroit	11.4	28.4	39.8
17 – Houston	9.5	26.2	35.7
18 – Orleans	9.5	26.4	35.9
19 – Memphis	4	12.8	16.8
20 – Atlanta	10.5	25.7	36.2
21 – Miami	7.5	24.9	32.4
22 – Hampton	5.5	13.8	19.3
23 – Baltimore	16.2	29.9	46.1
24 – Honolulu	2.7	5.6	8.3
25 – Puerto	8.4	21.3	29.7
Total	307.1	835.1	1142.2

of global cities. By 1950, each city and nation had a population estimate, and thus the data could be further contextualized with continent and global populations.

The population data is displayed in Table 14. In early stages, from 1850 to 1900, there are many times when the population changes more than 50 percent, and it regularly changes by over 30 percent. There is only one decline reported in this era. Memphis had a population decline of −16.49 percent between the 1870 and 1880 censuses, which was associated with Yellow Fever deaths and flight from the city to avoid the Yellow Fever. So many people left Memphis that the city went bankrupt, lost its charter, and only regained its status as a city in 1893. However, for the most part, overall growth at rates of

50 percent, 100 percent, 200 percent (and even more) were a regular occurrence on the sites with census data between 1850 and 1900.

Growth continues into the 1900 to 1950 data for most sites, but it is somewhat slower growth. South Bronx, Queens, Staten Island, LA, Oakland, Gary, Hampton, and Hempstead experience more growth in population percentage than most other sites during this time.

Table 15 shows the number of Black people on each site. This is an important analysis point because it goes beyond percentage and looks at raw numbers of Black people in locations. The table shows how many Black people lived in the highly populous sites of Manhattan, NYC, Brooklyn, Philadelphia, LA, Chicago, and Detroit over time. There are also many Black people on some sites with smaller overall site populations, such as New Orleans, Memphis, Atlanta, DC, and Baltimore. Newark also somewhat fits this characteristic.

There are also some additional observations. New Orleans had a Black population of over twenty-five thousand in 1830 and of over forty-two thousand in 1840—both significant populations of Black people at the time. In 1860, Philadelphia, New Orleans, Baltimore had significant numbers of Black people. By 1870, St. Louis would be added to this list, New Orleans doubled its Black population, and DC and Baltimore continued to grow their Black populations. By 1890, Memphis and Atlanta had major Black populations on site. After 1900, NYC and Manhattan grew significant Black populations. By 1920, Chicago would also be on this list, and by 1940, Detroit as well. In 1970, LA also had a significant Black population. There were lower populations of Black people in the West in general and in Midwestern cities of Minneapolis and St. Paul. Overall, this table indicates where Black people went directly after emancipation and the travels and ongoings through 1990.

Table 16 shows the number of Latinx people on each site. This information is important as it shows larger numbers on sites such as the Bronx, Manhattan, Queens, Brooklyn, LA, San Jose, San Francisco, Chicago, Houston, and NYC. Philadelphia, Newark, Boston, and Oakland also show larger numbers of Latinx people than most other sites. There are generally very low Latinx populations in some sites in the Mid-Atlantic, South, and Deep South (Hampton, Memphis, Atlanta, Baltimore, and New Orleans) and in some parts of the Midwest (Gary, St. Louis, Minneapolis, and St. Paul).

More Technical Observations and Data

There are some technical observations and data to report as well. Before 1898, Brooklyn was not yet a borough of NYC. The 1850–1890 decennial census data is reported here (organized by year, population number, and percentage change from prior census): 1850, n=96,838, 167.26 percent; 1860, n=266661, 175.37 percent; 1870, n=396099, 48.54 percent; 1880, n=566663, 43.06 percent; and 1890, n=806343, 42.30 percent. This is important to note for two reasons: (1) to have complete data, and (2) to establish the point that there was tremendous growth prior to the Great Migration, allowing Whites to establish networks before Black migrants and other immigrants would arrive.

The are some additional data notes related to migration data sources. The book largely uses long-range data from Honolulu County and Island, San Juan, and Saint Thomas. However, there are times when this data is different or less comprehensive than mainland data. In particular, San Juan and Saint Thomas include the use of Puerto Rican Island and USVI data, respectively, in addition to city data. It is indicated throughout the book whether city or territory data is being used. There are some data records missing for San Francisco in 1850, as the records were destroyed in a fire. The 1852 population was 34,776. Also, in 1850, Portland was unincorporated.

For use of data sources around race (Black percentage) and ethnicity (Latinx percentage), 15 percent US census samples were used over 5 percent US census samples. Although the survey was typically markedly shorter for 15 percent US census samples, the larger sample percentage seemed to be more appropriate when looking at matters of race and ethnicity. Questions of race were not asked in Puerto Rico between 1970 and 1990. In 1980, the USVI listed fifteen local West Indie locations under "place of birth." This data was not comparable to data taken for the US mainland at the time.

For statistical areas, some areas overlapped and appeared multiple times in the study: New York–Newark–Jersey City, NY–NJ–CT–PA metro area (nine times); San Francisco-Oakland-Berkeley, CA MSA (two times); and Minneapolis-St. Paul-Bloomington, MN-WI MSA (two times). This issue was accounted for by only using each statistical area once in averages and other calculations.

For NYC, any city data or averages used NYC as a city. NYC city boroughs were discussed as "sites," and this was actually the core reason for usage of the term "sites" in the book and "locations" in the book's title. Also, when taking the average population of scenes, the average population of borough sites (not NYC) was used.

Conclusion

Survey Development

These simple questions have been refined over the past ten years into a more comprehensive survey. The survey has been used in workshops, classrooms, and on local rap scenes. The process began with the types of questions initially asked of some artists on local scene:

If you were making a mixtape, which ten songs would be most essential?

Which ten rappers are the most important rappers ever to emerge from your
town, city, or area?

Who are the top five current rappers in your town, city, or area?

How long have you currently lived in your town, city, or area?

Appendix A

Table 14 Changes in Population of Scenes 1850–2020.

Scene Number	City or Site	1850	1860	1870	1880	1890	1900	1910	1920
1	South Bronx							114.95%	69.39%
2	Manhattan and Harlem							26.02%	−2.03%
3	Queens							85.65%	65.13%
4	Brooklyn							40.10%	23.50%
5	Staten Island							28.27%	35.55%
	New York City	64.86%	57.83%	15.81%	28.02%	25.62%	126.83%	44.50%	13.15%
6	Hempstead	15.80%	40.46%	13.11%	29.75%	30.79%	13.93%	63.66%	59.81%
7	Philadelphia	29.59%	365.93%	19.18%	25.69%	23.58%	23.57%	19.73%	17.74%
8	Newark	124.95%	84.97%	46.03%	29.93%	33.20%	35.33%	41.21%	19.30%
	Jersey City	123.18%	326.28%	182.44%	46.25%	35.02%	26.64%	29.72%	11.32%
9	Boston	46.58%	29.92%	40.87%	44.83%	23.60%	25.07%	19.56%	11.55%
10	Los Angeles		172.36%	30.63%	95.23%	350.64%	103.35%	211.48%	80.66%
11	Oakland			580.49%	229.10%	40.88%	37.55%	124.27%	44.01%
	San Francisco			163.15%	56.52%	27.80%	14.64%	21.63%	21.53%
	San Jose				38.27%	43.71%	19.05%	34.63%	36.95%
12	Seattle				219.15%	1112.48%	88.32%	194.03%	32.93%
	Portland		250.06%	188.55%	111.95%	163.90%	94.95%	129.15%	24.65%
13	Chicago	570.31%	274.37%	166.53%	68.30%	118.58%	54.44%	28.65%	23.63%
	Gary								229.59%
14	St. Louis	372.77%	106.49%	93.36%	12.76%	28.89%	27.33%	19.43%	12.50%
15	Minneapolis			409.59%	258.85%	251.35%	23.05%	48.68%	26.27%
	St. Paul		835.34%	92.58%	107.05%	221.07%	22.46%	31.69%	9.29%
16	Detroit	130.93%	117.04%	74.44%	46.20%	76.96%	25.66%	80.04%	113.34%
17	Houston		102.21%	93.64%	76.01%	66.88%	61.97%	76.55%	75.48%
18	New Orleans	13.88%	44.94%	13.48%	12.89%	12.01%	18.62%	18.10%	14.20%
19	Memphis		155.89%	77.81%	−16.49%	92.00%	58.65%	28.13%	23.83%
20	Atlanta		271.46%	128.06%	71.69%	75.18%	37.14%	72.29%	29.56%
21	Miami								440.50%
22	Hampton						9.99%	99.17%	11.50%
23	Washington, DC	71.21%	52.80%	78.66%	34.88%	56.42%	20.98%	18.78%	32.17%
	Baltimore	65.23%	25.65%	25.86%	24.30%	30.73%	17.15%	9.73%	38.56%
24	Honolulu								
25	San Juan								
	Saint Thomas								
	Population of Scenes								
	US Population								
	North American Population								
	Global Population								

1930	1940	1950	1960	1970	1980	1990	2000	2010	2020
73.32%	10.23%	4.06%	−1.82%	3.29%	−20.57%	2.98%	10.70%	3.94%	6.32%
−18.25%	1.21%	3.71%	−13.36%	−9.37%	−7.21%	4.15%	3.34%	3.17%	6.83%
130.07%	20.25%	44.94%	−3.79%	9.78%	−4.79%	3.19%	14.23%	0.06%	7.83%
26.86%	5.39%	1.48%	−4.05%	−0.96%	−14.26%	3.13%	7.16%	1.60%	9.24%
35.88%	10.16%	9.81%	15.89%	33.09%	19.18%	7.63%	17.09%	5.63%	5.76%
23.32%	7.57%	5.86%	−1.39%	1.45%	−10.43%	3.55%	9.36%	2.08%	7.69%
163.79%	38.87%	66.79%	71.27%	8.22%	−7.87%	−1.74%	4.17%	0.51%	4.43%
6.97%	−1.01%	7.26%	−3.34%	−2.69%	−13.36%	−6.08%	−4.29%	0.56%	5.10%
6.95%	−3.06%	2.10%	−7.65%	−5.63%	−13.90%	−16.41%	−0.61%	1.31%	12.42%
6.24%	−4.91%	−0.72%	−7.66%	−5.63%	−14.21%	2.24%	5.04%	3.14%	18.11%
4.43%	−1.33%	3.97%	−13.01%	−8.05%	−12.18%	2.01%	2.59%	4.83%	9.40%
114.69%	21.50%	30.98%	25.82%	13.60%	5.35%	17.48%	6.00%	2.65%	2.80%
31.35%	6.37%	27.27%	−4.43%	−1.63%	−6.15%	9.70%	7.32%	−2.19%	12.78%
25.21%	0.02%	22.19%	−4.52%	−3.33%	−5.13%	6.63%	7.29%	3.67%	8.54%
45.43%	18.74%	39.18%	114.31%	118.31%	41.20%	24.28%	14.40%	5.70%	7.11%
15.94%	0.74%	35.10%	11.96%	−4.71%	−6.97%	4.54%	9.13%	8.04%	21.09%
16.85%	1.12%	22.42%	−0.25%	2.67%	−4.24%	19.36%	20.99%	10.33%	11.77%
24.97%	0.60%	6.60%	−1.95%	−5.17%	−10.75%	−7.37%	4.03%	−6.92%	1.88%
81.35%	11.25%	19.86%	33.16%	−1.63%	−13.38%	−23.24%	−11.92%	−21.85%	−13.95%
6.35%	−0.71%	4.99%	−12.46%	−17.04%	−27.18%	−12.45%	−12.23%	−8.30%	−5.55%
22.01%	6.03%	5.96%	−7.45%	−10.04%	−14.61%	−0.69%	−0.40%	4.27%	12.38%
15.73%	5.94%	8.21%	0.66%	−1.09%	−12.82%	0.74%	1.83%	2.84%	9.28%
57.86%	3.49%	13.93%	−9.70%	−9.50%	−20.39%	−14.57%	−7.46%	−24.97%	−10.46%
111.43%	31.52%	55.04%	57.38%	31.40%	29.39%	2.22%	19.81%	7.46%	9.77%
18.48%	7.80%	15.35%	10.01%	−5.43%	−6.06%	−10.87%	−2.47%	−29.06%	11.68%
55.92%	15.72%	35.18%	25.64%	25.33%	3.66%	−5.57%	6.51%	−0.49%	−2.13%
34.77%	11.81%	9.60%	47.13%	1.95%	−14.48%	−7.29%	5.70%	0.85%	18.74%
274.14%	55.62%	44.78%	17.01%	14.80%	3.59%	3.37%	1.09%	10.20%	10.71%
3.98%	−7.58%	1.15%	1396.11%	35.31%	1.52%	9.11%	9.48%	−6.19%	−0.21%
11.27%	36.19%	20.98%	−4.76%	−0.97%	−15.62%	−4.92%	−5.74%	5.19%	14.60%
4.01%	6.74%	10.55%	−1.12%	−3.54%	−13.14%	-6.45%	−11.53%	−4.64%	−5.68%
	27.27%	36.69%	−16.66%	10.43%	12.37%	3.26%	−1.58%	−9.09%	3.72%
	47.54%	32.80%	100.94%	2.56%	−6.13%	0.67%	1.07%	−10.65%	−13.42%
		22.62%	17.29%	78.75%	53.22%	8.55%	6.26%	0.89%	−18.15%
			2.90%	1.74%	−6.77%	1.15%	5.25%	−0.09%	6.15%
			18.50%	13.32%	11.48%	9.78%	13.15%	9.71%	7.35%
			19.80%	14.26%	11.67%	11.34%	13.54%	10.24%	8.31%
			20.80%	22.39%	20.26%	19.63%	15.66%	13.61%	12.24%

Appendix A

Table 15 Black Population on Scenes 1790–1990.

Scene Number	City or Site	1790	1800	1810	1820	1830	1840	1850	1860	1870	1880
1	South Bronx										
2	Manhattan and Harlem										
3	Queens										
4	Brooklyn										
5	Staten Island New York City										
6	Hempstead										
7	Philadelphia	1630	4265	6354	7582	9806	10507	10736	22185	22147	31699
8	Newark					664	855	1230	1287	1789	3311
	Jersey City						34	122	355	705	1340
9	Boston	766	1174	1468	1690	1875	2427	1999	2261	3496	5873
10	Los Angeles							12	66	93	102
11	Oakland								18		593
	San Francisco								1176	1330	1628
	San Jose									105	91
12	Seattle									13	
	Portland							4	16	149	192
13	Chicago						53	323	958	3691	6480
	Gary										
14	St. Louis						2062	4054	3297	22088	22256
15	Minneapolis								8	109	362
	St. Paul							29	70	180	468
16	Detroit				67	126	193	587	1403	2235	2821
17	Houston							533	1077	3691	6479
18	New Orleans			10911	13592	26038	42674	26916	24074	50456	57617
19	Memphis							2468	3882	15471	14896
20	Atlanta							512	1939	9929	16330
21	Miami										
22	Hampton										
23	Washington, DC			2304	3641	5459	6521	10271	10983	35455	48377
	Baltimore	1598	5614	10343	14683	18910	2166	28388	27898	39558	53716
24	Honolulu Island and County										
25	San Juan USVI										

1890	1900	1910	1920	1930	1940	1950	1960	1970	1980	1990
	2370	4117	4803	12930	23529	97752	163896	357681	371926	449399
	36246	60534	409133	224670	296365	384482	397101	380442	309854	326967
	2611	3198	5120	18609	25890	51524	145855	258006	354129	423211
	18367	22708	31912	68921	107263	208478	371405	656194	722812	872305
	1072	1152	1499	2576	3397	5372	9674	15792	25616	30630
	60666	91709	152467	327706	458444	747608	1087931	1668115	1784337	2102512
							2518	46458	68682	87802
39371	62613	84459	134229	219599	250880	376041	529240	653791	638788	631936
4141	6475	9475	16977	38880	45760	74965	138035	207458	191745	160558
2099	3704	5690	8000	12575	13416	20758	36692	54595	61954	67864
8125	11591	13564	16350	20574	23679	40057	63165	104707	126229	146945
1258	2131	7599	15579	38894	63774	171209	334916	503606	505210	487674
644	1026	3055	5489	7503	8462	47562	83618	124710	159281	163335
1847	1654	1642	2414	3803	4864	43502	74383	96078	86414	79039
184	209	182	191	240	291	591	1955	10955	29186	36790
286	406	2296	2894	3303	3789	15666	26901	37868	46755	51948
480	775	1045	1556	1559	1931	9529	15637	21572	27734	33530
14271	30150	44103	109458	233903	277731	492265	812637	102620	1197000	1263524
		383	5299	17922	20394	39253	69123	92695	107644	93982
26865	35516	43960	69854	93580	108765	153766	214377	254191	206386	188408
1320	1548	2592	3927	4176	4646	6807	11785	19005	28433	47948
1476	2263	3144	3376	4001	4139	5665	8240	10930	13305	20083
3431	4111	2741	40838	120066	149119	300506	482223	660428	758939	777916
10370	14608	23929	33960	63337	86302	124766	215037	316551	440346	457990
64491	77714	89262	100930	129632	149034	181775	233514	267308	308149	307728
28706	49910	52441	61181	66550	121498	147141	184320	242513	307702	334737
28098	35727	51902	62796	90075	104533	121285	186464	255051	282911	264262
		2258	9270	25116	36857	40262	66213	76156	87110	98207
1183	1507	3320	3964	3574	4146	3744	70163	89376	78338	78149
75572	86702	94446	109966	132068	187266	280803	411737	537712	448906	399604
67104	79258	84749	108322	142106	165843	225099	325589	420210	431151	435768
								2400	4247	4821
								45309		78003

Table 16 Latinx Population on Scenes 1970–90.

Scene Number	City or Site	1970	1980	1990
1	South Bronx	407322	396353	523111
2	Manhattan and Harlem	312722	336247	386630
3	Queens	153691	262422	381120
4	Brooklyn	393575	392118	462411
5	Staten Island	12320	18884	30239
	New York City	1278630	1406024	1783511
6	Hempstead	1341	3613	9132
7	Philadelphia	45798	63570	89193
8	Newark	45771	61254	71761
	Jersey City	23729	41672	55395
9	Boston	17984	36068	61955
10	Los Angeles	481668	816076	1391411
11	Oakland	27541	32492	51711
	San Francisco	82797	83373	100717
	San Jose	85478	140529	208388
12	Seattle	10835	12646	18349
	Portland	224	355	513
13	Chicago	247343	422063	545852
	Gary	14241	10793	6690
14	St. Louis	5946	5531	5124
15	Minneapolis	3940	4684	7900
	St. Paul	6512	7864	11476
16	Detroit	27038	28970	28473
17	Houston	139673	281331	450483
18	New Orleans	26408	19226	17238
19	Memphis	2804	5225	4455
20	Atlanta	5074	5842	7525
21	Miami	151914	194037	223964
22	Hampton	1625	1703	2636
23	Washington	15671	17679	32710
	Baltimore	8435	7638	7602
24	Honolulu Island and County	8250	19127	16704
25	San Juan			
	USVI			

How many years total have you lived in your town, city, or area over the course of your life?

What are the five most important movies or TV shows about your town, city, or area?

Who are the five most underrated rap artists in your town, city, or area?

Who are the five most important DJs/producers/radio hosts in your town, city, or area?

This survey was then developed into an audience-, participant-, or student-facing questionnaire for presentations, workshops, and classes. This instantly transformed the presentation, workshop, or class space into focus groups for local scene analysis. Survey participants mentioned new, undiscovered, and forgotten artists, new discussion points, criticism of topics and approaches, and so on.

Survey Instrument for Future Research

For further research on the topic, the following questionnaire was developed and tested in presentations, workshops, and classes. These questions (or a modification of these questions) will be used moving forward to interview participants on the scenes.

Example Interview Questions

Q1: Name, Race/Ethnicity, Pronouns for Addressing You, Income, Current Zip Code, Email (all Q1 questions are for survey tracking and follow up purposes)
Q2: Which rap music scene have you been a part of the longest?

1. South Bronx, NY
2. Manhattan and Harlem, NY
3. Queens, NY
4. Brooklyn, NY
5. Staten Island, NY
6. Hempstead, NY
7. Philadelphia, PA
8. Newark, NJ and Jersey City, NJ
9. Boston, MA
10. Los Angeles and Compton, CA
11. Oakland, CA and the San Francisco Bay Area
12. Seattle, WA and Portland, OR
13. Chicago, IL and Gary, IN
14. St. Louis, MO
15. Minneapolis, MN
16. Detroit, MI
17. Houston, TX
18. New Orleans, LA
19. Memphis, TN
20. Atlanta, GA

21.   Miami, FL
22.   Hampton, VA
23.   Washington, DC and Baltimore, MD
24.   Hawai'i
25.   Puerto Rico and the US Virgin Islands
26.   Other scene in the US: Write in/Specify
27.   Other international scene: Write in/Specify
28.   Virtual scene: Write in/Specify

Q3: In approximate number of years, how long have you been involved with rap music from the local scene from Q2?

- 1 Year
- 2–3 Years
- 4–5 Years
- 5–10 Years
- 10–20 Years
- 20–30 Years
- 30–40 Years
- 40 or more years

Q4: Thinking about your involvement in the local rap music scene from Q2, which of the following best describes your role?

- Participant/Artist
- Label/Club Owner
- Fan/Supporter

Q5: Please list the ten most important rap albums from your scene.

Q6: Please list the ten most important rap songs from your scene.

Q7: Please list the ten most important rappers or rap groups from your scene.

Q8: Please list any neighborhoods within your scene that have been major influences on the production of rap music.

Q9: Please list any movie, television, or video game references to or about your scene.

Q10: If you were making a documentary about your scene, including the start of rap music on your scene, its changes, and its current status, where would you begin the story?

Q11: Is there anything else that you think is important to know about rap music from your scene?

Appendix B

List of Known Studies of Rap on Scenes from *American Rap Scenes*

Table 17 outlines twenty-five rap scenes that have had a major influence on rap's development in the US.[1] The sources in the table became the basis for information on the local scenes.

Hess's *Hip Hop in America* helped transform this study's inquiry from a regional to a local level.[53] From this starting point, numerous investigations of local scenes helped augment the book's list of musical artists—including studies of New Orleans, Houston, Seattle, and Oakland.[54] There was additional sourcing used for LA, Atlanta, Puerto Rico, and other scenes.[55] Also, there are many sources that are not regionally based, but that also feature locally-based rap artists.

For many scenes, three types of website resources were vital to creating thorough artist lists and keeping artist lists current. The first two resources were actual websites—The Good Ol'Dayz and Kulture Vulturez, and the third resource was the collection of journalistic news articles related to the 50th Anniversary of Hip Hop. The Good Ol'Dayz maps out most US rap scenes and in a way that includes many more artists and scenes than the current book could possibly cover. The Good Ol'Dayz also includes album covers, which act as a sort of verification that the rap product, artist, or group existed.[56] The Good Ol'Dayz scene lists are incredibly thorough in many places. For example, during the last check for Houston, there were over 156 artists listed, with 1,542 albums listed. Also, during the last check for Memphis, there were 129 artists listed, with 1,096 albums listed. Each of these entries included a tracklist and cover.

The other website that was essential to better understanding these scenes was Kulture Vulturez.[57] However, rather than mapping the city sites, the Kulture Vulturez website specializes in contextualized artist updates. While The Good Ol'Dayz offered a solid picture of underground Golden Era rap on local scenes, Kulture Vulturez offered (very brief) comparative analysis of legendary artists, active artists, and new artists on local scenes. Kulture Vulturez's lists were very accurate and included YouTube listings of artists on the scene. This website was essential given the nature of the Music 3.0 industry, with new artists using their own distribution and social media. Kulture Vulturez also helped by making sure the recent artists listed were established beyond the level of simply using search engine optimization (SEO) to have their names appear in a search for local artists

Table 17 Existing Studies of Twenty-Five Local Rap Scenes and Starting Points for Artist Sourcing on Local Scenes.

Scene	Location	Books, Articles, or Other Works
1	South Bronx, NY	• "Hip Cats in the Cradle of Rap: Hip hop in the Bronx"[2] • *Foundation: B-boys, B-girls and Hip-hop culture in New York*[3] • *Break Beats in the Bronx: Rediscovering Hip-hop's Early Years*[4]
2	Manhattan and Harlem, NY	• "Uptown Baby!: Hip Hop in Harlem and Upper Manhattan"[5]
3	Queens, NY	• "From Queens Come Kings: Run DMC Stomps Hard out of a 'Soft' Borough"[6]
4	Brooklyn, NY	• "Brooklyn Beats: Hip-hop's Home to Everyone from Everywhere"[7] • *Push Hip Hop History [Volume 1], the Brooklyn Scene*[8]
5	Staten Island, NY	• *The Wu-Tang Clan and RZA: A Trip Through Hip Hop's 36 Chambers*[9] • "A Black Sheep Borough, an Island of All White People: Staten Island Steps Up"[10]
6	Long Island, NY	• "From Queens Come Kings: Run DMC Stomps Hard out of a 'Soft' Borough"[11]
7	Philadelphia, PA	• "The Sound of Philadelphia: Hip Hop History in the City of Brotherly Love"[12]
8	Newark, NJ and Jersey City, NJ	• "The Bricks and Beyond: Hip Hop in Newark and Northern New Jersey"[13]
9	Boston, MA	• "Hip Hop in the Hub: How Boston Rap Remained Underground"[14] • "Tales of the Tape: Cassette Culture, Community Radio, and the Birth of Rap Music in Boston"[15]
10	Los Angeles and Compton, CA	• *It's Not About a Salary--: Rap, Race, and Resistance in Los Angeles*[16] • "Kickin' Reality: Kickin' Ballistics: 'Gangsta Rap' and Postindustrial Los Angeles"[17] • *The Real HipHop: Battling for Knowledge, Power, and Respect in the LA Underground*[18] • *Nuthin' But a 'G' Thang: The Culture and Commerce of Gangsta Rap*[19] • *Holy Hip Hop in the City of Angels*[20]
11	Oakland and the San Francisco Bay Area	• *Hip Hop Underground: The Integrity and Ethics of Racial Identification*[21] • *Rap and Politics: A Case Study of Panther, Gangster, and Hyphy Discourses in Oakland, CA (1965–2010)*[22]
12	Seattle, WA and Portland, OR	• "From the SEA to the PDX: Northwest Hip Hop in the I-5 Corridor"[24] • *Emerald Street: A History of Hip-hop in Seattle*[23]
13	Chicago, IL and Gary, IN	• "The Evolution of the Second City Lyric: Hip Hop in Chicago and Gary, Indiana"[25] • "True School: Situational Authenticity in Chicago's Hip-Hop Underground"[26]
14	St. Louis, MO	• "Heartland Hip Hop: Nelly, St. Louis, and Country Grammar"[27]
15	Minneapolis, MN	• "From St. Paul to Minneapolis, All the Hands Clap for this: Hip Hop in the Twin Cities"[28]

Table 17 (*Continued*)

Scene	Location	Books, Articles, or Other Works
16	Detroit, MI	• "Welcome to tha D: Making and Remaking Hip Hop Culture in Post-Motown Detroit"[29] • *Women Rapping Revolution: Hip Hop and Community Building in Detroit*[30]
17	Houston, TX	• *Hip-hop in Houston: The Origin & the Legacy*[31] • *Houston Rap Tapes: An Oral History of Bayou City Hip-Hop*[32] • "The Long, Hot Grind: How Houston Engineered an Industry of Independence"[33] • "Hustle in H-Town: Hip Hop Entrepreneurialism in Houston"[34] • *Welcome 2 Houston: Hip Hop Heritage in Hustle Town*[35]
18	New Orleans, LA	• "Bouncin' Straight Out the Dirty Dirty: Community and Dance in New Orleans"[36] • *Bounce: Rap Music and Local Identity in New Orleans*[37] • *The Definition of Bounce: Between Ups and Downs in New Orleans*[38]
19	Memphis, TN	• "Soul Legacies: Hip Hop and Historicity in Memphis"[39] • "The Lo-Fi Lens: Interpretations of Memphis Rap Tape Rips in the Online Mediascape"[40]
20	Atlanta, GA	• "The Sound of Money': Atlanta, Crossroads of the Dirty South"[41] • *Rap Capital: An Atlanta Story*[42]
21	Miami, FL	• "Tropic of Bass: Culture, Commerce, and Controversy in Miami Rap"[43]
22	Hampton, VA	• "Virginia—Transmissions from the Edge"[44] • "Virginia is for Lovers and Rappers: Hampton Roads Rappers Changing the Game"[45]
23	Washington, DC and Baltimore, MD	• *The Beat: GoGo Music from Washington, D.C.*[46] • *Diamonds in the Raw: "the Past, Present and Future of DC's Hip-hop Movement*[47]
24	Honolulu, HI	• "Paradise Lost and Found: Hip Hop in Hawai'i"[48]
25	San Juan, PR and Saint Thomas, VI	• *Reggaeton*[49] • "Rap in Puerto Rico: Reflections from the Margins"[50] • "Researching Steelband and Calypso Music in the British Caribbean and the U.S. Virgin Islands"[51] • "Jazz in the U.S. Virgin Islands"[52]

from a given scene. There were other websites and resources that would have an artist listed as new and emerging from a scene, and within weeks, the artist was no longer there. Lists such as Kulture Vultures, sites such as The Good Ol' Dayz, and texts such as Hess's *Hip Hop in America* (and texts inspired by the volume) were essential to keeping a detailed record of local scenes and helped form the musical corpus in the Scenes chapter of this book. These resources will likely be helpful to archivists seeking to preserve a record of these products for future generations.

In addition to these main sources, musical sources were found in work on regional rap. For the East Coast, Toop's work was essential.[58] For the West Coast, Abe and Westhoff were extremely helpful in building initial lists.[59] For the South, Palmer, Sarig, and Westhoff offered essential information.[60] Additionally, there were many sources used for lists of general rap artists who were then placed in their respective scenes. Some of these sources included Bogdanov, Coleman, Gray, Mook, and Shelowitz.[61] The local producer sections of Chapter 1 were created by looking into who produced song content for local artists and groups. However, additional sources that were helpful in locating DJ and producers included Souveignier's study of DJ culture and technology and Said's two major studies of production technology.[62]

American Rap Scenes Spotify and YouTube Playlists

This Appendix was created by searching for songs and videos from rap artists and producers discussed in Chapter 1 of this book. Spotify playlists focus on songs, and YouTube playlists focus on music videos. The playlists were originally created in December 2023, and all information below is related to that playlist creation stage. However, *American Rap Scenes* playlists are active and will change with community and social media input. Playlist content will increase as new songs are suggested, and playlist content will decrease as some songs are removed from the playlist. In December 2023, the complete *American Rap Scenes* Spotify playlist was about 8.5 days of music. There were over 3,000 songs on the initial Spotify playlist and over 2,300 videos on the initial YouTube playlist.

The basic method used to build the song and video playlists involved searching for up to two songs from each artist and producer listed in Chapter 1. Some artists and producers listed in this chapter did not have Spotify or YouTube content. For Spotify, top songs from the artists were used. For the most part, interludes, introductions, skit, and outros were not considered. For YouTube videos, only live-action music videos were considered. This not only eliminated many YouTube videos featuring images of rap artists, vinyl records, cassette tapes, or CDs but also other types of lyrical, visual, or live performance videos.

American Rap Scenes playlists are curated, but songs and videos on playlists are not censored for content. Unless otherwise noted, all songs and videos on all playlists should be considered explicit in content. Songs and/or videos can be explicit or suggestive in terms of mature, sexual, or violent content. As active playlists, community feedback (and emerging content) will continually shape these playlists. There will be an effort to add songs (on Spotify) and videos (on YouTube) to the local playlists and the overall *American Rap Scenes* playlists. There will also be an effort to replace or remove songs with outright mature, sexual, or violent content.

Table 18 lists summary data for the *American Rap Scenes* playlist (all twenty-five scenes combined as one playlist) and data for each scene's playlist—including number of songs, duration of song playlists, number of videos, and Spotify and YouTube playlist URLs.

Table 18 *American Rap Scenes* Spotify and YouTube Playlist Summary.

Playlist	# Songs	Duration	# Videos	URLs
American Rap Scenes Playlists (All Local Scenes)	**3,021 (2,965 unique)**	**204h, 36 m (~8.5d)**	2,362 videos	https://open.spotify.com/playlist/1J3rSoHF9Xe0g8dRnsUYkL https://youtube.com/playlist?list=PLezaLsTizx4XyK5yP35lwwoSwQ-lrzLXS
01 - South Bronx	87	6h	67	https://open.spotify.com/playlist/2QDihMDmZNkdNFglF1HWuz https://youtube.com/playlist?list=PLezaLsTizx4WTzzIf2LAjA8UYCToxvJ5T
02 - Manhattan and Harlem	144	10h	107	https://open.spotify.com/playlist/15LSgJJgI79IXBR91ST4zi https://youtube.com/playlist?list=PLezaLsTizx4VsGRGXFuxb53mO_1A_pG2e
03 - Queens	101	6h	88	https://open.spotify.com/playlist/071RBUZXzpLxytVmB4sqvr https://youtube.com/playlist?list=PLezaLsTizx4ULhAZ1olG6GwJbzkN7chv6
04 - Brooklyn	143	10h	130	https://open.spotify.com/playlist/39UsdA8jPyfCWyQPGlL9HT https://youtube.com/playlist?list=PLezaLsTizx4UAwKtg_f8nkuAh4xAIZlJc
05 - Staten Island	40	2h, 30m	30	https://open.spotify.com/playlist/2igEFR1RPWlU36TEAsSdcu https://youtube.com/playlist?list=PLezaLsTizx4Vv53msBQVkam7KosGlaV7g
06 - Long Island	80	5h	69	https://open.spotify.com/playlist/0SACIYseoDQ1oIBsMxaLY7 https://youtube.com/playlist?list=PLezaLsTizx4Vw5qEqeEKxPhidTjJdQT70
07 - Philadelphia	101	6h, 30m	104	https://open.spotify.com/playlist/5C5Mtn0nQEonPxD7nroh9q https://youtube.com/playlist?list=PLezaLsTizx4Vw5qEqeEKxPhidTjJdQT70
08 - Newark and Jersey City	86	5h, 30m	84	https://open.spotify.com/playlist/0skD8NzQERoyY3rVL61GXb https://youtube.com/playlist?list=PLezaLsTizx4VPBZUxipowGBNauhjFGPGh
09 - Boston	89	5h, 30m	69	https://open.spotify.com/playlist/6bTxIvSQvtCiOhlibyCeXn https://youtube.com/playlist?list=PLezaLsTizx4XL7e3z4IUVxDMN6jVI-gbk
10 - Los Angeles and Compton	287	20h	248	https://open.spotify.com/playlist/2s73cl1z33nfN6PRX3zZtg https://youtube.com/playlist?list=PLezaLsTizx4WnqdVpgM8so7Y6OwNESvzx
11 - Oakland and the San Francisco Bay Area	271	21h	224	https://open.spotify.com/playlist/3aM9bXUgOsHdC6olUrMEwz https://youtube.com/playlist?list=PLezaLsTizx4WXFhWdMsarE-Pq65Ww9bj3
12 - Seattle and Portland	100	6h	48	https://open.spotify.com/playlist/49kLfsMpjVTtiMEtz0rdjw https://youtube.com/playlist?list=PLezaLsTizx4WafSKJP83BClKXC4Kxt_4X

Playlist	# Songs	Duration	# Videos	URLs
13 - Chicago and Gary	163	11h	114	https://open.spotify.com/playlist/3x52RUP0uFbOjOZlLc6hi6 https://youtube.com/playlist?list=PLezaLsTizx4Vu-uOxVB4U8G_ui1_ynuB2
14 - St. Louis	101	5h, 30m	60	https://open.spotify.com/playlist/53xKYKq8DeuiIkzQP8gt9v https://youtube.com/playlist?list=PLezaLsTizx4XWjyfxnMRffTilTHfWWjk_
15 - Minneapolis and St. Paul	84	5h	44	https://open.spotify.com/playlist/0e5jgmmSf8I5grMBGbjATm https://youtube.com/playlist?list=PLezaLsTizx4UDg6civBVaWKsgwmASnMdc
16 - Detroit	129	7h, 30m	100	https://open.spotify.com/playlist/1SYdKfl1CWqwk6aoN26wI5 https://youtube.com/playlist?list=PLezaLsTizx4W6eCvSyHXemaVD78gXEjnl
17 - Houston	199	13h	131	https://open.spotify.com/playlist/57CuUNNZnM9BylHPltbS1d https://youtube.com/playlist?list=PLezaLsTizx4VGuksEPcglXoy9fAVUEr5O
18 - New Orleans	148	10h	93	https://open.spotify.com/playlist/0I9aFFgyDtacz3HzfcITcp https://youtube.com/playlist?list=PLezaLsTizx4UvRoctMjAHrMIDjcRN3VS2
19 - Memphis	155	9h	104	https://open.spotify.com/playlist/0kvvsKtYN1Ijo9ocozNOVA https://youtube.com/playlist?list=PLezaLsTizx4UCc9jN4SAP0cp5n4qFkAdc
20 - Atlanta	203	15h	159	https://open.spotify.com/playlist/4bykGbW8CTX1ky0UP7FmoL https://youtube.com/playlist?list=PLezaLsTizx4VfSdu-83kkcAR78WZWKtKj
21 - Miami	105	6h, 30m	64	https://open.spotify.com/playlist/1Ed8Dect0uz901oltEdD0P https://youtube.com/playlist?list=PLezaLsTizx4V4luVA0gqAXBJQwLpohBnb
22 - Hampton	63	3h, 30m	45	https://open.spotify.com/playlist/2JhKIxBjzBZjo847rXismJ https://youtube.com/playlist?list=PLezaLsTizx4XTXBEwPMHWQb9HPoDCMXMe
23 - Washington, DC and Baltimore	134	8h	104	https://open.spotify.com/playlist/1B75Tq14tKh9JZdhSagabd https://youtube.com/playlist?list=PLezaLsTizx4XeH0vM3cZ8sjtsOa1N_Not
24 - Honolulu	22	1h, 21m	17	https://open.spotify.com/playlist/0Ksj0oB5lTImMUbeezmw0l https://youtube.com/playlist?list=PLezaLsTizx4VsBYE4aAzu8VmKNKHlx_4g
25 - Puerto Rico and US Virgin Islands	83	4h, 45m	48	https://open.spotify.com/playlist/0mRuqUszB05HAsZpkGkjl6 https://youtube.com/playlist?list=PLezaLsTizx4VJ27ve4llHqKFIPRhCz70C

Playlist links are active as of the publication of this book. If a Spotify or YouTube link shows an error, please check to see if "www." has been added to the address in your web browser. If so, remove the "www." portion and the link should work as intended.

The remainder of this Appendix lists ten song examples from Spotify and ten video examples from YouTube for combined *American Rap Scenes* playlists and for twenty-five scene-specific playlists. For Spotify playlists, the first ten songs are curated by the author, with the remaining songs initially added in order of the rap artist or rap producer listing in Chapter 1. The YouTube playlists are organized by popularity (as determined by YouTube's algorithm) at the time of publication.

American Rap Scenes (All Playlists Combined)

Spotify

Grandmaster Caz – "South Bronx Subway Rap"
A Tribe Called Quest – "Electric Relaxation"
Digable Planets – "Where I'm From"
Fugees – "Temple"
Ed O.G. & Da Bulldogs – "I Got to Have It"
The Lady of Rage – "Afro Puffs"
Mac Dre – "Feelin' Myself"
Paul Wall – "Sittin' Sideways" (featuring Big Pokey)
Killer Mike – "TALK'N THAT SHIT!"
Daddy Yankee – "Gasolina"

YouTube

Mark Ronson – "Uptown Funk" (featuring Bruno Mars)
50 Cent – "In Da Club"
Bruno Mars – "24K Magic"
Tyga – "Taste" (featuring Offset)
Coolio – "Gangsta's Paradise" (featuring L.V.)
Eminem – "Rap God"
Dr. Dre – "Still D.R.E." (featuring Snoop Dogg)
Pharrell Williams – "Happy"
DJ Snake, Lil Jon – "Turn Down for What"
Lil Pump – "Gucci Gang"

1: South Bronx Playlists

Spotify

Grandmaster Caz – "South Bronx Subway Rap"
Boogie Down Productions – "South Bronx"
T La Rock – "Lyrical King (From the Boogie Down Bronx)"
Kool Keith – "Poppa Large"
Cold Crush Brothers – "Feel the Horns"
Funky 4 + 1 – "Do You Want to Rock (Before I Let Go)"
Fat Joe, Remy Ma, French Montana, Infared – "All the Way Up"
Remy Ma – "Whuteva"
Hurby's Machine – "Antionette (I Got an Attitude)"
The Beatnuts – "Watch Out Now"

YouTube

DMX – "Ruff Ryders' Anthem," "Slippin'"
Slick Rick – "Children's Story"
KRS-One – "Sound of da Police"
Grandmaster Flash & The Furious Five – "The Message"
Big Pun – "It's So Hard" (featuring Donell Jones)
Remy Ma – "Conceited (There's Something About Remy)"
Slick Rick – "Hey Young World"
Swizz Beatz – "It's Me Snitches"
Boogie Down Productions – "My Philosophy"

2: Manhattan and Harlem Playlists

Spotify

Mantronix – "Bassline"
Rob Base & DJ EZ Rock – "It Takes Two"
Doug E. Fresh & The Get Fresh Crew – "The Show"
Kurtis Blow – "The Breaks"
Harlem World Crew – "Rappers Convention"
Biz Markie – "Vapors"
Beastie Boys – "Sabatoge"

Cannibal Ox – "Iron Galaxy"
GM Grimm – "All Y'all"
The Last Poets – "When the Revolution Comes"

YouTube

Mark Ronson– "Uptown Funk"
AZEALIA BANKS – "212" (featuring LAZY JAY)
Cardi B – "Money"
A$AP Ferg – "New Level" (featuring Future)
Beastie Boys – "Intergalactic," "No Sleep till Brooklyn"
Puff Daddy – "I'll Be Missing You" (featuring Faith Evans & 112)
Biz Markie – "Just A Friend"
Rob Base & DJ EZ Rock – "It Takes Two"
Immortal Technique – "Dance with the Devil"

3: Queens Playlists

Spotify

Salt-N-Pepa – "Push It"
Kool G Rap & DJ Polo – "Rhymes I Express"
Run-D.M.C. – "It's Like That"
Mobb Deep – "Shook Ones, Pt. II"
A Tribe Called Quest – "Electric Relaxation"
LL Cool J – "Loungin (Who Do Ya Luv)"
Lost Boyz – "Jeeps, Lex Coups, Bimaz & Benz"
Nicki Minaj – "Super Bass"
Prodigy – "Keep It Thoro"
Sweet Tee & Jazzy Joyce – "It's My Beat"

YouTube

50 Cent – "In Da Club"
Nicki Minaj – "Anaconda," "Barbie World" (with Ice Spice and Aqua)
Rich The Kid – "Plug Walk"

Mobb Deep – "Shook Ones, Pt. II," "Survival of the Fittest"
Salt-N-Pepa – "Push It," "Shoop"
RUN DMC – "Walk This Way" (featuring Aerosmith), "It's Tricky"

4: Brooklyn Playlists

Spotify

Masta Ace Incorporated – "Born to Roll"
Lil' Kim – "The Jump Off"
My Lyte – "Cha Cha Cha"
Gang Starr, Inspectah Deck – "Above the Clouds"
Digable Planets – "Where I'm From"
X-Clan – "Xodus"
Black Moon, Smif-N-Wessun – "I Got Cha Opin (Remix)"
Mos Def – "Brooklyn"
JAY-Z – "Streets is Watching"
The Notorious B.I.G. – "Party and Bullshit"

YouTube

6IX9INE – "GOOBA," "Shaka Laka" (featuring Kodak Black & Yailin la Mas Viral)
The Notorious B.I.G. – "Juicy," "Big Poppa"
JAY-Z – "The Story of O.J."
Young M.A – "PettyWap," "EAT"
Joey Bada$$ – "Christ Conscious"
Lil' Kim – "Lighters Up," "The Jump Off"

5: Staten Island Playlists

Spotify

Ol' Dirty Bastard – "Shimmy Shimmy Ya"
Method Man – "Stimulation"
Cappadonna – "Milk the Cow"
Raekwon – "Criminology" (featuring Ghostface Killah)

DJ Muggs, GZA, RZA – "All In Together Now"
The UMC's – "Blue Cheese"
Force M.D.s – "Tender Love"
Fes Taylor – "Pump Ya Fist"
Wu-Tang Clan – "Protect Ya Neck"
Carlton Fisk, Inspectah Deck, Streetlife – "A Star is Born"

YouTube

Wu-Tang Clan – "C.R.E.A.M.," "Protect Ya Neck"
Ol' Dirty Bastard – "Shimmy Shimmy Ya," "Got Your Money" (featuring Kelis)
Method Man – "Bring the Pain," "Release Yo' Delf"
Force M.D.s – "Tender Love"
Ghostface Killah – "Cherchez LaGhost" (featuring U-God)
GZA – "Shadowboxin'" (featuring Method Man), "Breaker, Breaker"

6: Long Island Playlists

Spotify

Busta Rhymes – "Everybody Rise"
Craig Mack – "Flava in Ya Ear"
Public Enemy – "Welcome to the Terrordome"
Biz Markie – "Make the Music with Your Mouth, Biz"
Doctor Dré & Ed Lover – "Who's the Man" (featuring King Just, The Notorious B.I.G.)
De La Soul – "Stakes Is High"
JVC Force – "Doin' Damage"
Aesop Rock – "9–5ers Anthem"
Prodigy – "New Yitty"
Eric B. & Rakim – "Paid in Full"

YouTube

Lil Tecca – "Ransom"
Lil Peep – "Awful Things" (featuring Lil Tracy)
Biz Markie – "Just A Friend"

Craig Mack – "Flava in Ya Ear (Remix)"
Busta Rhymes – "Put Your Hands Where My Eyes Could See," "Gimme
    Some More"
Eric B. & Rakim – "I Ain't No Joke"
Rakim – "When I B On Tha Mic"
Method Man – "Bring the Pain"
Public Enemy – "Fight the Power"

7: Philadelphia Playlists

Spotify

Schoolly D – "Gucci Time"
Bahamadia – "Spontaneity"
Monie Love – "Monie in the Middle"
The Roots – "100% Dundee"
Tuff Crew – "Tuff Crew"
DJ Jazzy Jeff & The Fresh Prince – "Summertime"
MC Breeze – "Discombobulatorbubalator (Original)" (featuring Hand
    Master Flash)
Lil Uzi Vert – "XO Tour Llif3"
Meek Mill – "Dreams and Nightmares"
Asher Roth – "I Love College"

YouTube

Will Smith – "Gettin' Jiggy Wit It," "Switch"
Meek Mill – "Dreams and Nightmares (Intro)"
Diplo – "Wish" (featuring Trippie Redd), "Get It Right" (featuring MØ)
DJ Jazzy Jeff & The Fresh Prince – "Summertime"
Beanie Sigel – "Feel It in the Air"
Jedi Mind Tricks – "Design in Malice" (featuring Young Zee & Pacewon)
Asher Roth – "I Love College (MTV Version)"
Freeway – "What We Do" (featuring JAY-Z and Beanie Sigel)

8: Newark and Jersey City Playlists

Spotify

Rah Digga – "Clap Your Hands"
Fugees – "Temple"
Queen Latifah – "Wrath of My Madness (Soulshock Remix)"
Ms. Lauryn Hill – "Lost Ones"
Naughty By Nature – "Feel Me Flow"
Lords Of the Underground – "Chief Rocka"
Wise Intelligent – "Mr. Rocket Launcher 04'"
Akon – "Locked Up"
Fetty Wap – "Trap Queen"
Dave Ghetto – "Hey Young World Pt.II" (featuring Phonte of Little Brother &
    Mystic)

YouTube

Akon – "Smack That" (featuring Eminem), "Don't Matter"
Fetty Wap – "679" (featuring Remy Boyz), "My Way" (featuring Monty)
Fugees – "Ready or Not"
Lauryn Hill – "Doo-Wop (That Thing)," "Ex-Factor"
Method Man and Redman – "Da Rockwilder," "How High Part 2"
Naughty by Nature – "Hip Hop Hooray"

9: Boston Playlists

Spotify

Ed O.G. & Da Bulldogs – "I Got to Have It"
The Almighty RSO – "One in the Chamba (The RSO Saga Part 1)"
Mr. Lif – "What About Us?"
Top Choice Clique – "Sing a Hymn"
Jonzun Crew – "Space Cowboy"
Maurice Starr – "Electric Funky Drummer"
Guru, Donald Byrd – "Loungin'"
Reks – "Say Goodnight (Dirty)"

Made Men, DJ Clue – "Made Men"
Slaine – "99 Bottles"

YouTube

New Edition – "Can You Stand the Rain," "If It Isn't Love"
Bobby Brown – "Every Little Step," "Rock Wit'cha"
Gang Starr – "Mass Appeal"
Bell Biv DeVoe – "Poison"
Gang Starr – "Full Clip"
Marky Mark and the Funky Bunch – "Good Vibrations"
La Coka Nostra – "Gun in Your Mouth," "Mind Your Business"

10: Los Angeles and Compton Playlists

Spotify

Snoop Dogg – "G Funk Intro"
Ice Cube – "Steady Mobbin'"
Aceyalone – "The Guidelines"
Kendrick Lamar – "N95"
Ice-T – "6 'N the Mornin'"
N.W.A. – "Boyz-N-The-Hood (Remix)"
Tha Alkaholiks – "Turn Tha Party Out"
DJ Quik – "Tonight"
Yo-Yo – "You Can't Play with My Yo-Yo" (featuring Ice Cube)
People Under the Stairs – "E Business"

YouTube

Coolio – "Gangsta's Paradise" (featuring L.V.)
Dr. Dre – "Still D.R.E." (featuring Snoop Dogg)
The Black Eyed Peas – "Pump It"
Roddy Ricch – "The Box"
Eazy-E – "Real Muthaphuckkin G's"
Warren G – "Regulate" (featuring Nate Dogg)
O.T. Genasis – "CoCo"

Blueface – "Thotiana Remix" (featuring Cardi B)
Nipsey Hussle – "Double Up" (featuring Belly & Dom Kennedy)
Cypress Hill – "Insane In The Brain"

11: Oakland and San Francisco Bay Area Playlists

Spotify

Mac Dre – "Feelin' Myself"
J-Diggs, Mistah F.A.B., Dem Hoodstarz – "Ghost Ride It"
E-40 – "Tell Me When to Go" (featuring Keak da Sneak)
JT Tha Bigga Figga – "The SFC" (featuring Gigolo G, San Quinn, RBL Posse, Seff Tha Gaffla, D-Moe)
N2DEEP – "24-7-365"
Kamaiyah, Capolow, Keak Da Sneak - "Oakland Nights"
Dru Down – "Pimp of the Year"
2Pac – "Trapped"
Sway & King Tech – "Concrete Jungle"
Cold World Hustler – "Cold Day in Hell"
Hieroglyphics – "At the Helm"

YouTube

Sage The Gemini – "Red Nose"
E-40 – "Choices (Yup)"
2Pac – "I Get Around"
Raphael Saadiq – "Ask of You"
Too $hort – "Blow the Whistle," "The Ghetto"
DJ Shadow – "Nobody Speak" (featuring Run the Jewels)
Digital Underground – "The Humpty Dance"
Souls Of Mischief – "93 'Til Infinity"
Luniz – "I Got 5 On It"

12: Seattle and Portland Playlists

Spotify

Sir Mix-A-Lot – "Posse on Broadway"
Kid Sensation – "Back 2 Boom"
Boom Bap Project – "Rock the Spot"
Nacho Picasso – "'89 Dope Spot"
Shabaaz Palaces, Thaddillac – "Shine a Light"
Blue Scholars – "Sagaba"
Lifesavas, DJ Shadow – "What If It's True"
Westcoast Stone, Temu – "Watch Yo Neck"
Macklemore & Ryan Lewis – "Thrift Shop" (featuring Wanz)
E-Dawg – "Clap"

YouTube

Macklemore & Ryan Lewis – "Downtown," "My Oh My"
Sir Mix-A-Lot – "Baby Got Back," "Posse on Broadway"
Lil Mosey – "Live This Wild"
GRYNCH – "My Volvo"
Shabazz Palaces – "Forerunner Foray"
Jake One – "Home" (featuring Vitamin D, Note, Maneak B and Ish)
MIKEJACK3200 – "ONNAT SHIT AGAIN"
Common Market – "Trouble Is"

13: Chicago and Gary Playlists

Spotify

Da Brat – "Fa All Y'All"
Common – "Take It EZ"
Mr. Lee – "Get Busy"
Crucial Conflict – "Hay"
Chief Keef – "Pick One"
Chance the Rapper – "Same Drugs"
Kanye West, GLC, Consequence – "Spaceship"

Daily Plannet – "Paragon"
Qwel – "Chicago Barbeque"
Kid Sister, Kanye West – "Pro Nails"

YouTube

Juice WRLD – "Robbery," "Armed & Dangerous"
Lil Durk – "All My Life" (featuring J. Cole)
Kanye West – "Homecoming," "Runaway (Video Version)" (featuring Pusha T)
Yungeen Ace & JayDaYoungan – "Opps"
Lil Zay Osama – "Changed Up"
L'A Capone x RondoNumbaNine – "Play for Keeps"
FBG Duck – "Dead Bitches"
Chief Keef – "I Don't Like" (featuring Lil Reese)

14: St. Louis Playlists

Spotify

Chingy – "Right Thurr"
Nelly – "Hot in Herre"
J-Kwon – "Tipsy (Club Mix)"
J.M.C. & Ronin – "Nikki"
Lil St. Louis – "Geeked"
Huey – "Pop, Lock & drop It (Video Edit)"
Murphy Lee – "St. Louis"
Dahol9 – "Da Hol 9"
Murphy Lee, Nelly, Diddy – "Shake Ya Tailfeather (Radio Edit)"
Ebony Eyez – "In Ya Face"

YouTube

Metro Boomin – "Space Cadet" (featuring Gunna), "Too Many Nights" (with Don Toliver and Future)
J-Kwon – "Tipsy," "Hood Hop"
Sexyy Red – "SkeeYee"
NUSKI2SQUAD – "Live On (Thuggin Days)"

30 Deep Grimeyy – "Dead Goofies," "STL Blues"
Day1ss – "Leave Me" (featuring 5ive), "Change Up Remix"

15: Minneapolis and St. Paul Playlists

Spotify

Micranots – "So Deep Remix"
Atmosphere – "Free or Dead"
Lizzo – "About Damn Time"
St. Paul Slim, Slug – "Fade Away"
Toki Wright – "Devil's Avocate"
Brother Ali – "Uncle Sam Goddamn"
Northside Hustlaz Clic – "Coming from The MW"
I Self Devine – "I Want It All"
Dessa – "Hurricane Party"
Eyedea & DJ Abilities – "Smile"

YouTube

Lizzo – "About Damn Time"
Yung Gravy – "Betty (Get Money)," "oops!"
Atmosphere – "Trying to Find a Balance," "Sunshine"
Brother Ali – "Uncle Sam Goddamn," "Own Light (What Hearts Are For)"
Eyedea & Abilities – "Smile"
Jam & Lewis x Babyface – "He Don't Know Nothin' Bout It"
KayCyy – "THE SUN"

16: Detroit Playlists

Spotify

J Dilla – "Don't Cry"
Smiley – "The Smile Gets Wild"
Cybotron – "Clear (Jose 'Animal' Diaz Remix)"
Detroit's Most Wanted – "The City of Boom"
Bo$$, Papa Juggy – "Deeper"

Eminem, Royce Da 5'9" – "Bad Meets Evil"
Kash Doll – "Ice Me Out"
DeJ Loaf – "No Fear"
Big Sean – "Bounce Back"
Royce da 5'9" – "Boom (Explicit Album Version)"

YouTube

Eminem – "My Name Is"
Rockwell – "Somebody's Watching Me"
DeJ Loaf – "Try Me"
Kash Doll – "For Everybody"
Royce da 5'9" – "Caterpillar" (featuring Eminem and King Green)
Eminem, Royce da 5'9", Big Sean, Danny Brown, Dej Loaf, Trick Trick – "Detroit
    vs. Everybody"
Kid Rock – "Bawitdaba"
Molly Brazy – "Trust None"
Insane Clown Posse – "Hokus Pokus"
Trick Trick – "Welcome 2 Detroit" (featuring Eminem)

17: Houston Playlists

Spotify

Paul Wall – "Sittin' Sidewayz" (featuring Big Pokey)
Mike Jones – "Still Tippin'" (featuring Paul Wall and Slim Thug)
UGK (Underground Kingz) – "Int'l Players Anthem (I Choose You)" (featuring
    OutKast)
Devin The Dude – "I-Hi"
Chamillionaire, Krayzie Bone – "Ridin'"
Monaleo – "Beating Down Yo Block"
Bun B – "Get Throwed"
Scarface – "No Tears"
Geto Boys – "Fuck a War"
The Terrorists, Bushwick Bill – "Blow Dem Hoes Up"

YouTube

Don Toliver – "No Idea," "After Party"
Lil' Troy – "Wanna Be a Baller"
Travis Scott – "STOP TRYING TO BE GOD"
Mike Jones – "Still Tippin'" (featuring Slim Thug and Paul Wall)
Geto Boys – "Mind Playing Tricks on Me"
Monaleo – "Beating Down Yo Block"
Scarface – "I Seen a Man Die"
UGK (Underground Kingz) – "Int'l Players Anthem (I Choose You)" (featuring OutKast)
Sauce Walka – "Ghetto Gospel"

18: New Orleans Playlists

Spotify

Choppa – "Choppa Style"
Lil Wayne – "A Milli"
DJ Jubilee, Partners-N-Crime – "N.O. Block Party"
Lady Red – "Smokin' Dat Weed (Original)"
DJ Jimi, JUVENILE – "Bounce (For the Juvenile)"
Big Tymers – "Still Fly"
Hot Boys – "We on Fire"
Silky Slim – "I Sold My Soul to the Hood"
Fiend – "Mr. Whomp Whomp"
Silkk The Shocker, Master P – "The Shocker"

YouTube

Big Tymers – "Still Fly"
Juvenile – "Back That Thang Up" (featuring Mannie Fresh and Lil Wayne)
Rob49 – "Vulture Island V2" (featuring Lil Baby)
Juvenile – "Ha"
Birdman – "Fire Flame," "Breathe"
Mannie Fresh – "Real Big"
Lil Wayne – "Something Different," "Mama Mia"
Jet Life – "1st Place"

19: Memphis Playlists

Spotify

Kia Shine – "Be Quiet (God Talking)" (featuring Kinfolk)
Jucee Froot – "Down in the Valley"
8Ball & MJG – "Comin' Out Hard"
Project Pat – "Out There"
Kingpin Skinny Pimp – "King of da Playaz Ball"
Tela – "Tired of Ballin"
Gangsta Boo – "Mask 2 My Face"
Inner-City Clique – "Set It Off"
Lord T & Eloise, Muck Sticky – "Drastically Plastic"
Al Kapone – "Lyrical Drive By"

YouTube

Pooh Shiesty – "Neighbors" (featuring Big 30)
Three 6 Mafia – "Stay Fly"
Big Scarr – "SoIcyBoyz 2" (featuring Pooh Shiesty, Foogiano, and Tay Keith),
    "See Red"
Big Boogie – "Pop Out"
Duke Deuce – "Crunk Aint Dead"
GloRilla – "Lick or Sum"
Young Dolph – "Royalty"
Lil Wyte – "Plot Thickens"
Moneybagg Yo – "Ocean Spray"

20: Atlanta Playlists

Spotify

Killer Mike – "TALK'N THAT SHIT!"
Future – "Mask Off"
Jeezy, Bun B – "Trap or Die"
Kaliii – "Do a Bitch"
Goodie Mob – "Cell Therapy"
Prophetix – "Who Is This?"

Youngbloodz – "85/Billy Dee Interlude"
M.C. Shy-D – "Bust This"
Kris Kross – "Jump"
T.I. – "Bring Em Out"

YouTube

DJ Snake, Lil Jon – "Turn Down for What"
Mike WiLL Made-It – "23" (featuring Miley Cyrus, Wiz Khalifa, Juicy J)
Childish Gambino – "This Is America"
Outkast – "Hey Ya!"
21 Savage – "A Lot" (featuring J. Cole)
Soulja Boy Tell'em – "Crank That (Soulja Boy)"
Lil Nas X – "MONTERO (Call Me by Your Name)," "Industry Baby" (with Jack Harlow)
TLC – "No Scrubs"
Rich Homie Quan – "Type of Way"

21: Miami Playlists

Spotify

Pitbull, Ne-Yo – "Time of Our Lives"
Lil Pump – "Gucci Gang"
City Girls – "Act UP"
Rick Ross – "Hustlin' "
JT Money – "Who Dat"
Trina – "Pull Over"
2 LIVE CREW – "Me So Horny"
Vanilla Ice – "Play That Funky Music"
Ice Billion Berg, Jase – "I Get So High"
Bizzy Crook – "Luck You"

YouTube

2 Live Crew – "Me So Horny," "Pop That C"
3re Tha Hardaway – "Born in Tha Ghetto"

Bizzy Crook – "Oath"
Brisco – "In the Hood" (featuring Lil Wayne), "Slidin"
C-Ride – "Money Round Here" (featuring T-Pain)
City Girls – "Flashy" (featuring Kim Petras), "Twerk" (featuring Cardi B)
Denzel Curry – "WOO" (featuring PlayThatBoiZay & Chief Pound)

22: Hampton Playlists

Spotify

Missy Elliot – "Work It"
Clipse – "Grindin' "
Timbaland & Magoo – "Drop" (featuring Fatman Scoop)
N.E.R.D., Vita, Lee Harvey – "Lapdance"
Leikeli47 – "Money"
Bankroll Fresh – "Live Yo Life"
No Malice – "Shame the Devil" (featuring Pusha T)
Pusha T – "The Games We Play"
Danja Mowf – "Question"
Pretty Savage – "Ttu"

YouTube

Pharrell Williams – "Happy," "Freedom"
Clipse – "Grindin'," "When the Last Time"
N.E.R.D. – "She Wants to Move," "Rock Star"
Bankroll Fresh – "Walked In" (featuring Travis Porter & Boochie), "ESPN"
Pusha T – "Diet Coke," "If You Know You Know"

23: Washington, DC and Baltimore Playlists

Spotify

Rico Nasty – "Time Flies"
JPEGMAFIA – "HAZARD DUTY PAY!"
Q Da Fool – "Slick Talk"
DJ Kool – "Let Me Clear My Throat – Old School Reunion Remix Mix '96"

Logic – "Confessions of a Dangerous Mind"
E.U. – "Da' Butt (From the 'School Daze' Soundtrack)"
Nonchalant – "5 O'Clock"
Junkyard Band – "Sardines"
WillThaRapper – "Trappin' Ain't Dead"
Oddisee – "Beach Dr."

YouTube

Logic – "Take It Back," "The Spotlight"
DeStorm Power – "Tsunami"
Wale – "Chillin" (featuring Lady Gaga)
Juice WRLD & Cordae – "Doomsday"
ODDISEE – "OWN APPEAL"
Carnage – "Mase In '97" (featuring Lil Yachty), "Bricks" (featuring Migos)
3oh Black – "All Talk" (Official Video)
WillThaRapper – "Pull Up Hop Out"

24: Honolulu Playlists

Spotify

Ill Valley – "Old School Toyota"
Amphibeus Tungs – "Sermon on Da Mount"
Audible Lab Rats – "Breathe"
Bruno Mars – "24K Magic"
Sudden Rush – "We the People" (featuring Peni Dean Puaauli and Chiya Puaauli)
Amphibeus Tungs, Hott – "Freedom"
Kohomua – "Be Mine"
Bxmbz – "Hometown"
Creed Chameleon, Maddmatt – "Come Home"
Tassho Pearce – "Satellites" (featuring Kid Cudi)

YouTube

Bruno Mars – "24K Magic"
Sudden Rush – "Ready for Party," "Pure Aloha" (with B.E.T., Pito, and HHB)

Kohomua – "Unconditionally," "Hold Me in Your Arms"
BXMBZ – "Hometown (Kalihi, Honolulu Dedication)"
Tassho Pearce – "Broken Wings" (featuring Mark Nazal)
Creed Chameleon – "Morning Blessing," "Everything's Happening"
EMIRC – "Honolulu"

25: Puerto Rico and the US Virgin Islands Playlists

Spotify

Daddy Yankee – "Gasolina"
Bad Bunny – "MONACO"
Vico C, Dj Negro – "Me Acuerdo"
Voltio, Calle 13 – "Chulin Culin Chunfly"
Luny Tunes, Noriega, Tego Calderón – "Métele Sazón"
Wiso G – "Medley"
Ivy Queen – "Quiero Bailar"
Maicol y Manuel, DJ Blass – "La Noche"
Dezarie – "Defend Right"
R. City – "Locked Away" (featuring Adam Levine & Lil Wayne)

YouTube

R. City – "Locked Away" (featuring Adam Levine)
Calle 13 – "Atrevete te te"
Vico C – "Me Acuerdo," "Desahogo"
Daddy Yankee – "Lovumba," "Descontrol"
Baby Rasta y Gringo – "Me Niegas"
Ivy Queen – "La Vida Es Así"
Héctor El Father – "Payaso"
Bad Bunny – "MONACO"

Appendix D

Maps

This appendix contains twenty-four maps. This includes one US map and twenty-three city, area, or regional maps. All maps were created by International Mapping. The maps and their captions are listed below:

1. US map (including all scene locations in *American Rap Scenes*)
2. NYC regional map (with the Bronx, Manhattan, Queens, Brooklyn, Staten Island, Newark, and Jersey City)
3. Map of Long Island, including Hempstead
4. Philadelphia city-level map
5. Boston city-level map
6. LA area map
7. San Francisco Bay Area map
8. Seattle city-level map
9. Portland city-level map
10. Chicago and Gary city-level map
11. St. Louis city-level map
12. Minneapolis and St. Paul area map
13. Detroit city-level map
14. Houston city-level map
15. New Orleans city-level map
16. Memphis city-level map
17. Atlanta city-level map
18. Miami area map
19. Hampton region map (including Newport News, Norfolk, Chesapeake, and Virginia Beach)
20. Washington DC map
21. Baltimore city-level map
22. Honolulu city-level map
23. San Juan area map (with tourist area as map inset)
24. USVI map

Most maps (city, area, or regional) identify major highways, waterways, and transportation hubs. The major highways include interstate highways, US highways, state highways, county roads, and local roads. Many of the sites are located *near* or *on* major US Interstates. Created in the 1950s, the US Interstate system set up two interlocking grids over the contiguous US. The horizontal, latitudinal, or "East and West" running roads include interstates ending in "0." This includes highways from the South's Interstate 10 to the North's Interstate 90. The vertical, longitudinal, or "North and South" running roads include highways ending in "5." This includes highways from the West's Interstate 5 to the East's Interstate 95.

The maps below also include points of interest such as universities, major entertainment venues (such as stadiums), and airports. They include urban areas, parks, and open spaces as well. Overall, they should provide additional tools for anyone interested in learning more about the physical locale, both in general and with regard to the subject matter of this book.

Figure D.1 US map (including all scene locations in *American Rap Scenes*).

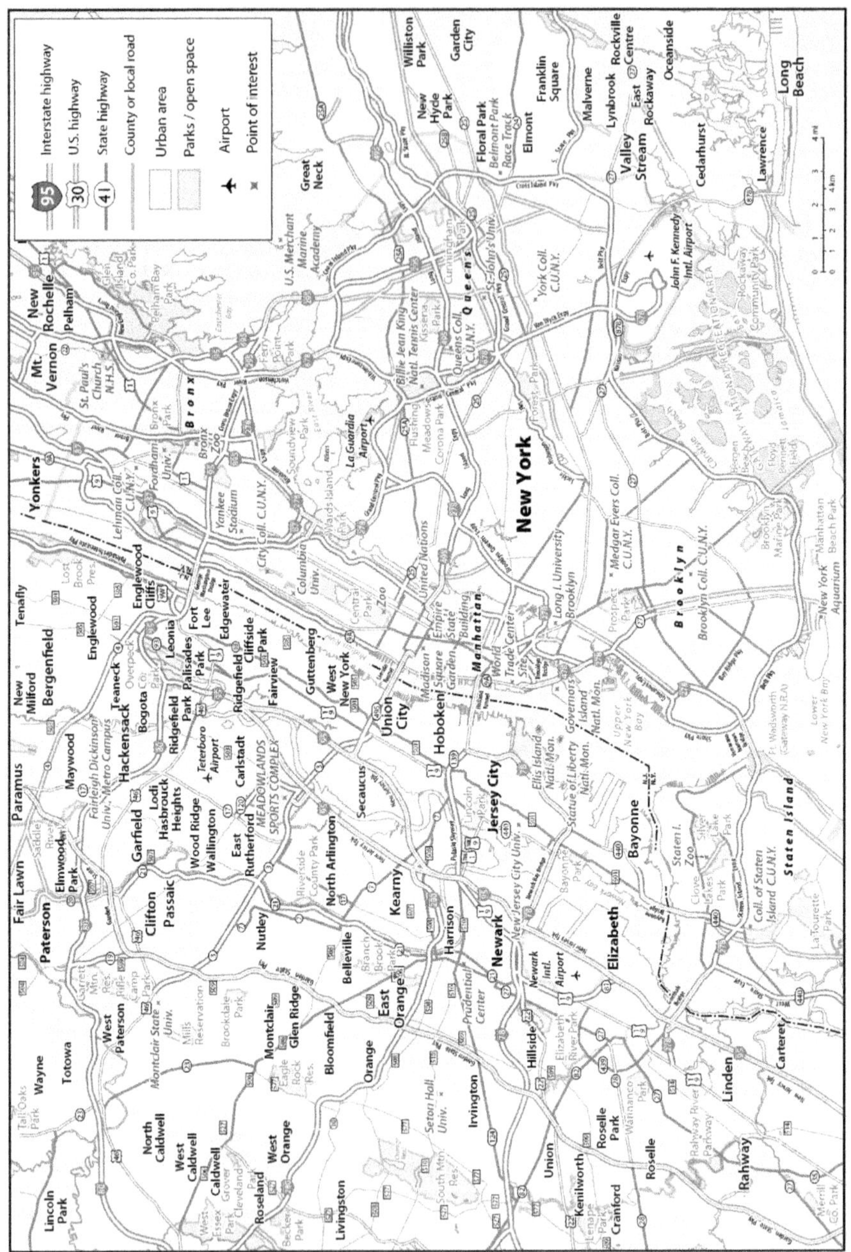

Figure D.2 NYC regional map (with the Bronx, Manhattan, Queens, Brooklyn, Staten Island, Newark, and Jersey City).

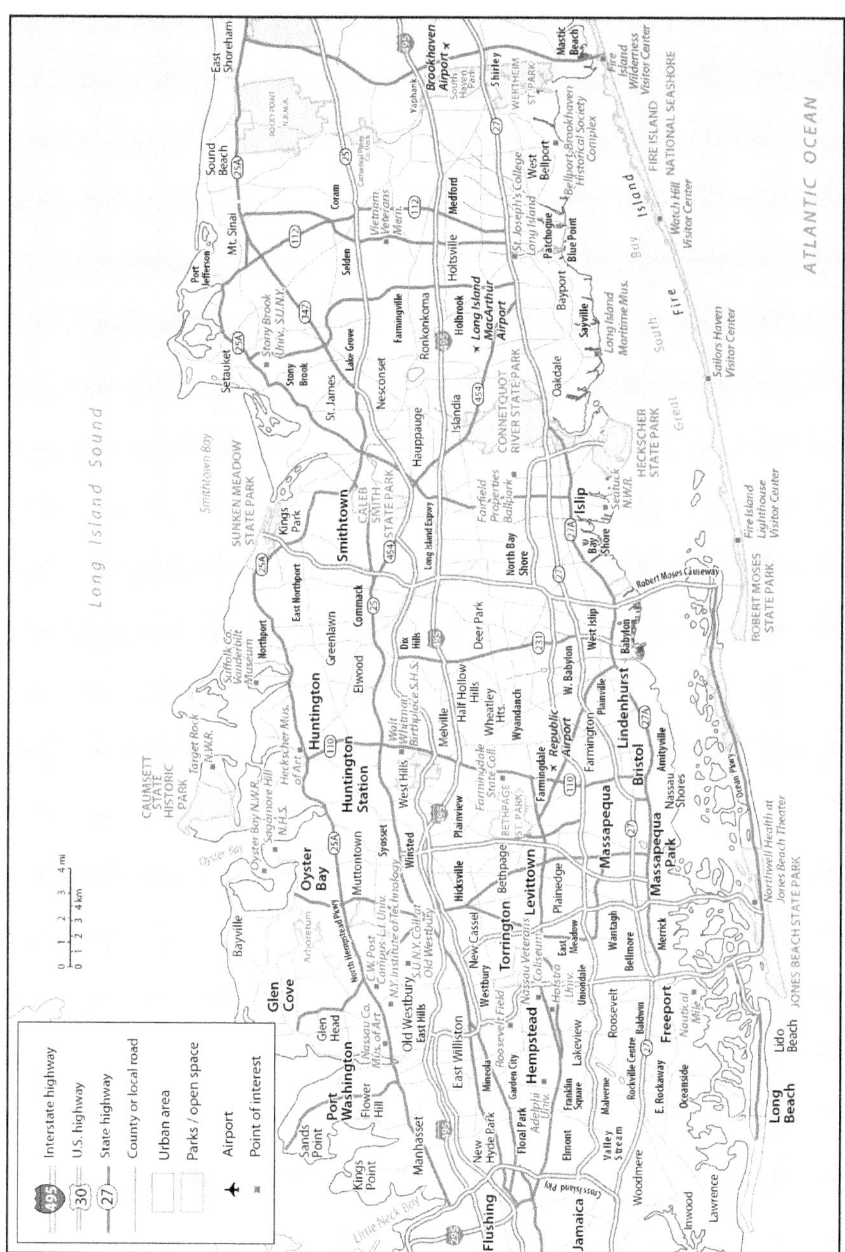

Figure D.3 Long Island map, including Hempstead.

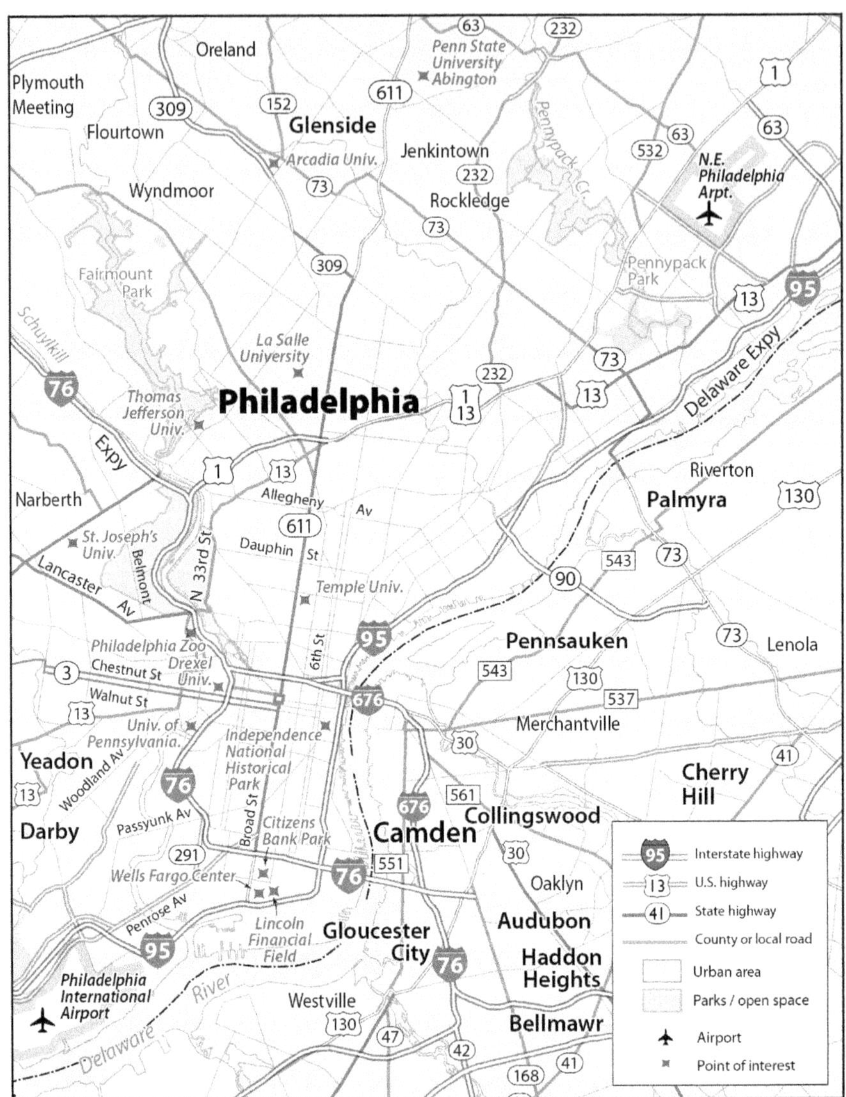

Figure D.4 Philadelphia city-level map.

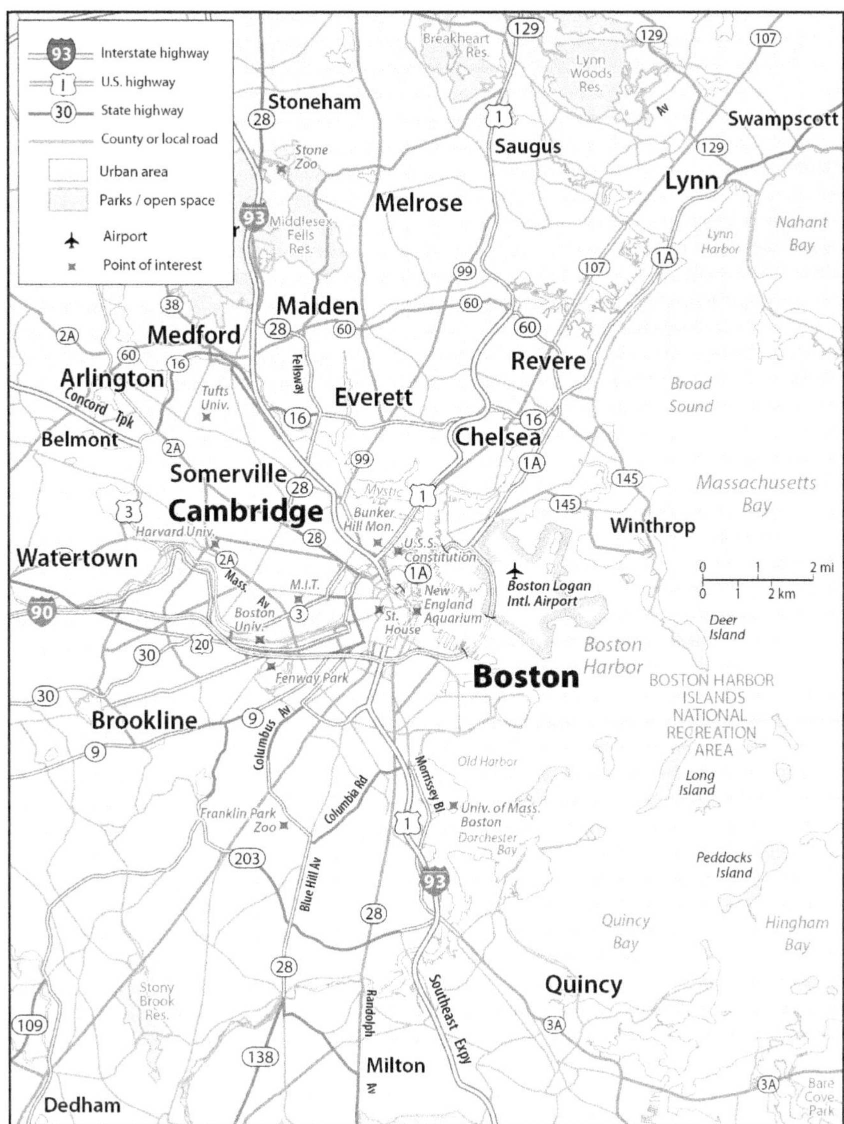

Figure D.5 Boston city-level map.

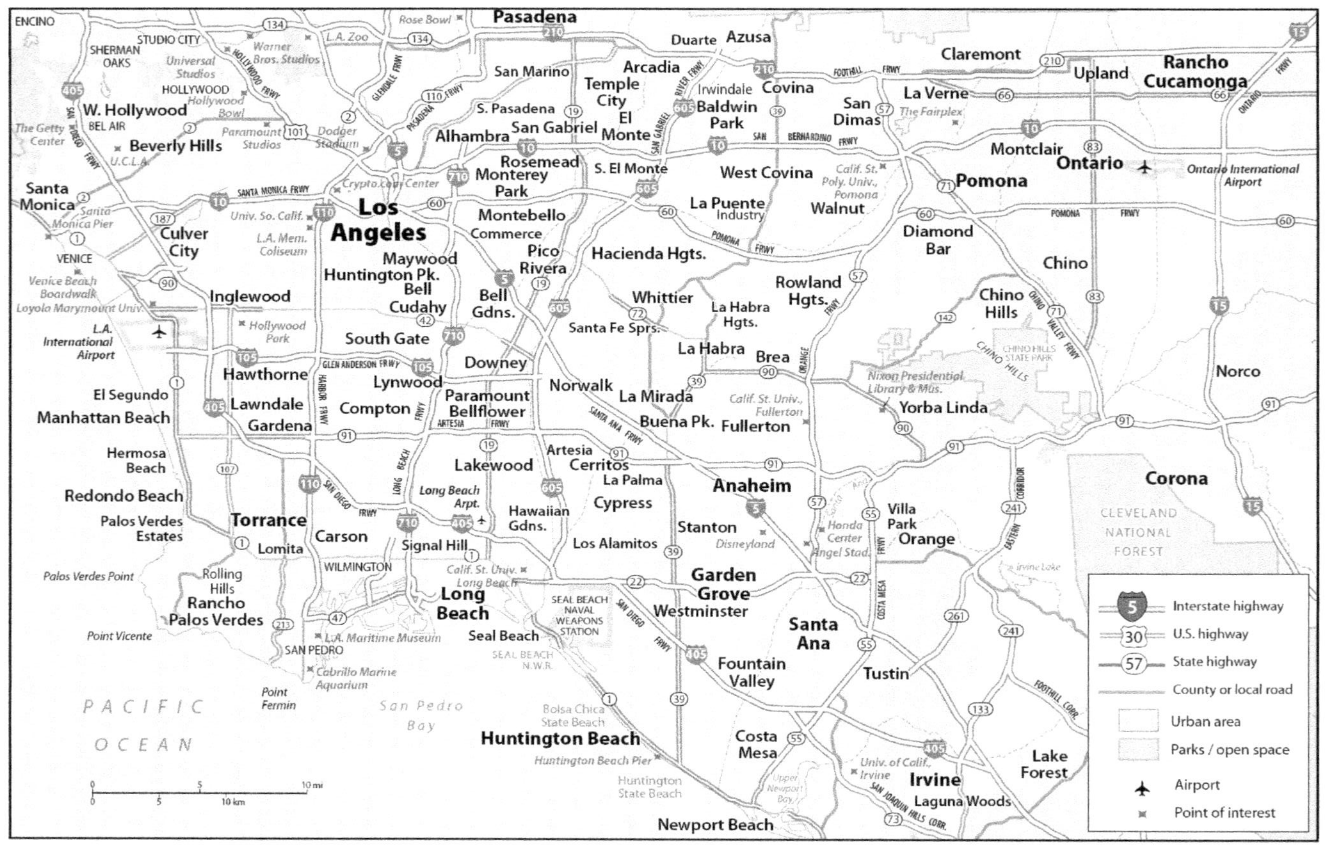

Figure D.6 LA area map.

Figure D.7 San Francisco Bay Area map.

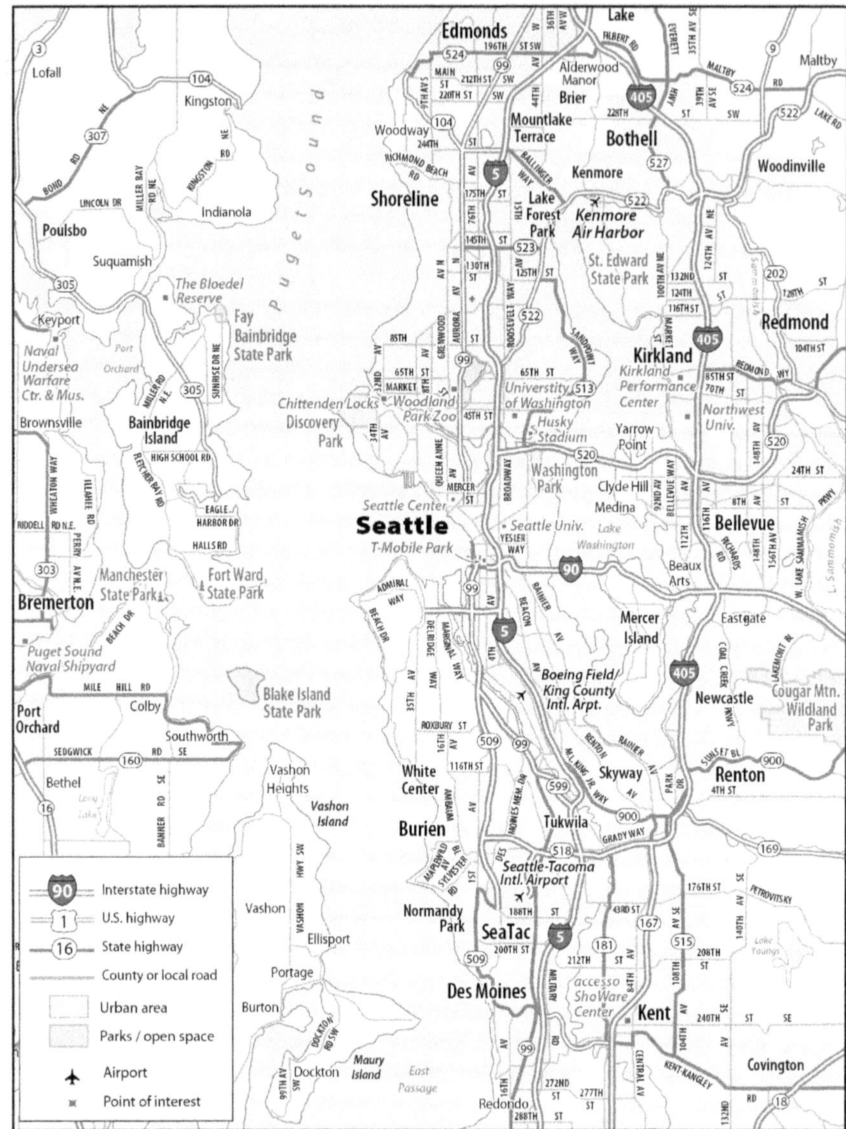

Figure D.8 Seattle city-level map.

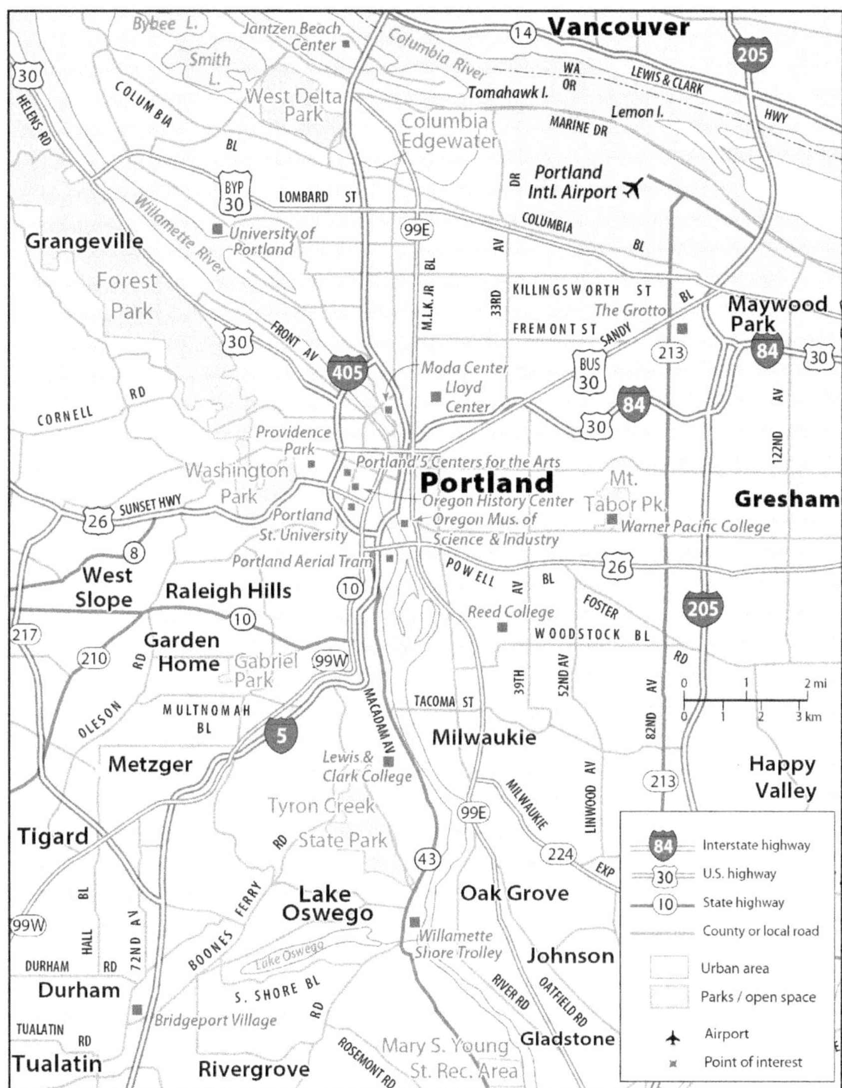

Figure D.9 Portland city-level map.

Figure D.10 Chicago and Gary city-level map.

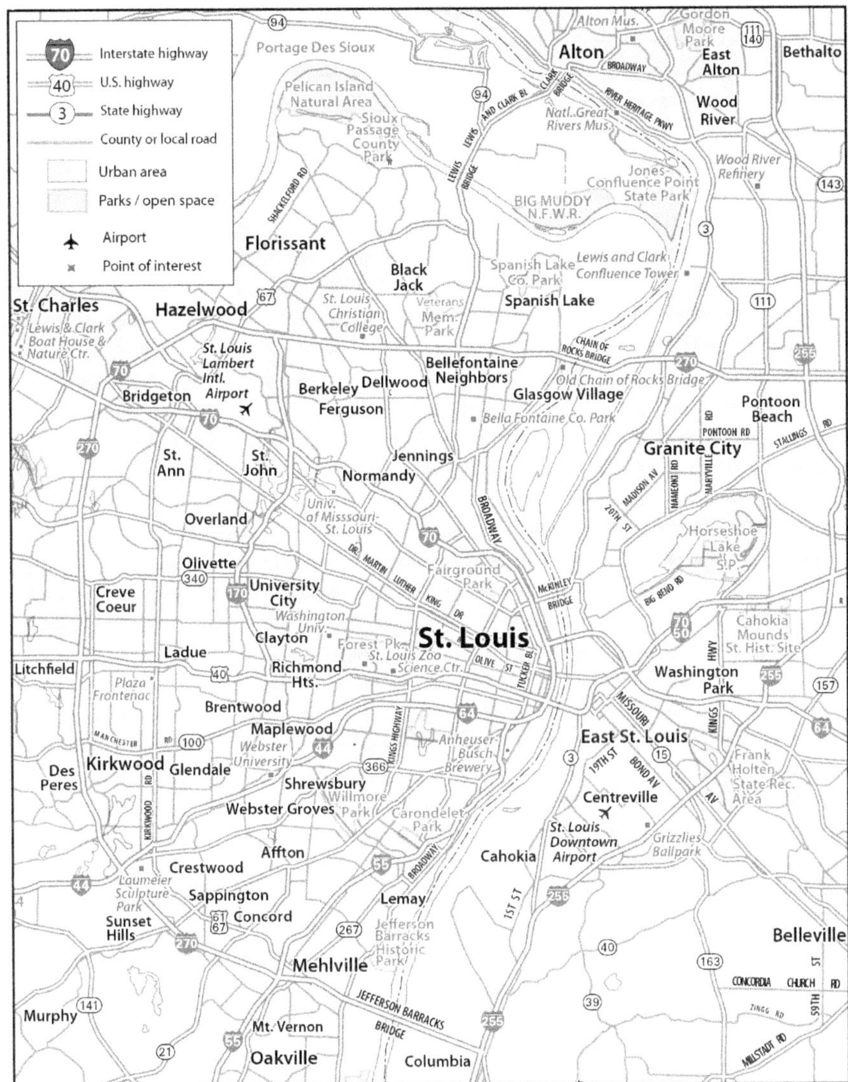

Figure D.11 St. Louis city-level map.

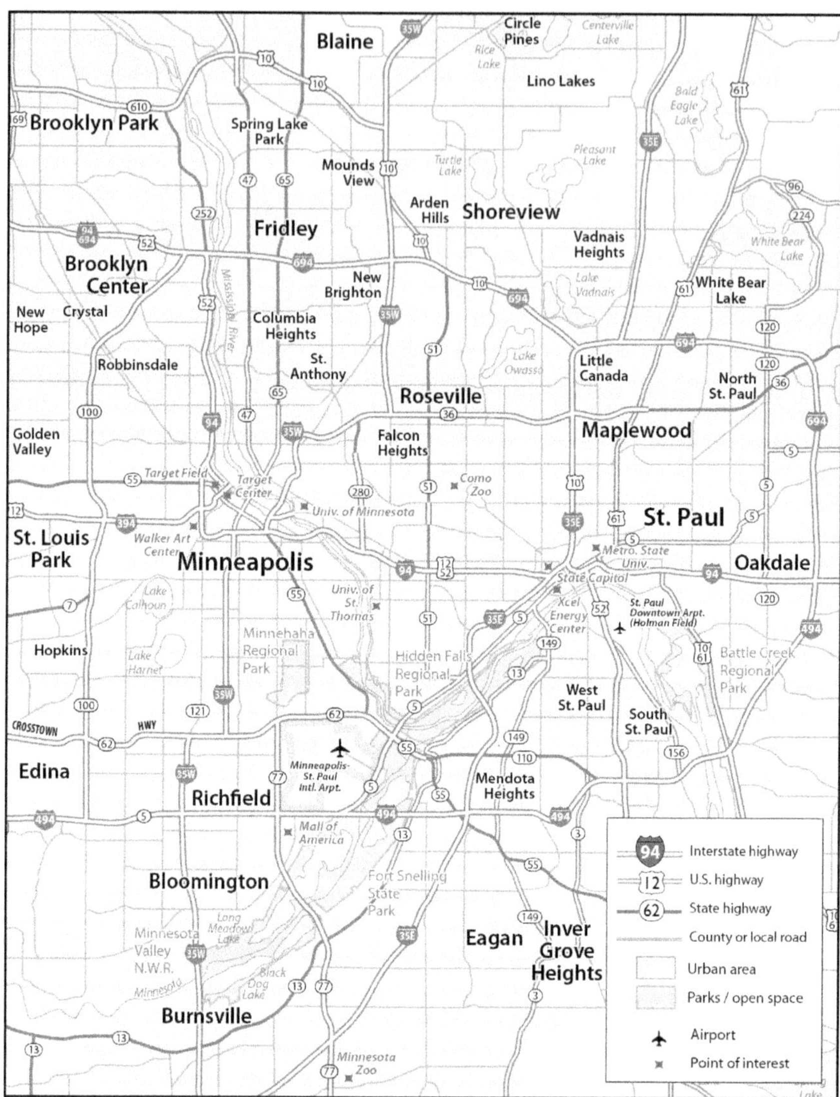

Figure D.12 Minneapolis and St. Paul area map.

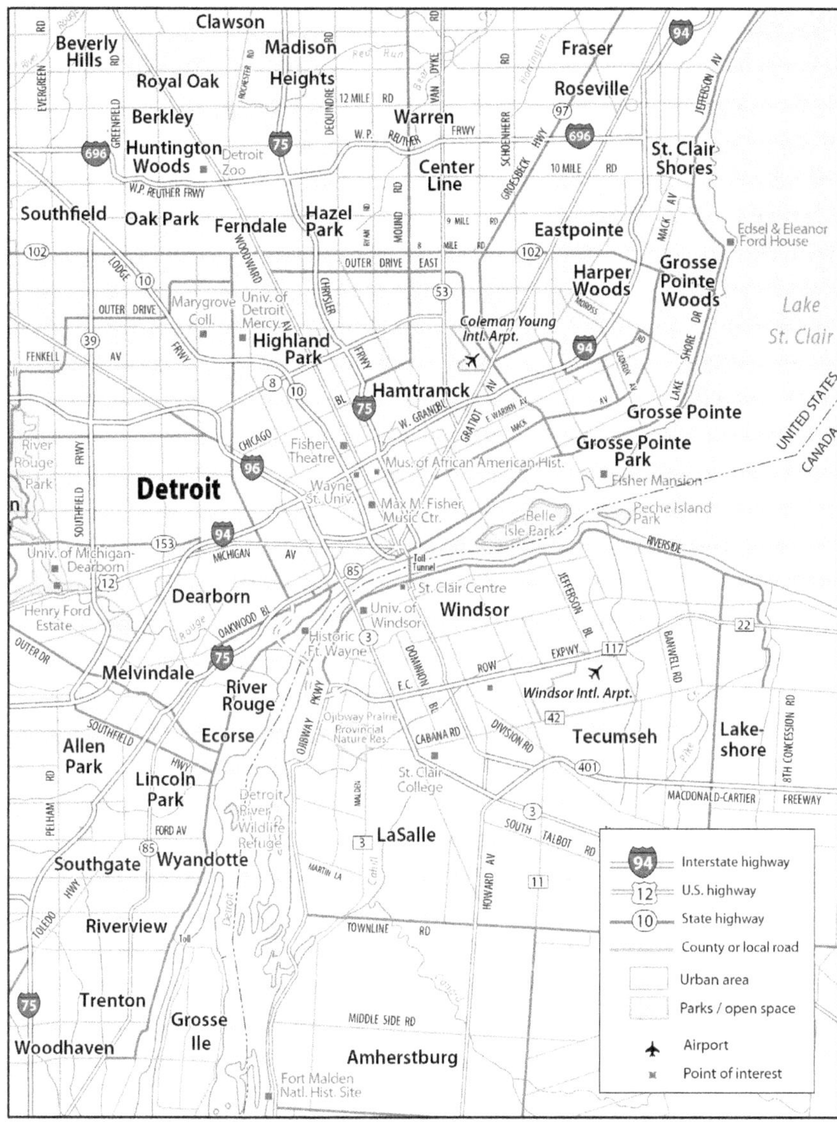

Figure D.13 Detroit city-level map.

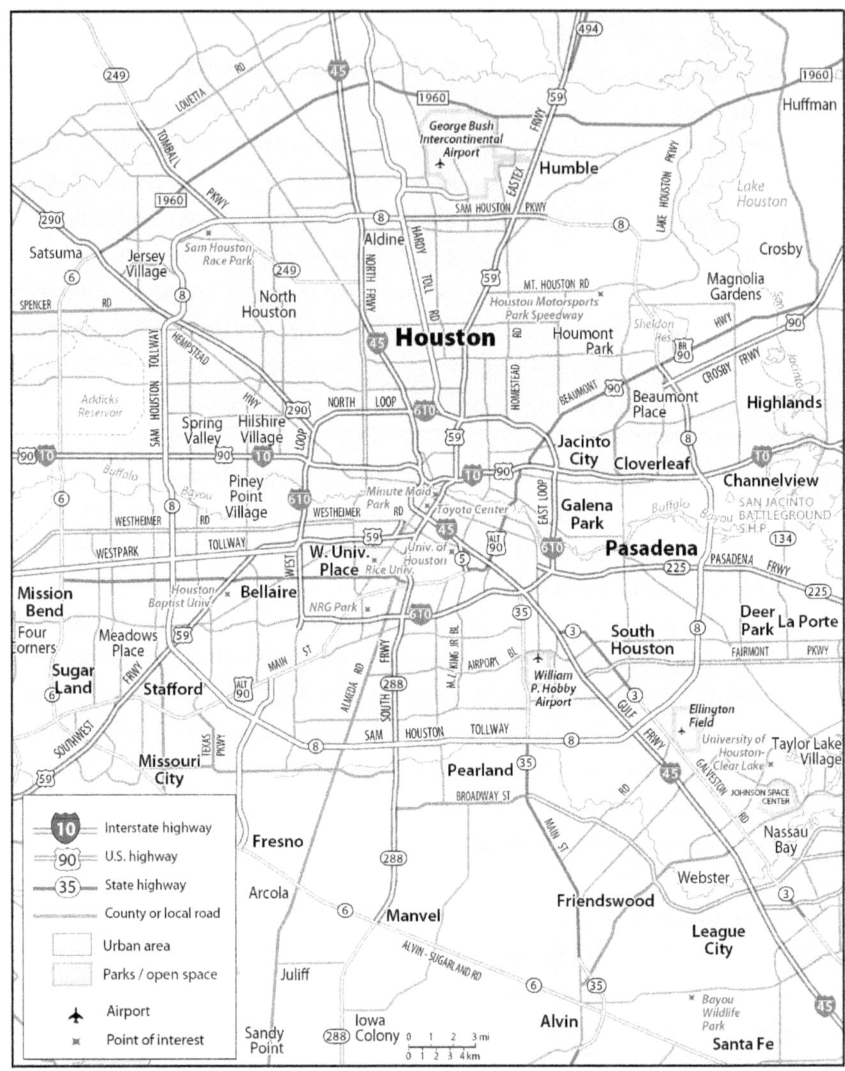

Figure D.14 Houston city-level map.

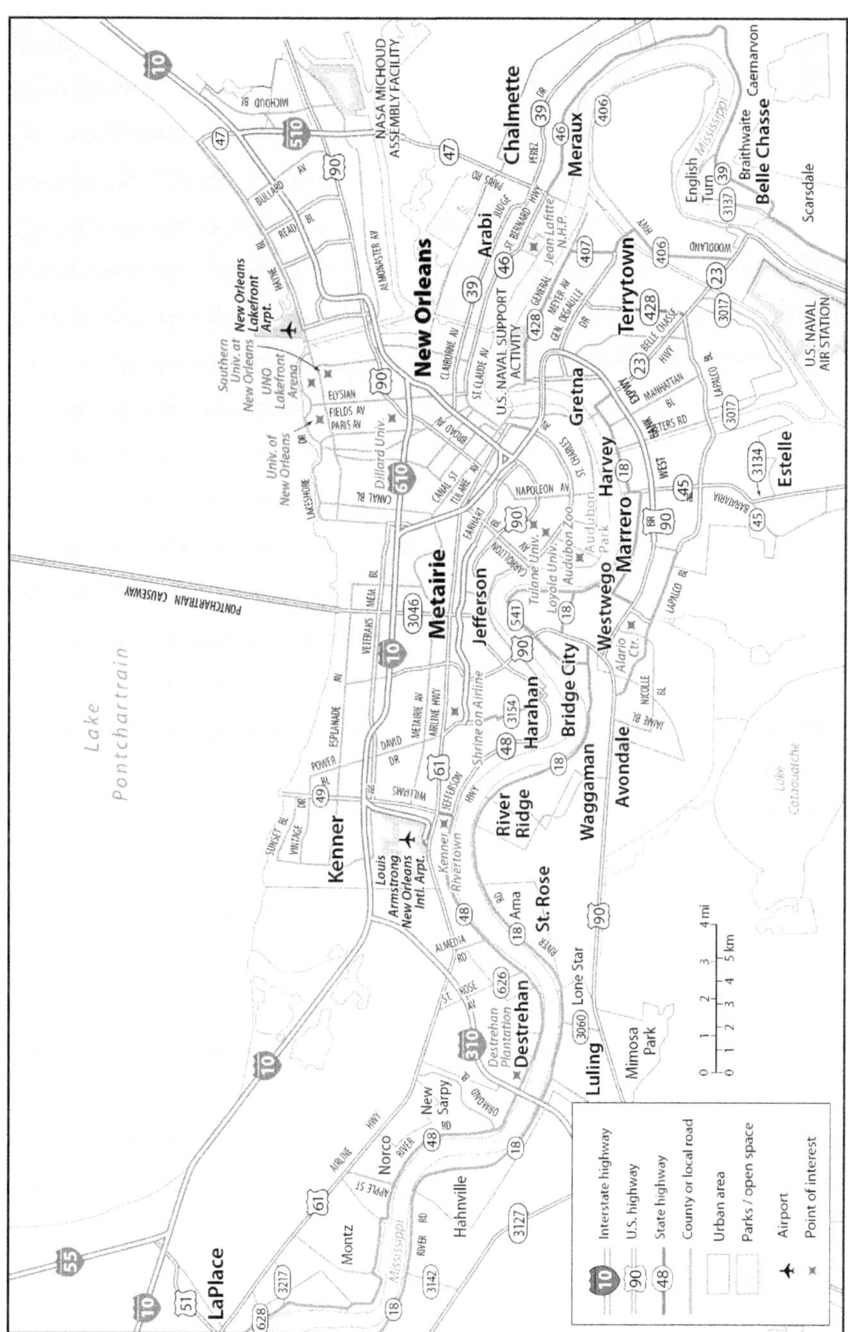

Figure D.15 New Orleans city-level map.

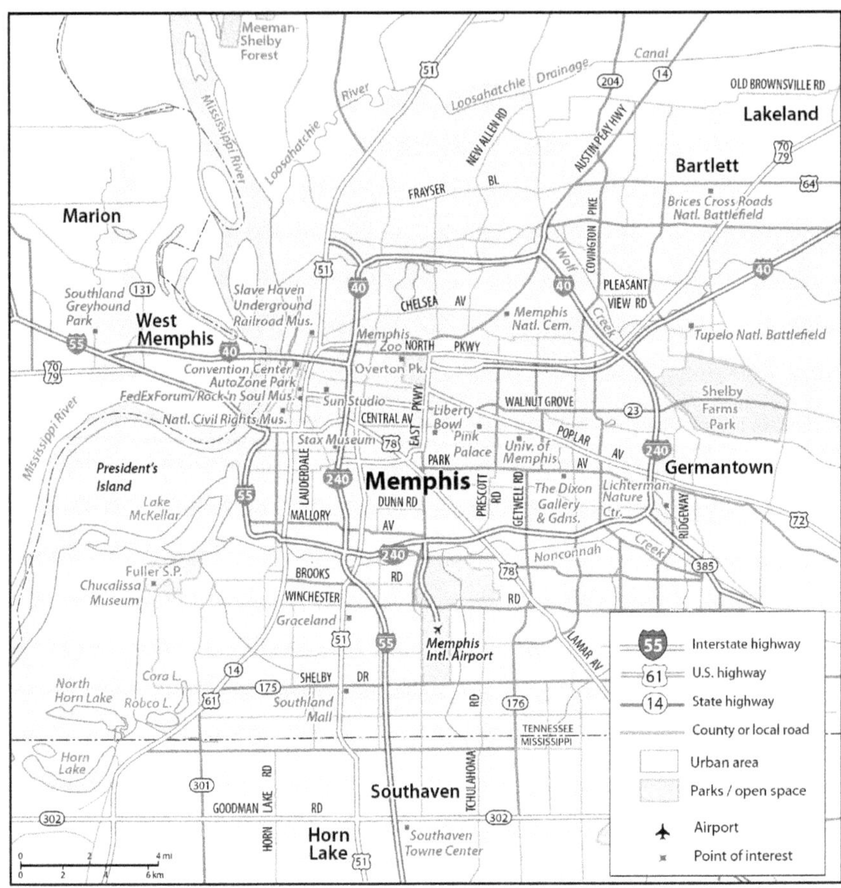

Figure D.16 Memphis city-level map.

Figure D.17 Atlanta city-level map.

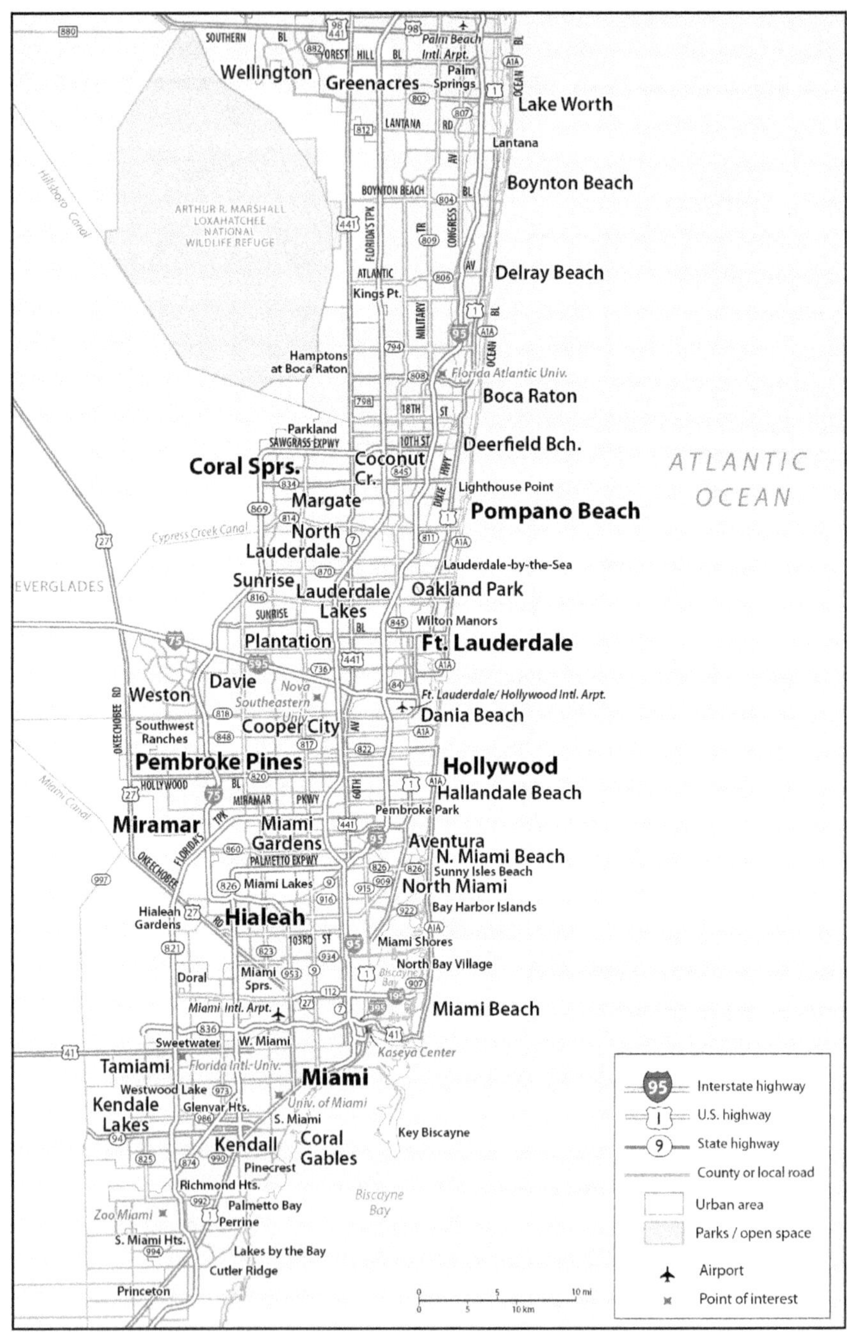

Figure D.18 Miami area map.

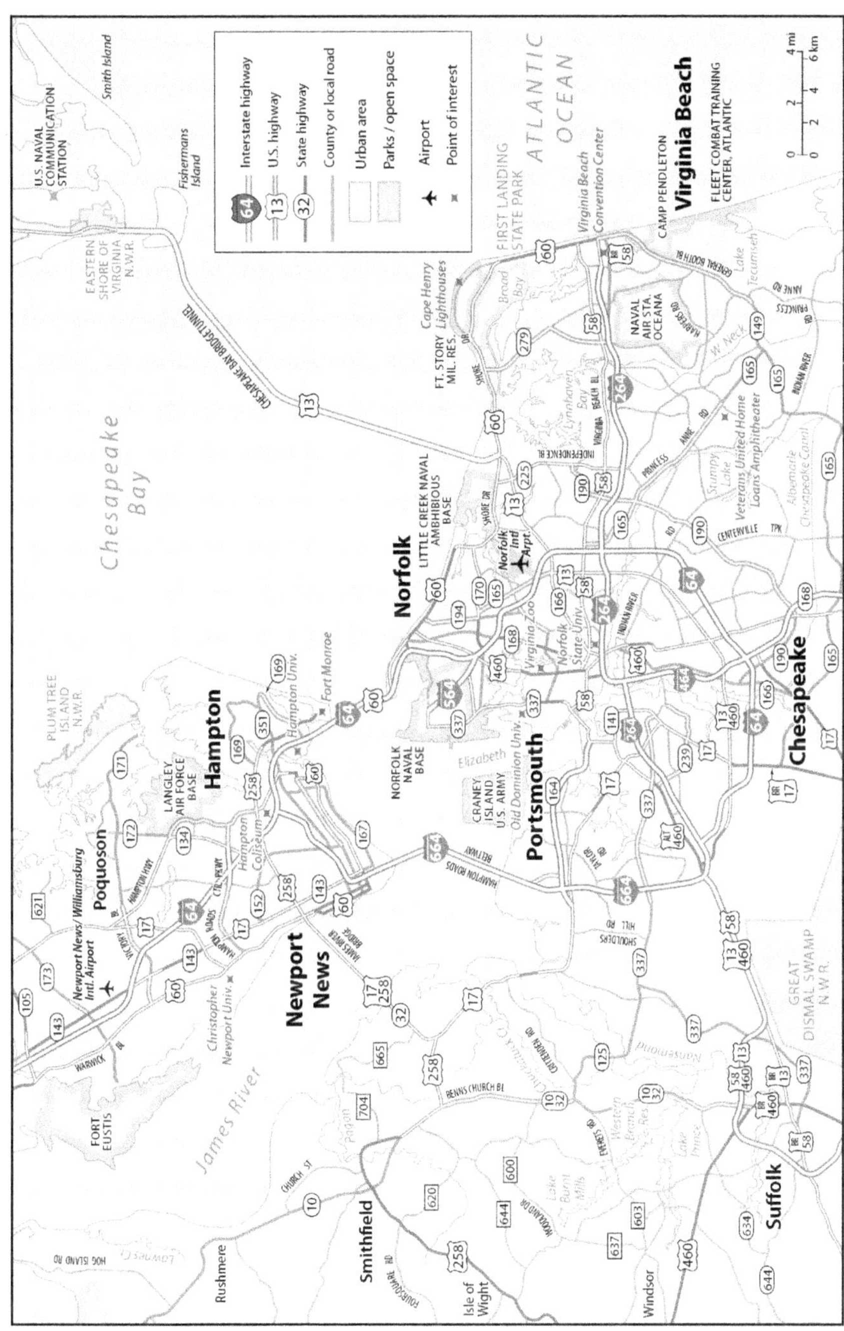

Figure D.19 Hampton region map (including Newport News, Norfolk, Chesapeake, and Virginia Beach).

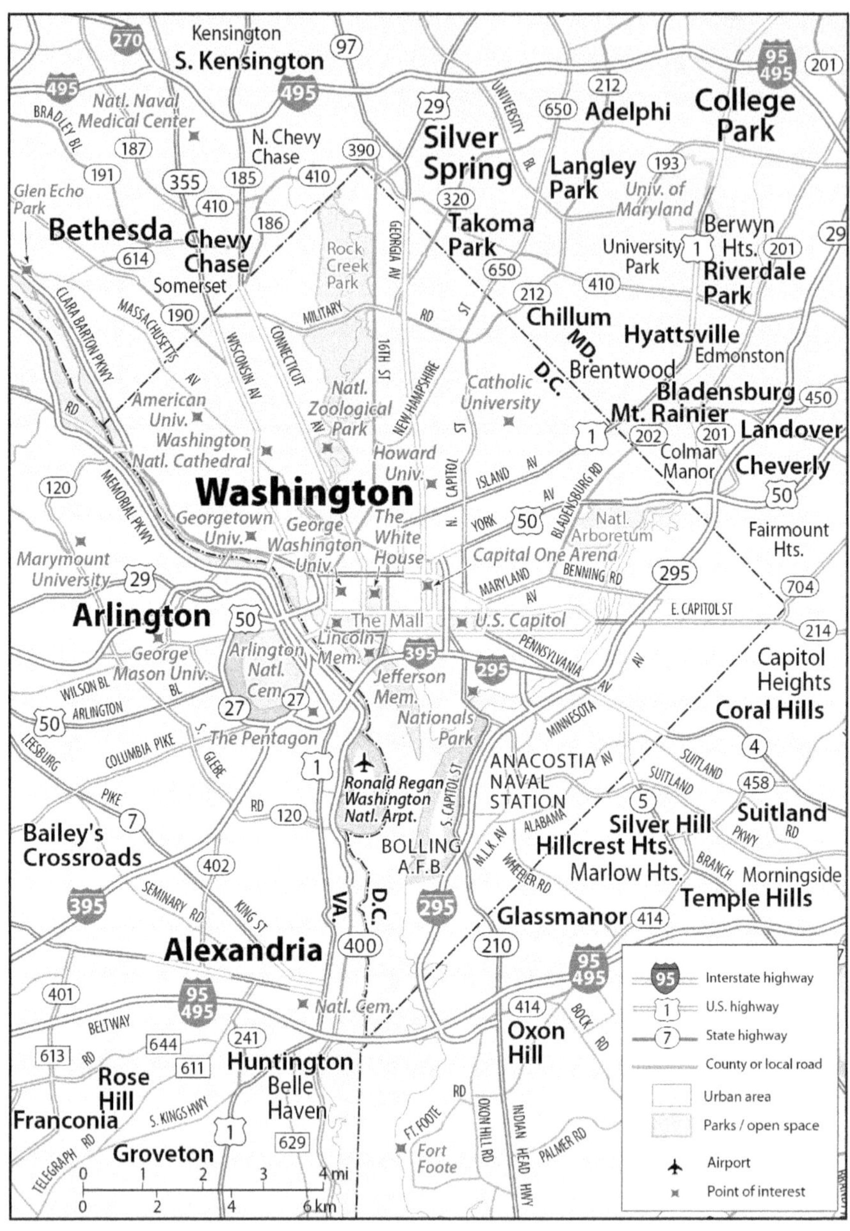

Figure D.20 Washington DC map.

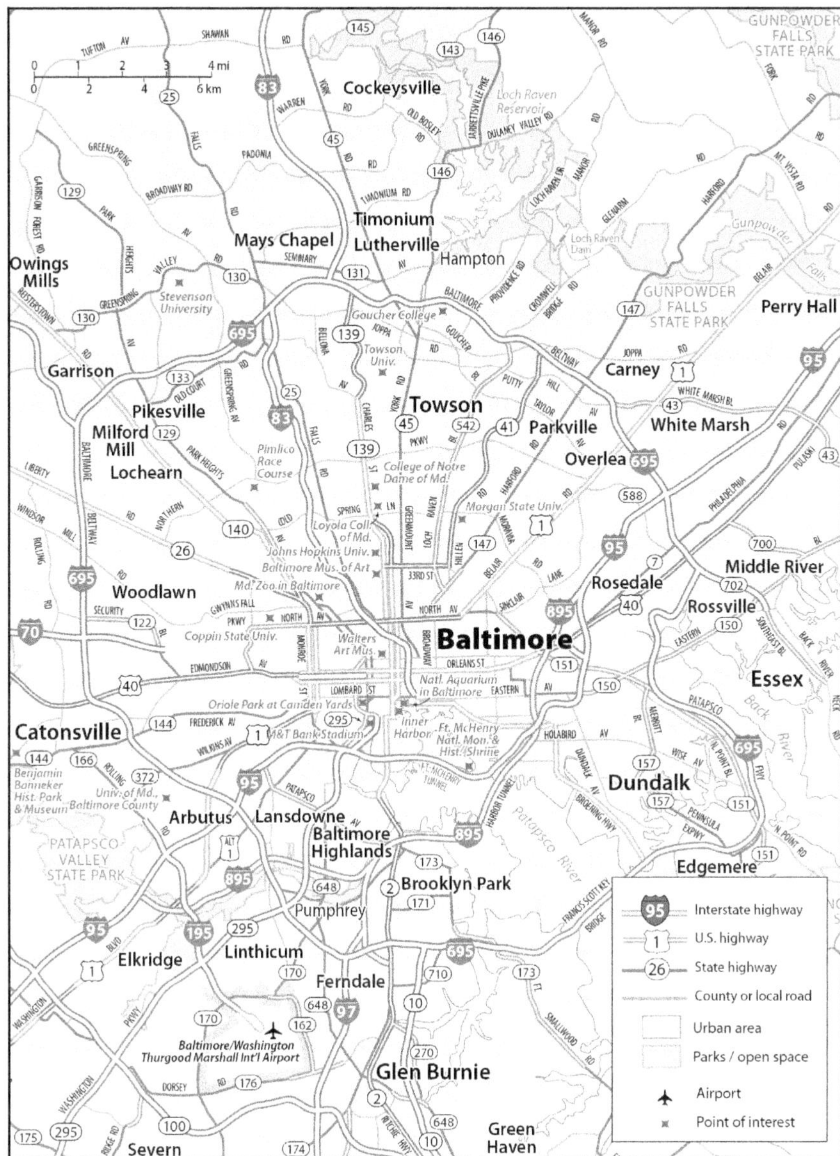

Figure D.21 Baltimore city-level map.

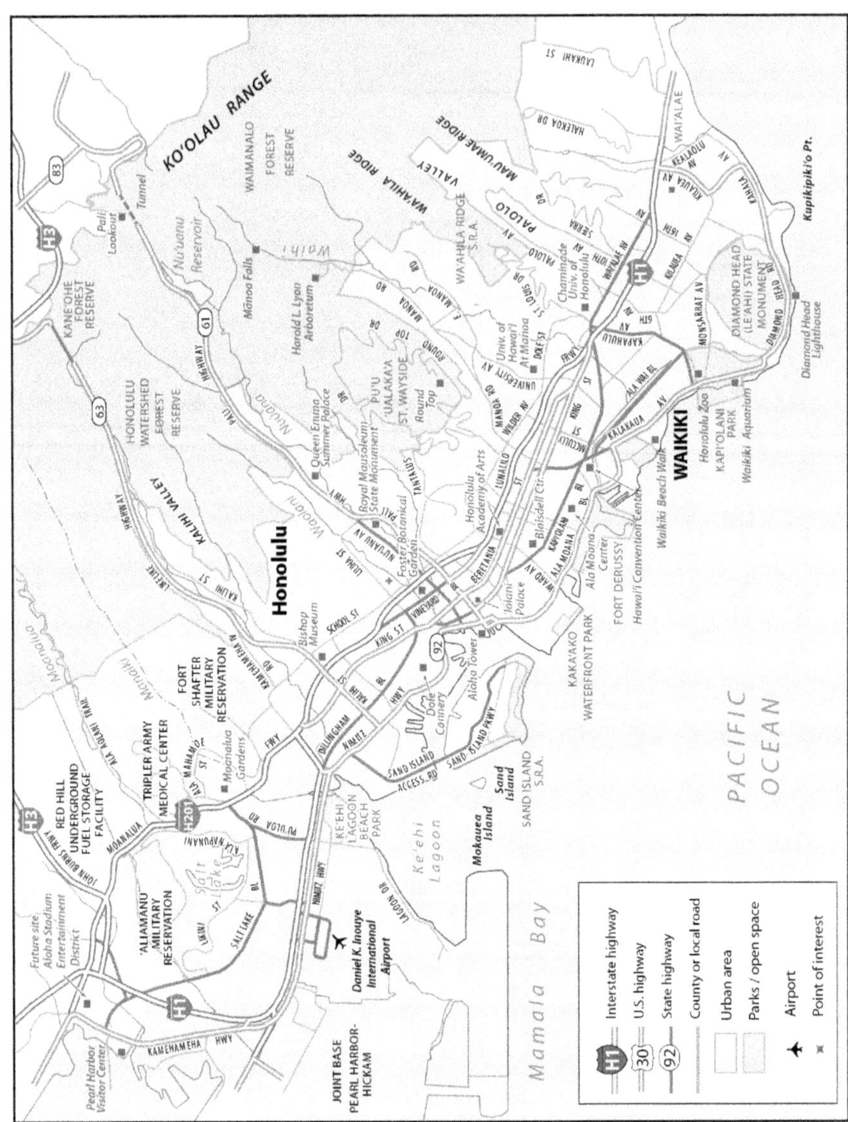

Figure D.22 Honolulu city-level map.

Figure D.23 San Juan area map (with tourist area as map inset).

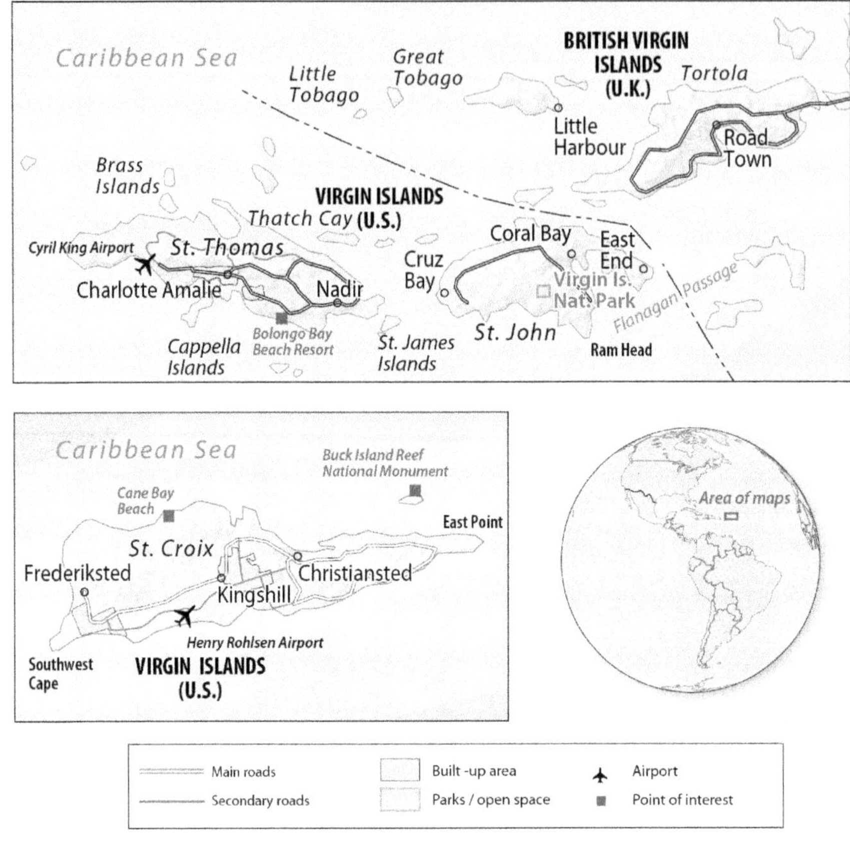

Figure D.24 USVI map.

Notes

Introduction

1   KRS ONE, "Underground," in *Kristyles [Sound recording]* (MNRK Music Group, 2003).

2   Jonathan Abrams, *The Come Up: An Oral History of the Rise of Hip-Hop* (New York: Crown, 2022), 150.

3   Fernando Orejuela, *Rap and Hip Hop Culture* (New York: Oxford University Press, 2015), 174.

4   Najja K. Baptist, "Rap and Politics: A Case Study of Panther, Gangster, and Hyphy Discourses in Oakland, CA (1965–2010). By Lavar Pope. New York: Palgrave Macmillan, 2020. 338p. $89.99 Cloth," *Perspectives on Politics* 20, no. 4 (2022): 1460.

5   Andy Bennett, "The Post-Subcultural Turn: Some Reflections 10 Years On," *Journal of Youth Studies* 14, no. 5 (2011): 496.

6   Fabian Holt, *Genre in Popular Music* (Chicago: University of Chicago Press, 2007), 16.

7   Cheryl L. Keyes, "Verbal Art Performance in Rap Music: The Conversation of the 80s," *Folklore Forum* 17, no. 2 (1984): 151.

8   Andy Bennett, "Hip Hop Am Main: The Localization of Rap Music and Hip Hop Culture," *Media, Culture & Society* 21, no. 1 (1999): 78.

9   Keyes, "Verbal Art Performance in Rap Music," 143.

10 Geneva Smitherman, *Talkin' and Testifyin': The Language of Black America* (Detroit, MI: Wayne State University Press, 1986), 55.

11 Travis Harris, Scott "lyfestile" Woods, Dana Horton, Nicole M. Horsley, and Shayne McGregor, "Funk What You Heard: Hip Hop Is a Field of Study," *Journal of Hip Hop Studies* 9, no. 1 (2022): 18.

12 Ibid., 19.

13 Ibid., 18.

14 Andy Bennett and Richard A. Peterson, eds., *Music Scenes: Local, Translocal and Virtual* (Nashville, TN: Vanderbilt University Press, 2004), 12.

15 Imani Perry, *Prophets of the Hood: Politics and Poetics in Hip Hop* (Dunham, NC: Duke University Press, 2004), 188.

16 Ibid.

17 Tricia Rose, *Black Noise: Rap Music and Black Culture in Contemporary America* (Middletown, CT: Wesleyan University Press, 1994).

18 Ibid.

19 For studies of the West Coast, see: Daubi Abe, *6 N the Morning: West Coast Hip-Hop Music 1987–1992 & the Transformation of Mainstream Culture* (Los Angeles: Over the Edge, 2013); Ben Westhoff, *Original Gangstas: The Untold Story of Dr. Dre, Eazy-E, Ice Cube, Tupac Shakur, and the Birth of West Coast Rap* (New York: Hachette Books, 2016). For studies of the South, see: Tamara Palmer, *Country Fried Soul: Adventures in Dirty South Hip-Hop* (San Francisco, CA: Backbeat, 2005); Roni Sarig, *Third Coast: Outkast, Timbaland, and How Hip-Hop Became a Southern Thing* (Cambridge, MA: Da Capo Press, 2007); Ben Westhoff, *Dirty South: Outkast, Lil Wayne, Soulja*

Boy, and the Southern Rappers Who Reinvented Hip-Hop (Chicago: Chicago Review Press, 2011).

20 Mickey Hess, ed. *Hip Hop in America: A Regional Guide* (Westport, CT: Greenwood, 2009).

21 For example, see: Anthony Kwame Harrison, *Hip Hop Underground: The Integrity and Ethics of Racial Identification* (Philadelphia: Temple University Press, 2009); Marcyliena Morgan, *The Real Hiphop: Battling for Knowledge, Power, and Respect in the LA Underground* (Durham, NC: Duke University Press Books, 2009); Eithne Quinn, *Nothing but a "G" Thang: The Culture and Commerce of Gangsta Rap* (New York: Columbia University Press, 2005).

22 Gail Hilson Woldu, "The Kaleidoscope of Writing on Hip-Hop Culture," *Notes* 67, no. 1 (2010): 10.

23 Ibid.

24 Ibid., 12.

25 For an analysis of local rap music in New Orleans, see: Matt Miller, *Bounce: Rap Music and Local Identity in New Orleans* (Amherst, MA: University of Massachusetts Press, 2012). For analyses of local rap music in Houston, see: Maco L. Faniel, *Hip-Hop in Houston: The Origin & the Legacy* (Charleston, SC: The History Press, 2013); Lance Scott Walker, *Houston Rap Tapes: An Oral History of Bayou City Hip-Hop* (Austin: University of Texas Press, 2018); Langston Collin Wilkins, *Welcome 2 Houston: Hip Hop Heritage in Hustle Town*, African American Music in Global Perspective (Urbana: University of Illinois Press Urbana, 2023). For an analysis of Oakland, see: Lavar Pope, *Rap and Politics: A Case Study of Panther, Gangster, and Hyphy Discourses in Oakland, CA (1965–2010)* (New York: Palgrave Macmillan, 2020). For an analysis of Seattle, see: Daubi Abe, *Emerald Street: A History of Hip-Hop in Seattle* (Seattle: University of Washington Press, 2020). For an analysis of local rap music in Atlanta, see: Joe Coscarelli, *Rap Capital: An Atlanta Story* (New York: Simon & Schuster, 2022).

26 Miller, *Bounce*.

27 Faniel, *Hip-Hop in Houston*.

28 Ibid., 41.

29 Walker, *Houston Rap Tapes*.

30 Wilkins, *Welcome 2 Houston*, 11.

31 Ibid., 48.

32 Ibid., 95.

33 Abe, *Emerald Street*.

34 Pope, *Rap and Politics*.

35 Helen Myers, *Ethnomusicology: Historical and Regional Studies* (New York: W. W. Norton, 1993), 3.

36 Ibid., 22.

37 Will Straw, "Systems of Articulation, Logics of Change: Communities and Scenes in Popular Music," *Cultural Studies* 5, no. 3 (1991): 373.

1 Scenes

1 Grandmaster Caz, "South Bronx Subway Rap (Original Version)," in *Wild Style Original Soundtrack [Sound Recording]* (Animal Records, 1983).

2 Perry, *Prophets of the Hood*, 23.

3 Jim Vernon, " 'The Fifth Element': Knowledge, or Hip Hop's Struggle Against Post-Rap Subversion," in *Sampling, Biting, and the Postmodern Subversion of Hip Hop* (Cham, Switzerland: Springer, 2021), 67–8.

4 Richard A. Peterson and Andy Bennett, "Introducing Music Scenes," in *Music Scenes: Local, Translocal and Virtual*, ed. Andy Bennett and Richard A. Peterson (Nashville, TN: Vanderbilt University Press, 2004), 1.

5 Ibid., 2.

6 Ibid.

7 Will Straw, "Some Things a Scene Might Be: Postface," *Cultural studies* 29, no. 3 (2015): 477, emphasis in original. This quote is not completely italicized, as compared to other quotes used in this book's chapter openings because the original quote contains italicized information.

8 Will Straw, "Scenes and Sensibilities" (paper presented at the E-compós, 2006); Martin Allor, "Placing Sites: Modeling Mediations of Local Cultural Activity" (paper presented at the Annual Conference of the Canadian Communications Association, Edmonton, Canada, May 28, 2000).

9 Straw, "Scenes and Sensibilities"; Allor, "Placing Sites: Modeling Mediations of Local Cultural Activity."

10 Holly Kruse, *Site and Sound: Understanding Independent Music Scenes* (New York: P. Lang, 2003), 145.

11 Barry Shank, *Dissonant Identities: The Rock 'N' Roll Scene in Austin, Texas* (Hanover, NH: University Press of New England, 1994), xiii.

12 Fabian Holt and Carsten Wergin, *Musical Performance and the Changing City: Post-Industrial Contexts in Europe and the US* (New York: Routledge, 2013), 15.

13 Benjamin Klement and Simone Strambach, "How Do New Music Genres Emerge? Diversification Processes in Symbolic Knowledge Bases," *Regional Studies* 53, no. 10 (2019): 1447.

14 Peterson and Bennett, "Introducing Music Scenes."

15 Straw, "Systems of Articulation, Logics of Change," 373.

16 Ibid., 378.

17 Bennett, "The Post-Subcultural Turn," 496.

18 Mark Katz, *Music and Technology: A Very Short Introduction* (New York: Oxford University Press, 2022), 108.

19 Thank you to the anonymous peer reviewer who made this great point. It opens questions about locational research on the periphery of the major and mid-sized cities.

2 Geography

1 Goodie Mob, "Cell Therapy," in *Soul Food [Sound recording]* (LaFace, 1995).

2 Kenneth French, "Geography of American Rap: Rap Diffusion and Rap Centers," *GeoJournal* 82 (2017): 265.

3 Ibid., 270.

4 Ibid.

5 Ibid.

6   Thomas Sigler and Murali Balaji, "Regional Identity in Contemporary Hip-Hop Music: (Re) Presenting the Notion of Place," Communication, Culture & Critique 6, no. 2 (2013): 345.

7   Nelson George, *Hip Hop America* (New York: Penguin, 2005), 130–1.

8   Rose, *Black Noise*, 50.

9   David Samuels, "The Rap on Rap: The 'Black Music' That Isn't Either," in *That's the Joint!: The Hip-Hop Studies Reader*, ed. Murray Forman and Mark Anthony Neal (London: Psychology Press, 2004), 169.

10 Murray Forman, "'Represent': Race, Space and Place in Rap Music," Popular Music 19, no. 01 (2000): 204.

11 Ibid., 209.

12 Quinn, *Nothing but a "G" Thang*, 11.

13 Ibid., 94–5.

14 Felicia A. Viator, "West Coast Originals: A Case for Reassessing the 'Bronx West' Story of Black Youth Culture in 1980s Los Angeles," American Studies 58, no. 3 (2019): 92.

15 Ibid.

16 Ibid.

17 Josh Sides, "Straight into Compton: American Dreams, Urban Nightmares, and the Metamorphosis of a Black Suburb," American Quarterly 56, no. 3 (2004): 596.

18 Cheryl L. Keyes, "Empowering Self, Making Choices, Creating Spaces," *That's the Joint! the Hip-hop Studies Reader* (2004): 99.

19 Pope, *Rap and Politics*.

20 Ibid.

21 Abe, *Emerald Street*, 19.

22 Ibid.

23 Ibid., 5.

24 Ibid.

25 Ibid., 3.

26 Ibid.

27 French, "Geography of American Rap," 265.

28 Abrams, *The Come Up*, 443.

29 Ibid.

30 Sarig, *Third Coast*, xv.

31 Ibid.

32 Ibid., xvi–xix.

33 Palmer, *Country Fried Soul*, 122–89.

34 Ibid., 153–66.

35 Ibid., 176–80.

36 Ibid., 143–6.

37 For rap music in New Orleans, see: Miller, *Bounce*. For rap music in Houston, see: Faniel, *Hip-Hop in Houston*.

38 *Hip-Hop in Houston*, 22–3.

39 Ibid., 23.

40 Walker, *Houston Rap Tapes*, ix.

41 Wilkins, *Welcome 2 Houston*, 162.

42 Ibid., 21.

43 Ibid., 47.

44 Ibid., 29.

45 Ibid., 38.

46 Miller, *Bounce.*

47 Ibid.

48 Ibid.

49 Laurie Cannady, "Virginia Is for Lovers and Rappers: Hampton Roads Rappers Changing the Game," in *Hip Hop in America: A Regional Guide*, ed. Mickey Hess (Westport, CT: Greenwood, 2009), 497.

50 Roni Sarig, "Virginia—Transmissions from the Edge," in *Third Coast: Outkast, Timbaland, and How Hip-Hop Became a Southern Thing* (Cambridge, MA: Da Capo Press, 2007), 167.

51 Colita Nichols Fairfax, *Hampton, Virginia* (Charleston SC: Arcadia, 2005), 7.

52 Ibid., 7–8.

53 Sidney Thomas, *Diamonds in the Raw: The Past, Present and Future of DC's Hip-Hop Movement* (Indianapolis, IN: Dog Ear, 2009), 1.

54 Ibid., 2.

55 Ibid., 76.

56 French, "Geography of American Rap," 263.

57 Ibid., 266–8.

58 Ibid., 265.

59 Ibid., 263.

60 Ibid., 265.

61 Ibid., 264.

62 Ibid., 265.

63 Ibid., 269.

64 Sigler and Balaji, "Regional Identity in Contemporary Hip-Hop Music."

65 Ibid., 337.

66 Murali Balaji, "The Construction of 'Street Credibility' in Atlanta's Hip-Hop Music Scene: Analyzing the Role of Cultural Gatekeepers," Critical Studies in Media Communication 29, no. 4 (2012): 314–15.

67 Sigler and Balaji, "Regional Identity in Contemporary Hip-Hop Music," 337.

68 Ibid., 343.

69 Ibid.

70 Ibid.

71 Ibid.

72 Ibid.

73 Ibid., 348.

74 Tricia Rose, *The Hip Hop Wars: What We Talk about When We Talk about Hip Hop— and Why It Matters* (New York: Basic Books, 2008), 55.

75 Ibid.

76 Perry, *Prophets of the Hood*, 197.

77 Stefano Barone, "Under a Groove: Rap, Hip-Hop and Their Glocalization," in *The Bloomsbury Handbook of Popular Music and Youth Culture*, ed. Andy Bennett (New York: Bloomsbury Publishing, 2022), 291.

78 Nina Baur, Linda Herring, Anna Laura Raschke, and Cornelia Thierbach, "Theory and Methods in Spatial Analysis: Towards Integrating Qualitative, Quantitative and Cartographic Approaches in the Social Sciences and Humanities," *Historical Social Research/Historische Sozialforschung* 2, no. 39 (2014): 25.

79 Mark Fossett, "Urban and Spatial Demography," in *Handbook of Population*, ed. Dudley L. Poston and Michael Micklin (Cham, Switzerland: Springer, 2005), 487.

80 Sarah F. Anzia, *Local Interests: Politics, Policy, and Interest Groups in US City Governments* (Chicago: University of Chicago Press, 2022), 5.

81 Ibid.

82 Ibid.

83 Houston A. Baker, *Black Studies, Rap, and the Academy* (Chicago: University of Chicago Press, 2018), 90.

84 James G. Spady, Samir Meghelli, and H. Samy Alim, *Tha Global Cipha: Hip Hop Culture and Consciousness* (Philadelphia, PA: Black History Museum Press, 2006), 10.

85 Olaf Kaltmeier and Wilfried Raussert, *Sonic Politics: Music and Social Movements in the Americas*, Interamerican Research (Abingdon: Routledge, 2019), 78.

86 John Klaess, *Breaks in the Air: The Birth of Rap Radio in New York City* (Durham, NC: Duke University Press, 2022), 123.

87 Jack Lucas, "Urban Governance and the American Political Development Approach," Urban Affairs Review 53, no. 2 (2017): 340.

88 Ibid., 341.

89 Ibid.

90 Michael Javen Fortner, "Racial Capitalism and City Politics: Toward a Theoretical Synthesis," Urban Affairs Review 59, no. 2 (2023): 630–1.

91 Ibid., 631.

92 Lucas, "Urban Governance and the American Political Development Approach," 344.

93 Ibid., 356.

94 Colin Woodard, *American Nations: A History of the Eleven Rival Regional Cultures of North America* (New York: Penguin Books, 2012), 5.

95 Ibid., 13.

96 Marcus Anthony Hunter and Zandria F. Robinson, *Chocolate Cities: The Black Map of American Life* (Berkeley: University of California Press, 2018), 5.

97 Ibid., 10.

98 Ibid., xiii.

99 Ibid., 179.

100 Ibid., 181.

101 Benjamin Woo, Jamie Rennie, and Stuart R. Poyntz, "Scene Thinking: Introduction," Culural Studies 29, no. 3 (2015): 289.

102 R. D. Enos, *The Space between Us: Social Geography and Politics* (Cambridge: Cambridge University Press, 2017), 20.

103 Ibid., 21.

104 George Philip & Son, *Oxford Atlas of the World*, 28th ed. (New York: Oxford University Press USA, 2021), 64.

105 Richardson Dilworth, ed. *Cities in American Political History* (Thousand Oaks, CA: CQ Press, 2011).

106 Ibid.

107 Dennis R. Judd and Todd R. Swanstrom, *City Politics* (Saddle River, NJ: Pearson Education, 2014).

3 Migration

1 Masta Ace Incorporated, "Born to Roll," in *Sittin' on Chrome [Sound Recording]* (Delicious Vinyl, 1995).
2 Smitherman, *Talkin' and Testifyin'*, 37.
3 Ibid., 73.
4 Alexander G. Weheliye, *Phonographies: Grooves in Sonic Afro-Modernity* (Dunham, NC: Duke University Press, 2005), 5.
5 Sheila Whiteley, Andy Bennett, and Stan Hawkins, *Music, Space and Place: Popular Music and Cultural Identity* (London: Routledge, Taylor & Francis Group, 2017), 8.
6 Jeff Chang, *Can't Stop, Won't Stop: A History of the Hip-Hop Generation* (New York: St. Martin's Press, 2005), 12.
7 Ibid.
8 Jill Jonnes, *South Bronx Rising: The Rise, Fall, and Resurrection of an American City*, 3rd ed. (New York: Empire State Editions, an imprint of Fordham University Press, 2022), 2–3.
9 Ibid., xviii.
10 Ibid., 8.
11 Juan Flores, "Puerto Rican and Proud, Boyee!," in *Microphone Fiends: Youth Music & Youth Culture*, ed. Andrew Ross and Tricia Rose (New York: Routledge New York, 1994), 92.
12 Juan Flores, *From Bomba to Hip-Hop: Puerto Rican Culture and Latino Identity* (New York: Columbia University Press, 2000), 55.
13 Jonnes, *South Bronx Rising*.
14 Isabel Wilkerson, *The Warmth of Other Suns: The Epic Story of America's Great Migration* (New York: Random House, 2010), 251.
15 Alejandro Chomski, "*Feel the Noise* [Motion Picture]" (Culver City, CA: Sony Pictures Home Entertainment, 2008).
16 From the circulation of the film: Spike Lee, "*Do the Right Thing* [Motion Picture]," (Universal City, CA: Universal Home Video, 1989).
17 W. E. B. Du Bois, *The Philadelphia Negro: A Social Study* (New York: Oxford University Press, 2007).
18 Brian Cross, *It's Not About a Salary--: Rap, Race, and Resistance in Los Angeles*, Haymarket Series (London: Verso, 1993), 6.
19 Ibid.
20 Ibid.
21 Ibid.
22 Jordan T. Camp, "Blues Geographies and the Security Turn: Interpreting the Housing Crisis in Los Angeles," *American Quarterly* 64, no. 3 (2012).
23 Cedric Johnson, *After Black Lives Matter* (London: Verso Books, 2023), 150.
24 Abe, *Emerald Street*, 27.
25 Margaret Garb, *Freedom's Ballot: African American Political Struggles in Chicago from Abolition to the Great Migration* (Chicago: University of Chicago Press, 2014), 2.
26 Ibid., 4.
27 Wilkerson, *The Warmth of Other Suns*, 386.
28 Ibid.
29 Enos, *The Space between Us*, 1.

30   John A. Agnew, "Slums, Ghettos, and Urban Marginality," *Urban Geography* 31, no. 2
     (2010): 145.

31   Justin Schell, "From St. Paul to Minneapolis, All the Hands Clap for This: Hip Hop
     in the Twin Cities," in *Hip Hop in America: A Regional Guide*, ed. Mickey Hess
     (Westport, CT: Greenwood, 2009), 383.

32   Gucci Mane and Neil Martinez-Belkin, *The Autobiography of Gucci Mane*
     (New York: Simon and Schuster, 2017), 18.

33   Coscarelli, *Rap Capital*, 1–15.

34   Hunter and Robinson, *Chocolate Cities*, 181.

35   Sarig, "Virginia—Transmissions from the Edge," 147.

36   Kip Lornell and Charles C. Stephenson, *The Beat!: Go-Go Music from Washington, DC*
     (Jackson: University Press of Mississippi, 2009), 40.

37   Ibid., 11.

38   Ibid., 12.

39   H. S. Jaffe and T. Sherwood, *Dream City: Race, Power, and the Decline of Washington,
     D.C* (Washington, DC: Argo Navis, 2014).

40   Lornell and Stephenson, *The Beat!*, 39.

41   Ibid., 40.

42   DC Statehood, https://statehood.dc.gov/page/new-columbia-statehood-commission.

43   Melanie A. Medeiros and Jennifer R. Guzmán, *Ethnographic Insights on Latin America
     and the Caribbean* (Toronto: University of Toronto Press, 2023).

44   Ramón A. Gutiérrez, "Internal Colonialism: An American Theory of Race," *Du Bois
     Review: Social Science Research on Race* 1, no. 2 (2004): 281.

45   Ibid., 282.

46   Ibid., 290; Robert Blauner, "Internal Colonialism and Ghetto Revolt," *Social Problems*
     16, no. 4 (1969): 51–81.

47   "Internal Colonialism and Ghetto Revolt," 396; Gutiérrez, "Internal Colonialism," 289.

48   Loïc Wacquant, "Urban Desolation and Symbolic Denigration in the Hyperghetto,"
     Social Psychology Quarterly 73, no. 3 (2010): 217.

49   Ibid.

50   Ibid.

51   Loïc Wacquant, "Deadly Symbiosis: When Ghetto and Prison Meet and Mesh,"
     Punishment & Society 3, no. 1 (2001): 98.

52   Dilworth, *Cities in American Political History*, 5.

53   Leah Platt Boustan and the National Bureau of Economic Research, *Competition in
     the Promised Land: Black Migration and Racial Wage Convergence in the North, 1940–
     1970*, Working Paper Series (National Bureau of Economic Research) (Cambridge,
     MA: National Bureau of Economic Research, 2008), 32.

54   William J. Collins, "The Great Migration of Black Americans from the US South: A
     Guide and Interpretation," *Explorations in Economic History* 80 (2021): 18.

55   Boustan and the National Bureau of Economic Research, *Competition in the Promised
     Land*, 4.

56   Ibid.

57   D. Marvin Jones, *Fear of a Hip-Hop Planet* (Santa Barbara, CA: ABC-CLIO, 2013).

58   Ibid.

59   Ibid.

60   Wilkerson, *The Warmth of Other Suns*, 537.

61   Ibid.

62 Rogers M. Smith, *Civic Ideals: Conflicting Visions of Citizenship in U.S. History* (New Haven, CT: Yale University Press, 1997), 101.

63 Patricia Hill Collins, *From Black Power to Hip Hop: Racism, Nationalism, and Feminism* (Philadephia: Temple University Press, 2006), 33.

64 Ibid., 35.

65 Ibid., 49.

66 Smith, *Civic Ideals*, 429.

67 Synthesized from: Todd Shaw, Louis DeSipio, Dianne Pinderhughes, and Toni-Michelle C. Travis, *Uneven Roads: An Introduction to US Racial and Ethnic Politics* (Washington, DC: CQ Press, 2014), 108; Henry Louis Gates et al., "*The African Americans: Many Rivers to Cross* [Motion Picture]," (2013).

68 Smitherman, *Talkin' and Testifyin'*, 35.

69 Robin D. Moore, *Music in the Hispanic Caribbean: Experiencing Music, Expressing Culture* (New York: Oxford University Press, 2010), 52.

70 Michael E. McGerr, Jan Ellen Lewis, James Oakes, Nick Cullather, Mark Summers, Camilla Townsend, and Karen M. Dunak, *Mapping US History: Coloring and Exercise Book* (New York: Oxford University Press, 2019), 4.

71 Moore, *Music in the Hispanic Caribbean*, 53–4.

72 K. Maurice Jones, *Say It Loud! The Story of Rap Music* (Brookfield, CT: Millbrook Press, 1994), 18.

73 Smith, *Civic Ideals*, 52.

74 Ibid.

75 Ibid.

76 Ibid., 63.

77 Ibid., 73.

78 Moore, *Music in the Hispanic Caribbean*, 55.

79 Myers, *Ethnomusicology: Historical and Regional Studies*, 419.

80 Whiteley, Bennett, and Hawkins, *Music, Space and Place*, 26.

81 Smitherman, *Talkin' and Testifyin'*, 12.

82 Orejuela, *Rap and Hip Hop Culture*, 7.

83 Jones, *Say It Loud! The Story of Rap Music*, 189.

84 David Toop, *The Rap Attack: African Jive to New York Hip Hop* (Boston: South End Press, 1984), 31–2.

85 Sarig, *Third Coast*, x.

86 Ibid.

87 Smitherman, *Talkin and Testifyin*, 12.

88 For example, see: Collins, "The Great Migration of Black Americans from the US South"; Garb, *Freedom's Ballot*; Wilkerson, *The Warmth of Other Suns*; Marco Martiniello and Jean-Michel Lafleur, "Ethnic Minorities' Cultural and Artistic Practices as Forms of Political Expression: A Review of the Literature and a Theoretical Discussion on Music," *Journal of Ethnic and Migration Studies* 34, no. 8 (2008).

89 Wilkerson, *The Warmth of Other Suns*, 9.

90 Ibid.

91 Ibid.

92 Ibid.

93 Collins, "The Great Migration of Black Americans from the US South," 17.

94   William Jelani Cobb, *To the Break of Dawn: A Freestyle on the Hip Hop Aesthetic* (New York: New York University Press, 2007), 31–2.

95   Hunter and Robinson, *Chocolate Cities*, 127.

96   Ibid.

97   Ibid.

98   Wilkerson, *The Warmth of Other Suns*, 178.

99   Ibid.

100   Ibid.

101   Ibid.

102   Ibid., 216.

103   Ibid.

104   Hunter and Robinson, *Chocolate Cities*, 46.

105   Ira Katznelson,*When Affirmative Action Was White: An Untold History of Racial Inequality in Twentieth-Century America* (New York: WW Norton, 2005), 43.

106   Molefi K. Asante, *It's Bigger Than Hip-Hop: The Rise of the Post-Hip-Hop Generation* (New York: Griffin, 2009), 39–40.

107   Collins, "The Great Migration of Black Americans from the US South," 14.

108   Wilkerson, *The Warmth of Other Suns*, 536.

109   Boustan and the National Bureau of Economic Research, *Competition in the Promised Land*, 4.

110   Toop, *The Rap Attack*, 4.

111   Ibid.

112   John Connell, *Sound Tracks: Popular Music Identity and Place* (London: Routledge, 2003), 85.

113   Whiteley, Bennett, and Hawkins, *Music, Space and Place*, 2.

114   Toop, *The Rap Attack*, 6.

4   Movement

1   Wise Intelligent, "Mr. Rocket Launcher," in *Blessed Be the Poor? [Sound recording]* (Intelligent Muzik, 2007).

2   Yvonne Bynoe, *Stand and Deliver: Political Activism, Leadership, and Hip Hop Culture* (Brooklyn: Soft Skull Press, 2004), vii.

3   Julian L. D. Shabazz, *The US of America vs. Hip-Hop* (Hampton, VA: United Brothers & Sisters, 1992), 6.

4   Pancho McFarland and Jared A. Ball, "The Re-Indigenization and Re-Africanization of Hip Hop," in *La Verdad: An International Dialogue on Hip Hop Latinidades*, ed. Melissa Castillo Planas and Jason Nichols (Columbus: Ohio State University Press, 2016), 44–5.

5   Asante, *It's Bigger Than Hip-Hop*, 8.

6   Ron Eyerman and Andrew Jamison, *Music and Social Movements: Mobilizing Traditions in the Twentieth Century* (Cambridge: Cambridge University Press, 1998), 1.

7   Ibid., 105.

8   Shana L. Redmond, *Anthem: Social Movements and the Sound of Solidarity in the African Diaspora* (New York: NYU Press, 2014), 1.

9   Ibid.

10   Pope, *Rap and Politics*, 113.

11 Josue Estrada, "Brown Beret Chapters 1969–1972," University of Washington, https://depts.washington.edu/moves/brown_beret_map.shtml.

12 Katherine Anastas and James Gregory, "SNCC Timeline 1960–1970," University of Washington, https://depts.washington.edu/moves/SNCC_database.shtml.

13 Amanda Miller, "May 1970 Student Antiwar Strikes," University of Washington, https://depts.washington.edu/moves/antiwar_may1970.shtml.

14 Andrew Witt, *The Black Panthers in the Midwest: The Community Programs and Services of the Black Panther Party in Milwaukee, 1966–1977* (New York: Routledge, 2013), 31.

15 Ibid.

16 Ibid., 87.

17 Ibid.

18 Judson L. Jeffries, *The Black Panther Party in a City Near You* (Athens: University of Georgia Press, 2018), 5.

19 Ibid.

20 Perry, *Prophets of the Hood*, 47.

21 Cheryl L. Keyes, "The Aesthetic Significance of African American Sound Culture and Its Impact on American Popular Music Style and Industry," *The World of Music* 45, no. 3 (2003): 113.

22 Reiland Rabaka, *Hip Hop's Amnesia: From Blues and the Black Women's Club Movement to Rap and the Hip Hop Movement* (Lanham, MD: Lexington Books, 2012), 268, emphasis in original.

23 For the August 1980 *Washington Post* use of "rap" and the infamous ABC 20/20 report on rap, see: David Diallo, "'Every MC Raps, but Not Every Rapper is an MC: Examining the MC/Rapper Rivalry in American Rap Music," *Volume!* (2022): 202–3.

24 Ibid., 203–4.

25 Chang, *Can't Stop, Won't Stop*, 17.

26 Sara Towe Horsfall, "Understanding Deviant Music," *Sociology of Crime Law and Deviance* 18 (2013): 214.

27 Ibid.

28 Jonnes, *South Bronx Rising*, 3.

29 Jeffrey Ogbonna Green Ogbar, *Hip-Hop Revolution: The Culture and Politics of Rap* (Lawrence: University Press of Kansas, 2007), 48.

30 Chang, *Can't Stop, Won't Stop*, 49.

31 Ibid., 50.

32 Marcus Reeves, *Somebody Scream!: Rap Music's Rise to Prominence in the Aftershock of Black Power* (New York: Faber and Faber, 2008), 15.

33 Ibid., 14.

34 Martin Lamotte, "Rebels without a Pause: Hip-Hop and Resistance in the City," *International Journal of Urban and Regional Research* 38, no. 2 (2014): 689.

35 Loren Kajikawa, *Sounding Race in Rap Songs* (Oakland: University of California Press, 2015), 26.

36 Ibid.

37 Reeves, *Somebody Scream!*, 28.

38 Bill Brewster, *Last Night a DJ Saved My Life: The History of the Disc Jockey* (New York: Grove/Atlantic, 2014), 255.

39 Charlie Ahearn, "*Wild Style* [Motion Picture]," (US: Wild Style Productions, 1983); Diana Darzin, "Breakdancing's Big Break," *The Rocket* (February 1984).

40 Hess, *Hip Hop in America*, xxxi–xxxii.

41 Nate Patrin, *Bring That Beat Back: How Sampling Built Hip-Hop* (Minneapolis: University of Minnesota Press, 2020).

42 For example, see: Kevin J. Mumford, *Newark: A History of Race, Rights, and Riots in America* (New York: New York University Press, 2007).

43 Katie L. Mullins, "Black Female Identity and Challenges to Masculine Discourse in Rah Digga's Dirty Harriet," *Popular Music and Society* 36, no. 4 (2013): 430.

44 Kathy Iandoli, *God Save the Queens: The Essential History of Women in Hip-Hop* (New York: Dey Street Books, 2019), 178.

45 Felicia Angeja Viator, *To Live and Defy in LA: How Gangsta Rap Changed America* (Cambridge, MA: Harvard University Press, 2020), 16.

46 Ibid., 61.

47 Philip V. Bohlman, "Musicology as a Political Act," *The Journal of Musicology* 11, no. 4 (1993).

48 Abrams, *The Come Up*, 206.

49 Pope, *Rap and Politics*, 178.

50 Himanee Gupta-Carlson, "Planet B-Girl: Community Building and Feminism in Hip-Hop," *New Political Science* 32, no. 4 (2010): 520.

51 Ibid., 518.

52 Ibid.

53 Bynoe, *Stand and Deliver*, 42.

54 Wilkerson, *The Warmth of Other Suns*, 386.

55 Ibid., 388.

56 Hess, *Hip Hop in America*, xxxiii.

57 Peter Katel, "Debating Hip-Hop: Does Gangsta Rap Harm Black Americans?," in *Issues for Debate in Sociology: Selections from CQ Researcher* (Thousand Oaks, CA: Sage, 2010), 126.

58 Schell, "From St. Paul to Minneapolis, All the Hands Clap for This," 383.

59 For example, see: Rebekah Farrugia and Kellie D. Hay, *Women Rapping Revolution: Hip Hop and Community Building in Detroit* (Oakland: University of California Press, 2020).

60 Ibid.

61 Ibid., 16.

62 Brittany L. Long, "Hustle in H-Town: Hip Hop Entrepreneurialism in Houston," *Journal of Hip Hop Studies* 9, no. 1 (2022): 61.

63 Walker, *Houston Rap Tapes*, 39.

64 Ibid., 269.

65 Ibid., 269, emphasis in original.

66 Ibid., 4–5.

67 Iandoli, *God Save the Queens*, 286.

68 Nik Cohn, *Triksta: Life and Death and New Orleans Rap* (New York: Vintage, 2009), 19.

69 Ibid., 95.

70 Daron Crawford and Pernell Russell, *Beyond the Bricks* (New Orleans, LA: Neighborhood Story Project, 2009).

71 10th Ward Buck, *The Definition of Bounce: Between Ups and Downs in New Orleans* (New Orleans, LA: Lancaster, 2011), 90.

72 Ibid., 97.

73 Jeffries, *The Black Panther Party in a City Near You*, 198.

74 Min Bee and Jordan Anthony Kapono Bee, "Finding Agency in Hawaiian Online Collaborative Music Videos: Reclaiming "Kaulana Nā Pua" in a Contemporary Context," in *Sound Communities in the Asia Pacific: Music, Media, and Technology* (New York: Bloomsbury, 2021), 225.

75 Ibid., 229.

76 Flores, *From Bomba to Hip-Hop*, 35.

77 Jorge L. Giovannetti, "Popular Music and Culture in Puerto Rico: Jamaican and Rap Music as Cross-Cultural Symbols," in *Musical Migrations: Transnationalism and Cultural Hybridity in Latin/O America*, ed. Frances R. Aparicio and Cándida F. Jáquez (New York: Palgrave Macmillan, 2003), 89.

78 Ibid., 90.

79 Jonnes, *South Bronx Rising*, 9.

80 Sydney Hutchinson, *Focus: Music of the Caribbean* (New York: Routledge, 2019), 39.

81 US Bureau of the Census, *Geographic Areas Reference Manual* (Washington, DC: U.S. Department of Commerce, Economics and Statistics Administration, Bureau of the Census, 1994), 7–37.

82 Ibid., 7–38.

83 Norwell Harrigan and Pearl I. Varlack, "The US Virgin Islands and the Black Experience," *Journal of Black Studies* 7, no. 4 (1977): 389.

84 Ibid.

85 Smitherman, *Talkin' and Testifyin'*, 2.

86 Ibid.

87 Cross, *It's Not About a Salary*, 3.

88 George Lipsitz, *Dangerous Crossroads: Popular Music, Postmodernism, and the Poetics of Place* (London: Verso, 1994), 35.

89 Eyerman and Jamison, *Music and Social Movements*, 7.

90 Mark Mattern, *Acting in Concert: Music, Community, and Political Action* (New Brunswick, NJ: Rutgers University Press, 1998), 35.

91 Ibid., 19.

92 Ibid.

93 Ibid., 25.

94 Sarig, *Third Coast*, x.

95 Ibid.

96 Ibid.

97 James C. Scott, *Weapons of the Weak: Everyday Forms of Peasant Resistance* (New Haven, CT: Yale University Press, 1985), xvi.

98 Perry, *Prophets of the Hood*, 139.

99 Wilkerson, *The Warmth of Other Suns*, 529.

100 Collins, *From Black Power to Hip Hop*, 9.

101 Wilkerson, *The Warmth of Other Suns*, 535–6.

102 Collins, *From Black Power to Hip Hop*, 9.

103 Asante, *It's Bigger Than Hip-Hop*, 36.

104 Robin D. G. Kelley, *Freedom Dreams (Twentieth Anniversary Edition): The Black Radical Imagination* (Boston: Beacon Press, 2022).

105 Ibid., 45.

106 Ibid., 62.

107 Ibid., 123.

108 Eric Harvey, *Who Got the Camera?: A History of Rap and Reality* (Austin: University of Texas Press, 2021), 69.

109 Perry, *Prophets of the Hood*, 148.

110 Smitherman, *Talkin' and Testifyin'*, 177.

111 Eyerman and Jamison, *Music and Social Movements*, 83.

112 Ibid.

113 Erik Nielson and Andrea L. Dennis, *Rap on Trial: Race, Lyrics, and Guilt in America* (New York: The New Press, 2019), 36.

114 William Eric Perkins, *Droppin' Science: Critical Essays on Rap Music and Hip Hop Culture* (Philadelphia, PA: Temple University Press, 1996), 4.

115 Ibid.

116 Reeves, *Somebody Scream!*, 7–8.

117 Sarah RudeWalker, *Revolutionary Poetics: The Rhetoric of the Black Arts Movement* (Athens: University of Georgia Press, 2023), 15; Kalamu ya Salaam, *The Magic of Juju: An Appreciation of the Black Arts Movement* (Chicago: Third World Press, 2016), x–xi.

118 Collins, *From Black Power to Hip Hop*.

119 James Edward Smethurst, "The Black Arts Movement and Historically Black Colleges and Universities," in *New Thoughts on the Black Arts Movement*, ed. Lisa Gail Collins and Margo Natalie Crawford (New Brunswick, N.J.: Rutgers University Press, 2006).

120 RudeWalker, *Revolutionary Poetics*, 132.

121 Ibid., 120.

122 Bynoe, *Stand and Deliver*, 182.

123 Ibid., 148.

124 Ibid., 182.

125 Perkins, *Droppin' Science*, 16.

126 Dianna Watkins Dickerson, "A Call (and Response) to Battle Rap," *Journal of Contemporary Rhetoric* 12, no. 2 (2022): 107.

127 Salaam, *The Magic of Juju*, x.

128 Ibid., xii–xvii.

129 Kelley, *Freedom Dreams (Twentieth Anniversary Edition)*, 8.

130 For example, see: Michael C. Dawson, *Black Visions: The Roots of Contemporary African-American Political Ideologies* (Chicago: University of Chicago Press, 2001); Melissa Victoria Harris-Lacewell, *Barbershops, Bibles, and BET: Everyday Talk and Black Political Thought* (Princeton, NJ: Princeton University Press, 2004); Lester K. Spence, *Stare in the Darkness: The Limits of Hip-Hop and Black Politics* (Minneapolis: University of Minnesota Press, 2011); Lakeyta M. Bonnette, *Pulse of the People: Political Rap Music and Black Politics* (Philadelphia: University of Pennsylvania Press, 2015); Cathy J. Cohen, *Democracy Remixed: Black Youth and the Future of American Politics* (New York: Oxford University Press, 2010).

131 John W. Roberts, *From Trickster to Badman: The Black Folk Hero in Slavery and Freedom* (Philadelphia: University of Pennsylvania Press, 1990), 11.

132 Ibid.

133 Smitherman, *Talkin' and Testifyin'*, 73.

134 For US-specific examinations, see: Reiland Rabaka, *Civil Rights Music: The Soundtracks of the Civil Rights Movement* (Lanham, MD: Lexington Books, 2016). For extensions into R&B and Hip Hop, see: Reiland Rabaka, *The Hip Hop Movement: From R & B and the Civil Rights Movement to Rap and the Hip Hop Generation* (Lanham, MD: Lexington Books, 2013). For connections to the African diaspora, see: Redmond, *Anthem*.

135 Jones, *Fear of a Hip-Hop Planet*, 21.

136 Ibid., 211.

137 Leah Tonnette Gaines, " 'This Ain't Just a Rap Song': 2Pac, Sociopolitical Realities and Hip Hop Nation Language," *Journal of Hip Hop Studies* 9, no. 1 (2022): 95–7.

138 Ibid., 102.

139 Ibid., 114.

140 Perry, *Prophets of the Hood*, 10.

141 Barone, "Under a Groove," 282.

142 Raquel Z. Rivera, *New York Ricans from the Hip Hop Zone*, New Directions in Latino American Cultures (New York: Palgrave Macmillan, 2003), x.

143 Ibid., x–xii.

144 Ibid., 3.

145 Ibid.

146 Ibid., 25.

147 Ibid., 59.

148 Ibid.

149 Flores, *From Bomba to Hip-Hop*, 137.

150 Kyra Danielle Gaunt, *The Games Black Girls Play: Learning the Ropes from Double-Dutch to Hip-Hop* (New York: New York University Press, 2006), 118.

151 Ibid., 9, 36.

152 Ibid., 56.

153 Ibid.

154 Ibid., 58.

155 Ibid., 2–3.

156 Perry, *Prophets of the Hood*, 115.

157 Paula Guerra and Thiago Pereira Alberto, eds., *Keep It Simple, Make It Fast!: An Approach to Underground Music Scenes* (Porto, Portugal: Universidade do Porto, Faculdade de Letras [University of Porto, Faculty of Arts and Humanities], 2019), 452–53.

158 Gwendolyn D. Pough, *Check It While I Wreck It: Black Womanhood, Hip-Hop Culture, and the Public Sphere* (Lebanon, NH: University Press of New England, 2004), 57.

159 Gail Hilson Woldu, "Women, Rap, and Hip-Hop the Challenge of Image," in *The Routledge History of Social Protest in Popular Music*, ed. Jonathan C. Friedman (New York: Routledge/Taylor & Francis Group New York, 2017), 173.

160 Keyes, "The Aesthetic Significance of African American Sound Culture and Its Impact on American Popular Music Style and Industry," 113.

161 Perry, *Prophets of the Hood*, 160.

162 Cheryl L. Keyes, *Rap Music and Street Consciousness* (Champaign: University of Illinois Press, 2002), 187.

163 Woldu, "Women, Rap, and Hip-Hop the Challenge of Image," 173.

164 Pough, *Check It While I Wreck It*, 164.

165 Ibid., 57.

166 Orejuela, *Rap and Hip Hop Culture*, 167.

167 Toop, *The Rap Attack*, 95.

168 Anthony Kwame Harrison and Craig E. Arthur, "Hip-Hop Ethos," *Humanities* 8, no. 1 (2019): 1.

169 Ibid.

170 Timothy J. Brown, "Welcome to the Terrordome: Exploring the Contradictions of a Hip-Hop Black Masculinity," in *Progressive Black Masculinities*, ed. Athena D. Mutua (New York: Routledge, 2006), 205.

171 Ibid.

172 Gupta-Carlson, "Planet B-Girl," 520.

173 Ibid., 519.

174 Harrison and Arthur, "Hip-Hop Ethos," 7.

175 Klaess, *Breaks in the Air*, 64.

176 Clarence Lusane, "Rap, Race and Politics," *Race & Class* 35, no. 1 (1993): 43.

177 Asante, *It's Bigger Than Hip-Hop*, 43.

178 Wacquant, "Urban Desolation and Symbolic Denigration in the Hyperghetto," 216.

179 Max Torvald Ryynänen, "Can the (Non-) Subaltern (Understand) Rap?: Rap as Vernacular Critical Theory," *Journal of Asia-Pacific Pop Culture* 6, no. 2 (2021): 218.

180 JloveCalderon and Marcella Runell Hall, *Love, Race, & Liberation:'Til the White Day Is Done* (New York: Love-N-Liberation Press, 2010), 14.

181 Ibid., 15, adapted from the text and emphasis was removed.

182 Pope, *Rap and Politics*, 9–10.

183 Smitherman, *Talkin' and Testifyin'*, 199.

184 Collins, *From Black Power to Hip Hop*, 21.

185 Smith, *Civic Ideals*; Nikole Hannah-Jones, *The 1619 Project: A New American Origin Story* (New York: Random House, 2021).

186 Smith, *Civic Ideals*, 130–3.

187 Pancho McFarland, *Toward a Chican@ Hip Hop Anti-Colonialism* (New York: Routledge, 2019), 10.

188 Smith, *Civic Ideals*, 131.

189 Ibid., 67.

190 Collins, *From Black Power to Hip Hop*, 21–2.

191 Barone, "Under a Groove," 283.

192 Collins, *From Black Power to Hip Hop*, 181.

193 Pough, *Check It While I Wreck It*, 21.

194 Iandoli, *God Save the Queens*, 23.

195 Ibid.

196 Ibid., 23–5.

197 Ibid.

198 Pough, *Check It While I Wreck It*, 165.

199 Ibid., 85.

200 Ibid.

201 Harvey, *Who Got the Camera?*, 140.

202 Pough, *Check It While I Wreck It*, 107.

203 Ibid.

204 Iandoli, *God Save the Queens*, 244.

205 Collins, *From Black Power to Hip Hop*, 150.

206 Ibid.

207 Tia Tyree and Melvin Williams, "Black Women Rap Battles: A Textual Analysis of US Rap Diss Songs," *Women and Music: A Journal of Gender and Culture* 25, no. 1 (2021): 70.

208 Collins, *From Black Power to Hip Hop*, 12.

209 Ibid., 165.

210 Pough, *Check It While I Wreck It*, 46.

211 Ibid., 61.

212 Layli Phillips, Kerri Reddick-Morgan, and Dionne Patricia Stephens, "Oppositional Consciousness within an Oppositional Realm: The Case of Feminism and Womanism in Rap and Hip Hop, 1976–2004," *The Journal of African American History* 90, no. 3 (2005).

213 Jožef Kolarič, "Homophobia in Rap," *Words, Music and Gender* 119 (2020): 128.

214 Ibid., 119–22.

215 Ibid., 128.

216 Matthew Oware, "Brotherly Love: Homosociality and Black Masculinity in Gangsta Rap Music," *Journal of African American Studies* 15, no. 1 (2011); M. Miller-Young, "Hip-Hop Honeys and Da Hustlaz: Black Sexualities in the New Hip-Hop Pornography," *Meridians: Feminism, Race, Transnationalism* 8, no. 1 (2008); LaToya E. Eaves, "Interanimating Black Sexualities and the Geography Classroom," *Journal of Geography in Higher Education* 44, no. 2 (2020); Nikki Lane, "Black Women Queering the Mic: Missy Elliott Disturbing the Boundaries of Racialized Sexuality and Gender," *Journal of Homosexuality* 58, nos. 6–7 (2011); Beverley Skeggs, "Two Minute Brother: Contestation through Gender, 'Race' and Sexuality," *Innovation: The European Journal of Social Science Research* 6, no. 3 (1993).

217 Susan Gillman and Alys Weinbaum, *Next to the Color Line: Gender, Sexuality, and W. E. B. Du Bois* (Minneapolis: University of Minnesota Press, 2007).

218 Barone, "Under a Groove," 291.

219 Eleni Dimou and Jonathan Ilan, "Taking Pleasure Seriously: The Political Significance of Subcultural Practice," *Journal of Youth Studies* 21, no. 1 (2018): 3.

220 Barone, "Under a Groove," 283.

221 Richard E. DeLeon and Katherine C. Naff, "Identity Politics and Local Political Culture: Some Comparative Results from the Social Capital Benchmark Survey," *Urban Affairs Review* 39, no. 6 (2004): 694–5.

222 Bynoe, *Stand and Deliver*.

223 Smitherman, *Talkin and Testifyin*, 31.

224 George, *Hip Hop America*, 154–5.

5 Music

1 Sir Quick Draw, "Rapaholic," in *Rapaholic VLS [Sound Recording]* (Bay Wave Records, 1987).

2 Harris et al., "Funk What You Heard," 21.

3 Kool Moe Dee, in *How Ya Like Me Now [Sound recording]* (Rooftop Records/Jive, 1987).

4 Joseph C. Ewoodzie, *Break Beats in the Bronx: Rediscovering Hip-Hop's Early Years* (Chapel Hill: University of North Carolina Press, 2017), 164.

5 Ibid.

6 Amir Said, *The Beattips Manual: The Art of Beatmaking, the Hip Hop-Rap Music Tradition, and the Common Composer*, 6th ed. (Brooklyn, NY: Superchamp Books, 2016), 49.

7 Ewoodzie, *Break Beats in the Bronx*, 166–7.

8 Ibid., 185.

9 Jonathan Mael, *Harlem World: How Hip Hop's Early Innovators Took Over New York and Changed Music Forever* (Baltimore, MD: Johns Hopkins University Press, 2023).

10 Mabusha Cooper, *Push Hip Hop History. [Volume 1], the Brooklyn Scene* (Bloomington, IN: 1stBooks Library, 2003), 4.

11 Ibid.

12 Hess, *Hip Hop in America*, xxxv.

13 Ibid., xxxvi.

14 Ibid., xlii.

15 French, "Geography of American Rap."

16 Ibid., 269.

17 Schoolly D, "Park Side Killers (PSK What Does It Mean?)," in *PSK What Does It Mean? VLS [Sound recording]* (Schoolly D, 1985).

18 Robin D. G. Kelley, "Kickin' Reality, Kickin' Ballistics: Gangsta Rap and Postindustrial Los Angeles," in *Race Rebels: Culture, Politics, and the Black Working Class* (New York: The Free Press, 1994), 191; Pope, *Rap and Politics*, 13.

19 French, "Geography of American Rap," 267.

20 Harvey, *Who Got the Camera?*, 214.

21 Ibid., 39–40.

22 Martin Butler, "Sonic Maps: On the Acoustic (Trans) Formation of Urban Space in Straight Outta Compton (2015) and Grand Theft Auto (1997–2013)," *AVANT* 11, no. 3 (2020): 9.

23 Ibid., 5.

24 Ibid.

25 Ibid.

26 Quinn, *Nothing but a "G" Thang*, 14.

27 Orejuela, *Rap and Hip Hop Culture*, 188–9.

28 Ibid.

29 Christina Zanfagna, *Holy Hip Hop in the City of Angels* (Oakland: University of California Press, 2017).

30 Perry, *Prophets of the Hood*, 150.

31 Geoffrey Victor Harkness, *Chicago Hustle and Flow: Gangs, Gangsta Rap, and Social Class* (Minneapolis: University of Minnesota Press, 2014), 4.

32 Ibid.

33 Ben Duinker, "Good Things Come in Threes: Triplet Flow in Recent Hip-Hop Music," *Popular Music* 38, no. 3 (2019): 11.

34 Ibid.

35 Ibid., 1.

36 Westhoff, *Dirty South*, 9.

37 Ibid.

38 Faniel, *Hip-Hop in Houston*, 23.

39 Walker, *Houston Rap Tapes*.

40 Wilkins, *Welcome 2 Houston*, 15.

41 Ibid.

42 Zanfagna, *Holy Hip Hop in the City of Angels*.

43 Wilkins, *Welcome 2 Houston*, 13.

44 Lance Scott Walker, *DJ Screw: A Life in Slow Revolution* (Austin: University of Texas Press, 2022), xi.

45 Ibid., 90.

46 Ibid., 124, emphasis in original.

47 Ibid., 104.

48 S. Charters, *A Trumpet around the Corner: The Story of New Orleans Jazz* (Jackson: University Press of Mississippi, 2010).

49 Miller, *Bounce*, 57.

50 Ibid., 4–6.

51 Ibid., 7.

52 Ibid., 55.

53 Lauron J. Kehrer, "'Sissy Style': Gender, Race, and Sexuality in New Orleans Bounce Dance," *Journal of Popular Music Studies* 35, no. 3 (2023): 62.

54 Ibid.

55 French, "Geography of American Rap," 264.

56 Coscarelli, *Rap Capital*, 3.

57 Ibid.

58 French, "Geography of American Rap," 268.

59 Cannady, "Virginia Is for Lovers and Rappers," 495.

60 Ibid., 497.

61 Halifu Osumare, *The Africanist Aesthetic in Global Hip-Hop: Power Moves* (New York: Palgrave Macmillan, 2008), 106.

62 Ibid., 114.

63 Ibid., 118.

64 Ibid., 126.

65 Frances R. Aparicio, Cándida Frances Jáquez, and María Elena Cepeda, *Musical Migrations* (New York: Palgrave Macmillan, 2003), 81.

66 Flores, *From Bomba to Hip-Hop*, 3.

67 Ibid.

68 Portia K. Maultsby, "Africanisms in African American Music," in *A Turbulent Voyage: Readings in African American Studies*, ed. Floyd Windom Hayes (Lanham, MD: Rowman & Littlefield, 2000), 159; Pope, *Rap and Politics*, 5–6.

69 Connell, *Sound Tracks*, 138.

70 Kip Lornell, *Exploring American Folk Music: Ethnic, Grassroots, and Regional Traditions in the US*, 3rd ed. (Jackson: University Press of Mississippi, 2012), 189.

71 Ibid.

72 Myers, *Ethnomusicology: Historical and Regional Studies*, 425.

73 Wilkerson, *The Warmth of Other Suns*, 531.

74 Ibid., 528.

75 Ibid., 529–30.

76 Ibid., 528.

77 Tony Mitchell, *Popular Music and Local Identity: Rock, Pop, and Rap in Europe and Oceania* (London: Burns & Oates, 1996), 22.

78 Toop, *The Rap Attack*, 16.

79 Ibid.

80 Said, *The Beattips Manual*, 60–6; Tariq Nasheed, "*Microphone Check: The Hidden History of Hip Hop* [Motion Picture]," (USA: Melanoid Nation, 2024).

81 Said, *The Beattips Manual*, 60–6; Dick Hebdige, *Cut 'N' Mix: Culture, Identity and Caribbean Music* (New York: Routledge, 2003), 136–8.

82 Said, *The Beattips Manual*, 60–6.

83 Ibid.

84 Ibid., 65.

85 Nasheed, "*Microphone Check*."

86 Keyes, *Rap Music and Street Consciousness*, 30.

87 Perkins, *Droppin' Science*, 4.

88 Keyes, *Rap Music and Street Consciousness*, 31.

89 Perkins, *Droppin' Science*, 5.

90 Toop, *The Rap Attack*, 104.

91 Serouj Aprahamian, *The Birth of Breaking: Hip-Hop History from the Floor Up*, Black Literary and Cultural Expressions (New York: Bloomsbury Academic, 2023), 164–65.

92 Chang, *Can't Stop, Won't Stop*, 23.

93 Keyes, *Rap Music and Street Consciousness*, 50.

94 Dick Hebdige, *Subculture, the Meaning of Style* (London: Routledge, 1979), 36–7.

95 Cobb, *To the Break of Dawn*, 18.

96 Said, *The Beattips Manual*, 61–5.

97 Perry, *Prophets of the Hood*, 13.

98 Ibid., 4–15.

99 Ibid., 16.

100 Keyes, "The Aesthetic Significance of African American Sound Culture and Its Impact on American Popular Music Style and Industry," 121.

101 Toop, *The Rap Attack*, 8.

102 Connell, *Sound Tracks*, 182.

103 Perkins, *Droppin' Science*, 6.

104 Adam Bradley, *Book of Rhymes: The Poetics of Hip Hop* (New York: Civitas Books, 2017), xxxii.

105 V. Alexandra de F. Szoenyi, "14 Latinxs Who Contributed to the Birth of Hip Hop," https://hiplatina.com/latinxs-hip-hop-originators/.

106 Fantastic Freaks, "Fantastic Freaks at the Dixie," in *Wild Style Original Soundtrack [Sound Recording]* (Animal Records, 1983).

107 Connell, *Sound Tracks*, 139.

108 Spady, Meghelli, and Alim, *Tha Global Cipha*, 35.

109 Adam Patrick Bell, *Dawn of the DAW: The Studio as Musical Instrument* (New York: Oxford University Press, 2018), 69.

110 Bradley, *Book of Rhymes*, xxxii.

111 Adam Krims, *Rap Music and the Poetics of Identity* (Cambridge: Cambridge University Press, 2000), 3.

112 Bennett, "Hip Hop Am Main," 78.

113 Diallo, " 'Every MC Raps, but Not Every Rapper Is an MC,' " 196.

114 Ahearn, "*Wild Style* [Motion Picture]."

115 Pough, *Check It While I Wreck It*, 5.

116 Ryynänen, "Can the (Non-) Subaltern (Understand) Rap?," 217.

117 Keyes, "Verbal Art Performance in Rap Music," 150.

118 Barone, "Under a Groove," 285.

119 Ibid., 284.

120 Diallo, "'Every MC Raps, but Not Every Rapper Is an MC,'" 196.

121 Ibid., 198.

122 Ibid., 196.

123 Ibid., 199.

124 Ibid., 198.

125 Ibid., 198–9.

126 Samuels, "The Rap on Rap," 169.

127 Diallo, "'Every MC Raps, but Not Every Rapper Is an MC,'" 201.

128 Ibid.

129 David Diallo, *Collective Participation and Audience Engagement in Rap Music* (Cham, Switzerland: Springer Nature, 2019), 67.

130 Ibid., 110.

131 Ibid., 72.

132 Ibid., 67.

133 Perry, *Prophets of the Hood*, 107.

134 Bradley, *Book of Rhymes*, xv.

135 Ibid., 4.

136 Keyes, "Verbal Art Performance in Rap Music," 144.

137 Ibid., 145.

138 Ibid., 146.

139 Ibid., 147.

140 Ibid., 150.

141 Smitherman, *Talkin' and Testifyin'*, 99.

142 Ibid., 94.

143 Bradley, *Book of Rhymes*, ix.

144 Ibid., 137.

145 Ibid.

146 Christopher Emdin, "Pursuing the Pedagogical Potential of the Pillars of Hip-Hop through Urban Science Education," *The International Journal of Critical Pedagogy* 4, no. 3 (2013): 88.

147 Ibid.; Robert E. Kohler, *Landscapes and Labscapes: Exploring the Lab-Field Border in Biology* (Chicago: University of Chicago Press, 2010).

148 Keyes, "Verbal Art Performance in Rap Music," 150–1.

149 Bradley, *Book of Rhymes*, xiv.

150 Cobb, *To the Break of Dawn*, 87.

151 Bradley, *Book of Rhymes*, 43.

152 Ibid., 41.

153 Ibid., 78.

154 David Toop, *Rap Attack 2: African Rap to Global Hip Hop* (London: Serpent's Tail, 1994), ix.

155 Ibid., 169.

156 Wilkins, *Welcome 2 Houston*.

157 Holt, *Genre in Popular Music*, 2.

158 Ibid., 20–4.

159 Jennifer C. Lena and Richard A. Peterson, "Classification as Culture: Types and Trajectories of Music Genres," *American Sociological Review* 73, no. 5 (2008): 708.

160 Ibid.

161 Klement and Strambach, "How Do New Music Genres Emerge?," 1447.

162 Ibid., 1450.

163 Ibid., 1452.

164 Barone, "Under a Groove," 288.

165 Abrams, *The Come Up*, 469.

166 Smitherman, *Talkin' and Testifyin'*, 52.

167 Bradley, *Book of Rhymes*, xv.

168 Perry, *Prophets of the Hood*, 43.

169 Barone, "Under a Groove," 285.

170 Greg Dimitriadis, *Performing Identity/Performing Culture: Hip Hop as Text, Pedagogy, and Lived Practice* (New York: Peter Lang, 2009), 41.

171 Ibid.

172 Regina N. Bradley, *An Outkast Reader: Essays on Race, Gender, and the Postmodern South* (Athens: University of Georgia Press, 2021), 9.

6 Technology

1 Bahamadia, "Spontaneity," in *Kollage [Sound Recording]* (Chrysalis, 1996).

2 Iandoli, *God Save the Queens*, 103.

3 Perry, *Prophets of the Hood*, 71.

4 Harris et al., "Funk What You Heard," 21.

5 For discussion of turntables as Hip Hop's original instrument, see: Mark Katz, *Groove Music: The Art and Culture of the Hip-Hop DJ* (New York: Oxford University Press, 2012), 43–69; Michail Exarchos, "Boom Bap Ex Machina: Hip-Hop Aesthetics and the Akai MPC," in *Producing Music: Perspectives on Music Production* (New York: Routledge, 2019), 2.

6 "Boom Bap Ex Machina," 3.

7 Mark Katz, *Capturing Sound: How Technology Has Changed Music* (Berkeley: University of California Press, 2004), 147.

8 Ibid., 148.

9 Perry, *Prophets of the Hood*, 70.

10 Bell, *Dawn of the DAW*, 63.

11 James E. Perone, *Music and Technology: A Historical Encyclopedia* (Santa Barbara, CA: Greenwood, 2022), ix.

12 Rose, *Black Noise*, 27.

13 Ibid., 33.

14 Steven Hager, *Hip Hop: The Illustrated History of Break Dancing, Rap Music, and Graffiti* (New York: St. Martin's Press, 1984), 42–3.

15 Abrams, *The Come Up*, 22.

16 Toop, *The Rap Attack*, 78.

17 Perkins, *Droppin' Science*, 10.

18 Toop, *The Rap Attack*, 63.

19 Katz, *Capturing Sound*, 126.

20 Ewoodzie, *Break Beats in the Bronx.*
21 Rose, *Black Noise*, 41.
22 Ibid., 52.
23 Ibid., 36.
24 Said, *The Beattips Manual*, 33–5.
25 Bell, *Dawn of the DAW*, 59.
26 Exarchos, "Boom Bap Ex Machina," 4.
27 Abrams, *The Come Up*, 150.
28 Klaess, *Breaks in the Air*, 70.
29 Ibid., 86.
30 Ibid., 81.
31 Ibid., 6.
32 Ibid., 108.
33 Hess, *Hip Hop in America*, xxxi–xxxii.
34 Cobb, *To the Break of Dawn*, 68, emphasis in original.
35 Brian Coleman, *Check the Technique: Liner Notes for Hip-Hop Junkies* (New York: Villard, 2009), 144.
36 Barone, "Under a Groove," 286.
37 Cross, *It's Not About a Salary*, 20.
38 Viator, "West Coast Originals," 89.
39 Ibid., 93.
40 Ibid., 101–2.
41 Ibid.
42 Ibid., 95.
43 Viator, *To Live and Defy in LA*, 116.
44 Guerra and Alberto, *Keep It Simple, Make It Fast!*, 452.
45 Ibid.
46 Quinn, *Nothing but a "G" Thang*, 64–5.
47 Ibid., 64.
48 Chang, *Can't Stop, Won't Stop*, 422.
49 Ibid.
50 Joseph Glenn Schloss, *Making Beats: The Art of Sample-Based Hip-Hop* (Middletown, CT: Wesleyan University Press, 2004).
51 Ibid.
52 Ibid., xiii.
53 Ibid.
54 Forrest Stuart, *Ballad of the Bullet: Gangs, Drill Music, and the Power of Online Infamy* (Princeton, NJ: Princeton University Press, 2021), 5.
55 Hess, *Hip Hop in America*, xxxv.
56 Barone, "Under a Groove," 287.
57 Ibid.
58 Ibid.
59 Long, "Hustle in H-Town," 64.
60 Ibid., 63.
61 University of Houston Libraries, "DJ Screw Photographs and Memorabilia," (Houston, TX: University of Houston Libraries, 2012).
62 10th Ward Buck, *The Definition of Bounce*, 161.
63 Ibid.

64 Abrams, *The Come Up*, 398.

65 Joseph Coughlan-Allen, "The Lo-Fi Lens: Interpretations of Memphis Rap Tape Rips in the Online Mediascape," *Popular Music and Society* (2024), 67–8, emphasis in original.

66 Ibid., 1, emphasis in original.

67 Ibid., 3–4.

68 Ibid., 5–6.

69 Ibid., 4.

70 Ibid., 2.

71 Ibid., 6.

72 Balaji, "The Construction of 'Street Credibility' in Atlanta's Hip-Hop Music Scene," 319.

73 Sarig, "Virginia—Transmissions from the Edge," 154.

74 Cannady, "Virginia Is for Lovers and Rappers," 519.

75 Sarig, "Virginia—Transmissions from the Edge," 154.

76 Harris et al., "Funk What You Heard," 21.

77 Exarchos, "Boom Bap Ex Machina," 2.

78 Baker, *Black Studies, Rap, and the Academy*, 88.

79 Emdin, "Pursuing the Pedagogical Potential of the Pillars of Hip-Hop through Urban Science Education," 90.

80 George, *Hip Hop America*, 19.

81 Barone, "Under a Groove," 285.

82 Brett Milano, *Vinyl Junkies: Adventures in Record Collecting* (New York: St. Martin's Griffin, 2003), 19.

83 Katz, *Groove Music*, 67–8, emphasis in original.

84 Ibid., 16.

85 Ibid., 62–3.

86 Todd Souvignier, *The World of Djs and the Turntable Culture* (Milwaukee, WI: Hal Leonard Corp., 2003).

87 Ibid., ix.

88 Ibid., 43.

89 Ibid., 41.

90 Ibid.

91 Katz, *Capturing Sound*, 125.

92 Tricia Rose, "A Style Nobody Can Deal With," in *Microphone Fiends: Youth Music & Youth Culture*, ed. Andrew Ross and Tricia Rose (New York: Routledge, 1994), 78.

93 Ibid., 73.

94 Barone, "Under a Groove," 289.

95 Ibid., 285.

96 Hager, *Hip Hop*, 51.

97 Alejandro Nava, *Street Scriptures: Between God and Hip-Hop* (Chicago: University of Chicago Press, 2022), 45.

98 Perry, *Prophets of the Hood*, 203.

99 Phil Morse and Digital DJ Tips, "The 2024 Global DJ Census," https://www.digitaldjtips.com/census-results-2024/. I would like to thank my colleague DC Cochrane for informing me about this survey.

100 Ibid., 5.

101 Ibid.

102 Ibid., 3–4.

103 Ibid., 6–12.

104 Ibid., 13–23.

105 Ibid., 24–37.

106 Ibid., 38–49.

107 Ibid., 50–53.

108 Patrin, *Bring That Beat Back*, 80.

109 Bell, *Dawn of the DAW*, 4.

110 Perry, *Prophets of the Hood*, 72.

111 Exarchos, "Boom Bap Ex Machina," 4.

112 Attorney Richard Stim, "Fair Use: What Is Transformative?," Nolo.com, https://www.nolo.com/legal-encyclopedia/fair-use-what-transformative.html.

113 Ibid.

114 For example, see: Paul Harkins and Nick Prior, "(Dis) Locating Democratization: Music Technologies in Practice," *Popular Music and Society* 45, no. 1 (2022): 87–8; Joseph G. Schloss, *Foundation: B-Boys, B-Girls and Hip-Hop Culture in New York* (New York: Oxford University Press, 2009).

115 "(Dis) Locating Democratization," 88.

116 Ibid., 89.

117 Ibid., 90.

118 George, *Hip Hop America*, 92.

119 Ibid.

120 Exarchos, "Boom Bap Ex Machina," 1.

121 Harkins and Prior, "(Dis) Locating Democratization," 87.

122 Exarchos, "Boom Bap Ex Machina," 7–8.

123 Ibid., 8.

124 Ibid., 1.

125 Ibid., 3.

126 Ibid., 9–11.

127 Malte Pelleter, "Chopped and Screwed," *IM KONTEXT* (2022): 19.

128 Harkins and Prior, "(Dis) Locating Democratization," 90–1.

129 Ibid., 97.

130 Exarchos, "Boom Bap Ex Machina," 21.

131 Perone, *Music and Technology*, xxi.

132 Forman, " 'Represent,' " 205.

133 Cross, *It's Not About a Salary*, 3.

134 Ibid.

135 Robin den Drijver and Erik Hitters, "The Business of DIY: Characteristics, Motives and Ideologies of Micro-Independent Record Labels," *Cadernos de Arte e Antropologia* 6, no. 1 (2017): 20.

136 Anthony J. Fonseca, *Listen to Rap!: Exploring a Musical Genre* (Santa Barbara, CA: Greenwood, 2019), xiv.

137 Forman, " 'Represent,' " 204.

138 Ibid.

139 Barone, "Under a Groove," 281.

140 Bell, *Dawn of the DAW*, 28.

141 Rose, *Black Noise*, 2–3.

142 Ibid., 25.

143 Harris et al., "Funk What You Heard," 23.

144 Harkins and Prior, "(Dis) Locating Democratization," 86.

145 Perry, *Prophets of the Hood*, 7.

146 Jonathan Kabongo, Craig Arthur, and Freddy Paige, "Dusty & Digital Media Literacy Workshops," *The International Journal of Information, Diversity, & Inclusion* 6, no. 1/2 (2022): 66.

147 Ibid., 64.

148 Asante, *It's Bigger Than Hip-Hop*, 6.

149 Ogbar, *Hip-Hop Revolution*, 41.

150 Andreas Gebesmair, "The Transnational Music Industry," in *The Ashgate Research Companion to Popular Musicology*, ed. Derek B. Scott (London and New York: Routledge, 2016).

151 Weheliye, *Phonographies*, 20.

152 Drijver and Hitters, "The Business of DIY," 21.

153 Ibid., 20.

154 Rabaka, *Hip Hop's Amnesia*, xxiv.

155 Forman, "'Represent,'" 88.

156 Jennifer C. Lena, "Social Context and Musical Content of Rap Music, 1979–1995," *Social Forces* 85, no. 1 (2006).

157 Katel, "Debating Hip-Hop," 118.

158 Robert Strachan, *Sonic Technologies: Popular Music, Digital Culture and the Creative Process* (New York: Bloomsbury Academic, 2017), 4.

159 Ibid.

160 Ibid., 6.

161 Ibid., 29.

162 Ibid.

163 Wilkins, *Welcome 2 Houston*, 15.

164 Bobby Oswinski, *Social Media Promotion for Musicians: The Manual for Marketing Yourself, Your Band, and Your Music Online*, 3rd ed. (Burbank, CA: Bobby Owsinski Media Group, 2020), 22.

165 Ibid.

166 Amy Coddington, *How Hip Hop Became Hit Pop: Radio, Rap, and Race* (Oakland: University of California Press, 2023), 128.

167 Katz, *Music and Technology*, 81.

168 Will Straw, "Mediality and the Music Chart," *SubStance* 44, no. 3 (2015): 133, emphasis in original.

169 Perone, *Music and Technology*, xxi.

170 metav3rse, https://www.instagram.com/p/CqN6TSVMAOs/?hl=en.

171 XXL Staff, "Virtual Rapper FN Meka Powered by Artificial Intelligence Signs to Major Label," XXL, https://www.xxlmag.com/fn-meka-virtual-rap per-signs-major-label/.

172 Gerry Bloustien, Margaret Peters, and Susan Luckman, eds., *Sonic Synergies: Music, Technology, Community, Identity* (Aldershot: Ashgate, 2008), xxv.

173 David Sax, *The Revenge of Analog: Real Things and Why They Matter* (New York: Public Affairs, 2016), xvi-xvii.

174 Ibid., 11.

175 Ibid., 13.

176 Patrin, *Bring That Beat Back*, xi.

177 Perry, *Prophets of the Hood*, 67.

178 Ibid.

179 Raphael Travis Jr., *The Healing Power of Hip Hop* (Santa Barbara, CA: Praeger, 2016), 13.

7 More Scenes

1 Busta Rhymes, "Everybody Rise," in *Extinction Level Event: The Final World Front [Sound recording]* (Elektra Records, 1998).

2 Spady, Meghelli, and Alim, *Tha Global Cipha*, 8. Miami is mentioned twice in original source.

3 Peterson and Bennett, "Introducing Music Scenes," 7.

4 Ibid.

5 Ibid., 8.

6 Ibid.

7 Thank you to the anonymous peer reviewer who made this important observation. It opens questions about the limits of urban geography and the importance of both rural and suburban settings and themes.

8 Faniel, *Hip-Hop in Houston*, 25.

9 David Banner, "Foreward," in *Country Fried Soul: Adventures in Dirty South Hip-Hop*, ed. Tamara Palmer (San Francisco, CA: Backbeat, 2005), 8.

10 David Grazian, "Digital Underground: Musical Spaces and Microscenes in the Postindustrial City," in *Musical Performance and the Changing City: Post-Industrial Contexts in Europe and the US*, ed. Fabian Holt and Carsten Wergin (New York and London: Routledge, 2013), 131.

11 Ibid.

12 Harris et al., "Funk What You Heard," 19.

13 Toop, *The Rap Attack*, 8.

14 Paul Khalil Saucier, *Native Tongues: An African Hip-Hop Reader* (Trenton, NJ: Africa World Press, 2011), xi.

15 Bradley, *Book of Rhymes*, xxxii.

16 Rebecca J. Haines, "Break North: Rap Music and Hip-Hop Culture in Canada," in *Ethnicity, Politics, and Public Policy: Case Studies in Canadian Diversity*, ed. Harold Martin Troper and M. Weinfeld (Toronto, Canada and Buffalo, NY: University of Toronto Press, 1999), 61.

17 F. W. Hayes, *A Turbulent Voyage: Readings in African American Studies* (Lanham, MD: Collegiate Press, 2000), 41.

18 Lipsitz, *Dangerous Crossroads*, 39.

19 Weheliye, *Phonographies*, 147.

20 Samuel A. Floyd, "Black Music and Writing Black Music History: American Music and Narrative Strategies," *Black Music Research Journal* 28, no. 1 (2008): 119.

21 Jesse Stewart and Niel Scobie, "Fantastic Voyage: The Diasporic Roots and Routes of Early Toronto Hip Hop," in *Contemporary Musical Expressions in Canada*, ed. Anna Hoefnagels, Judith Klassen, and Sherry Johnson (Montreal: McGill-Queen's University Press, 2019), 306.

22 Ibid., 312.

23 Tony Mitchell, *Global Noise: Rap and Hip Hop Outside the USA* (Middletown, CT: Wesleyan University Press, 2001), 10.

24 George, *Hip Hop America*, 203.

25 Barone, "Under a Groove," 293.

26 Frederick W. Gooding, *The Griot Tradition as Remixed through Hip Hop: Straight Outta Africa* (Lanham, MD: Lexington Books, 2023), xv–xvi.

27 Ibid.

28 Connell, *Sound Tracks*, 182.

29 Ibid., 139.

30 Aparicio, Jáquez, and Cepeda, *Musical Migrations*, 3.

31 Barone, "Under a Groove," 295.

32 David Buckingham and Liesbeth de Block, *Global Children, Global Media: Migration, Media and Childhood* (London: Palgrave Macmillan UK, 2007), viii.

33 Stuart Borthwick, *Positive Vibrations: Politics, Politricks and the Story of Reggae* (London: Reaktion Books, 2022), 17.

34 Brian Meeks, "The Rise and Fall of Caribbean Black Power," in *From Toussaint to Tupac: The Black International since the Age of Revolution*, ed. Michael O. West, William G. Martin, and Fanon Che Wilkins (Chapel Hill: University of North Carolina Press, 2009), 197.

35 Ibid., 198.

36 Borthwick, *Positive Vibrations*, 101.

37 Kaltmeier and Raussert, *Sonic Politics*, 1.

38 Stewart and Scobie, "Fantastic Voyage," 326.

39 Ibid., 313.

40 Barone, "Under a Groove," 296.

41 The Movement for Black Lives, "Black August Hip Hop Concert," https://m4bl. org/black-august/#:~:text=The%20Black%20August%20Hip%2DHop,between%20 the%20years%201998%20–%202010.

42 S. Fernandes, *Close to the Edge: In Search of the Global Hip Hop Generation* (London: Verso, 2011).

43 Dominic Power and Daniel Hallencreutz, "Profiting from Creativity? The Music Industry in Stockholm, Sweden and Kingston, Jamaica," *Routledge Studies in International Business and the World Economy* 33 (2004): 258.

44 Borthwick, *Positive Vibrations*, 217.

45 Eric Charry, *Hip Hop Africa: New African Music in a Globalizing World* (Bloomington: Indiana University Press, 2012), xi.

46 Ibid., 3.

47 Ibid., 3–9.

48 Bell, *Dawn of the DAW*, 54.

49 Ibid.

50 Chang, *Can't Stop, Won't Stop*, 30.

51 Power and Hallencreutz, "Profiting from Creativity?," 258.

52 Mitchell, *Global Noise*, 2.

53 Oswinski, *Social Media Promotion for Musicians*, 29.

54 Ibid.

55 Holly Kruse, "Local Identity and Independent Music Scenes, Online and Off," *Popular Music and Society* 33, no. 5 (2010).

56 Ibid.

57 Ibid., 625.

58 Shane Blackman, "Youth Subcultural Theory: A Critical Engagement with the Concept, Its Origins and Politics, from the Chicago School to Postmodernism," *Journal of Youth Studies* 8, no. 1 (2005): 16.

59 Najja K. Baptist, "And When They Wake Up: Black Lives Matter, Rap, and Activism," in *For the Culture: Hip-Hop and the Fight for Social Justice*, ed. Lakeyta Bonnette-Bailey and Adolphus Belk (Ann Arbor: University of Michigan Press, 2022), 88.

60 Jeffrey Lane, "The Digital Street: An Ethnographic Study of Networked Street Life in Harlem," *American Behavioral Scientist* 60, no. 1 (2016): 1.

61 For local to regional scene analysis, see: Hess, *Hip Hop in America*. For South Bronx, see: Ewoodzie, *Break Beats in the Bronx*. For New Orleans, see: Miller, *Bounce*. For Houston, see: Faniel, *Hip-Hop in Houston*; Walker, *Houston Rap Tapes*; Wilkins, *Welcome 2 Houston*. For Seattle, see: Abe, *Emerald Street*. For the Oakland and San Francisco Bay Area, see: Pope, *Rap and Politics*. For Atlanta, see: Coscarelli, *Rap Capital*.

62 For developments in ethnographic methods, see: Harrison, *Hip Hop Underground*; Morgan, *The Real Hiphop*; Quinn, *Nothing but a "G" Thang*.

63 For New Orleans, see: Miller, *Bounce*. For Houston, see: Faniel, *Hip-Hop in Houston*; Walker, *Houston Rap Tapes*; Wilkins, *Welcome 2 Houston*. For Oakland and the San Francisco Bay Area, see: Pope, *Rap and Politics*. For Seattle, see: Abe, *Emerald Street*.

64 Pope, *Rap and Politics*, 278.

65 Ibid., 278–88.

66 Ibid., 288.

67 Terror Squad, "Lean Back (Featuring Fabolous)," in *True Story [Sound recording]* (Terror Squad/SRC/Universal, 2004).

68 Fat Joe, "Make It Rain (Featuring Lil Wayne)," in *Me, Myself, and I [Sound recording]* (Imperial/Terror Squad, 2006).

69 Onyx, *Bacdafucup [Sound recording]* (JMJ Records, 1993).

70 Mobb Deep, *The Infamous [Sound recording]* (Loud/RCA/BMG Records, 1995).

71 Nas, *It Was Written [Sound recording]* (Columbia, 1996).

72 Junior M.A.F.I.A., *Conspiracy [Sound recording]* (Undeas/Big Beat Records, 1995).

73 Smif-N-Wessun, *Dah Shinin [Sound recording]* (Wreck Records, 1995).

74 The Notorious B.I.G., *Life After Death – CD1 [Sound recording]* (Bad Boy, 1997).

75 Jay-Z, *Vol. 2…Hard Knock Life [Sound recording]* (Roc-A-Fella/Def Jam, 1998).

76 "Empire State of Mind (Featuring Alicia Keys)," in *The Blueprint 3 [Sound recording]* (Roc Nation/Atlantic, 2009).

77 Genius/GZA, *Liquid Swords [Sound recording]* (Geffen/MCA Records, 1995).

78 Public Enemy, in *Apocalypse 91…The Enemy Strikes Black [Sound recording]* (Def Jam/Columbia, 1991).

79 EPMD, *Business as Usual [Sound recording]* (Def Jam/RAL/Columbia, 1993).

80 Public Enemy, *Greatest Misses [Sound recording]* (Def Jam/Columbia/SME Records, 1992).

81 Santana, "Maria Maria (Featuring Wyclef)," in *Maria Maria (CD Single) – Side B [Sound recording]* (Arista, 1999).

82 Shakira, "Hips Don't Lie (Featuring Wyclef Jean)," in *Oral Fixation Vol. 2 [Sound recording]* (Epic, 2005).

83 Ice-T, *Power [Sound recording]* (Sire/Warner Bros. Records, 1988).

84 Cypress Hill, *Cypress Hill [Sound recording]* (Ruffhouse/Columbia/SME Records, 1991).

85 Ice Cube, *Death Certificate [Sound recording]* (Priority/EMI Records, 1991).

86 Eazy-E, *It's On (Dr. Dre 187um) Killa [Sound recording]* (Ruthless/Relativity/Epic, 1993).

87 Snoop Doggy Dogg, *Doggystyle [Sound recording]* (Death Row Records, 1993).

88 Cypress Hill, *Black Sunday [Sound recording]* (Ruffhouse/Columbia, 1993).

89 Coolio, "Gangsta's Paradise," in *Dangerous Minds Soundtrack [Sound recording]* (MCA, 1995).

90 Mack 10, *Mack 10 [Sound recording]* (Priority, 1995).

91 Snoop Dogg, "I Wanna Rock," in *Malice N Wonderland [Sound recording]* (Doggy Style/Priority, 2009).

92 Jamie Foxx, "DJ Play a Love Song (Featuring Twista)," in *Unpredictable [Sound recording]* (J, 2006).

93 Bo$$, *Born Gangstaz [Sound recording]* (DJ West/Chaos/Columbia/SME Records, 1993).

94 Eminem, "Lose Yourself," in *8 Mile Soundtrack [Sound recording]* (Shady/Interscope, 2002).

95 Scarface, *The Untouchable [Sound recording]* (Rap-A-Lot Records, 1997).

96 Chamillionaire, "Ridin' (Featuring Krayzie Bone)," in *The Sound of Revenge [Sound recording]* (Chamillitary/Universal Records, 2006).

97 Hot Boys, *Guerrilla Warfare [Sound recording]* (Cash Money Records, 1999).

98 Eightball, *On Top of the World [Sound recording]* (Suave House Records/Relativity Records, 1995).

99 Goodie Mob, *Soul Food [Sound Recording]* (LaFace, 1995).

100 OutKast, *ATLiens [Sound recording]* (LaFace/Arista, 1996).

101 "Ms. Jackson," in *Stankonia [Sound recording]* (LaFace/Arista, 2000).

102 Purple Ribbon All-Stars, "Kryptonite (I'm on It) (Featuring Big Boi)," in *Got Purp? Vol 2 [Sound recording]* (Virgin, 2005).

103 Yung Joc, "It's Goin' Down," in *New Joc City [Sound recording]* (Bad Bad South/Block Entertainment/Atlantic Record, 2006).

104 Young Dro, "Shoulder Lean (Featuring T.I.)," in *Best Thang Smokin' [Sound recording]* (Grand Hustle Records/Atlantic Records/Warner Bros. Records, 2006).

105 Young Jeezy, "Lose My Mind (Featuring Plies)," in *Lose My Mind (CD Single) [Sound recording]* (Corporate Thugz/Def Jam, 2006).

106 T.I., "Live Your Life (Featuring Rihanna)," in *Paper Trail [Sound recording]* (Grand Hustle/Atlantic, 2008).

107 Rick Ross, "The Boss (Featuring T-Pain)," in *Trilla [Sound recording]* (Slip-n-Slide/Def Jam/Poe Boy, 2008).

108 Pope, *Rap and Politics*, 271.

109 Dilworth, *Cities in American Political History*.

110 It's About Time, "Chapter History," http://www.itsabouttimebpp.com/BPP_Newspapers/bpp_newspapers_index.html; Pope, *Rap and Politics*, 113.

111 Andy Avgousti (MPC-Tutor), *The MPC Bible: For the MPC X, MPC Live, MPC One & MPC Key*, 19th ed. (Sheffield: MPC-Samples.com, 2017–24).

Conclusion

1   MF Grimm, "Stable," in *Digital Tears: E-mail from Purgatory [Sound recording]* (Day By Day Entertainment, 2004).

2   Woo, Rennie, and Poyntz, "Scene Thinking," 288.

3   US Census Bureau, "Historical Delineation Files: Area History Metadata," https://www2.census.gov/programs-surveys/metro-micro/geographies/reference-files/2020/historical-delineation-files/area_history_metadata.doc.

4   Enos, *The Space between Us*, 40.

5   Bradley, *Book of Rhymes*, 153.

6   Hager, *Hip Hop*, 103.

7   Shabazz, *The US of America vs. Hip-Hop*, 6.

8   Osumare, *The Africanist Aesthetic in Global Hip-Hop*, 7.

9   Harvey, *Who Got the Camera?*

10 Ibid., 141.

11 Baptist, "Rap and Politics: A Case Study of Panther, Gangster, and Hyphy Discourses in Oakland, CA (1965–2010). By Lavar Pope. New York: Palgrave Macmillan, 2020. 338p. $89.99 Cloth," 1460.

12 Bynoe, *Stand and Deliver*, 148.

13 Schloss, *Foundation*, 5.

14 Ibid.

15 Adam de Paor-Evans, "Urban Myths and Rural Legends: An Alternate Take on the Regionalism of Hip Hop," *Popular Music and Society* 43, no. 4 (2020): 415.

16 Kevin C. Holt, "Emcee Ethnographies: A Brief Sketch of US Hip-Hop Ethnography," *Current Musicology* 105 (2019): 11.

17 Harris et al., "Funk What You Heard," 10.

18 Gaines, "'This Ain't Just a Rap Song,'" 114.

19 Pough, *Check It While I Wreck It*, 8.

20 Johnson, *After Black Lives Matter*, 151.

21 Jones, *Fear of a Hip-Hop Planet*, 4.

22 Ibid., 175.

23 Rose, *Black Noise*, 19.

24 Perry, *Prophets of the Hood*, 137.

25 Mara Persello, "The Subculture Archive Manifesto: The Role of Scholars in the Preservation of Subcultural Heritage," in *Keep It Simple, Make It Fast!: An Approach to Underground Music Scenes*, ed. Paula Guerra and Thiago Pereira Alberto (Porto, Portugal: Universidade do Porto, Faculdade de Letras [University of Porto, Faculty of Arts and Humanities], 2019), 82.

26 Ibid., 80.

27 John Vallier, "Preserving the Past, Activating the Future: Collaborative Archiving in Ethnomusicology," in *Ethnomusicology: A Contemporary Reader, Volume II*, ed. Jennifer C. Post (New York: Routledge, Taylor & Francis Group, 2018), 312–14.

28 Morgan, *The Real Hiphop*, 15.

29 Ibid.

30 Ibid.

31 Geoff Harkness, "True School: Situational Authenticity in Chicago's Hip-Hop Underground," *Cultural Sociology* 6, no. 3 (2012): 277.

32 Lavar Pope, "Internal Colonization and Revolt: Rap as an Underground Political Discourse in Oakland, CA from 1965–2010" (PhD dissertation, University of California Santa Cruz, 2012), 31–2.
33 Harris et al., "Funk What You Heard," 6.
34 Ibid., 7.

Appendix A

1 Edith Cowan University Library, "Search Engines and Library Databases: Google Scholar," Edith Cowan University, https://ecu.au.libguides.com/search-engines/google-scholar.
2 For US data, see: Campbell Gibson and Kay Jung, "Historical Census Statistics on Population Totals by Race, 1790 to 1990, and by Hispanic Origin, 1790 to 1990, for the US, Regions, Divisions, and States" (Washington, DC: US Census Bureau, 2002). For large city and other urban place data, see: "Historical Census Statistics on Population Totals by Race, 1790 to 1990, and by Hispanic Origin, 1970 to 1990, for Large Cities and Other Urban Places in the US" (Washington, DC: US Census Bureau, Population Division, 2005).

Appendix B

1 This is adapted from the twenty-five scene list in Pope, *Rap and Politics*, 271. The twenty-five scene list in *Rap and Politics* is adapted from the regional and local analysis in Hess, *Hip Hop in America*.
2 David Diallo, "Hip Cats in the Cradle of Rap: Hip Hop in the Bronx," in *Hip Hop in America: A Regional Guide*, ed. Mickey Hess (Westport, CT: Greenwood, 2009).
3 Schloss, *Foundation*.
4 Ewoodzie, *Break Beats in the Bronx*.
5 David Shanks, "Uptown Baby!: Hip Hop in Harlem and Upper Manhattan," in *Hip Hop in America: A Regional Guide*, ed. Mickey Hess (Westport, CT: Greenwood, 2009).
6 Ericka Blount Danois, "From Queens Come Kings: Run DMC Stomps Hard out of a 'Soft' Borough," ibid.
7 Jennifer R. Young, "Brooklyn Beats: Hip-Hop's Home to Everyone from Everywhere," ibid.
8 Mabusha Cooper, *Push Hip Hop History. [Volume 1], the Brooklyn Scene* (Bloomington, IN: 1stBooks Library, 2003).
9 Alvin Blanco, *The Wu-Tang Clan and RZA: A Trip through Hip Hop's 36 Chambers* (Santa Barbara, CA: Praeger, 2011).
10 Matthew Brian Cohen, "A Black Sheep Borough, an Island of All White People: Staten Island Steps Up," in *Hip Hop in America: A Regional Guide*, ed. Mickey Hess (Westport, CT: Greenwood, 2009).
11 Blount Danois, "From Queens Come Kings."
12 Mickey Hess, "The Sound of Philadelphia: Hip Hop History in the City of Brotherly Love," ibid.

13 Andrea Roberts, "The Bricks and Beyond: Hip Hop in Newark and Northern New Jersey," ibid.

14 Pacey C. Foster, "Hip Hop in the Hub: How Boston Rap Remained Underground," ibid.

15 Pacey Foster and Wayne Marshall, "Tales of the Tape: Cassette Culture, Community Radio, and the Birth of Rap Music in Boston," *Creative Industries Journal* 8, no. 2 (2015).

16 Cross, *It's Not About a Salary*.

17 Kelley, "Kickin' Reality, Kickin' Ballistics."

18 Morgan, *The Real Hiphop*.

19 Quinn, *Nothing but a "G" Thang*.

20 Zanfagna, *Holy Hip Hop in the City of Angels*.

21 Harrison, *Hip Hop Underground*.

22 Pope, *Rap and Politics*.

23 Abe, *Emerald Street*.

24 Rachael Key, "From the SEA to the PDX: Northwest Hip Hop in the I-5 Corridor," in *Hip Hop in America: A Regional Guide*, ed. Mickey Hess (Westport, CT: Greenwood, 2009).

25 Warren Scott Cheney, "The Evolution of the Second City Lyric: Hip Hop in Chicago and Gary, Indiana," ibid.

26 Harkness, "True School."

27 Amanda Lawson, "Heartland Hip Hop: Nelly, St. Louis, and Country Grammar," in *Hip Hop in America: A Regional Guide*, ed. Mickey Hess (Westport, CT: Greenwood, 2009).

28 Schell, "From St. Paul to Minneapolis, All the Hands Clap for This."

29 Carleton S. Gholz, "Welcome to Tha D: Making and Remaking Hip Hop Culture in Post-Motown Detroit," ibid.

30 Farrugia et al., *Women Rapping Revolution*.

31 Faniel, *Hip-Hop in Houston*.

32 Walker, *Houston Rap Tapes*.

33 Jamie Lynch, "The Long, Hot Grind: How Houston Engineered an Industry of Independence," in *Hip Hop in America: A Regional Guide*, ed. Mickey Hess (Westport, CT: Greenwood, 2009).

34 Long, "Hustle in H-Town."

35 Wilkins, *Welcome 2 Houston*.

36 Rich Paul Cooper, "Bouncin' Straight out the Dirty Dirty: Community and Dance in New Orleans," in *Hip Hop in America: A Regional Guide*, ed. Mickey Hess (Westport, CT: Greenwood, 2009).

37 Miller, *Bounce*.

38 10th Ward Buck, *The Definition of Bounce*.

39 Zandria F. Robinson, "Soul Legacies: Hip Hop and Historicity in Memphis," in *Hip Hop in America: A Regional Guide*, ed. Mickey Hess (Westport, CT: Greenwood, 2009).

40 Coughlan-Allen, "The Lo-Fi Lens."

41 Miller, "'The Sound of Money': Atlanta, Crossroads of the Dirty South."

42 Coscarelli, *Rap Capital*.

43 Matt Miller, "Tropic of Bass: Culture, Commerce, and Controversy in Miami Rap," in *Hip Hop in America: A Regional Guide*, ed. Mickey Hess (Westport, CT: Greenwood, 2009), 10.

44 Sarig, "Virginia—Transmissions from the Edge."

45 Cannady, "Virginia Is for Lovers and Rappers."

46 Lornell and Stephenson, *The Beat!* For DMV artist information, many sources are from searches of websites and fanzines, as there is not a lot of comprehensive academic or journalistic accounting of the scene. Many of the go-go bands and references are from the 1980s and 1990s, which is not necessarily the same musical soundscape of the local and current rap scene. However, the interplay is noted and analyzed in the main text of *American Rap Scenes*.

47 Thomas, *Diamonds in the Raw.*

48 Rohan Kalyan, "Paradise Lost and Found: Hip Hop in Hawai'i," in *Hip Hop in America: A Regional Guide*, ed. Mickey Hess (Westport, CT: Greenwood, 2009). For Honolulu, additional material was sourced from Osumare, *The Africanist Aesthetic in Global Hip-Hop*, 105.

49 Raquel Z. Rivera, Wayne Marshall, and Deborah Pacini Hernandez, eds., *Reggaeton* (Durham, NC: Duke University Press, 2009).

50 Raquel Z. Rivera, "Rap in Puerto Rico: Reflections from the Margins," in *Globalization and Survival in the Black Diaspora: The New Urban Challenge*, ed. Charles St. Clair Green (Albany, NY: SUNY Press, 1997).

51 Hollis Urban Liverpool, "Researching Steelband and Calypso Music in the British Caribbean and the U.S. Virgin Islands," *Black Music Research Journal* 14, no. 2 (1994).

52 Warren R. Pinckney, "Jazz in the U.S. Virgin Islands," *American Music* 10, no. 4 (1992).

53 Hess, *Hip Hop in America.*

54 For New Orleans, see: Miller, *Bounce.* For Houston, see: Faniel, *Hip-Hop in Houston*; Walker, *Houston Rap Tapes.* For Seattle, see: Abe, *Emerald Street.* For the Oakland and San Francisco Bay Area, see: Pope, *Rap and Politics.*

55 For LA, see: Cross, *It's Not About a Salary.* For Atlanta, see: Coscarelli, *Rap Capital.* For Puerto Rico, see: Rivera, *New York Ricans from the Hip Hop Zone.*

56 The Good Ol'Dayz, "Maps," https://www.thegoodoldayz.com/map.html.

57 Kulture Vulturez, "Rap/Hip Hop," https://www.kulturevulturez.com.

58 Toop, *The Rap Attack*; *Rap Attack 2.*

59 Abe, *6 N the Morning*; Westhoff, *Original Gangstas.*

60 Palmer, *Country Fried Soul*; Sarig, *Third Coast*; Westhoff, *Dirty South.*

61 Vladimir Bogdanov, *All Music Guide to Hip-Hop: The Definitive Guide to Rap & Hip-Hop* (San Francisco, CA: Backbeat Books, 2003); Coleman, *Check the Technique.* Richard Mook, *Rap Music and Hip Hop Culture: A Critical Reader*, 2nd ed. (Dubuque, IA: Kendall/Hunt Pub. Co., 2009). John Gray, *Hip-Hop Studies: An International Bibliography and Resource Guide*, Black Music Reference Series (Nyack, NY: African Diaspora Press, 2016).

62 Souvignier, *The World of Djs and the Turntable Culture*; Amir Said, *The Art of Sampling: The Sampling Tradition of Hip Hop* (New York: Superchamp Books, 2015); *The Beattips Manual.*

Index